Case Studies in **Abnormal Psychology**

CASE STUDIES IN
ABNORMAL PSYCHOLOGY

Ethan E. Gorenstein
Behavioral Medicine Program,
Columbia-Presbyterian Medical Center

Ronald J. Comer
Princeton University

WORTH PUBLISHERS

Case Studies in Abnormal Psychology

Sponsoring Editor: Marjorie Byers
Senior Marketing Manager: Renee Altier
Associate Managing Editor: Tracey Kuehn
Production Manager: Sarah Segal
Art Director: Barbara Reingold
Cover Illustrator: Wiktor Sadowski
Cover and Interior Designer: Ana Linnemann
Composition: Compset, Inc.
Printing and Binding: R. R. Donnelly and Sons, Harrisonburg

HarperCollins College Publishers previously published this book.

Library of Congress Cataloging in Publication Data available upon request.

Worth Publishers
41 Madison Avenue
New York, NY 10010
www.worthpublishers.com

For Margee, Eleazer, and Julian
—E.E.G.

For Marlene, Greg, and Jon
—R.J.C.

Contents

There are several fine case study books available today that provide in-depth descriptions of psychological disorders and treatments. In writing *Case Studies in Abnormal Psychology*, we wanted to maintain the clinical richness of such books and, in addition, offer a number of important and unique features that truly help bring clinical material to life. Our approach helps readers to appreciate the different perspectives of clients, friends, relatives, and therapists; reveals the nitty-gritty details of treatment programs; and challenges readers to apply their clinical insights, think critically, and make clinical decisions. We believe that *Case Studies in Abnormal Psychology* can stimulate a greater understanding of abnormal psychology by use of the following features that set it apart from other clinical case books:

1. **Multiple perspectives:** Like other case books, our cases offer in-depth descriptions of clinical symptoms, histories, and treatments. In addition, however, each case looks at a disorder from the point of view of the client, the therapist, and a friend or relative. These different points of view demonstrate that a given disorder typically affects multiple persons and help readers to empathize with the concerns and dilemmas of both clients and those with whom they interact.

2. **In-depth treatment presentations:** Extra attention is paid to treatment in this book, particularly to the interaction between client and therapist. Our detailed treatment discussions help readers to fully appreciate how theories of treatment are translated into actual procedures and how individuals with particular problems respond to a clinician's efforts to change those problems.

3. **Research-based treatments, integrated approaches:** The treatments described throughout the book represent approaches that are well supported by empirical research. In most of the cases, the

treatment is actually an *integration* of several approaches, again reflecting current trends and findings in the clinical research.

4. **Balanced, complete, accurate:** Overall, a very balanced view of current practices is offered, with cases presented free of bias. Readers will find each of the major models of abnormal psychology—behavioral, cognitive, psychodynamic, humanistic, biological, and sociocultural—represented repeatedly and respectfully throughout the book, with particular selections guided strictly by current research and applications.

5. **Stimulating pedagogical tools:** An array of special pedagogical tools helps students process and retain the material, appreciate subtle clinical issues, and apply critical thinking. For example, every page of the book features marginal notes that contain important clinical and research points as well as other food for thought, each introduced at precisely the right moment. Testing shows that readers enjoy this exciting technique and that it helps them to learn and retain material more completely.

6. **Reader interaction and application:** The final three cases in the book are presented without diagnosis or treatment so that readers can be challenged to identify disorders, suggest appropriate therapies, and consider provocative questions (stated in the margins). By taking the perspective of the therapist, readers learn to think actively about the cases and apply their clinical knowledge and insights. These three special cases, each entitled "You Decide," are followed by corresponding sections in the appendix that reveal probable diagnosis, treatment approaches, and important clinical information about the disorder under discussion.

7. **DSM-IV checklists:** Each case is accompanied by a DSM-IV checklist, a detailed presentation of the DSM criteria for arriving at the diagnosis in question.

8. **Real clinical material:** The cases presented in this book are based on real cases, as are the treatments and results obtained. They are taken from our own clinical experiences and from those of respected colleagues who have shared their clinical cases with us.

9. **Interwoven clinical material, theory, and research:** Each case weaves together clinical material, theoretical perspectives, and empirical findings so that readers can appreciate not only the fascinating clinical details and events but also what they mean. Similarly, they can

recognize not only what and how treatment techniques are applied, but why such techniques are chosen.

10. **Current references:** The theories and treatment approaches that are described reflect current writings and research literature.

11. **Readability:** Of course, every book tries to be interesting, readable, and widely appealing. But case books provide a unique opportunity to bring material to life in a manner that deeply engages and stimulates the reader. We have worked diligently to make sure that this opportunity is not missed through not only showing the diversity of our clients and therapists but by making sure that readers walk away from the book with the same feelings of deep concern, passion, fascination, wonder, and even frustration that we experience in our work every day.

It is our fervent hope that reading these cases inspires empathy for clients, their relatives, their friends, and their therapists. The practitioners described in these pages struggle mightily to maintain both their humanity and their scientific integrity, and we believe that humanity is indeed served best when scientific integrity is maintained.

A number of people helped to bring this project to fruition. Foremost are the clinicians and patients who dedicated themselves to the efforts described in these pages. We are particularly grateful to Cindy Bott, Alan Fruzzetti, Kenneth Gorfinkle, Alex Kopelowicz, Philip Muskin, Helen Raytek, James Swanson, and Tim Wigal for serving as clinical consultants. We are also indebted to Cindy Bott, Greg Comer, Jonathan Comer, and Amy Dierberger for their superb drafts of clinical and related material which set the foundation for and added clinical flavor to case discussions throughout the book. And we thank Marion Kowalewski and Marlene Comer for their outstanding and tireless preparation of the book's manuscript, and Marlene Comer again and Margaret Gorenstein for their discerning commentaries and skilled editing throughout the process.

Finally, we are indebted to the extraordinary people at Worth Publishers, whose superior talents, expertise, and commitment to the education of readers guided us at every turn. They are Marge Byers, Catherine Woods, Barbara Reingold, Tracey Kuehn, and Sarah Segal. They have all been superb, and we deeply appreciate their invaluable contributions.

Ethan E. Gorenstein
Ronald J. Comer
April, 2001

CASE 1

Posttraumatic Stress Disorder

Table 1-1

DSM-IV Checklist

Posttraumatic Stress Disorder

1. A history of having experienced, witnessed, or confronted event(s) involving death, serious injury, or threat to the physical integrity of self or others. Reaction of intense fear, helplessness, or horror produced by event.

2. Event persistently reexperienced in at least one of the following ways:
   a. Recurrent distressing recollections.
   b. Recurrent distressing dreams, illusions, flashbacks, or a sense of reliving the experience.
   c. Distress caused by reminders of event.
   d. Physical arousal produced by reminders of event.

3. Persistent avoidance of reminders of the event and a subjective sense of numbing, detachment, or emotional unresponsiveness.

4. At least two marked symptoms of increased arousal:
   a. Difficulty sleeping.
   b. Irritability.
   c. Poor concentration.
   d. Hypervigilance.
   e. Exaggerated startle response.

5. Significant distress or impairment, with symptoms lasting at least one month.

Based on APA, 1994, 2000.

At age 71, Sofia, a retired professor of social work, was living a full and active life. Although retired, she had never been one to sit back and let life pass her by. She had always been an energetic and outgoing woman, something of a bon vivant who enjoyed good friends and good food. She was a regular subway rider, traveling all over the city to go to her favorite shops, restaurants, museums, and lectures, and to visit her numerous friends from the university community.

Sofia—A Woman of Energy and Optimism

In fact, Sofia's energetic and optimistic life in retirement was consistent with the robust and challenging state of mind with which she had always approached life. Indeed, she had never had any psychological difficulties to speak of, or even a sig-

Interest in stress disorders intensified during the Vietnam War, when clinicians observed that increasing numbers of returning veterans were experiencing *flashbacks* (intense recollections of combat traumas) and were generally estranged from everyday life.

nificant physical illness. On the other hand, she had certainly had her share of trauma earlier in her life. She had spent her late teens and early 20s in war-ravaged Poland, under Nazi occupation. As a Catholic, she was spared automatic deportation to the concentration camps. However, in Warsaw, where she lived, sudden deportation to a labor camp was a constant threat. According to prevailing procedure, German soldiers would cordon off a street without warning, and all able-bodied Poles who were captured would be loaded onto trucks. They would then be taken to munitions factories, rock quarries, or other war-related industries, where they would reside in barracks and perform slave labor for an indefinite period, sometimes just days, other times weeks or months.

Sofia had taken pride in her skill at evading capture. Athletic and in her prime, she had developed almost a sixth sense for evading German patrols. Her ability to cope with such dangers had instilled in her a fierce pride in her self-sufficiency, mental acuity, and physical resilience. She likened herself in those times to a cat: someone who quickly sized up a situation and made the right move almost instinctively, always landing on her feet.

Following the war, Sofia went to London to study for a bachelor's degree in classics. Upon graduation, she emigrated to the United States to study social work, eventually earning a doctorate and obtaining a faculty appointment at a major university, where she remained for 40 years.

At the university, she threw herself wholeheartedly into her career, devoting her life to teaching, research, and writing. Her intense involvement in her work was legendary, and there were anecdotes circulating in her department of how she had occasionally been found asleep at her desk when colleagues arrived in the morning; apparently, she had become so absorbed in her work that she had ended up staying the night.

With her devotion to her career, there was no doubt in Sofia's mind that her personal life had suffered. As she remained unmarried, her colleagues and students became her family (her family of origin had remained in Poland). Sensing her devotion, students flocked to receive the benefits of her wisdom and experience, which she generously bestowed. She, in turn, took great personal interest in her students' progress, maintaining contact with them and following their careers, sometimes for decades, after they had graduated.

And so it was, both prior to and during retirement; Sofia was a picture of emotional and physical strength—a woman of self-confidence and direction. Then, in one brief moment, everything seemed to change. She was struck by a catastrophe that took her life and state of mind in a direction that she could never have anticipated or imagined.

> Stress disorders can occur at any age, even in childhood.

Sofia—Disaster Strikes

Sofia was taking the subway home from a shopping trip when it struck a stationary train on the track ahead. Although her train was not traveling at high speed—perhaps 20 miles an hour at most—the impact was forceful enough to hurl the passengers from their seats, and partially crush the metal cars. Sofia herself had been standing at the moment of impact. As she was thrown forward, her left leg struck a seat jutting out in front of her, wrenching her knee, and her head struck a metal pole, knocking her out. When Sofia regained consciousness, she was lying in a pile of other passengers who had been thrown together in the same corner of the car. As far as she could make out in the dim light, most were unconscious and bleeding. Sofia put her hand to her own forehead and it came back wet with blood. She was horrified. What if she was bleeding to death and no one could reach her to stop the flow? She tried to get up, but could not overcome the weight of the other passengers. She spent the next half hour lying there, paralyzed with fear, wondering if she would be able to survive until help arrived.

When the rescue squad finally did arrive on the scene, the injured passengers were taken out of the train on stretchers. Only four were judged to require hospitalization—Sofia among them—and they were taken to separate emergency rooms in the vicinity of the train wreck.

The initial examination in the emergency room determined that Sofia had not suffered a critical loss of blood. Now, as she lay on a gurney awaiting further tests, the terrified woman stared wide-eyed at the gruesome scenes paraded before her: people being brought in as a result of stabbings, shootings, drug overdoses, and the like. A tough-looking stabbing victim, one with only superficial wounds, seated himself next to Sofia and winked at her. Sofia was aghast. She turned her head away from the derelict, hoping to escape his further notice, but she felt she might be set upon at any moment.

Sofia spent 3 hours in this highly anxious state, restrained by the straps on the gurney, until she was finally taken to the radiology department for tests. At first, she was relieved to be removed from the throng, but then, as she was wheeled down a dark corridor, she began to wonder if her relief was premature. Overcome by her fears, she even wondered whether she was being taken away to be raped or killed by the hospital orderly, of all people.

Once her X rays and a CT scan were completed, Sofia was returned to the waiting area, where her fears further intensified. Now she began to focus on the risk of contagion. Numerous patients were coughing persistently, and Sofia became alarmed that she was being exposed to tuberculosis, which had been making a well-publicized comeback in city hospitals. She glanced at the disreputable-looking man hacking away next to her. He seemed extremely haggard and sickly, practically spitting on the floor, and she became convinced she was about to contract a drug-resistant strain of tuberculosis.

After another 2 hours, the doctor finally arrived and informed Sofia that the X rays and CT scan had revealed no fracture or brain hemorrhage. He then helped her up from the gurney and tested her gait, physical mobility, and neurological signs. Everything seemed normal. The doctor told Sofia she was free to go home as soon as the nurse dressed her head wound. To play things safe, however, he also advised Sofia to see a doctor for follow-up.

Sofia was relieved to be released finally. However, she glanced at the clock and saw that it was now 1:00 a.m., 6 hours from when she had originally been brought to the hospital. The idea of venturing out into the night at this hour, in this condition, in this neighborhood, was, like everything else, terrifying. She was in a tremendous conflict. This horrifying emergency room was the last place on earth that she wanted to be in. But the alternative, leaving the emergency room to be discharged into the unknown, seemed even worse right now. She soon positioned herself in the same waiting area that moments before she had so fervently been hoping to flee. The frightened woman sat there amid the other patients' coughing, shaking, vomiting, and bleeding. In fact, she waited there until the first glimmer of dawn, and then hobbled out to a taxi waiting at curbside.

The taxi shepherded her through the awakening city. It was a strangely quiet, dreamy ride, completing the journey Sofia had begun on the subway some 12 hours before. She arrived at her apartment house in 20 minutes, dragged herself out of the cab and into her building, where she took the elevator up to her floor. Once inside her apartment, she collapsed on her bed, happy to be home at long last. What had begun as a simple trip home from a downtown shopping expedition had turned into a nightmare. Sofia slept for almost a full 24 hours.

Sofia—Aftermath of the Trauma

The next day, Sofia called some close friends to tell them what had happened. In the light of day, she now realized that one of the most disturbing elements of the whole experience had been coming face-to-face with the prospect of physical disability. As someone who lived alone and had no close living relatives, it occurred to her that even a temporary inability to care for herself could be disastrous. Fortunately, she had a close-knit network of friends and colleagues from the university where she had taught until a few years ago. With her calls this morning, she hoped to reassure herself that her friends would indeed step in if the need arose.

Her friends were sympathetic, and asked her if she needed anything. But, oddly, Sofia felt disoriented and found it difficult to answer their questions. The previous day's experience was now jumbled in her mind, and explaining it required considerable effort. It was tiring just to talk for a few minutes. By the time she had made the third call, her voice was so weak that her friend felt great concern, and suggested she see a doctor sooner rather than later.

Sofia set up an appointment with a neurologist for 3 days later. In leaving her apartment—for the first time since the accident—she was alarmed at how noisy and confusing it was just to be outside. The city traffic seemed unbearably loud, and Sofia wondered if she would even be able to cross the street. Her body still

> Women are at least twice as likely as men are to develop a stress disorder. About 20% of women who are exposed to a severe trauma develop such a disorder, compared to 8% of men.

ached from the accident, but more important, she became concerned that history might repeat itself. She had never been in an accident before and had never been concerned about crossing the street. Now, however, she found herself jumping back and running from cars as they zoomed past, even though she was still on the sidewalk.

Eventually, Sofia reached the doctor's office exhausted and out of breath. She was panting noticeably, as much from running as from her anxiety about the traffic. She didn't even speak to the receptionist when she first arrived. Instead, she collapsed on the nearest seat, closed her eyes and gulped for air, as though having just escaped some grave danger. After a few minutes, the receptionist noticed her sitting there and walked up to greet her. At the sound of the receptionist's voice, Sofia practically jumped out of her seat, she was so startled to find someone suddenly upon her.

The neurologist gave her a thorough examination and reviewed the X rays and CT scan taken in the hospital emergency room. He said that all results seemed normal, but that judging from the cuts and bruises on her head and her complaints about fatigue, noise sensitivity, and disorientation, she might well have sustained a concussion. He told her it was mild, but the symptoms could take several days or even weeks to go away. In the meantime, she should take it easy and get all the rest she needed.

> **Studies indicate that survivors of severe stress, especially those who develop stress disorders, experience abnormal activity of the neurotransmitter norepinephrine and the hormone cortisol.**

Noticing that Sofia's knee seemed quite swollen, the neurologist also referred her to an orthopedist. Two days later, the latter physician determined that Sofia must have torn the cartilage in her knee as a result of the accident, and now it was becoming inflamed. He stated that, for the time being, he would treat the knee with an anti-inflammatory drug; but should the inflammation not improve, or even worsen, arthroscopic surgery to remove the inflamed tissue would be necessary.

Sofia returned home from her appointment with the orthopedist with a vague sense of unease that gradually built to a feeling of impending doom. She had not expected to hear surgery mentioned, and the idea was unusually threatening to her. She shuddered at the thought of going back into a hospital. She recalled her emergency room experience and practically shook with fear as she considered the terrifying scene.

As time passed, Sofia's postconcussion symptoms—her fatigue, noise sensitivity, and disorientation—improved. Physically, she started to feel more her old self, but what she couldn't seem to shake was her fearfulness. Each trip outdoors was extraordinarily stressful. Crossing the street was consistently anxiety provoking, as she couldn't get over her preoccupation with becoming involved in another accident, this time as a pedestrian. Taking the bus or subway was simply out of the question. The very thought of getting on a train made her shudder. Accordingly, her travels were confined to small local trips in her neighborhood, just to do the necessities: buy food and go to doctors' appointments.

It seemed that Sofia's accident and emergency room experience had transformed her entire outlook on life. Somehow, having spent several hours in a highly charged emotional state, focusing almost exclusively on the prospect of dying, or being raped or murdered, her mind had started to see everything through this lens. And there was no escaping the memories. When home, in what she considered a safe environment, her memories of the subway car or the emergency room would constantly intrude. As she watched television, her eyes would glaze over as some particularly harrowing element of her experience forced itself into her consciousness: the pile of bodies in the subway car, the grim ride down the hall to the X-ray room, or one of the bleeding or coughing "thugs" sitting just a few seats away. Then she would try to shake the memory loose, forcing it out of her mind and trying to focus on something more pleasant, only to find it returning in bits and pieces throughout the evening.

Previously a sound sleeper, she now found herself waking frequently from dreams that contained images of her subway or emergency room experiences. They were not exactly nightmares; rather, they were mostly accurate renditions of her all-too-real experience. She couldn't escape the images, even in sleep.

> People who generally view life's negative events as beyond their control seem more prone to develop a stress disorder when confronted with a traumatic event (Regehr et al., 1999). Nevertheless, even people like Sofia, who have "hardy" attitudes and personalities, may experience a stress disorder.

Sofia Drifts Away—A Friend's Perspective

During the weeks immediately following the accident, Sofia talked on the phone to friends regularly, endlessly sharing her experience. At first, her friends were deeply interested and supportive. It pained them to consider what this grand elderly lady had gone through. But after a while, as Sofia turned every conversation back to her "horrible experience," her friends began to lose patience.

Even Fiona, perhaps Sofia's closest friend, came to dread her daily phone calls from Sofia. In a later conversation with her sister, Fiona tried to explain such a reaction and to describe the course that her relationship with Sofia had traveled in the months following the accident.

> At first, I hung on every word, trying to grasp the horror that had befallen her. I worried about her terribly, wanted to help her through this, wanted to be there for her. But after a few weeks, a sameness began to set in in our conversations. No matter what we talked about, Sofia found a way of turning the discussion back to her accident or her fears. If I told her about a film I saw, she would ask, "Did you take the subway?", and then she'd tell me, for the fiftieth time, how dangerous the subway is, how many crimes are committed in movie theaters, or some other tale of peril. Eventually, I felt unimportant to her, just an excuse to describe the danger she now saw everywhere. Sometimes, it didn't even seem as if she was even talking *to* me—just reciting her terrible litany out loud. It didn't matter that I was her best friend—anyone would have done fine.
>
> Once I realized what was happening, I would try to divert her attention from these topics. I would offer gossip about someone at the university, bring up items

from the news, or recall a funny or interesting event from past times. Nothing. Sofia showed no interest in anything except her newfound fears.

I would try to make plans to see her in person, rather than just talk on the phone. Sofia would not consider going out to a restaurant or movie; however, she would "let me" come over to visit her. Of course, during these visits we would just wind up talking about her fears again. Over time, the visits became shorter and shorter. Finally, I began to feel like a delivery person. Sofia would "allow me" to bring groceries to her or to pick up some laundry from the cleaners. Our whole relationship became empty and superficial. I tried letting her talk about her fears; I tried *not* letting her talk about her fears. But nothing seemed to help. In time, it became a moot point, because Sofia pushed me out of her life.

By 3 months after the accident, she had stopped calling me and would only occasionally answer my calls. Our communications were brief and very superficial, as if Sofia couldn't wait for them to end. She seemed very fearful over what had happened to her and, worse, over what might happen to her in the future. And, loving her, I truly felt for her. But, she also seemed to become increasingly angry, nasty, and cynical. Not at all the friendly and warm woman I have known for so many years. She acted as if she blamed me—I'm not sure for what—perhaps for not having gone through the same ordeal, or maybe for not seeming to care enough or to do enough now. All I know is that after a while, conversations or interactions with me seemed to further agitate Sofia. If I were to suggest that she see her doctor again or if I were to give her advice regarding her bad knee, she would act like I was bothering her and sticking my nose where it didn't belong. So I pretty much stopped. I stopped making suggestions or trying to coax her back into the world. It seemed easier for Sofia that way; it was certainly easier for me.

You know, in an odd way, I feel like I was a victim of that train accident. For the most part, I have lost my dearest friend. I have been forced to stand by and watch her drift away. This warm, energetic, and worldly woman who had added so much richness and love to my life has been replaced by a stranger—an obsessive, self-centered, angry woman—who seems to resent me and wants little to do with me. I am just so frustrated and sad and a little angry as well, I guess. For now, Sofia and I have an implicit understanding to keep some distance between us.

> One third of victims of serious traffic accidents may develop a stress disorder within a year of the accident (Stallard et al., 1998).

Sofia in Treatment—The Journey Back to Normalcy

Over the next few months, Sofia's life became more isolated. Her fearfulness did not improve, and her outdoor activities remained restricted to what she considered "safe" situations, although nothing felt completely safe. At the same time, her injured knee became more and more painful. When the orthopedist, during a subsequent visit, talked more certainly about the need for surgery, she burst into tears and cried out, "I cannot face going back into that horrible place. My life has already been ruined by this accident. If I go back into the hospital once more, I know I will never survive." Soon realizing that his patient was in need of more than physical help, the physician suggested that Sofia make an appointment with Dr. Martin Fehrman, a psychologist, just to discuss her situation and see if the psychologist had any helpful suggestions about her lingering fears and upsets. The next morning, after yet another fitful night's sleep, she decided to call Dr. Fehrman.

At the psychologist's office, Sofia recounted her "nightmare," and how her life had unraveled overnight. As a former professor of social work, she was rather sophisticated about psychological matters and had spent some time pondering her predicament. She told Dr. Fehrman that, on the one hand, she felt that her current state was an understandable result for anyone undergoing such a horrifying experience. But on the other hand, given her previous level of functioning, she would not have expected to become so completely undone by what she knew objectively to be a "just an accident." Her whole identity had become consumed by this accident and its aftermath. She felt like a different person.

After listening to Sofia's story, Dr. Fehrman concluded that her condition met the DSM-IV criteria for *posttraumatic stress disorder*. First, she had been exposed to a traumatic event that posed a threat of death or serious injury; moreover, her response to the event entailed intense fear. Second, the traumatic event was persistently reexperienced—in Sofia's case, in the form of intrusive recollections and intense psychological distress in response to cues that resembled the original trauma (subways, buses, traffic, and strangers on the street). Third, Sofia persistently avoided stimuli associated with the trauma, and experienced *numbing* (in the form of diminished interest or participation in activities, and the sense of a foreshortened future). Fourth, she exhibited persistent symptoms of increased arousal, including sleep difficulties, hypervigilance, and exaggerated startle response. This had been going on for 5 months now, and her functioning had been greatly impaired as a result. Dr. Fehrman believed that Sofia had experienced an *acute stress disorder* in the immediate aftermath of the train crash, but that as her early symptoms continued and even intensified after the first month, she was now experiencing posttraumatic stress disorder.

A specialist in stress disorders, Dr. Fehrman knew that both behavioral and cognitive approaches have often proved helpful in cases of posttraumatic stress disorder. The behavioral approach involves *exposing* the person—with either in vivo or imaginal exposure—to anxiety-provoking stimuli. The cognitive approach, called *cognitive restructuring,* guides the individual to think differently about the trauma itself and about possible current dangers. Dr. Fehrman typically used a combination of the approaches when treating clients.

In vivo exposure is used to help clients react less fearfully to stimuli and events around them. The in vivo exposure procedure for the posttraumatic stress disor-

If the stress symptoms begin within 4 weeks of the traumatic event and last for less than a month, the person is suffering from *acute stress disorder*. If the symptoms continue longer than a month, a diagnosis of *posttraumatic stress disorder* is appropriate.

der client is similar to that used with other anxiety disorders, such as phobias. A hierarchy of anxiety-provoking situations, ranging from the least to most threatening, is constructed by the client and therapist. The individual is then given assignments to enter these situations and to remain there for a period of time, usually until he or she experiences a significant drop in anxiety. The therapist generally has the individual repeat the exposures on several occasions until only minimal anxiety is experienced during the exposure. Such exposure assignments proceed up the hierarchy until the most threatening item is mastered.

Imaginal exposure is used to help clients with posttraumatic stress disorder react less fearfully when recalling the original trauma. The individual *visualizes* the entire sequence of events involved in the trauma for a prolonged period, on a repeated basis. In visualization exercises, the client usually listens to a lengthy tape-recorded description that he or she has provided. The purpose of the exposure is to desensitize the client to the memory of the trauma, in the same manner that someone would be desensitized to any phobic object through repeated exposure. In essence, the meaning of the traumatic memory as a danger signal is changed by the exposure experience, and it eventually stops producing a sense of threat. Ultimately, the traumatic memory can be readily put aside like any other long-term memory.

Cognitive therapy, which more directly challenges the accuracy of the individual's negative cognitions, can further bring about changes in the fearful reactions of persons with posttraumatic stress disorder. In one cognitive strategy, a client might be guided to write down or practice less catastrophic, less self-damaging interpretations of the trauma, often in connection with exposure exercises. Thus, Dr. Fehrman, like a number of professionals, included this approach in his treatment program. Under his care, Sofia embarked on a treatment program that extended over 19 sessions.

Session 1 In the first session, Sofia described the anxiety she had been suffering for the past 5 months. She also described the accident and its aftermath in the emergency room. She explained that the feelings resulting from that experience—mainly the fear of injury or attack—seemed to have colored her entire approach to life. "I just can't seem to get past this horrible experience. This is not me. It's like I've become somebody else. I've got to get my old self back."

Dr. Fehrman said he was optimistic that Sofia would be able to get back to her former self. He explained that she was suffering from posttraumatic stress disorder, the anxiety syndrome that arises following an intensely frightening experience. He also explained that, following such an event, most people go through a stressful period in which they feel especially vulnerable.

The psychologist then outlined the basic treatment strategy. He said one component of the treatment would involve surveying all the different ways in which

Sofia's life had been changed by her current fears and anxieties, paying particular attention to activities that had been curtailed. Then, the two of them would arrange the activities along a scale ranging from the least to the most threatening. Together, they would construct weekly exercises in which Sofia would enter— "expose" herself to—the situations she was avoiding, according to carefully specified procedures. Dr. Fehrman explained that Sofia's anxiety should ultimately improve after she repeatedly entered situations for specified durations and frequencies each week.

The second component of treatment, the psychologist explained, also involved exposure, but in this case, exposure to the traumatic memory itself. He noted that the memory of the trauma was provoking a strong emotional reaction in Sofia, and so long as this was the case, it would intrude on both her waking and sleeping life. He indicated that the emotional reaction provoked by the traumatic memory could be reduced by prolonged exposure to the memory itself.

Sofia was puzzled by the logic of this approach. She remarked that she already was experiencing repeated exposure to the traumatic memory; indeed, it seemed to intrude numerous times each day, but her emotional reaction remained as strong as ever. Dr. Fehrman noted that with these naturally occurring intrusions, the exposure often lasts only a few minutes; in addition, people are inclined to block out some of the more disturbing elements of the intrusion. The psychologist explained that, in general, improvement occurred only with prolonged exposure, perhaps 45 to 60 minutes at a time, and only when all the elements, including the most disturbing ones, were faced.

For the coming week, he asked Sofia to start monitoring her feelings and behavior. She was to note particularly any instances of fear and anxiety, including the *circumstances* that provoked the anxious reaction and any associated thoughts. In addition, the psychologist asked Sofia to start taking note of the various activities she was avoiding, so that he and she could begin constructing a series of in vivo behavioral exposure exercises.

> In many cases of stress disorder, antianxiety drugs are also used to help control the client's tension and exaggerated startle responses; antidepressants may help reduce the occurrence of nightmares, panic attacks, flashbacks, unwanted recollections, and feelings of depression (Friedman, 1999).

Session 2 Sofia began the next session by reporting that she had not kept any of the requested records. She explained that at her most recent visit to the orthopedist, he had once again voiced his skepticism that her knee would improve without surgery, although he could not rule it out. Sofia said that since this consultation, she had been completely consumed with the question of whether or not to have the surgery. The decision laid before her by the orthopedist had sent her into a state of anxiety and conflict that was overshadowing everything else.

Dr. Fehrman suggested that inasmuch as the orthopedist had told Sofia that there was no immediate need to make a decision, the client might consider removing that pressure entirely for a defined period. Specifically, the psychologist suggested that Sofia shelve the whole question of surgery for 1 month. Sofia expressed tremendous relief at this idea. Suddenly the future seemed brighter to her. She said she now felt prepared to throw herself wholeheartedly into the treatment.

At the same time, Sofia expressed concern that her physical limitations might prevent her from proceeding at a reasonable pace with in vivo exercises (that is, doing things she had been avoiding). It was decided, therefore, that for the time being, greater emphasis should be given to the imaginal exposure, and that the next session would be devoted to discussing the subway and emergency room experiences in more detail. Still, Sofia would try a couple of brief shopping trips in the coming week if she felt physically capable.

Session 3 Dr. Fehrman asked Sofia to relate the details of her traumatic episode, including the accident and its aftermath in the emergency room. Sofia began describing the episode matter-of-factly into a tape recorder, but soon closed her eyes in a trancelike fashion, as if trying to focus her efforts on an intensely painful task. She then described the whole episode in a detailed monologue lasting approximately 45 minutes. She included the bodies in the darkened subway car, the blood on her forehead, her helpless posture on the gurney, the threatening characters in the emergency room, and so on.

When she had finished, Sofia appeared drained. Dr. Fehrman praised her for her tremendous effort in recounting those experiences. He then asked her to estimate her level of anxiety at its peak during the monologue, and at the end of the monologue, using a 0-to-10 scale. Sofia assigned ratings of 8 and 5, respectively, indicating that some reduction of anxiety had occurred by the end of the monologue.

In one form of exposure therapy, *eye movement desensitization and reprocessing*, clients move their eyes in a saccadic or rhythmic manner from side to side, while recalling or imaging traumatic and phobic objects and situations. Some people with stress disorders have been helped by this approach (Cahill et al., 1999).

Session 4 Sofia and the psychologist listened to the tape together. While listening, Sofia closed her eyes and, as instructed, tried to imagine the events as vividly as possible. This time, she said she seemed to have experienced some new insights. First, she said that she now realized that one of the most troubling elements of the whole experience was the sense of "loss of control"—in this case, being at the mercy of various ambulance and hospital workers, and not being able to fend for herself. She drew a direct connection to her wartime experience, when physical and mental quickness were her most prized possessions, which she equated with life itself. She now realized that her accident and emergency room experience had dealt a severe blow to this most precious aspect of her self-image.

Dr. Fehrman tried to offer Sofia a means of viewing the experience in a less negative fashion, suggesting that occasional episodes of "loss of control" are a normal part of life, and that people are not necessarily diminished or demeaned by their occurrence. On hearing this, Sofia seemed tentatively prepared to accept the idea. She herself noted that, yes, even during wartime, when she felt so independent and vital, she had once been completely subjugated to the Nazi authorities for several days while temporarily imprisoned in a labor camp. Nevertheless, she had later been able to view that episode as a transient interlude in an otherwise independent existence. When freed, she had felt prepared to pursue her independence even more vigorously than before. She said she could now see how it might be possible to view the recent accident in a similar light, perhaps like a war injury.

Sessions 5–8 During the next 4 weeks, Sofia was instructed to listen to the tape almost every day. She recorded her peak anxiety level for about half of these imaginal exposures. Sofia's anxiety level declined progressively, and by the end of the 4th week, her anxiety reaction to the tape was virtually extinguished. Decided shifts in Sofia's thinking accompanied these reductions in anxiety. After about 2 weeks, when the client's peak anxiety had lessened considerably, Sofia told Dr. Fehrman that listening to the tape was making her feel that many of her fears had been overblown. By the 3rd week, when Sofia's anxiety had decreased still further, she stated that the reduction in anxiety seemed to be carrying over to other parts of her life. She had resumed taking short bus and subway trips, at first with friends and then alone; moreover, she said she felt much "looser" with her friends, who had remarked on and rejoiced over the improvement in her spirits. Sofia also observed that repeated listening to the tape had made her feel that the episode was "now part of my experience." The memory was no longer constantly "in the back of my mind"; nor did she feel compelled any longer to shut it out when she did think of it. In other words, its intrusive properties had been eliminated. By the eighth therapy session, Sofia reported that she had actually fallen asleep during a couple of listenings, so relaxing had the tape become.

During these same 4 weeks, Sofia also spontaneously began to take trips downtown, both by subway and bus, to places that she hadn't visited since the accident (again, first with friends and later on her own). At the about same time, her fear of youths on the street also declined.

The psychologist felt Sofia no longer needed to listen to the tape at this point, suggesting that the most benefit would come from Sofia's increasing the range of her behavioral activities through in vivo exposure. The therapist and client designed a plan for Sofia to take at least one local shopping or subway trip per day, plus a couple of downtown shopping trips per week.

Sessions 9–13 During these sessions, held over a 4-week period, the emphasis remained on the in vivo behavioral exercises. Sofia continued to become more comfortable using public transportation, and now did so without hesitation. At the same time, however, her physical condition was starting to deteriorate. Her

Some people with stress disorders also benefit from group therapy, where they can discuss with other trauma victims their lingering fears and other symptoms, their feelings of guilt or anger, and the impact that the trauma has had on their personal and social lives.

Survivors of train or plane crashes, hurricanes, tornados, or other large-scale disasters now sometimes receive on-site treatment from teams of mental health professionals immediately after the disaster.

knee had now grown so tender that she was finding it difficult to walk at all. The orthopedist was again pushing for surgery.

Intellectually, Sofia felt that the surgery was the rational solution to her problem at this point, but she didn't know if emotionally she could face going into a hospital. Thus, Dr. Fehrman suggested that perhaps this anxiety could be reduced through some exposure to preliminary aspects of the medical process. He suggested that Sofia begin taking some of the steps that would be involved if the surgery were *hypothetically* to take place, as a type of mock exercise. The first step would be to make an appointment with the orthopedic surgeon to inquire about the surgical procedure, including such matters as the preoperative testing involved, the duration of the surgery, the length of the hospital stay, and the recovery process.

Sessions 14–15 Sofia carried out the assignment and reported back on the information received from the orthopedic surgeon. It turned out that surgery would be arthroscopic, a couple of small incisions, through which the inflamed and torn cartilage would be removed. There would be a recovery period of several weeks, but after the first week she shouldn't be any more debilitated than she was now, and she should steadily improve after that point. Acquiring this information seemed to allow Sofia to consider the idea with some objectivity for the first time.

To further promote Sofia's psychological preparedness, Dr. Fehrman suggested that she now look into the arrangements that would have to be made for a home recovery—again, should the surgery "hypothetically" occur. At Session 15, Sofia reported that the home recovery arrangements could apparently be made without much difficulty. The psychologist then asked her to call the orthopedist's office manager and ask, once again hypothetically, how one would go about actually scheduling the surgery, should she decide to do so.

Sessions 16–19 Returning for Session 16, Sofia discussed her phone call to the orthopedic surgeon's office. In fact, she had gone ahead and scheduled the surgery, reminding herself that she could always cancel or reschedule it. By Session 19, the surgery date was only 1 week away and she felt only limited hesitation about proceeding.

According to one survey, posttraumatic stress symptoms last an average of 3 years with treatment, but 5½ years without treatment (Kessler & Zhao, 1999).

Epilogue

Sofia had the surgery and reported to Dr. Fehrman that it had gone "marvelously." From beginning to end, she was impressed with the professionalism and caring of the medical staff. Her only remaining task was to recover physically, which she expected would take several weeks. From a psychological standpoint, she felt she had now come full circle. It had been just about a year since her accident, and here she was, once again emerging from a hospital, but this time in good spirits and filled with optimism for the future, this time embracing her friends and their offers of help, rather than pushing them away.

Dr. Fehrman contacted Sofia by phone 3 months later and learned she had made a full recovery from the surgery. She said she now felt fully restored, both physically and mentally. Her traumatic accident had finally come to an end.

Around one third of the adults who were inside or just outside the Oklahoma City federal building at the time of the 1995 bombing developed posttraumatic stress disorder (North et al., 1999).

CASE **2**

Panic Disorder

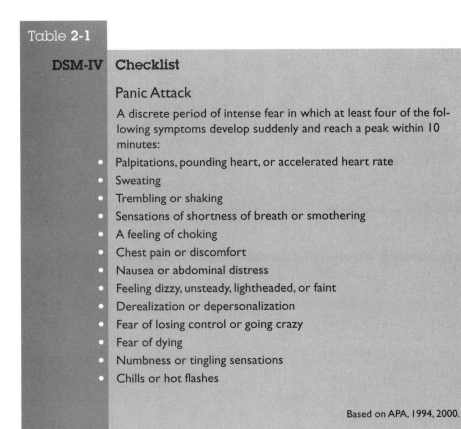

Table 2-1

DSM-IV Checklist

Panic Attack

A discrete period of intense fear in which at least four of the following symptoms develop suddenly and reach a peak within 10 minutes:

- Palpitations, pounding heart, or accelerated heart rate
- Sweating
- Trembling or shaking
- Sensations of shortness of breath or smothering
- A feeling of choking
- Chest pain or discomfort
- Nausea or abdominal distress
- Feeling dizzy, unsteady, lightheaded, or faint
- Derealization or depersonalization
- Fear of losing control or going crazy
- Fear of dying
- Numbness or tingling sensations
- Chills or hot flashes

Based on APA, 1994, 2000.

Table 2-2

DSM-IV Checklist

Panic Disorder with Agoraphobia

1. Recurrent unexpected panic attacks.
2. A month or more of one of the following after at least one of the attacks.
   a. Persistent concern about having additional attacks.
   b. Worry about the implications of consequences of the attack.
   c. Significant change in behavior related to the attacks.
3. Anxiety about being in places or situations from which escape might be difficult (or embarrassing) or in which help might not be available if paniclike symptoms were to occur.

(continued)

Table **2-2**	
DSM-IV	**Checklist**
	Panic Disorder with Agoraphobia *(continued)*
4.	Situations either avoided, endured with marked distress, or manageable only with the presence of a companion.
5.	Panic attacks are not due to the direct physiological effects of a substance or general medical condition.
6.	Panic attacks are not better accounted for by another mental disorder such as another anxiety disorder.

Based on APA, 1994, 2000.

> Panic disorder is twice as common among women as men.

Joe's childhood was a basically happy one. At the same time, it was steeped in financial hardship as his Hungarian immigrant parents struggled to keep the family afloat in the United States during the Depression. Joe's father, after a series of jobs as a laborer, ultimately scraped together enough money to start a small hardware store, which survived, but not without Joe's having to quit school in the ninth grade in order to help run the business. He put in 9 years at the store before eventually being drafted for World War II at the age of 23.

Joe: An American Success Story

When Joe returned from the army, he took a more studied interest in the store, and with some far-sighted marketing strategies turned it into a successful enterprise that ultimately employed six full-time workers. Joe was proud of what he had accomplished, but harbored lifelong shame and regret over his shortened education, especially as he had been an outstanding student. The store was thus both the boon and the bane of his existence.

Joe met Florence at age 45, after he had already taken over the store from his father and established himself as a respectable neighborhood businessman. Before meeting Florence, the energetic businessman's social life had been spare; his goal of making a success of himself was his overriding concern. Florence was a 40-year-old, college-educated administrator for an insurance company when they met. She was impressed with Joe's intelligence and wisdom, and would never have suspected that his education stopped at the ninth grade. As soon as they became serious, Joe revealed his lack of education to her as though making a grave confession. Far from being repelled, Florence was all the more impressed with Joe's accomplishments. The couple married within a year.

Joe and Florence worked hard, raised a daughter, saved what they earned, and eventually enjoyed the fruits of their labor in the form of a comfortable retirement when he was 70. The couple continued to live in the neighborhood where Joe grew up and had his business. They spent much of their time with friends at a public country club that was popular among local retirees. Joe also enjoyed tinkering daily with the couple's modest investments.

Six years into Joe's retirement, at age 76, Joe and Florence were returning from a Florida vacation when catastrophe struck. The catastrophe was not an airplane accident or anything like that. It was a more private event—a happening that was not even apparent to anyone but Joe. Nevertheless, it had a profound and expanding impact on the retired veteran, and it began a journey that Joe feared would never end.

> Unlike Joe's case, panic disorder usually first begins between late adolescence and the mid-30s.

Joe: The Attack

After their plane had taken off from the Miami airport, and Joe had settled back in his seat, he noticed that it was getting difficult to breathe. It felt as if all the air had been sucked out of the plane. As Joe's breathing became increasingly labored, he began staring at the plane's sealed door, contemplating the fresh air on the other side. Then, suddenly, he had another thought, which frightened him. He wondered if he might feel so deprived of oxygen that he would be tempted to make a mad dash for the door and open it in midflight. He struggled to banish this vision from his brain, but soon became aware of his heart flailing away furiously in his chest cavity. The pounding became almost unbearable. He could feel every beat. The beating grew so strong that he thought he could actually hear it.

Joe looked over at his wife, Florence, in the seat next to his. She was peacefully immersed in a magazine, oblivious to his condition. He stared at her fixedly, wondering what he must look like in such a state. His spouse glanced up for a moment, gave Joe the briefest of smiles, and went back to her reading. She obviously hadn't a clue as to what he was going through. Joe felt as if he were about to die or lose his mind—he couldn't tell which at this point—and she continued reading as if nothing were happening. Finally Joe had to say something. He asked Florence if the air in the plane felt stuffy to her. She said it seemed fine, but suggested that her husband open the valve overhead if he felt uncomfortable. He did so and felt only slightly better.

The rest of the plane ride was sheer torture. Joe spent the entire time trying to get the cool air to flow directly onto his face from the valve above. This activity sustained him until the plane landed. When the passengers were finally permitted to disembark, Joe couldn't get to the door fast enough. As he emerged from the plane, he felt released from a horrible confinement.

After arriving home at his apartment in the city, the retired store owner felt better. He was still shaky, but said nothing to Florence, who remained unaware of what had happened. Joe slept well that night and by the next morning felt like his old self. He decided to put the whole episode behind him.

Joe continued to feel fine for the next few days. Then, one night, he awoke at 2:00 a.m. in a cold sweat. His heart felt as though it were about to leap out of his chest; his lungs seemed incapable of drawing any oxygen from the air. His first thought was to open the bedroom window, to make it easier for him to breathe. But as Joe got out of bed, he suddenly drew back in alarm. He recalled the airplane door and what had seemed like an almost uncontrollable urge to force it open in midflight. He wondered if this meant he had an unconscious desire to commit suicide. Joe concluded he should stay away from the window. Instead, he sat motionless on the edge of the bed while his thoughts raced along with his heart toward some unreachable finish line. The man was frightened and confused. He was also gasping loud enough to awaken Florence. She asked him what was wrong and he told her his physical symptoms: He couldn't breathe and his heart was pounding so hard that his chest ached. Florence immediately concluded that her husband was having a heart attack and called an ambulance.

The ambulance workers arrived, administered oxygen, and rushed Joe to the hospital emergency room. By the time the patient got there, however, he was feeling much better. A cardiologist examined him, performed a battery of tests, and eventually informed Joe that he had not had a heart attack. In fact, there was nothing obviously wrong with him. The doctor told Joe he could go home, that the episodes he experienced were probably "just anxiety attacks."

Joe felt relieved that his heart seemed to be okay, but was confused as to exactly what was wrong with him. He wanted nothing more than to forget the whole matter. However, as time passed, that became increasingly difficult. In fact, over the course of the next few weeks, he had two more attacks in the middle of the night. In both cases, he just lay in bed, motionless, praying that the symptoms would go away.

Then there was a new development. One morning, Joe was walking down a busy street in his neighborhood, on a routine trip to the store, when he was overcome by the same symptoms he had previously experienced at night. Out of the blue, his heart started pounding, his breathing became labored, and he felt dizzy; also, he couldn't stop trembling. He looked around for a safe haven—a store or restaurant where he could sit down—but he felt as if he were in a kind of dream world. Everything around him, the people, the traffic, the stores, seemed unreal. He felt bombarded by sights and sounds, and found it impossible to focus on anything. The overwhelmed man then recalled the cardiologist's mention of the term *anxiety attack* and came to the sickening realization that the doctor must have detected that he had mental problems. Joe feared that he was on the verge of a nervous breakdown.

He was several blocks from home but discovered, to his relief, that he could make his way back to the apartment with less difficulty than he anticipated. Once inside, Joe sat down on the living room sofa and closed his eyes. He felt certain he was losing his mind; it was just a matter of time before the next attack sent him

> Many people (and their physicians) mistake their first panic attack for a general medical problem.

off the deep end. As he became caught up in his private terror, he heard a sound at the front door. It was Florence returning home from her shopping.

Once again, Florence appeared to have no inkling that anything was amiss. She cheerfully related the details of her shopping trip: the neighbors she met at the store, the things she bought, and the like. Joe could barely follow what she was saying, further proof, in his mind, that he was rapidly losing his grip. Finally, his wife suggested that they go out for a walk. At this, Joe realized that the very thought of leaving the apartment was terrifying to him. What if he had an attack in the middle of the street and could no longer function, physically or mentally? He felt as if he had a time bomb inside him. In response to Florence's suggestion, he simply broke down in tears.

Florence begged her husband to tell her what was wrong. Joe confessed that he had just had another one of his "attacks," this time on the way to the store, and that this one was so bad he was forced to return home. Now he dreaded going outside.

Florence could see that Joe was extremely upset, but at the same time she was puzzled. There didn't seem to be anything wrong with him. He was in no obvious physical pain, and he appeared vigorous and alert. She insisted they make an appointment with their regular doctor.

In the week before the appointment, Joe made a few tentative forays onto the street, in Florence's company. He felt some symptoms while outside, but did not have as intense an attack as he had that one time when he had been alone. His nighttime episodes increased in frequency, however—to the point where he could count on waking up with an attack almost every time he went to bed.

The Family Doctor: Armed with New Knowledge

At the doctor's office, Joe recounted his repeated attacks of racing heart, breathlessness, and tremulousness. He didn't know quite how to describe his fear of losing his mind, nor did he really want to, so he left that part out. He did convey, however, that he had now become so apprehensive about the attacks that he was reluctant to venture outside for fear of being overwhelmed. In describing his symptoms, Joe noticed that he was actually starting to experience some of them.

As he continued, his physician became increasingly confident that the patient was suffering from panic disorder. The doctor marveled to himself at how far medicine had come during the past decade. Not that long ago, a patient like Joe would have been hospitalized for weeks with a suspected heart problem and subjected to literally dozens of tests. If no major disease turned up, he would be released, but even then the suspicion would linger that he was on the verge of a major cardiac problem, and the patient would be advised to cut back on his activities and keep on the lookout for further symptoms. Far from being reassured, the person would feel like a ticking time bomb.

Around 2.3% of all people in the United States suffer from panic disorder in a given year; 3.5% develop the disorder at some point in their lives (Kessler & Zhao, 1999).

Now physicians were very aware of the power of panic attacks, and of how their symptoms mimicked those of a heart attack. As soon as cardiac and other physical conditions were ruled out, practitioners usually turned their attention to the possibility of panic attacks. Indeed, Joe's was the fourth case of probable panic disorder that the doctor had seen this month alone. Even more gratifying, effective treatments for panic disorders had been developed during the past several years. Now he could offer patients two forms of good news: one, that their hearts were fine; and two, that their condition was fully treatable.

After examining Joe, the doctor informed him that, other than a slightly elevated heart rate, everything seemed normal. He told his patient that his symptoms were by no means imaginary; rather, he had a well-known condition known as panic disorder. He suggested that Joe see Dr. Barbara Geller, a professor of clinical psychology at the nearby university, who also saw clients two evenings each week in private practice. Dr. Geller specialized in panic-related problems.

Joe was encouraged by his doctor's pronouncement that his condition could be helped, but he was leery of the idea of seeing a "shrink." He had never had any psychological treatment of any kind, and the whole idea fueled his secret fear, not yet expressed to anyone, that he was on the brink of insanity.

When they returned home, Florence urged Joe to call Dr. Geller, but he continued to put it off for a few more days. Florence, growing increasingly impatient, said she would call the psychologist herself to arrange the appointment, and Joe reluctantly agreed.

> Today's physicians must also be careful to consider possible medical explanations before making a diagnosis of panic disorder. Certain medical problems, such as *thyroid disease, seizure disorders, cardiac arrhythmias,* and *mitral valve prolapse* (a cardiac malfunction marked by periodic episodes of palpitations) can cause panic attacks. Medical tests can rule out such causes.

Joe in Treatment: Regaining Control Over His Mind and Body

After Joe recounted his experiences of the past few weeks in minute and animated detail, Dr. Geller asked him if he could recall ever having had similar attacks or sensations prior to these. Upon reflection, Joe realized that he had had these sensations before, during the Florida vacation itself. He recalled that the day after arriving in Florida he suffered a fall as he was walking down some steps toward the outdoor pool. His injuries were not serious, but a cut on his chin was deep enough to require a couple of stitches from the house physician. For the remainder of the vacation, Joe had momentary "jolts" of anxiety—including heart palpitations and mild dizziness—at the slightest indication of physical imbalance. He also realized now that, since falling, he had been very tentative in his walking.

Joe strained his memory to recall whether he had ever had similar attacks or sensations even before the Florida incident. The only thing he recalled in this connection was an extremely upsetting experience he had had more than 50 years ago, when he was in his 20s. It was something that he had never discussed with anyone.

When he was in the army, stationed in the Philippines after World War II, he and some buddies were driving a jeep back to base when they passed a local man

> According to research, people who are prone to panic attacks typically have a high degree of *anxiety sensitivity*. That is, they generally are preoccupied with their bodily sensations and interpret them as potentially harmful.

walking along the side of the road. To demonstrate goodwill, Joe offered him a ride. The man was grateful for this kindness and took a seat in the open vehicle. After traveling only a few hundred yards, however, the jeep hit an enormous pothole, throwing the man onto the road, where his leg fell under the jeep's wheel. The soldiers quickly loaded him carefully back onto the jeep and raced to the nearest civilian hospital. They had to leave the injured man there and depart, however, as they were already close to being AWOL.

When Joe visited the hospital the next day to assure himself that their passenger would recover satisfactorily, he was shocked at what he saw. Due to lack of staffing or supplies, or some such difficulty, the hospital had done nothing more than provide a bed for the injured man. As Joe tried to talk to him, the man just lay there, obviously traumatized, gazing absently into space. Joe left the hospital even more shaken than when he had witnessed the actual accident. He was certain he had ruined the life of another human being. He drove back to the base in a trancelike state, with his heart pounding and his eyes barely able to focus on the road. That intensity of feeling was the closest he had ever experienced to what he was currently going through.

After interviewing Joe and reviewing his medical reports, Dr. Geller concluded that his condition met the DSM-IV criteria for a diagnosis of *panic disorder*. His attacks typically included several of the required symptoms: breathlessness, heart palpitations, chest discomfort, tremulousness, sweating, and fear of losing control or going crazy. Moreover, he currently experienced almost constant apprehension over the possibility of further attacks. Finally, his panic disorder was also accompanied by *agoraphobia*, as he was beginning to avoid leaving the house, except in Florence's company.

Dr. Geller's reading of psychological literature and her own research on panic disorders had convinced her, along with many other clinicians, that panic attacks and disorders can best be explained by a combination of biological and cognitive factors. On the biological side, she believed that panic attacks are similar to the so-called *fight-or-flight response*, the normal physiological arousal experienced by humans and other animals in response to danger. The difference is that, with a panic attack, there is no external triggering event. From this standpoint, a panic attack can be considered a false alarm of sorts. The body produces its reaction to danger in the absence of any objective, dangerous event. People whose bodies repeatedly experience such false alarms are candidates for panic disorder.

On the cognitive side, Dr. Geller believed that a full-blown disorder is experienced by those individuals who repeatedly interpret their attacks as something more than false alarms. They typically identify the physiological reactions as a real source of danger. They may conclude that they are suffocating, or having a heart attack or stroke; or they may believe they are "going crazy" or out of control. Such interpretations produce still more alarm and further arousal of the sympathetic nervous system. As the nervous system becomes further aroused, the

The *fight-or-flight response* is so named because it prepares an organism to cope with a dangerous predicament either by fighting or fleeing. It primes the organism for a rapid use of energy by increasing heart rate, breathing rate, perspiration, blood flow to large muscles, and mental alertness.

person's sense of alarm increases, and a vicious cycle unfolds in which anxious thoughts and the sympathetic nervous system feed on each other.

For many people with panic disorder, the panic experience is aggravated by *hyperventilation*. As part of their sympathetic nervous system arousal, they breathe faster and deeper, ultimately causing a significant drop in their blood's level of carbon dioxide. This results in feelings of breathlessness, light-headedness, blurred vision, dizziness, or faintness—sensations that lead many people to further conclude there is something physically or mentally wrong with them.

Even if people with panic disorder eventually come to recognize that their attacks are false alarms set off by their nervous system, they may live in a heightened state of anxiety: anxiety over what their sympathetic nervous system might do. Many also develop anxieties about situations in which they feel a panic attack would be especially unwelcome (in crowds, closed spaces, airplanes, trains, or the like). Because of such *anticipatory anxiety*, their sympathetic nervous system becomes aroused whenever those situations are approached, and the likelihood of a panic attack in such situations is increased. The individuals may even avoid many such situations entirely—a pattern known as agoraphobia.

Given this integrated view of panic attacks and panic disorder, Dr. Geller used a combination of cognitive and behavioral techniques, each chosen to help eliminate the client's anxiety reaction to his or her sympathetic nervous system arousal. The cognitive techniques were designed to change the individual's faulty interpretations of sympathetic arousal. The behavioral component of treatment involved repeated exposure to both internal (bodily sensations) and external triggers of the person's panic attacks.

Session 1 To begin treatment, Dr. Geller showed Joe a list of typical symptoms associated with panic attacks, including the mental symptoms of "unreality" and "fear of going crazy or losing control." She asked the client which symptoms he had personally experienced. Joe was astonished to see his most feared symptoms actually listed on paper, and he seized the opportunity to discuss them openly at long last.

Dr. Geller explained to Joe that fears of going crazy were very common among panic sufferers; indeed, many people found them to be the most disturbing aspect of the disorder. She emphasized, however, that the fear of losing one's mind on account of the panic disorder, although common, was completely unfounded. There was no chance of Joe's going "insane." Although visibly relieved to hear this, he wondered aloud why it seemed as if he were coming apart mentally.

The psychologist gave him a quick sketch of the workings of the autonomic nervous system and the fight-or-flight response. She explained that Joe's disorientation on the street had been due to extreme arousal of his central nervous system, a useful feature in an actual emergency but confusing when there is no concrete

> Panic disorder is analogous to a phobia. However, rather than fearing an external object or situation, sufferers come to distrust and fear the power and arousal of their own autonomic nervous system.

> About 85% of those who receive cognitive–behavioral treatment for their panic disorder fully overcome their disorder (Clark & Wells, 1997).

danger. This hyperarousal, Dr. Geller indicated, made it hard—but not impossible—for Joe to focus his thoughts, leading to the feeling of disorientation. As for Joe's thoughts about rushing for the door of the airplane (and, later, the window at home), the psychologist emphasized that these were simply ideas: fleeting thoughts associated with the fight-or-flight response, but not actions that he was ever close to carrying out. And as far as Joe's disorientation on the street was concerned, she noted that in spite of it all, he had made it home satisfactorily and was in complete command of his faculties at all times. Increasingly, Joe seemed ready to entertain the possibility that his condition was not as dire as he originally had believed.

Dr. Geller further outlined for him the steps that would be taken to treat his panic disorder, and the rationale behind them. There would be four basic components of treatment: (a) training in relaxation and breathing techniques, (b) changing his cognitive misinterpretations of panic sensations, (c) repeated exposure to sensations of panic under controlled conditions, and (d) repeated practice in situations that Joe was currently avoiding or apprehensive about. For the coming week, he was instructed to monitor his anxiety and panic attacks.

Session 2 At the next session, the psychologist reviewed the records Joe had kept during the week. It turned out that he had not had any panic attacks during the day—he was still avoiding going out except with Florence—but that he was waking up almost every night with symptoms of breathlessness, palpitations, unreality, and fear of losing control. Dr. Geller asked Joe what he did when these symptoms occurred, and the client explained that he simply lay in bed, fervently hoping that the symptoms would subside. In order to help him recognize some of his cognitive misinterpretations and to begin changing them, Dr. Geller had the following exchange with Joe:

Dr. Geller: You said that when you got those attacks in the middle of night, you just lay in bed. Why is that?

Joe: Well, it could be dangerous if I got up.

Dr. Geller: Why would it be dangerous?

Joe: I might have a heart attack or something else serious might happen.

Dr. Geller: What did the cardiologist say about your heart?

Joe: He said it was fine; all the tests were normal. But my heart is pounding so hard, and it's so hard to breathe, I can't think of any other explanation.

Dr. Geller: Let's review what we discussed last time about the physiology of panic attacks and why people get certain symptoms with these attacks. . . .

Dr. Geller described in greater detail the fight-or-flight response, the physiological changes it produces in various organ systems, and the role of hyperventilation. In addition, she gave Joe a written summary of this material for him to study at his leisure. She explained that the most important conclusion to be drawn from this

Panic disorder can also be treated by medications that lower the arousal of a person's sympathetic nervous system. About 40 to 60% of those who receive the antianxiety drug *alprazolam* or certain antidepressant medications fully overcome their disorder (Lecrubier et al., 1997).

The close biological relatives of people with panic disorder are up to eight times more likely than the general population to develop the disorder.

material was that his panic attacks, although extremely unpleasant, were ultimately harmless, both to his physical and his mental well-being. Then the psychologist resumed the discussion with Joe about his nightly panic attacks.

Dr. Geller: In light of what we just discussed, how might you respond differently to the attacks you're getting at night?

Joe: Well, according to what you say, there would be no danger in my getting up. After all, the cardiologist did say my heart was fine. But I wonder if I might keel over just from the panic attack.

Dr. Geller: What has happened on other occasions when you had panic attacks and were sitting or standing up?

Joe: I certainly never keeled over. In fact, when I had the big one out in the street I even managed to walk several blocks to get back home.

Dr. Geller: So it seems that your fear of keeling over might be unfounded. Do you think you would prefer to get up for a while when you wake up with an attack, rather than lie in bed?

Joe: I suppose it would make more sense. When I have trouble falling asleep under normal conditions I certainly don't just lie in bed doing nothing. I usually get up and putter around or do a little paperwork at my desk.

Dr. Geller: From now on, why don't you try getting up when you awaken with a panic attack and do the things you would normally do. We'll discuss how this works out next time.

In the remainder of the session, the psychologist had Joe carry out a standard *progressive muscle relaxation* exercise. Under her direction, he alternately tensed and relaxed various muscle groups, with the goal of achieving complete relaxation in all muscle groups by the end of a 20-minute training session. This widely used exercise teaches clients to recognize excess muscle tension and to relax the tension at will. Dr. Geller felt that Joe could benefit from the relaxed feelings that the exercise produces and that the relaxation training might also lay the groundwork for an additional exercise in *breathing control*.

> At least 10% of people with panic disorder also experience major depressive disorder. In two thirds of such cases, the panic disorder precedes the onset of depression (APA, 1994, 2000).

The breathing control exercise trains clients both to prevent hyperventilation and to cope effectively when hyperventilation occurs. For this exercise, patients practice breathing using the diaphragm as opposed to the chest. Use of the chest is discouraged because it fosters pressured breathing, promotes hyperventilation, and can produce chest pain or discomfort when employed regularly. With diaphragm breathing (the so-called natural way to breathe), the chest is almost immobile; only the abdomen moves, ballooning out as the person inhales and collapsing as the person exhales. Use of the diaphragm promotes slow, unpressured breathing of the sort necessary to prevent or counteract hyperventilation.

The complete exercise, progressive muscle relaxation plus breathing control training, was tape-recorded during the session, and Joe was to practice it once a day by following the instructions on the tape.

Session 3 Joe and Dr. Geller again reviewed the records he kept during the preceding week. As advised, Joe had changed his response during the nightly panic attacks. Rather than lying in bed, he got up and did minor chores, reminding himself as he did so that the sensations he was experiencing were not dangerous. After following this practice every night, Joe noted that the nightly attacks were getting shorter; one attack subsided after only 5 minutes, as opposed to the 20 minutes or so that the attacks used to last.

Dr. Geller took this result as an opportunity to point out the cognitive component of panic, specifically, how overestimating the danger of panic sensations fuels the attacks, whereas assessing the sensations realistically allows the sensations to subside. Joe's more realistic mind-set about the nightly attacks this past week had resulted in shorter and less intense attacks by the end of the week.

Session 4 When Joe returned the following week, he reported that he still was waking every night with his panic symptoms; but as instructed, he was trying to appraise the sensations realistically and function normally, regardless. As a result, the symptoms seemed to be getting weaker and not lasting as long; in most cases now, it was only a matter of minutes before they subsided, aided, he felt, by his use of slow, diaphragm breathing. Still, he was leery of venturing outside on his own.

Dr. Geller gave Joe several instructions for the coming week. First, he was to continue with his current strategy for handling the nightly attacks and to continue practicing the diaphragm breathing exercise daily. In addition, he was to venture out at least three times on his own, if only to walk to the end of the block and back. If he experienced any panic sensations, he was to handle them as he did the nightly sensations: breathe slowly and with his diaphragm, appraise the sensations rationally, and behave normally.

> Between one third and one half of people with panic disorder also suffer from agoraphobia (APA, 1994, 2000).

Session 5 Joe reported that he had slept through the night three times this week, and on those nights when he was awakened, his symptoms had subsided within a few minutes. As instructed, he had gone out three times to the end of his block and back. In so doing, he experienced typical panic symptoms: heart palpitations, breathlessness, light-headedness, and unreality. The first time he did this exercise, Joe had felt so fearful he almost returned home before completing it. However, he followed the psychologist's instruction to complete the assignment regardless of the symptoms that arose. The second and third times, Joe had also experienced symptoms, but was more prepared for them and carried out the assignment without any thoughts of abandoning it.

Next, Dr. Geller proceeded with the *interoceptive exposure exercises*—repeated exposures to panic sensations under controlled conditions. She explained that he would do several exercises designed to produce sensations similar to those arising from autonomic arousal, and which therefore might trigger panic

Procedures that are used by researchers or therapists to induce hyperventilation or other panic sensations are called *biological challenge tests.*

symptoms. The goal was to progressively extinguish his anxiety reactions to these sensations, to give Joe opportunities to practice more accurate cognitive appraisals of such sensations, and to help him develop behavioral coping skills. The specific exercises that were carried out are listed in Table 2-3.

After each exercise, Joe reported the specific physical symptoms he experienced, and rated the symptoms with respect to (a) intensity, (b) resemblance to panic, and (c) level of anxiety provoked. Dr. Geller instructed Joe to practice the mildest of the three panic-producing exercises—holding his breath for 30 seconds—three times a day in the coming week. In addition, Joe was to continue taking short trips on his own, this week to a nearby store at least three times.

Sessions 6–9 Joe continued to progress over the next few weeks. By Session 9, he was carrying out on a daily basis three interoceptive exposure exercises—shaking his head from side to side for 30 seconds, staring at a spot on the wall for 90 seconds, and hyperventilating for 60 seconds—and getting minimal panic effects. In addition, his nightly awakenings were becoming infrequent, and he was traveling farther and farther from home without Florence. For Session 9, he traveled to see Dr. Geller alone by subway for the first time. Although Joe, in fact, ar-

Table **2-3** | **Interoceptive Exposure Exercises and Individual Reactions***

Activity	Duration	Intensity of Symptoms	Resemblance to Panic	Anxiety Level
1. Whole body tension	60 sec	3	0	0
2. Breathe through straw	120 sec	1	0	0
3. Shake head from side to side	30 sec	6	1	1
4. Place head between legs, and then lift	30 sec	3	2	2
5. Stare at spot on wall	90 sec	2	2	0
6. Hold breath	30 sec	5	5	3
7. Run in place	60 sec	6	6	4
8. Hyperventilate	60 sec	7	7	5

*Joe's ratings on a 0–10 scale. Exercises were derived from Craske & Barlow (1993).

rived at that session with stronger panic sensations than he had experienced in weeks, he simply mentioned his symptoms to the psychologist and proceeded to describe the other details of his week as if the symptoms themselves were a minor annoyance. Within a few minutes, they subsided.

Joe's instructions for the coming week were to continue practicing the interoceptive exposure exercises three times a day, and to travel freely, without restricting his behavior due to panic fears. The next session was scheduled for 2 weeks away.

Session 10 Joe reported that he had been panic-free for the entire 2 weeks. In addition, he was going wherever he needed to go, on his own, and without apprehension. He continued to perform the interoceptive exposure exercises, but at this stage they evoked no reaction; they mainly bored him.

Now he had a new concern. Florence was determined that they take a trip to Europe in the next couple of months. They would have to fly, of course, and the very idea revived painful memories of his experience on the plane from Florida, where his problem began. Joe had visions of reliving that terrible episode. Dr. Geller outlined a program of progressive exposure over the next couple of weeks to images and situations involving airplanes. This would include multiple viewings of movies involving airplanes, and trips to the airport twice each week.

Sessions 11–12 When Joe returned 2 weeks later for Session 11, he had spent the intervening time immersing himself in airplane-related imagery and situations. As anticipated, he had initially been anxious while watching the airplane movies, but by the 2nd week he was watching them without emotional reaction; he and Florence had also made it out to the airport three times, and each time Joe felt more at ease. Two weeks later, Joe and Dr. Geller met for the last time before the trip to Europe. At this meeting, he was panic-free, but still apprehensive about the trip. His parting words were, "I'll see you in a month—if I survive."

Around half of all people with panic disorder receive treatment for it (Narrow et al., 1993).

Epilogue: The Final Conquest

Joe returned triumphant from his trip to Europe. He had had no problems on the plane, or anywhere else. He felt his problem was behind him now. Dr. Geller chatted with him for a while about the trip, and stated she was glad that things had turned out so well. She and Joe reviewed the treatment program, including strategies he would follow should he have any symptoms in the future. Joe was feeling better—enormously better than he had for many months. Most of all, he felt that he had regained control over his body and his mind.

CASE **3**

Obsessive-Compulsive Disorder

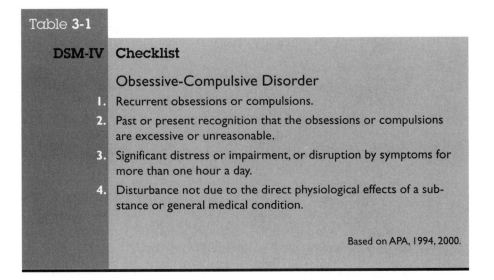

Table 3-1

DSM-IV Checklist

Obsessive-Compulsive Disorder

1. Recurrent obsessions or compulsions.
2. Past or present recognition that the obsessions or compulsions are excessive or unreasonable.
3. Significant distress or impairment, or disruption by symptoms for more than one hour a day.
4. Disturbance not due to the direct physiological effects of a substance or general medical condition.

Based on APA, 1994, 2000.

Sarah, a 26-year-old accountant, recalled her childhood as basically happy and carefree. She and her younger brother grew up in a comfortable middle-class environment in a racially integrated suburb. Although race relations in her neighborhood and school were considered good, as an African American she felt some pressure both to perform well in school and to conduct herself in a manner that was beyond reproach, as though the slightest misstep might increase her vulnerability to bigotry.

Sarah was in fact an excellent student and was considered a model for other children to follow. By junior high school, it was apparent that she excelled in mathematics, and even at that early age she had set her sights on a career in accountancy.

Her seriousness as a student continued through high school, where she described her social life as "conservative." In college, where she majored in mathematics and accounting, her commitment to academics continued. She also became more involved with boys, and developed a serious relationship with one boyfriend by her senior year.

Sarah: Early Worries and Odd Behaviors

Despite her generally happy youth, Sarah had been a "worrier" for as long as she could remember. For example, she always seemed more concerned about safety than other people did. She recalled that in college she had to check the lock on her door three or four times before she could walk away from her dormitory room. And even then, she was often left with a feeling of doubt, as though the door still hadn't been locked properly and a thief might get in due to her negligence. She dreaded the losses her roommate might sustain if there was a theft.

Obsessive-compulsive disorder usually begins in adolescence or early adulthood, although it may begin in childhood (APA, 1994, 2000).

Curiously, her own losses didn't seem to matter so much; it was more the idea of being responsible for another person's misfortune that troubled her.

Similarly, other areas of anxiety had produced some difficulties for Sarah over the years. For example, mailing a letter often posed minor problems. Although she always wrote, addressed, and stamped her mail with the utmost care, when it came time to deposit the letter in the mailbox she experienced doubts about whether everything had been done properly. Thus, she would stand at the mailbox, rereading the address three to four times and checking the stamp and return address as well, before actually dropping the letter in the box. After releasing the letter, she was always left with a sense of unease, as though something irrevocable had just taken place. Occasionally, Sarah's doubts were so strong that she would have to reopen the envelope and verify its contents.

Sarah: Beyond Worrying

Around four years back, soon after graduating from college, Sarah's worries and excessive behaviors had begun to take an extreme form. This change first occurred on the heels of a traumatic experience. Specifically, Sarah had been the target of an attempted sexual assault. About to enter her car after seeing a movie with some friends, she was accosted from behind by a stranger who tried to talk her into letting him into the vehicle with her. When Sarah refused, the man tried physically to force his way in, with the clear intention of sexually assaulting her. Sarah struggled and screamed for help, and the attacker was scared off. Hearing her cries, two ushers ran to the scene and apprehended the man as he was fleeing.

Eventually, the man was sentenced to four years in prison. Nevertheless, as time passed, Sarah began to experience increasing feelings of insecurity. She started to check her door lock several times before going to bed at night. Gradually, this extended to the checking of windows, faucets, appliances, and the like.

Sarah's feelings of insecurity and her accompanying rituals continued to expand during the next several years, to the point where they were currently making it impossible for her to lead a fully normal life. Mornings were a particular problem: She was finding it more and more difficult to leave her apartment and get to work. Each morning, the young woman felt compelled to perform a large number of rituals to verify that everything in the apartment was being left in a safe condition. She was concerned that her negligence might bring about some terrible event (a fire or flood) that would cause damage both to her apartment and, more importantly it seemed, to her neighbors' apartments.

Thus, Sarah would check that the stove had been turned off, the faucets turned off, and the windows closed, and that various appliances were unplugged, including the hair dryer, the microwave, the toaster oven, and the television, among others. Just checking all the different items once would have been a chore, but Sarah

> Studies reveal that many people with obsessive-compulsive disorder have unusually high standards of conduct and morality (Rachman, 1993).

typically felt compelled to check each item several times. Often, after checking one item, she would lose track of what she had already checked and so would have to go back and check everything all over again.

Sometimes she would go back to check an item even after having checked it seconds before. It seemed she could never be reassured completely. Sometimes she would stand and stare at an item for a full 5 minutes, hoping that this would be enough to persuade her that the item had been properly checked. However, even this was often not enough and, within a few minutes, she would find herself checking the item all over again.

On a bad morning, it could take Sarah up to 2 hours to get out of the apartment. Occasionally, after completing all her checking and getting out of her apartment building, she was suddenly seized with doubt about a particular item—Had she really checked the stove satisfactorily or did she just think she had?—and she would have to return to her apartment to end her suspense. A few times, she missed work altogether due to this checking. More often, she was able to break away after a certain point and would arrive at work late.

Fortunately, in her job as an accountant, she had a flexible schedule and it didn't matter when she showed up at the office, only that she get her work done. This she was able to accomplish by staying late. Indeed, she was highly valued for her abilities and had been promoted several times since beginning work at her firm 2 years before. However, her life in the morning had become, in her mind, a "living hell."

When Sarah returned home in the evening, the urge to check would be revived; she felt compelled to make sure that all was in order before going to bed. This nighttime checking was not as severe as the morning routine, however. She was somehow able to tell herself that everything had been checked earlier that day and, if she avoided using the stove or appliances before going to bed, a less thorough inspection would suffice. The next morning, however, the urge to carry out the complete checking routine would start anew.

Sarah also had another set of symptoms, which she would experience as she was driving to work. These other symptoms had begun a while back, after she had driven past a minor accident one day. Soon after passing the accident, the young woman ran over a bump of some kind. She looked in the rearview mirror to see what she might have hit, but observed nothing. After driving for another 15 minutes, Sarah was suddenly seized by the thought that she had struck another car or person. In the throes of this anxiety, she got off the highway and doubled back to where she had felt the bump. She was trying to determine if there was any evidence of an accident there—a disabled car or a body in the road—to confirm or disconfirm her fears. She discovered nothing, however, so she continued on to work, but still in a state of anxiety that she might have been responsible for some accident.

One survey indicates almost half of all adults have occasionally doubled back to make sure they turned off an appliance (Kanner, 1995).

As many as 2% of people in the United States and Great Britain suffer from obsessive-compulsive disorder in any given year (APA, 2000).

The next morning, similar doubts arose on the way to work, and the problem continued thereafter. Now, almost every day while driving, she would wonder if she had accidentally hit a person or another car. Any irregularity in the feel of the car could set her off: a bump, a swerve, or even just the realization that she hadn't been concentrating very hard on her driving. To reassure herself, Sarah would scrutinize the road through the rearview mirror. Most of the time she could reassure herself enough to keep on driving. Occasionally, though, she would be forced to double back on her route in order to confirm that no accident had occurred.

Since these driving doubts had arisen, Sarah had also been experiencing other images of havoc and destruction. The slightest thing could provoke them. For example, if she saw a set of matches on a desk at work, she would get an image of setting fire to her office building. Sometimes, after walking away from the matches, she would half wonder if she actually had set fire to the building; she would then review in her mind the sequence of events to reassure herself that no such thing had occurred. Occasionally, she would go back to obtain visual proof that the matches were still resting safely on the desk. In another case, she might see a knife on a table in a restaurant and get an image of stabbing somebody. Again, as she walked away, she would half wonder if she actually had stabbed someone; and then, as with the matches, she would review the sequence of events in her mind or return to the scene to establish that the knife was still there and she had not in fact carried out the imagined act. At other times, she would imagine less catastrophic events, insulting someone, for example, or neglecting to leave her car keys with the parking lot attendant.

James: Trying to Understand

Sarah and James had met during their senior year at college. They were in an accounting class together and, as James would tell friends, "The numbers added up quickly." He was totally taken with Sarah. He found her to be beautiful, effervescent, and caring. She took herself seriously, in a good way he thought—always wanting to be of service to others and to do the right thing in the right way. And as a bonus, they had similar interests, particularly interests in the business world: She wanted to be an accountant and he was determined to make it as a stockbroker. He felt that she was perfect and that their relationship was perfect.

Well, as it turned out, not entirely perfect. In fact, perfection was part of the problem. As James and Sarah grew closer, he became aware that she had some very odd habits—behaviors that she would repeat again and again according to certain rules, until she was certain that everything was okay. At first, he found her behaviors—checking locks again and again, addressing envelopes just so, and the like—to be kind of funny, like a personality quirk. But over time they became less funny. He saw that Sarah was a prisoner of her rituals. They made her very unhappy, they made her late for everything, and they prevented her from living a spontaneous life; but she could not stop them. When James pushed her for explanations, Sarah was clearly embarrassed. She would say that she just felt that she had to do these things, that she felt very anxious otherwise, but she didn't offer much more.

Concerned (and often annoyed) though he was, James believed that Sarah's behaviors were more or less tolerable—a price that he had to pay in order to have a relationship with an otherwise great woman. The two of them continued to grow close, and in fact they had become engaged two years before.

Unfortunately, his fiancée's strange habits had grown stranger still since the start of their engagement. The behaviors that he himself witnessed—constant checking, no longer just of locks, but of windows, faucets, appliances, and more—were certainly odd; but even more disturbing were the rituals that a desperate Sarah told him about one evening: the endless morning rituals in her apartment and the doubt-ridden drives to work. And then there were those mystery areas, the way she would go cold and freeze with apparent fear whenever she saw matches or came into contact with a knife. What was going through her head at these times? What was she worried about? These reactions she would not discuss with James at all, as close as they were and as much as she trusted him. She confided only that it was too dark to discuss and that if he loved her, he would let it go and let her be.

James did love her, and so, after much thought and heartfelt talks with a close friend, he decided to stay in the relationship with Sarah. Their wedding date was now 6 months away and he decided to focus on all the positive things about Sarah and go full-steam ahead with the marriage plans. He asked one thing of her, however—that she seek treatment for her problem, whatever it was. His request was not an ultimatum or condition of marriage, but rather, he explained, a plea from the man who loved her greatly and who worried that all of their wonderful future plans could unravel if she continued on as she was doing. Sarah more than understood the request. She knew, even better than James, how disturbed she was and how much worse she had been getting. And although James was not threatening to end the relationship, she knew that there was probably only so much that he could take. She loved him and didn't want to lose him. Even more, she was tired of living this way. Within a few days, she made an appointment with Dr. Marlene Laslow, a psychologist whose treatment of obsessive-compulsive disorders had received some attention in a recent newspaper article.

Treatment for Sarah: Eliminating Obsessions and Compulsions

Sarah recognized that her fears and rituals were in some sense absurd, but also acknowledged that she found them too compelling to resist. As she put it during her first visit with Dr. Laslow, "When I describe it to you here, I can practically

> Compulsive acts are often a response to obsessive concerns. People who repeatedly perform cleaning rituals may be reacting to obsessive fears of contamination. Similarly, individuals who repeatedly check locks and gas jets may be reacting to obsessive fears that their lives are unsafe.

> Obsessive-compulsive disorder is equally common in men and women (APA, 2000).

laugh about it, because I know it's so dumb. But when I'm in the situation, I just can't stop myself, the feeling is so overpowering."

After hearing Sarah's description of her thoughts and rituals, Dr. Laslow concluded that the client did indeed suffer from *obsessive-compulsive disorder*. Like most people with this disorder, the client exhibited both obsessions *and* compulsions. Her obsessions consisted of thoughts that some disaster (fire, flood, burglary) might be visited upon her apartment or her neighbors' if she did not take special precautions; thoughts that she might have caused a serious road accident; and thoughts and images of setting fires, stabbing people, or carrying out other, more minor, antisocial or negligent acts. Sarah's compulsions included her morning and evening checking routines, her unusual driving habits, and her repeated mental reviews of events to reassure herself that she had not run anyone over or had not burned down the house or stabbed someone.

Research indicates that antidepressant drugs, particularly the selective serotonin reuptake inhibitors, significantly reduce the obsessions and compulsions of many people with this disorder. But so does the behavioral approach called *exposure and response prevention*. Dr. Laslow's usual practice was to try the behavioral approach first, referring clients to a psychiatrist for drug therapy only if they failed to improve with this approach.

In the procedure of exposure and response prevention, clients are repeatedly exposed to anxiety-provoking stimuli, typically stimuli that are the subjects of their obsessive fears and thoughts. Then they are prevented from performing the anxiety-reducing compulsions that they would usually feel obligated to follow. The repeated prevention of compulsive behaviors eventually shows clients that the compulsions serve no useful purpose. The rituals are not needed in order to prevent or undo the clients' obsessive concerns, nor are they needed to reduce anxiety. In short, clients learn that nothing bad will happen if they fail to perform compulsive behaviors. At the same time, this approach helps them increasingly learn that their obsessive concerns are groundless and harmless, and so their anxious reactions to the obsessions lessen. In many cases, to help clients react less anxiously to their obsessive thoughts, Dr. Laslow also used a cognitive approach, in which the clients reexamined the actual sources of the obsessions and learned to interpret their repeated thoughts more accurately.

In the past, only repetitive behaviors could be considered compulsions. Today, however, repetitive "mental" acts (such as Sarah's frequent review of events to make sure that she had not run anyone over) can also be considered compulsions.

Session 1 In the first session, after Sarah described her current symptoms and their background, Dr. Laslow spent some time discussing the young woman's views on the danger posed by the objects of her obsessions. Sarah could see objectively that her morning efforts were excessive. She acknowledged that the danger from plugged-in appliances or dripping faucets was minuscule, but she felt compelled to take repeated measures "just in case, because, if anything did go wrong, it would be horrible." Sarah was also aware that it was extremely unlikely that she could hit someone on the road and not know it, or set a fire or stab someone and not know it. "It just seems that I want to know for certain that it isn't true; if I review it in my mind or go back to check that the person is okay, I feel relieved."

Sarah was less confident about her violent thoughts and imagery. Occasionally, when talking to someone, she would get an image of a knife in the person's chest; or, on seeing a book of matches, she might get the thought of setting fire to the building. Sarah was frightened by these images and thoughts because she assumed they indicated she was capable of committing such acts, even though all her life she had been someone who conscientiously obeyed every rule and regulation.

Dr. Laslow explained that these images should be viewed in the same spirit as the dripping faucet or the plugged-in hair dryer: They provoked anxiety, but they posed no objective danger. The psychologist pointed out that most people occasionally experience a bizarre image, or a thought of doing something outlandish or destructive; however, they just dismiss these thoughts as meaningless or unimportant. Sarah, on the other hand, kept reading disproportionate significance into such images; thus, she kept monitoring them closely and becoming extremely anxious in their presence.

Sarah:	But isn't there a problem with these thoughts? I mean, if I am thinking such things, doesn't it mean I'm capable of doing such things, or I want to do such things?
Dr. Laslow:	Do you have any conscious desire to do these things?
Sarah:	Of course not. They are the last things I would ever want to do.
Dr. Laslow:	I think the reason the thoughts scare you so much is that you've been assuming that their very presence means that you are in danger of carrying them out. Just because you think something, doesn't mean you want to carry it out or would ever carry it out. In fact, in spite of having the thoughts hundreds of times, you've never once made even the smallest gesture implied by the thoughts.
Sarah:	True. But sometimes I feel so close, like I have to put away the knives if anyone comes over, or if I were to touch a knife in someone's presence I would lose control.
Dr. Laslow:	Again, these are just assumptions on your part. The problem is not the thoughts or images themselves, but your incorrect assumptions about them and your excessively anxious reaction. During this treatment, you will learn through experience that these assumptions are not valid. When you are ready, we will do certain exercises in which you start coming into contact with knives more frequently, in fact more frequently than the average person. In doing this, you will learn that your fears are unfounded, and you will become less anxious when these

People with obsessive-compulsive disorder tend to believe that their intrusive negative thoughts are equivalent to actions and capable of causing harm to themselves or to others (Wilson & Chambless, 1999).

thoughts and images arise. As you become less anxious, you will also become less preoccupied with the thoughts and images, and will probably start experiencing them less frequently.

Sarah: Are there are other people with the same problem as me? With thoughts about stabbing people or setting fires?

Dr. Laslow: Yes, lots. In fact, the thoughts and images you describe are very typical of people with obsessive-compulsive disorder.

Sarah: That makes me feel better somehow. I guess I assumed I was the only person in the world with such bizarre and perverse thoughts.

Dr. Laslow: No, not at all. In fact, as I said, most so-called normal people will have a bizarre or perverse thought on occasion. Your problem is that you become excessively preoccupied with these thoughts.

For the remainder of the session, the psychologist further explained the exposure and response prevention treatment, describing the principles behind it and indicating how it would be applied to Sarah. The client indicated that the treatment plan made sense to her and she was ready to proceed.

For the coming week, Dr. Laslow asked Sarah to keep a diary of her obsessions and compulsions, using a form provided for that purpose.

Session 2 Sarah kept the requested records and, from these, three separate categories of obsessive-compulsive anxieties were identified: (a) household anxieties, (b) driving anxieties, and (c) anxieties over destructive thoughts and imagery. The session was spent setting up exercises that would pertain to the household anxieties.

To begin, a complete listing of all Sarah's household checking compulsions was made. The items that Sarah felt compelled to keep unplugged included the hair dryer, the microwave, the toaster, the toaster oven, the television, and the air conditioner. Light switches and lamps merely had to be shut off, not unplugged, to Sarah's way of thinking. Other items that she felt compelled to check were the stove (to make sure the flame was out), the faucets (to make sure they were not dripping), and the door (to make sure it was locked).

For exposure and response prevention exercises, Dr. Laslow proposed focusing first on the items that Sarah felt had to be unplugged or turned off. The psychologist suggested not only that Sarah plug these items in before leaving for work, but also that she turn a few of them on (specifically, the television, the air conditioner, and some lights) and leave them running for the whole day.

Sarah stated that she couldn't see any way she could bring herself to do what Dr. Laslow was proposing. Accordingly, a less extreme procedure was devised. Sarah would not be required to leave any items on; instead, she would simply plug them in. Beginning the next morning, she was to plug in each of the feared appliances and leave them that way for the rest of the day. Sarah felt that this exercise was within her capability and agreed to carry it out. In addition, she was to allow herself only one check of the lights, faucets, stove, and lock each morning.

Dr. Laslow cautioned Sarah about not surrendering to any urges to do unauthorized checks, no matter how strong. She compared obsessive-compulsive disorder to a machine that needed fuel, explaining that every time Sarah yielded to a compulsion to check, she was adding fuel to that machine, whereas every time she resisted the urge, she was taking fuel away. Therefore, whatever benefit might be provided by the exposure exercises would be undone if Sarah gave in to the urge to check.

Session 3 Sarah reported that she had carried out the instructions every day in the past week. By the end of the week, she found to her surprise that plugging in the appliances was producing no anxiety whatsoever. On the other hand, the urge to recheck the stove, lights, faucets, and lock was still present, although reduced. Nevertheless, as instructed, she had succeeded in limiting herself to one check for each item.

Sarah was pleased by her accomplishment and encouraged by the practical benefits of the new morning procedure. Instead of spending an hour or more with her checking routine, the current procedure could be accomplished in a few minutes, essentially just the time it took to briefly unplug and then replug the various appliances. This was already having a significant impact on her quality of life. Dr. Laslow suggested that now was the time to start limiting the checking even further. After some discussion, it was decided that Sarah would stop checking all light switches, while still allowing herself one check of the stove, faucets, and lock.

The psychologist also spent some time reviewing with Sarah her ultimate fears about household items. Sarah reiterated what she had stated in the first interview: Her greatest fear seemed to be a fire or a flood due to her negligence. She could envision the havoc and destruction, and being blamed; the very thought of it made her visibly upset.

Dr. Laslow suggested that in order for Sarah to overcome her preoccupation with this thought, some of the emotionality associated with it would have to be reduced. She proposed that the treatment of Sarah's household anxieties include prolonged and repeated exposure to images of her building being destroyed.

Sarah: You are saying it would be beneficial to eliminate or reduce the anxiety I feel when thinking of my building being destroyed. But isn't this anxiety appropriate? I mean, isn't it normal not to want the building destroyed?

Dr. Laslow: Yes, that is normal. But there is a difference between not wanting the building destroyed and getting anxious at the very thought of it. The first is appropriate, but the second is causing you difficulties. Of course you don't want the building to be destroyed, but you also don't want to be getting anxious at the very thought of it.

Certain antidepressant drugs (for example, *clomipramine, fluoxetine,* and *fluvoxamine*) also bring improvement to between 50 and 80% of those with obsessive-compulsive disorder (Taylor, 1995). However, in most cases, at least some of the patients' symptoms continue.

Dr. Laslow then explained the mechanics of exposure to anxiety-provoking thoughts or imagery. Sarah would have to develop a detailed description of the building being destroyed, perhaps both by fire and flood simultaneously. The description would include the hideous aftermath, the people whose lives would be lost or ruined, their awareness that Sarah was to blame, and their everlasting loathing of her. Together, the psychologist and Sarah worked on a written scenario. Next week, the session would be devoted to recording a 45- to 60-minute description of the event. Sarah would then take the tape home and listen to it.

Sarah's instruction for the coming week was simply to keep all appliances plugged in and not do any checking, except once for the stove, faucets, and door lock. The same procedure was to be followed at night before going to bed.

Session 4 Sarah reported that she had been able to keep to the new morning and evening checking procedure 95% of the time during the past week. She continued to keep appliances plugged in all the time, saying it now felt totally normal to her. She mentioned, however, that she did make one or two unauthorized checks of the stove. These extra checks seemed to have been provoked by her use of the stove that morning or evening.

On hearing this, Dr. Laslow instructed Sarah on a new exposure and response prevention exercise. Specifically, Sarah was to use the stove at least once in the morning and once in the evening every day, even if only to turn it on and off in some token fashion. Then she was to walk away without checking it further.

> Most people with compulsions recognize that their repeated acts are unreasonable, but they believe that something terrible will happen if they do not perform them (Foa & Kozak, 1995).

The remainder of the session was devoted to making the tape recording. According to this procedure, Sarah sat back with her eyes closed and imagined the scene as vividly as possible. She then began her verbal description: "I accidentally leave the water running as I leave the apartment. The overflowing water reaches an electric outlet, causing a short circuit. The walls ignite. Flames start shooting up to the apartment above me. The people are trapped . . ." Sarah continued for about 10 minutes, ending with the destruction of the building and her being blamed by the survivors. The psychologist then provided a second description, Sarah a third, and so on until a tape of 50 minutes in length was produced.

In addition to the stove exercises discussed earlier in the session, Sarah was given an assignment to listen to the tape daily, rating her anxiety prior to each visualization, at its peak during each visualization, and at the end of each visualization.

Session 5 Sarah reported she had been able to listen to the tape five times during the week, and she was indeed becoming less reactive to it. She also reported that her general feelings about causing a disaster seemed to be undergoing a shift of sorts, as a consequence of listening to the tape. She noted that, in thinking about being blamed for a disaster, her reaction was becoming one of "healthy defiance." Specifically, in her current frame of mind she was thinking, "I suppose I could cause a disaster, but so could anybody; if I did do it, it wouldn't be on purpose, and to hate me for it would be ridiculous."

Sarah was enthusiastic about the positive effects the tape appeared to be having on her, and she even seemed to look forward to listening to it again this week, feeling it led to more positive attitudes with each listening.

Regarding her other exercises, Sarah continued to keep all appliances plugged in. She also limited herself to one check of the stove, faucets, and lock in the morning and evening. As a new exercise, Dr. Laslow asked Sarah now to leave several lights on every day while she was away at work, and to stop checking faucets.

Next the psychologist raised the idea of Sarah's starting to limit some of her compulsions during the drive to work: the excessive inspection of the rearview mirror, driving too slowly, mentally reviewing events on the road to reassure herself, and keeping lane changes to a minimum. Dr. Laslow suggested that instead the client now start normalizing her driving habits, driving at least 50 miles per hour on the highway and making at least five unnecessary lane changes while driving both to and from work. She also instructed Sarah to check the rearview mirror only as required for monitoring traffic.

> Repeated cleaning and repeated checking are the most common kinds of compulsions.

Sessions 6–7 At the sixth session, Sarah reported that she had been able to follow through with the new instructions about changing her driving habits. To all outward appearances, her driving habits probably now seemed normal to onlookers. More important, these changes seemed to have reduced Sarah's obsessions about causing accidents.

It was decided that the next 2 weeks would be devoted to consolidating all of the changes that Sarah had made thus far. In addition, during the 1st of the 2 weeks, the client was to leave the radio on all day while she was away at work, and, during the 2nd week, the television. In the driving area, she was to continue with the current procedures.

Regarding the tape recording, by Session 7 Sarah reported that she could listen to the disaster scenario with hardly any reaction at all; if anything, she was getting bored with it. Accordingly, it was decided that she could stop listening to the tape.

In summary, by Session 7, Sarah's household obsessions and compulsions had virtually been eliminated. When driving, she was checking the rearview mirror much less frequently and even felt free enough to listen to morning radio broadcasts rather than obsessing over the possibility of an accident.

The next step was to work on the client's anxiety about committing deliberate, destructive acts: stabbing people and setting fires. For the coming week, Sarah's task in this area was simply to keep written records of the thoughts and her behavioral responses.

Session 8 Sarah reported that over the past week she had continued to maintain her gains in the household and driving areas. In fact, she sometimes amazed herself with how different she had become in household matters.

As instructed, she had kept records of any anxieties associated with destructive thoughts. She reported several typical incidents. Twice, while out to lunch at a restaurant, she was disturbed by the thought of stabbing her lunch companion. More frightening to Sarah, the same thought occurred when James, her fiancé, came over for dinner at her apartment. Similarly, thoughts and images about setting fires arose whenever Sarah came in contact with matches.

She also tried to observe her behavioral responses to these images or to her obsessions about knives and matches in general. She noted that she took pains to keep all knives hidden away in drawers while at home, particularly if she had company. She also made a point of never having any matches in the house.

Dr. Laslow proposed that they begin working on this problem with some in vivo exposures. First, as a response prevention measure, Sarah was to stop avoiding knives or matches. Indeed, she was to make special efforts to start exposing herself to these items. Specifically, at home she was to take all the knives out of the drawers and leave them on the kitchen counters for the entire week. In addition, she was to buy a box of matchbooks and place several books of matches in plain view in each room of her apartment.

Session 9 Sarah reported that she had indeed carried out the instructions concerning knives and matchbooks throughout the week. At first it had made her quite anxious to have these items out in plain view, but after a couple of days her anxiety subsided and she became accustomed to it. Still, she wondered how she would fare if anybody came to her house while the knives were accessible. She was concerned that the thoughts of stabbing someone might be overwhelming.

At this point, Dr. Laslow proposed some new exposure exercises for the coming week. Sarah was now to carry a Swiss Army knife in her purse at all times, in order to give her prolonged experience with having a knife accessible. In addition, the psychologist suggested that Sarah have James over to dinner while she kept all the knives displayed on the kitchen counter. If practical, Sarah was actually to use a sharp knife in his presence; for example, she could have him come into the kitchen to chat while she cut vegetables.

In addition, Sarah was to increase the intensity of her exposure to matches. Specifically, she had to strike several matches every day, blow them out, and then discard them.

Finally, Dr. Laslow suggested that the next session be devoted to recording another imaginal exposure exercise, one involving the violent imagery associated with knives and matches. Sarah herself suggested that the taped scenario focus on

> Obsessions may take such forms as obsessive *wishes* (for example, repeated wishes that one's spouse would die), *impulses* (repeated urges to yell out obscenities at church), *images* (fleeting visions of forbidden sexual scenes), *ideas* (notions that germs are lurking everywhere), or *doubts* (concerns that one may make the wrong decision).

her fiancé, since he was often the subject of her violent imagery, a factor that made the images particularly disturbing.

Sessions 10–13 At Session 10, Sarah and Dr. Laslow recorded the new visualization exercise: a 50-minute description of Sarah stabbing James and then setting fire to his building. As with the first exercise, the client reported high anxiety while visualizing the scene, but the anxiety tapered off slightly by the end.

For the next 2 weeks, Sarah listened to the tape daily, and as with the first visualization exercise, her anxiety lessened with each listening. At Session 13, she informed Dr. Laslow that she was barely feeling any emotional reaction at all when listening to the tape.

During this 2-week period, Sarah also kept a Swiss Army knife with her constantly. At first, the knife made her anxious, fueling her image of herself as "some kind of secret killer." However, as time passed, the knife seemed no more remarkable than her keys or wallet. It was just another item in her purse. She even used it on several occasions to slice tomatoes for lunch at her desk.

Sarah also scheduled the fateful evening with her fiancé. James came for dinner and she deliberately handled knives in his presence in the kitchen. In so doing, she experienced the usual violent image—she had an image of stabbing him—but she followed the instruction not to try to force the image out, as she had in the past. Instead, she just let the image occur and carried on normally with her conversation and dinner preparations; in so doing, her anxiety eventually subsided. Sarah also invited James over a second and third time during this period. On each occasion, she still experienced the image, but she became less and less anxious and preoccupied with it.

In the other areas—household and driving—Sarah had been faithfully following the specified procedures, which were beginning to feel like second nature. Now, in the morning, she was free of any extraordinary urges to check, and often did not bother with her one allotted check of the stove and lock. In driving to work, she felt like any other bored commuter. Occasionally, she said, she had a flashback to one of her former obsessions (about causing a car accident), but now it felt like just a vague memory of former times.

At Session 13, it was decided that Sarah would stop carrying out any active therapeutic procedures, which by now consisted mainly of turning on items before leaving for work and listening to the taped "slash and burn" scenario (as Sarah called it).

Session 14 Sarah reported on her first week of "normal life." She was not experiencing anything more than an occasional urge to check, which she resisted. A plan was made to meet at 2-week intervals for the next two sessions, and at 3-

> The most common theme found in obsessions is a fear of dirt or contamination. Other common themes center on violence or aggression, orderliness, religion, and sexuality.

week intervals for the two sessions after that. The goal was simply to keep an eye on Sarah's status and advise her on adjustments to any new situations. As it happened, in 3 weeks' time, Sarah and her fiancé would be married and beginning their life together in a new apartment.

Sessions 15–18   These follow-up sessions were held over a period of 2½ months. Throughout this period, Sarah was free of obsessions and compulsions in the household and driving areas.

Living with James, now her husband, turned out to present few unexpected challenges. As expected, however—and Dr. Laslow had advised the client about this—Sarah had initially experienced more frequent violent images. However, in keeping with all she had learned, she did not try to force the images out and did not treat them as a threat. After the first couple of weeks with her husband, the imagery lessened markedly.

Because everything continued to go well during this period, it was decided not to schedule any more therapy sessions. The psychologist asked only that Sarah return for one more visit in 6 months' time to report on her progress.

Epilogue

At her 6-month follow-up visit, Sarah reported that all was continuing to go well. Her only lingering symptom was an occasional violent image. On the other hand, she said such images were causing hardly any anxiety. Generally, she was extremely pleased, and she expected that these images would continue to lessen with time. Overall, she reported feeling like a different person, certainly different from the woman who had entered therapy a year ago, and also different from the person who had been suffering from less severe obsessions and compulsions for several years prior to that. Now able to focus on events and activities without the constant intrusion of frightening thoughts and images, and without the burden of complex compulsions, she found life much easier and, in turn, more enjoyable, than she had ever thought it could be.

Although drug therapy and behavioral procedures are often combined, it is not clear from research that such integrated treatments are consistently superior to the use of one of the approaches alone.

Major Depressive Disorder

Table **4-1**	
DSM-IV	**Checklist**

Major Depressive Episode

1. The presence of at least five of the following symptoms during the same two-week period: • depressed mood most of the day, nearly every day • markedly diminished interest or pleasure in almost all activities most of the day, nearly every day • significant weight loss or weight gain, or decrease or increase in appetite nearly every day • insomnia or hypersomnia nearly every day • psychomotor agitation or retardation nearly every day • fatigue or loss of energy nearly every day • feelings of worthlessness or excessive guilt nearly every day • reduced ability to think or concentrate, or indecisiveness, nearly every day • recurrent thoughts of death or suicide, a suicide attempt, or a specific plan for committing suicide.

2. Significant distress or impairment.

3. Symptoms are not due to the direct physiological effects of a substance or general medical condition.

4. Symptoms are not better accounted for by bereavement.

Major Depressive Disorder

1. The presence of a major depressive episode.

2. No history of a manic or hypomanic episode.

Based on APA, 1994, 2000.

Most people with a mood disorder suffer from *unipolar* depression—that is, they have no history of mania and return to normal or nearly normal mood when their depression lifts. *Bipolar disorder,* in which people suffer from both depression and mania, is the subject of Case 5.

Carlos was born in 1959 in Philadelphia, Pennsylvania. His parents had both been born in Puerto Rico, but moved to the mainland before their four children were born. Trained in Puerto Rico as a plumber, Carlos's father readily found profitable work in the continental United States. Eventually, he moved into selling wholesale plumbing parts and supplies. He worked hard to make his business work, and involved all four children in the fledgling company at early ages.

Carlos: A Comfortable Climb

By the time Carlos graduated from high school and began working in the family business full-time, it was a solid company that sold supplies to plumbers, builders, and contractors in several states. Thus, Carlos's career in the plumbing supply business was foreordained. Only an average student in school, he couldn't imagine what would have become of him if he had had to make it on his own. He was proud to carry his load in the family business, and indeed, felt he had a certain business acumen that his father and brothers respected.

On the other hand, as the baby in a family business, he had a lower status than his brothers during the early years of the business. His brothers did not dominate him deliberately; there were just occasional moments when they would "pull rank," so to speak. At the same time, Carlos felt a certain safety and security in what was basically a loving family atmosphere.

At the age of 20, Carlos married Sonia, whose family had also come from Puerto Rico. They had dated in high school and became engaged upon graduation. Two years later they were married in a large church wedding. They set up a traditional household, with Carlos working in the business and Sonia tending to the home. She gave birth to a daughter within a year of their marriage; another daughter followed 4 years later, then a son, and then another son.

Carlos: A Sudden Decline

At the age of 39, Carlos, by now the successful part-owner of his family's plumbing supplies business and the proud father of four children, became increasingly preoccupied with his health. His cousin, who was about 15 years older than Carlos, had recently suffered a fatal heart attack. Carlos was saddened by the loss, but didn't think much more of it at the time. However, within a few months, he started to worry about himself, and ultimately became convinced that he might also have a heart condition. He began taking his pulse constantly and putting his hand to his chest to decide if his heartbeat was palpable, believing that a pounding heart could be the sign of a heart attack.

Eventually, Carlos went to see his doctor, even though he had just had a checkup a few months before. The doctor performed an electrocardiogram (EKG) in his office; the results were completely normal. Carlos left the doctor's office reassured in a factual sense; but somehow it didn't help his mood. "A heart attack is still possible," he thought to himself.

In the succeeding weeks, he could not get over the idea of disaster striking. He envisioned the effect his death would have on his wife, children, and brothers, and found it devastating. On several nights he awoke with an overwhelming sense of despair, and sobbed quietly to himself while Sonia lay asleep next to him.

At work, Carlos lost all interest in his usual activities and could barely focus his thoughts at times. What did anything matter, he now thought, when such tragedy could strike? At home, he just sat and moped. He looked at his children as if they were already orphans, and tears would come to his eyes.

Carlos decided to see his doctor again. This time, the physician told Carlos that his preoccupation with the idea of a heart attack was getting out of hand. "You're fine, my friend, so stop your worrying." As the doctor spoke, Carlos's eyes welled up

Forty-one percent of persons with depression initially go to a physician with complaints of feeling generally ill, 37% complain of pain, and 12% report fatigue (Katon & Walker, 1998).

with tears, and the doctor realized that this patient was further gone than he had at first suspected. The physician recommended that Carlos see a psychologist, Dr. Alex Willard, who was also a member of their church; and he told Carlos that just one visit with the psychologist would probably be enough to set him on the right track.

Upon hearing Carlos's recital of his symptoms—feelings of despair, poor concentration, difficulty sleeping, loss of interest in usual activities, and tearfulness—the psychologist told Carlos that he believed he was suffering from depression and would benefit from psychological treatment. Dr. Willard also recommended that Carlos consult a psychiatrist, who could advise him on the benefits of antidepressant medication.

Carlos left the psychologist's office shaken. He had not expected to hear an actual diagnosis pronounced, and the idea of medication gave him the feeling that the real threat to his well-being now was not a heart attack, but rather, mental illness. In fact, Carlos's older sister had been diagnosed with schizophrenia years ago and had spent the past 2 decades in and out of institutions. Despite the psychologist's assurances that Carlos did not have any symptoms of schizophrenia, the troubled man now focused on the possibility that a similar fate could befall him.

Eventually, he went to see the psychiatrist, Dr. Charles Hsu, who had been recommended by Dr. Willard. After interviewing Carlos, Dr. Hsu concurred with the diagnosis of depression. He also reiterated that Carlos's symptoms had nothing to do with schizophrenia. Dr. Hsu then recommended that Carlos begin taking antidepressant medications.

The psychiatrist explained that antidepressant drugs are ordinarily very effective. Carlos would simply have to follow the medication regimen, taking one or two capsules of *fluoxetine* (Prozac) per day, and this might well be enough to relieve his depression and tide him over this difficult period. When Carlos asked whether he would have to undergo psychotherapy as well, Dr. Hsu replied that many people found taking the medication and undergoing psychotherapy at the same time very helpful, while others improved with medication alone. Carlos decided to try sticking with the medication alone for the time being.

He began taking Prozac, but after a few days concluded that he didn't like the side effects. He called Dr. Hsu and told him that he felt like he was about to "jump out of his skin." The psychiatrist explained that jitteriness was sometimes an initial side effect of Prozac, but that it often dissipated with time. He urged Carlos to continue with the medication a bit longer. However, Carlos simply couldn't stand this feeling, and pushed for a change.

Dr. Hsu switched Carlos to a similar antidepressant, *sertraline* (Zoloft). Although the patient experienced fewer side effects, he didn't seem to derive much benefit from the new medication. His feeling of despair persisted, apparently fueled by his sense of defeat at not getting better with Prozac in the first place. And the longer Carlos remained depressed, the more he became convinced that

---

Between 5 and 10% of adults in the United States, Canada, and Great Britain suffer from a severe unipolar pattern of depression in any given year, while another 3 to 5% suffer from mild forms (Kessler & Zhao, 1999). About 17% of adults experience an episode of severe unipolar depression at some point in their lives (Angst, 1995, 1999).

About 60% of people with severe unipolar depression respond successfully to antidepressant medications (Hirschfeld, 1999).

he was indeed headed toward a nervous breakdown, like his sister before him. Eventually, he was refusing outright to go to work, and Dr. Hsu felt it would be best to hospitalize him so a concentrated effort could be launched to find an effective medication regimen. Unfortunately, this also meant that Carlos's worst fears were now (in his eyes) about to be realized.

Carlos spent 3 weeks in the hospital, where various combinations of antidepressant and antianxiety drugs were tried. Ultimately, one combination provided some relief. Carlos was soon discharged from the hospital, with the plan of continuing to see Dr. Hsu once a week.

Although no longer hospitalized, Carlos was nevertheless struggling mightily. He hoped that if he just continued to take the medication and kept the demands on himself to a minimum, he would gradually recover. Accordingly, he cut his work hours by half, stopped seeing customers, and restricted his activities at the office to paperwork and occasional meetings with his brothers. In his spare time, he thought it best to lead a minimalist existence. At home, he told his wife he could no longer help take care of the children or do any other household chores. Accordingly, he spent his spare time napping, jogging in the park, or trying to watch an occasional television show.

The summer went fairly well by Carlos's current standards. As in the past, the family made their weekend trips to the beach, and Carlos resumed playing softball in his summer league. He was starting to feel a little bit better. Maybe, he thought, this whole horrible business would soon be behind him. As the summer drew to a close, however, Carlos started to get an uneasy feeling, which gradually built into a sense of impending doom. Somehow, he had gotten it into his mind that the end of summer would signal a turning point for him. He became convinced that with the approaching fall, he would either recover or descend into an abyss.

Unfortunately, it was the latter. When fall arrived, and Carlos still did not feel completely better, he lost hope of ever recovering, and his condition started to deteriorate again. He became preoccupied with the possibility of becoming sick again and, in due time, this preoccupation grew into the previous symptom picture: depressed mood, poor concentration, and loss of interest in usual activities.

> Approximately two-thirds of people with unipolar depression recover within 4 to 6 months, some without treatment (APA, 1994, 2000).

Sonia's View: Sinking Along With Carlos

Carlos was not the only person affected by his depression. His wife, Sonia, and their children—the people who lived with him and cared about him—were hurt by it as well. And, like Carlos, they were confused by the dramatic changes that they had seen in him. As Sonia explained to her sister:

> For years I lived with this strong man who was a good father and caring husband and who worked hard every day to provide a good life for all of us. Then over the

course of weeks, I watched him change into a sad, frightened, and weak person who could think of nothing but himself—his pain, his health, his unhappiness.

It seemed innocent enough when it first started. When Frank [the cousin] died, we were all upset, and it was natural to think about how young he was and how something like that could happen to any of us. But while the rest of us—his brothers, his cousins, and I myself—got over it and got back to our lives, it seemed to trigger something in Carlos that wouldn't let go of him.

First, it was his fear of having a heart attack. Then, his concern about dying. Then, worrying about every little thing, overprotecting himself, seeing doom everywhere. I would walk into the family room and find him sobbing. Over what? He was healthy, he was successful, he had a beautiful family, yet he was sobbing.

Time and again, I tried to point out the brighter side of things, to snap him back to his old self, but nothing helped. I talked my guts out. But, it was always, "Yes, but this" or "Yes, but that." He felt doomed and hopeless about everything; nothing made a difference.

It was horrible to see him so upset, but worse was the way he stopped doing anything. At home, he stopped being a father and husband. The kids would need help with their homework or have to be driven somewhere. The sink or car would need fixing. Or I would need to talk about finances with him. He could do none of it. He would just sit there, usually staring into space, sighing or crying. He became like a fifth child. Actually, it was worse than that. At least, I could reason with the children, get them to do things, have fun with them.

At work it was the same. His brother Enrique called one day, worried to death about Carlos. He was no longer doing anything there; he hardly was coming into work at all. The brothers had to pick up his work. They were worried. And they were angry, too. They couldn't really understand what was going on, and sometimes they resented the way they had to cover for him, the way he pitied himself, the way he turned them away. What could I tell Ricky? I too was confused, and worried, and angry. I too was watching him sink.

I was relieved when he went to the hospital. The medicine was not helping and he was only getting worse, and his behavior was really upsetting the children. In addition, I felt that I was in over my head. He was sinking and nothing I did made a difference. What if he decided to do something to himself? He certainly was dropping enough hints in that direction. Finally, I thought, we'll get this fixed. Actually, it was much easier at home while he was hospitalized. We didn't have to tiptoe around Carlos or worry about upsetting him or disturbing him. We missed him and were worried about him, but, at the same time, the cloud of darkness was temporarily lifted from the house; our spirits improved as well.

Overall, the hospitalization seemed to help him and his new medications brought some relief. After his return home, he was very shaky at first. In fact, he did even less than before. But then, he seemed to gradually be getting better. By the middle of the summer, I was sure that he had turned the corner. He was more ac-

About half of all people with severe unipolar depression also suffer from an anxiety disorder (Fava et al., 2000). In most such cases, the anxiety symptoms precede the depressive symptoms, often by years (Regier et al., 1998).

Between 6 and 15% of people with severe unipolar depression commit suicide (Inskip et al., 1998; Rossow & Amundsen, 1995).

tive again, seeing friends and even playing ball again. And he started to do more with the children. I really felt hopeful that I was getting my husband back.

That was a big mistake. For some reason, Carlos crashed down once again in the autumn, just like the leaves falling from the trees. It was like the summer had been a vacation from his depression, and now the vacation was over. I love him, but I don't think I can take another bout of this. Neither can the children. I doubt that Carlos can take it anymore, either. You know, I used to dismiss it when he would say that he wasn't going to recover, wasn't going to ever feel happy again. Now I wonder whether he might be right. One thing is for sure. Something has to be done. I told Carlos, and his psychiatrist, that more must be done. The hospitalization did not work. The medications are not working. More must be done. Last night, I found a video that we made at the beach a year ago. It shocked me. Carlos was a totally different person. I had almost forgotten how confident and happy he used to be. I almost couldn't recognize him. For his sake, and for ours, we must find that man again. In the meantime, I've lost my husband and my children have lost their father.

Carlos in Treatment: Focusing on Cognitions

Given Carlos's latest decline, Dr. Hsu suggested to the patient that now was the time to consider psychotherapy, which Carlos had initially hoped to avoid by taking the medication. The psychiatrist explained that he would continue trying to find a medication combination that provided some benefit, but that they should now cover those bases that had been missed up to this point. In particular, Dr. Hsu explained there was a *cognitive* form of psychotherapy, suited specifically for depression, that might provide the missing ingredient in the treatment Carlos had received up to this point. He wanted very much for Carlos to see a specialist in this kind of psychotherapy.

Carlos, now more willing to pursue psychotherapy, began treatment with Dr. Robert Walden, a psychologist who had in fact trained with Aaron Beck, a pioneer in the development of cognitive therapy, at Beck's Center for Cognitive Therapy in Philadelphia. Dr. Walden agreed with Dr. Hsu and Carlos's previous practitioners that their client met the DSM-IV criteria for a diagnosis of *major depressive disorder*. He exhibited a depressed mood most of the time, had markedly reduced pleasure or interest in his usual activities, suffered from sleep difficulty, and had lost both his energy and his ability to concentrate.

Like other cognitive therapists and researchers, Dr. Walden explained and treated depression largely by focusing on a person's style of thinking. Although a disturbance in mood is the most obvious symptom in this disorder, research suggests that disturbances in *cognition* have an important—perhaps primary—role in the disorder. Cognitive therapists believe that depressed individuals have a severe negative bias in their perceptions and interpretations of events, a bias that leads them to experience themselves, events in their lives, and their futures in very neg-

About 60% of people with severe unipolar depression respond successfully to cognitive therapy (DeRubeis et al., 2000).

ative—depressing—terms. The goal of *cognitive therapy* is to change this negative bias and negative style of interpretation, and, in so doing, remove the source of depression.

Although straightforward in principle, the application of cognitive therapy is no small matter. Concentrated methods have to be brought to bear in order to rid depressed persons of their cognitive bias. The process includes psychoeducation, self-monitoring by clients, self-examination, sustained questioning by therapists, personal research by clients, and retraining in how to think about things. In addition, *behavioral methods* are typically used to enhance the cognitive techniques.

> As many as 20% of the relatives of severely depressed people are themselves depressed (Harrington et al., 1993).

Session 1 Most of the first session of psychotherapy was devoted to a discussion of Carlos's current condition and the events leading up to it. In spite of his obvious distress, Carlos related the events of the past year in a coherent and organized fashion. At the same time, the desperation on his face was almost painful to observe, and his voice trembled with distress. He said he just wanted to know one thing: whether Dr. Walden believed that he could ever be cured. He stated that he had been through a lot, and felt that he was down to his last hope. He said he just wanted the straight truth: Was he ever going to get back to normal or not?

Like most mental health professionals who encounter a seriously disturbed patient, Dr. Walden found himself wondering for a moment whether Carlos could indeed be restored to his former self. At the same time, the psychologist knew that his own fleeting misgivings were the last thing that Carlos needed to hear right now. The psychologist told him that nothing was guaranteed, but that he had agreed to treat Carlos because he had every expectation of bringing about a full recovery. Carlos pressed the matter further, wanting to know specifically *when* he could expect to be restored to normal. "How many months?" he asked, "Why can't you tell me?"

Dr. Walden felt no antagonism in Carlos's close questioning about the timetable. Rather, he knew the questioning reflected Carlos's sense of desperation, his utter fear that he might be a hopeless case. He was obviously hanging on the psychologist's every word, looking for some glint of reassurance.

The psychologist felt he had to walk a fine line. On the one hand, he wanted Carlos to have confidence in getting better. On the other hand, given Carlos's history of becoming unduly focused on his rate of progress and then alarmed at not improving according to a self-determined timetable, Dr. Walden wanted to avoid setting up expectations for improvement by specific dates, foreseeing that if expectations were not met, it would fuel Carlos's negative view of the future.

Dr. Walden: I know you're anxious to get better, and I don't blame you. It's natural to wonder when this is all going to end. As I said before, I'm seeing you because, as I told Dr. Hsu, I expect you will recover from this depression and I can hasten the process. At the same time, I am reluctant to place an exact timetable on it, simply because it has been my experience that the rate of improvement varies from person to person. I could, of course, hazard a guess as to when you'll be better, but I'm concerned that if you don't have a complete recovery by that date, you might think it means more than it really does.

Carlos: I know. I would be upset.

Dr. Walden: So I think it best that we leave the timetable open for now. If the time ever comes when I truly think we're not getting anywhere, I'll let you know honestly and we'll consider our options.

Carlos: OK. I guess I can live with that.

Dr. Walden spent the remaining 15 minutes of the session giving Carlos a brief overview of the cognitive theory of depression and the implied treatment. He used Carlos's sensitivity to the timetable of recovery as an example of how certain negative perceptions or interpretations can have powerful effects on the way one feels. In particular, the psychologist noted that a different point of view, one that placed less importance on the exact timetable of recovery, would result in a less catastrophic response to the absence of a full recovery by a certain date.

The psychologist went on to explain that a major part of therapy would be discovering those aspects of Carlos's thinking and behavior that were undermining his capacity to feel well, and then to help him develop alternative ways of thinking and behaving that would ultimately reduce his depression. To begin, the psychologist explained that Carlos would be asked to monitor his emotional reactions throughout the next week, recording all thoughts or events that produced distress (sadness, anger, anxiety, or whatever) and rating their intensity. In the next session, Dr. Walden explained, they would discuss these matters, so as to bring out Carlos's thinking about them. In addition, the psychologist asked him to keep a diary of his activities.

Later that evening, the psychologist called Dr. Hsu, as the two had agreed (with Carlos's permission) to keep in close contact in order to coordinate their treatments. Dr. Hsu indicated that, unless the psychologist had any particular objections, he would like to begin Carlos on a low starting dose of yet another antidepressant, Anafranil. The psychologist agreed, so the plan was for Carlos to start the new medication the next day.

Session 2 Dr. Walden reviewed the records Carlos had kept throughout the week of both his moods and his activities, and these provided the focus of discussion. A distressing thought that Carlos had written down several times each day pertained to the seriousness of his current condition, expressed in several forms: "I'm a basket case." "How did I get so sick?" "I can barely function." These thoughts seemed to arise spontaneously, particularly when Carlos was inactive.

Studies suggest that a combination of psychotherapy and drug therapy is modestly more helpful to depressed people than either treatment alone (Frank et al., 2000; Miller et al., 1999).

Dr. Walden engaged Carlos in the type of Socratic dialogue that is typical of cognitive therapy.

Dr. Walden: You say you are a "basket case" and can barely function. What leads you to those conclusions?

Carlos: Well, I've been hospitalized. That's how bad it's been. I just can't believe it.

Dr. Walden: I know we discussed it last time, but tell me again what led to that hospitalization.

Carlos: I sort of got panicked when the medicine didn't help, and I stopped going to work or doing anything else. Dr. Hsu figured that as long as I wasn't working, I might as well go into the hospital where I could try different drugs without having to manage all the side effects on my own. I also was pretty miserable at the time. I told Dr. Hsu my family might be better off without me.

Dr. Walden: Do you think they would be better off?

Carlos: I don't know. I'm not doing them much good.

Dr. Walden: What would life be like for them without you?

Carlos: It would be terrible for them. I suppose saying they'd be better off without me is going too far. As bad off as I am, I'm still able to do a few things.

Dr. Walden: What are you able to do?

Carlos: Well, I'm not in the hospital anymore. And I don't think I will be back either. When I went into the hospital, I didn't really feel any worse than I do now. I mainly went in because I thought I could get better treatment or whatever. But it didn't pan out, so what would be the point of going back in?

Dr. Walden: So the fact that you were in the hospital isn't really a sign that you are now or ever were a "basket case," which I take to mean someone who is completely helpless and can't function.

Carlos: No. If I knew then what I know now, I probably wouldn't have been hospitalized at all. In looking back on it now, it was all basically voluntary. But that doesn't erase the fact that I'm still a mess.

Dr. Walden: How much of a mess are you?

Carlos: I can't work, I can't help out at home, I can't even watch a television show. What else do you want to know?

Dr. Walden: A couple of minutes ago you said you were still able to do a few things. What are those?

Carlos: I can drive to work and . . . I guess it's an exaggeration to say that I can't work at all. There are a few things that I do at the office.

Dr. Walden: Like what?

> Studies have found that depressed subjects recall unpleasant experiences more readily than positive ones, denigrate their performances on various tasks, and expect to fail in various situations (Lloyd & Lishman, 1975; Cole & Turner, 1993).

With continued discussion, the psychologist helped Carlos to recognize the various capabilities that he did have, and how, in practical terms, he wasn't as compromised as the terms "basket case" and "barely able to function" implied. Dr. Walden also pointed out that Carlos really didn't know the limits of his capabilities because he had deliberately reduced the demands on himself under the questionable assumption that "stress" would worsen his condition. The psychologist suggested that they start testing this assumption by having Carlos make a few simple additions to his activities. After some discussion, it was decided that each day Carlos would make a concerted effort to get up and leave for work at 8:00 a.m., the same time he used to leave before becoming depressed. Second, it was decided that Carlos would read a bedtime story to his two younger children each night; moreover, it was specified that he try hard to attend to the content of the story, rather than allow his thoughts to drift off into his own concerns. He was to note on his activity record his daily success in carrying out these two assignments.

Finally, Dr. Walden asked that Carlos continue to keep a record of his unpleasant emotions and the thoughts associated with them. This time, however, the client was also to try to produce alternative, more realistic thoughts by considering whether his initial thoughts truly reflected all the evidence. Furthermore, the more realistic thoughts were to be written down.

> When nondepressed subjects are manipulated into reading negative statements about themselves, they become increasingly depressed (Bates et al., 1999).

Session 3 Carlos appeared upset when he came in for the third session. He said that he had begun taking the Anafranil 5 days ago—he had put off starting it, even though Dr. Hsu had written the prescription almost 2 weeks ago—and he was experiencing pronounced "light-headedness." He stated that the medication only made him feel worse, and he was inclined to stop.

The psychologist's private feeling was that Carlos, although experiencing actual side effects, was becoming unduly alarmed over the sensations and, as a result, was experiencing the effects more intensely than he might otherwise. He needed some help in tolerating the sensations psychologically, until such time as his body adjusted. Dr. Walden was particularly concerned that Carlos not repeat the scenario of 6 months ago with Prozac, when he became panicked over the initial side effects, insisted on going off the medicine, and lapsed into despair over his prospects of recovery.

> Sales of antidepressant drugs total $10 billion annually.

Dr. Walden:	Tell me exactly what you've been feeling since you started the medicine.
Carlos:	I feel light-headed, dizzy, especially when I get up suddenly.
Dr. Walden:	Have you spoken to Dr. Hsu about it?
Carlos:	Yeah. He says that this sometimes happens when people start this medicine, but it will probably get better.

Dr. Walden: Why does it bother you so much?

Carlos: I don't know. It makes me feel like I might topple over or something.

Dr. Walden: Have you toppled over?

Carlos: No. It just feels like I might.

Dr. Walden: Has the light-headedness prevented you from doing anything? Were you able to drive here, for example?

Carlos: I drove. In fact, while I'm driving I don't seem to notice it that much.

Dr. Walden: Is there anything that you feel you can't do because of the symptoms?

Carlos: Well, I didn't leave for work at 8:00, like we had agreed. I figured, given the way I'm feeling, why push myself?

Dr. Walden: What about reading to the kids?

Carlos: I did that! It worked out fine. I made a point of focusing just on the story for the 15 minutes or so that it lasted, and I was amazed I could actually do it. I've read them a story every night this week.

Dr. Walden: Great! I'm glad that you made that effort, and it sounds like you got some satisfaction from it.

Carlos: Yeah. But this light-headedness, it really bothers me.

Dr. Walden: Remember last week when I pointed out the principle of considering all the evidence both for and against a particularly upsetting thought that you have, and then trying to produce a more balanced thought? How about trying your skill at this situation with the light-headedness? What is your immediate thought about the light-headedness? Why does it bother you so much?

Carlos: Well, I guess my immediate thought is, "This light-headedness is terrible, I'm not going to be able to function at all."

Dr. Walden: What is the evidence?

Carlos: I guess the evidence shows that I'm still doing at least as much this week as I did last week, in spite of the light-headedness. Also, considering what Dr. Hsu said, it probably won't last, or it should get better.

Dr. Walden: So what is the more balanced thought?

Carlos: I guess it is: "This is a damn nuisance, but it's a known side effect of the medicine and does not mean that something is going wrong or that I'm going downhill."

Antidepressant drugs are the second most prescribed class of drugs, just behind drugs for high blood pressure (Express Scripts, 1999).

Based on his more balanced conclusion for his behavior, Carlos decided it was worth putting up with the light-headedness temporarily in order to see if the medicine would benefit him. Second, he decided he should not eliminate any of his activities on account of the light-headedness, unless there was clear evidence that carrying out the activity presented a physical hazard. This meant that if he noticed a surge of light-headedness, he would persevere with his ongoing activity. In addition, it was decided he would once again attempt last week's assignment of leaving for work every morning by 8:00 a.m., and continue reading to the kids for 15 minutes every night.

Session 4 Dr. Walden asked Carlos first about the behavioral assignments. The client reported that he had continued to read to the children each evening throughout the week, and was doing so with a "clear head." On the other hand, he complained that for the rest of the evening, he would just sit around and mope, sometimes sitting in the living room chair for an hour or more worrying about his condition and his inability—or lack of desire—to do anything else, while the rest of the family went about their normal activities. Dr. Walden asked him about his negative thoughts during this period, and the client replied that it was "the same old thing," meaning thoughts about being a basket case and unable to function. The psychologist asked Carlos if he was able to refute such thoughts when they arose. The client replied that he was carrying out the exercise of weighing the evidence and forming alternative thoughts, but that within a few minutes the negative thoughts would return. Then, he would carry out the thought exercise all over again. It was getting to be repetitive.

On hearing this, Dr. Walden reviewed with Carlos their earlier discussions about the objective extent of Carlos's disability. The client acknowledged that his characterization of his condition as being a basket case was exaggerated, but he seemed to have trouble holding on to this more accurate assessment and had to remind himself constantly that he was in fact functioning reasonably well, all things considered.

Dr. Walden felt that the next step was for Carlos to bring the force of behavior behind his reformulated thoughts. That is, it was time for Carlos to participate more fully in the family's evening routine. Such participation would help to refute his exaggerated perceptions of being dysfunctional, and promote greater belief in the alternative: that he was temporarily depressed but still capable of doing more than he currently allowed. Second, more activity would provide a wider range of stimulation, thus diverting Carlos's thinking from its strictly depressive content. Finally, from the standpoint of family dynamics, becoming more active would help to bring Carlos's existence more in tune with the family's, leading to a more normal family environment and, at the same time, reducing some of the tension with Sonia, who was becoming increasingly angry at being the only responsible adult in the household.

According to research, various kinds of regular exercise often help alleviate depression (Tkachuk & Martin, 1999).

A large portion of this session was therefore devoted to working out in detail the appropriate routine for Carlos to follow in the evening at home. It was decided that he would follow a set routine upon returning home from work: (a) talk to his wife about her day, (b) eat dinner with the family, setting aside his own concerns and attending as closely as possible to the conversation, including asking the children some questions about their day, (c) assist the children with their homework, (d) read the newspaper or watch television, (e) read to the children before bed, (f) do household or work-related paperwork, (g) go to bed.

At the end of the session, the psychologist asked Carlos about his success in leaving for work by 8:00 a.m. Carlos reported that he had found he could do it, but had learned that it was important not to get caught up in what he termed a "stall mode" in the morning—by which he meant becoming so wrapped up in his thoughts that he paused and brooded for several minutes at a time before proceeding to the next task. The best strategy, he observed, was to maintain his momentum by going directly from one task to another. As for the light-headedness, Carlos noted that it was greatly reduced this week, as Dr. Hsu had predicted, so he was less concerned about it.

The main assignments for the coming week were outlined on paper: (a) Continue to leave for work at 8:00 a.m. consistently, avoiding the "stall mode," (b) follow the new evening routine, (c) continue to record negative thoughts and to produce more balanced alternatives.

> **Women are at least twice as likely as men to experience episodes of severe unipolar depression (Weissman & Olfson, 1995).**

Session 5 Carlos reported that he had been able to follow the prescribed routine at home. He found that keeping his attention focused on the concrete tasks before him—reading the kids a story, asking them questions about school, doing some paperwork—had a way of reducing his pattern of depressive thinking. He told Dr. Walden he was pleased with his ability to do these things, and he was even starting to enjoy some activities. In fact, he spontaneously decided to go to the playground a couple of times to play catch with his older son, and had a pleasant time. His wife, on the other hand, was not so pleased with the changes, Carlos remarked.

Carlos: Well, she obviously prefers me this way as compared to the old way, but now she's asking me why I couldn't do these things before. Her idea, basically, is that it is too little too late. She said she's had a year of misery.

Dr. Walden: What are your thoughts on why you couldn't do those things before?

Carlos: I don't know. It's still sometimes a struggle to do them now, but I feel better doing them. I never realized the connection between how I was thinking and acting, and how I felt. Also, I wonder if the new medicine has anything to do with it. I'm feeling better, but I tried at least a dozen different medicines in the past, and none really seemed to do that much. Do you think this one is helping? I don't want to be taking something that isn't necessary.

Dr. Walden: There is no way of knowing for sure how much the medicine is helping. The two treatments—the psychotherapy and the drug therapy—were started more or less at the same time, so your improvement could be due to the medicine, the psychotherapy, or the combination. Regardless, the good news is that you *are* improving, so I don't think we should even consider your going off the medicine for the time being.

Further discussion returned to the question of Sonia and her resentment of the past. Carlos's initial thinking was: "She's self-centered; she has no appreciation for what I've been through; she's just going to make my condition worse and undo my progress. Pretty soon I'll just be back in the same boat." Dr. Walden had him weigh the evidence both for and against such notions. The client recognized that most of Sonia's actions in the past year had indeed been supportive, even if she did have occasional lapses into frustration. He also recognized that he would get worse only if he himself strayed from his current regimen, and he had no intention of doing so. His more rational conclusion was: "She's been a good wife throughout all of this, especially considering the hard time she's been through. If I just show some understanding, it will probably help her frustration. In the meantime, she's not doing anything that would prevent me from getting better."

The next discussion turned to Carlos's routine at work. He reported that he was spending about 6 hours a day at work (9:00 a.m. to 3:00 p.m.), but found himself feeling frequently depressed there. Apparently, he had severely cut down his activities at work under the assumption that stress could exacerbate his condition. As a result, he had a lot of dead time on his hands, which he would spend sitting at his desk, staring at his computer, and brooding over the extent of his disability and his rate of progress. Carlos was doing his best to refute his negative thinking—reminding himself of his improvements—but it seemed like a never-ending process.

Dr. Walden pointed out the inconsistency between Carlos's attempts to refute his negative thoughts and his actual behavior in the situation:

Dr. Walden:	It's good that you're challenging the incorrect idea that you're a basket case and can't function. But if you really know that such thinking is wrong, why are you still limiting your activities at work?
Carlos:	I guess I'm afraid that any increased stress might ruin my progress.
Dr. Walden:	What happened when you started taking on more responsibilities at home?
Carlos:	I got less wrapped up in my worries.
Dr. Walden:	What lesson does that seem to teach for the work situation?
Carlos:	That I should start doing more things. I'm not even doing the minimum. And I can't say that I ever had that much stress from work. I mean, I'm one of the owners. I set my own pace. I always put in a good day's work—at least I used to—but I never saw any point in going overboard.
Dr. Walden:	So, getting back to my original question about how to conduct yourself at work ...
Carlos:	I know, I know. It makes no sense at this point to be slacking off like I am.

As many as half of all depressed clients may experience marital problems. In such cases, couple therapy may be as helpful as cognitive therapy (Teichman et al., 1995).

People who consistently ruminate—that is, repeatedly dwell on their moods without acting to change them—are more likely to become clinically depressed than people who do not generally ruminate (Nolen-Hoeksema, 1995, 1998).

Carlos agreed to gradually start building up his activities at work. Specifically, he would (a) leave the office at 5:00 p.m., rather than 3:00 p.m., (b) resume handling telephone sales calls, and (c) resume attending the daily sales meetings with his brothers and the sales associates. For now, he would omit seeing customers face-to-face, going on sales visits, or taking overnight business trips.

All other aspects of the treatment program (record keeping, thought exercises, the home routine) remained in place.

Later, the psychologist once again called Dr. Hsu in order to exchange observations. Dr. Hsu said he had met with Carlos the previous day and was impressed with the gains he was making. He said he normally would be inclined to increase the Anafranil dose at this point, but decided to hold off since Carlos was doing so well at the low dose and, in Dr. Hsu's experience, every increase in medication caused a level of disturbance in Carlos that was probably better to avoid. Dr. Hsu indicated that he planned to maintain the low level of medication indefinitely.

> If people who respond to antidepressant medications stop taking the drugs immediately after obtaining relief, they run as much as a 50% risk of relapsing within a year (Montgomery et al., 1993). The risk of relapse decreases considerably if they continue taking the drugs for 5 months or so after being free of depressive symptoms (Kocsis et al., 1995).

Session 6 This session focused on Carlos's adjustment to the fuller day at work. The client's overall impression was that it was going well. He noted particularly that when he was actively engaged in practical activities—talking on the phone to customers, attending meetings, speaking to coworkers about business concerns—he tended not to brood. In contrast, when he retreated to his office and sat idly at his desk, he became caught up in depressive thoughts and images.

Dr. Walden suggested that Carlos use this observation to his advantage and do what he could to minimize the brooding. The psychologist recommended that he follow a four-step mental procedure to cope with periods of brooding. Step one was simply to recognize that he was becoming caught up in depressive thinking. Step two was to identify the specific negative thoughts involved. Step three was to consider the evidence, and then produce more rational or balanced thoughts. Step four was then to put the issue aside and turn his attention to practical matters.

Carlos liked the idea of having a concrete procedure to follow, and remarked that he had already applied a similar strategy on his own in a few situations. But why couldn't he just sit and "do nothing" without getting depressed? Dr. Walden explained that there was no such thing as "doing nothing." The mind is always active; if it is not engaged in one thing, it is engaged in something else. The point was for Carlos to keep his mind engaged in rational and constructive activities, rather than irrational and destructive ones.

Sessions 7–9 Over the course of the next 3 weeks, Carlos applied the four-step procedure as consistently as possible and was reaping the benefits. He was becoming more and more engaged in the practical aspects of daily life and less consumed with negative thinking. The result: He was feeling normal most of the time. He was participating fully in the family routine and, at work, was meeting the responsibilities he had set for himself. As he functioned better, it strengthened his conviction that he was not headed for a permanent mental collapse.

At the same time, during this period, Carlos had experienced an episode of anger after his eldest brother questioned a decision that he had made at work. An extended therapy discussion revealed Carlos's negative thinking: "Ricky thinks I'm incompetent; he has no respect for the good work I do around here; he thinks he's smarter than anybody." With Dr. Walden asking Carlos to weigh the evidence, he came to realize that this characterization was not accurate. Far from thinking he was smarter than anybody, Ricky was a nervous person who fretted constantly about the smallest business details, worrying about mistakes he might have made, and generally making a pest of himself with everybody. Carlos now recognized that when Ricky questioned one of Carlos's decisions, it reflected his brother's own insecurity more than anything else. With this understanding, Carlos felt he could take his brother's comments more in stride.

> Studies reveal that depressed people who lack social support remain depressed longer than those who have a supportive spouse or warm friendships (Moos & Cronkite, 1999).

Sessions 10–14 In the 4 weeks comprising sessions 10 to 14, Carlos had returned to full functioning and was in good spirits most of the time. He had even resumed going on overnight business trips. Accordingly, the therapy sessions themselves were now devoted to *relapse prevention*. The goal was to help Carlos understand the basic beliefs underlying much of his depressive thinking.

It was, for example, apparent that the client's most fundamental depressive belief was a so-called *vulnerability to harm and illness* schema—a belief that disaster is about to strike at any time and that the client is helpless to protect himself. This particular belief seemed to be the basis of Carlos's original preoccupation with heart disease and his preoccupation later on with the prospect of a total mental breakdown.

Session time was spent reviewing the various negative thoughts that had arisen due to this belief. The goal was to improve Carlos's ability to recognize when the belief was active and to take it as a cue to confront the resulting negative thoughts. As one exercise, the therapist had Carlos practice verbally refuting the negative thoughts that he had experienced thus far due to this belief.

In a related vein, Carlos's current behavior patterns were scrutinized for any remaining behavioral practices that might inappropriately be producing a sense of vulnerability in him. In this regard, he noted that he was still cutting short his exercise regimen, a remnant from the time when he was preoccupied with heart attacks. He decided he would now reinstate an exercise level more in tune with his athletic interests and his true physical capacity.

Epilogue

Because Carlos had had such a severe depression prior to cognitive therapy, both Dr. Walden and Dr. Hsu decided to follow him on a once-a-month basis and have him continue to take a low dose of Anafranil for at least 18 months. Carlos continued to feel well during this period and experienced no return of symptoms after the Anafranil was eventually withdrawn. With each day, he became more convinced that a dark cloud had been lifted from his life—more accurately, that he had lifted the cloud. It was not that he felt happy every minute of every day, but rather that he felt armed to cope with and even conquer life. Problems were now perceived as challenges—challenges that could be overcome, challenges from which he could grow. The dark cloud had indeed been lifted.

As many as 30% of depressed patients who respond to cognitive therapy may relapse within a few years after completing treatment (Cameron et al., 1999; Shea et al., 1992). A continuation of therapy, perhaps on a less frequent basis, seems to reduce the rate of relapse (Clarke et al., 1999; Spanier et al., 1999).

CASE 5

Bipolar Disorder

Table **5-1**	

DSM-IV Checklist

Manic Episode

1. A period of abnormally and persistently elevated, expansive, or irritable mood, lasting at least one week.
2. Persistence of at least three of the following: • inflated self-esteem or grandiosity • decreased need for sleep • more talkativeness than usual, or pressure to keep talking • flight of ideas or the experience that thoughts are racing • distractibility • increase in activity or psychomotor agitation • excessive involvement in pleasurable activities that have a high potential for painful consequences.
3. Significant distress or impairment.

Bipolar I Disorder

1. The presence of a manic, hypomanic, or major depressive episode.
2. If currently in a hypomanic or major depressive episode, history of a manic episode.
3. Significant distress or impairment.
4. Symptoms are not due to the direct physiological effects of a substance or general medical condition.

Based on APA, 1994, 2000.

Gina, an only child, was raised in a prosperous family. Her father was the chief executive officer of a major charitable organization, and much of his work involved the hosting of fund-raising events to support charitable projects. Through these events, Gina's family acquired a wide array of prominent people as family friends and acquaintances.

Gina attended an exclusive private school for girls, where she was an above-average student. She did not seem to experience any unusual psychological problems during childhood and early adolescence. A popular girl who got along well with others, she had many friends. At about age 17, however, there was an incident that, as it turned out, foreshadowed the problems to follow.

Bipolar disorders usually first occur between the ages of 15 and 44 years (APA, 2000).

Gina: The First Incident

In her senior year of high school, Gina became very involved in a school play production, in which she had a minor acting role. As the production progressed, she became more and more absorbed in the work. Her presentation on stage during rehearsals became increasingly theatrical, and she became more involved in her costuming and makeup. The other students initially were in awe of the teenager's increased level of creativity and comfort on stage. However, with time, her behavior became bizarre. Once, for example, in the soda shop where students would gather after rehearsals, Gina became so giddy and talkative that she approached strangers for rambling conversations, telling some that she was a famous actress. Once, she actually burst out in song, reveling in the attention she got, which was actually not admiring.

Soon the other cast members were distancing themselves from the high school senior. As matters progressed, Gina's joy shifted into a state of paranoia. She became convinced that the other students were plotting against her, trying to undermine her road to fame and glory. She became increasingly guarded and, ultimately, withdrawn. Soon she became depressed, crying all the time, and refusing to go to school; she believed that everyone hated her and she wished she were dead. Unable to cope with this dramatic downslide, her parents sought professional help, and Gina was soon admitted to a private psychiatric hospital.

While hospitalized, she improved with antidepressant medication and was released after 6 weeks, feeling more or less like her old self. She received her high school diploma after making up missed work over the summer, and began college, as planned, in the fall. Things progressed well during her first year in college, but in her sophomore year she experienced a manic episode that brought about another hospitalization.

> Bipolar disorders are equally common in women and men (APA, 2000).

Gina: The Roller Coaster Continues

During her sophomore year, Gina became increasingly absorbed in her course work in astronomy, to the point of neglecting her other studies. She would spend large amounts of time at the library, reading astronomy materials and becoming extremely excited about the idea of interplanetary travel. Eventually, she spent 3 days in her room almost without sleeping, plotting different voyages across the heavens and developing grandiose plans for colonizing the solar system.

The resident advisor (RA) of her dormitory eventually became aware that Gina had stopped attending classes and was up at all hours of the night. When the RA asked her about her activities, Gina offered an excited discourse on the benefits of space travel. Realizing something was amiss, the RA urged Gina to visit the student health center, telling her that she looked exhausted. In response, Gina got annoyed and stalked off. The RA finally decided that Gina's behavior might be a health emergency, and contacted the dean's office for guidance. The dean called Gina's parents, who drove to the campus and realized that their daughter was in a state similar to the one that had preceded her depression in high school. It was not long before the young woman found herself in a psychiatric hospital for a second time.

While she was hospitalized, Gina's mania received psychopharmacological attention. She was given an antipsychotic drug *haloperidol* (Haldol), which produced dramatic relief within a few days, restoring her to a normal condition. Then, an antidepressant, *amitriptyline* (Elavil), was added to help prevent any recurrence of depression.

This combination of medicines appeared to work well for her, and it became the mainstay of her treatment for the next several years. Later, *thioridizine* (Mellaril) replaced the haloperidol, and after that, she received *lithium carbonate* in combination with *chlorpromazine* (Thorazine) for sleep. The problem was that Gina felt incapable of staying on medications consistently. Although recognizing the benefits, she often felt "straitjacketed" by the drugs she was taking. When medicated, she was free of manic episodes, but at the same time she felt she had lost her spark; her emotions felt dulled, and she sometimes longed for a few mild "highs" in her emotional life, a feeling of excitement, or of "just being alive" as she put it. When the longing became intense, Gina would stop taking the medications, often without immediate negative consequences, and with a return of her desired emotional highs. Unfortunately, she also became more vulnerable to manic episodes and the depression that sometimes followed.

The result, over the years, was a life greatly hampered by periodic bipolar episodes. Because of several further hospitalizations during the next few years and other disruptions caused by more minor manic or depressive episodes, Gina was unable to complete her bachelor's degree on time. She moved back into her parents' apartment, and lived there for several years while taking a reduced course load at a community college. Ultimately, she earned a bachelor's degree and found work, ironically, as a sales representative for a pharmaceutical company.

Unfortunately, Gina continued to ride an emotional roller coaster after obtaining employment. Her manic episodes were more frequent than her depressive episodes and, in her opinion, more of an obstacle to her professional and social goals.

At the outset of each manic episode, there was no obvious indication that something was wrong. Rather, the first sign was usually a feeling of happiness that gradually grew to a glorious outlook on life. At this early stage, Gina felt immensely pleased, considering herself the smartest, sexiest, most talented woman alive. These feelings were in sharp (and initially welcome) contrast to the feelings she would have when depressed, when she would consider herself the most miserable failure who ever existed. Even when not depressed, Gina often would hold herself in somewhat low regard, unhappy with her work, her love life, and her appearance, which actually was attractive.

The feelings that preceded a manic episode were therefore hard to resist. Gina went shopping for new clothes, often spending large amounts of money, which forced her parents to provide her with financial assistance. Gina also became almost unbearably outgoing and friendly, chatting with strangers on the bus or subway and calling up friends, in search of stimulating conversation, late at night.

Lithium is a silvery white metallic element that occurs in nature as a mineral salt.

The depressive symptoms experienced by persons with bipolar disorders are virtually identical to those of people suffering from unipolar depression.

As the euphoric feelings progressed, her behavior crossed any acceptable boundaries. Of particular concern were her sexual impulses. Due to her family's social connections, Gina often attended society charity balls and other gala social events. When the young woman was manic, these parties were the focus of her sexual interests as she became intent on picking up men and having sex with them the same evening. There was one extremely short red dress that she favored for such events. Her typical strategy was to don that dress and then apply lavish makeup. When finished, she presented a striking figure.

At the party itself, she made a grand entrance, and soon became the focus of attention of several men with whom she flirted. Gina loved the attention, and her sense of euphoria and self-satisfaction increased with each passing hour. As the evening progressed, one of the men inevitably would suggest to Gina that they leave the party together, and Gina would almost automatically go. She had sex with 50 different men under such circumstances over the course of several years.

Her work activities also offered opportunities for picking up men when she was in a manic state. One of her functions in her capacity as sales representative at the pharmaceutical company was to coordinate conferences and meetings among doctors, in order to promote sales. When manic, Gina would arrive at the meeting wearing the provocative red dress or a similar outfit. Her language would become flowery and fast-paced. Although she was often noticed at the meeting, it was after the conference, at the customary social hour, that she made her presence truly felt. As at parties, she found men to flirt with and inevitably wound up in bed with one of them.

This behavior had its negative consequences. Aside from medical problems—she contracted a venereal disease—she acquired a reputation. Thus, even when no longer manic she might be approached by men who assumed they could take liberties with her, given her behavior on prior encounters. On one occasion, word got back to her employer when the director of a medical department requested that Gina's company send someone "a little more low-key" to organize the conference for the following year.

As her state of mania progressed, her contact with reality would increasingly slip away, and she was capable of developing many grandiose ideas. For example, she once became convinced that she had developed a cookie recipe that would render all other desserts obsolete. The cookies would be so perfect, and so irresistible, that all other recipes would wind up in the wastebasket. Completely taken with this idea, Gina got in her car and spent several days buying as much flour, sugar, butter, and eggs as she could from the stores in her neighborhood, both to corner the market on ingredients and to get busy mass-producing the cookies right away.

Gina ultimately purchased several hundred pounds of products and spent the next few days mixing and baking, a process she carried out on only a couple of hours of sleep per night. At one point, the young woman received a phone call

Like depressive episodes, some manic episodes include psychotic symptoms. Some persons with mania, for example, may hold delusions of grandeur: They believe that they have special powers or that they are especially important beings, even a deity.

from her mother who, upon hearing her daughter's confused recitation of her "ingenious" plan, knew that she was once again manic. Racing over to Gina's apartment, her mother found her in the kitchen, looking like a creature from another planet—white as a ghost, covered from head to toe with a thick coating of flour, her hair a tangled mess of sugar, butter, and eggs. The kitchen itself was piled high with mounds of malformed cookies, and the stove was sending out billows of smoke.

Gina excitedly told her mother that soon they would all be millionaires. She asked her mother to help out in the meantime by picking up 20 gallons of vanilla extract and a steel drum (for mixing) at the store. Only with patient questioning, which obviously annoyed Gina, was her mother able to coax out the full story of the cookie plans.

Her mother tried explaining that the cookie idea was unsound, but the young woman became irritated with her failure to cooperate. When her mother begged Gina to call her psychiatrist, she refused, saying she had finally discovered something important and all her mother could think about was putting her away. Eventually, Gina's mother phoned the psychiatrist herself, and was advised to call an ambulance.

When the paramedics arrived, they tried persuading Gina to come with them to a hospital where she had been taken once before. Only when they promised that she would be released right away if an examination by her psychiatrist proved that everything was all right, did she agree to go.

Gina was forcibly confined at the hospital on the basis of a *two-physician certificate,* which allowed the hospital to hold her for 2 days without a court order. She was put back on medications, and she lost her desire to return to her cookie project, which she eventually saw as absurd.

When depressed, Gina's feelings were almost the mirror image of what she experienced when manic. She lost all interest in normal activities, called in sick at work, and slept 16 hours each day. Even when awake she could barely leave her bed. Instead, she spent most of her conscious hours staring at a flickering television, sobbing, and thinking she was a miserable failure at every aspect of life. Occasionally, she might throw on some old clothes and go to the store to buy a few basic things, barely looking at anyone she might encounter. At such times, she had no concern for her appearance and ate only enough food to keep going.

In between her mood episodes, Gina was intelligent, responsible, serious about her work, and considered a capable sales representative by her employer. However, even then, she was not completely free of difficulties. She suffered from low self-esteem. Although perfectly capable in her work, for example, she often doubted her abilities; and after organizing successful meetings she would spend considerable amounts of time and energy analyzing flaws or faults. Similarly, any hint of criticism had a way of overshadowing the praise that she generally received in her work. This sensitivity led to great anxiety and suffering. In her love

Many states have established procedures by which clinicians can temporarily commit patients to a psychiatric hospital in an emergency situation. The procedure is usually called a *two-physician certificate* (or a *2 PC*), because in past times such hospitalizations had to be certified (ordered) by two physicians. Today, certification by nonphysician mental health professionals is allowed in many states.

life, Gina's lowered self-esteem would interfere with her ability to find a partner. Actually, her relations with men were mostly confined to sexual escapades while manic, as if she had nothing else to offer.

A Friend's View: Along for the Ride

It was a challenge, to say the least, to be friends with Gina. Actually, it was easy— even seductive—to *become* her friend, especially if a person were to meet her during the early stages of a manic episode. Her wit, energy, and upbeat disposition would bowl people over. But it was very hard indeed to *stay* friends with Gina. As she became increasingly manic, friends would find themselves confused, appalled, and ultimately frightened. If she crossed over into depression, they might feel pulled down by her misery and pain. After witnessing one of her manic or depressive episodes, some friends would decide to end the relationship. Others might understand that she was suffering from a severe disorder and would try to pick up the relationship where it had left off. But in many cases, such efforts were elusive. A line had been crossed; the friends' trust or confidence in Gina and in her stability had been broken, and so things were not quite the same. A line had also been crossed for Gina. Embarrassed and humiliated by how she might have acted, especially during a manic episode, she later found it hard to feel comfortable, or even respectable, in the presence of those who had witnessed her behaviors.

Cyndi, another sales representative at work, was one such individual. Her relationship with Gina started as a source of great joy, but it progressed, along with Gina's manic behaviors, into a troubling, painful, and desperate experience that Cyndi had trouble putting behind her. She later described the relationship to Andrea, one of the newer representatives in the pharmaceutical company:

I didn't think too much about Gina at first, because she generally kept to herself. The first year that I worked with her, we never talked too much, even when we were at a sales conference together. In fact, she kind of had a reputation of not talking to anyone. She didn't have a lot of friends. She was a damn good salesperson, but that was about all I knew about her. Everyone seemed to have their own theory about her, and I heard some talk about a psychiatric hospital, but I figured it was just hogwash.

So I was really surprised at one sales conference when Gina suddenly approached me and started talking to me with great gusto and interest. She told me that she'd always wanted to ask me if I spelled my name the way I do after Cyndi Lauper, and I told her that the singer had nothing to do with it. I said I took complete and utter credit for the name Cyndi, and we had a good laugh. It turned out that we both enjoyed pop music and we both enjoyed going out to clubs dancing. We also talked about movies and television. Looking back, it wasn't really what we talked about, I guess, but the way the talk happened. She seemed really excited to be getting to know me, and I was happy that I was making friends with someone at work.

Soon we arranged to sit next to each other at marketing meetings, and we would start to have little private jokes that we'd share.

I was really enjoying my friendship and having a lot of fun with Gina. I guess the first time I noticed that something might be a bit off was half a year or so after we started really being friends. One night, she called me up at 4:00 a.m., which was very unusual, and I immediately assumed there'd been some sort of emergency. She seemed extremely excited and when I could get her to calm down and tell me what was going on, she said, "You know that guy Dave who reps for us in Seattle. Well, you'll never guess. I made it with him! I went home with him and it was so great I just can't believe it!" I tried to find a way to get off the phone, but she just kept talking a mile a minute, telling me every detail I didn't want to know.

Mind you, I was pretty shocked that she was sleeping with someone we knew from our careers. Then she told me that she'd been with a whole lot of the guys who worked in the field offices. A few months later, as luck would have it, Dave was transferred to our office. By the end of his first week there, Gina was telling me that she was deeply in love. After a couple of weeks of hearing about her perfect relationship, I must admit I was getting pretty tired of it, but I had to be polite. Then, by the end of just 1 month, she was talking to me about marriage. I would say, "Listen, Gina, don't you think this is a little fast? I mean, you guys aren't ready to be talking about marriage." She wasn't even fazed. "Oh, Dave and I are going to do this; it's gonna be like that." She even asked me my opinions on flower arrangements for the wedding.

Finally, I said to her, "Listen, I think this is too soon. As your friend, I have to say I just don't think you're ready to get married and it doesn't sound like Dave is either. I mean, you guys haven't even told anyone at work besides me that you're seeing each other, and you won't even let me tell him that I know."

She then screamed at me, "But I love him so much! We're going to be together forever! You're the best friend I've ever had and you're going to be my maid of honor. How dare you say we're not ready to get married!" This really scared me, not least because I hardly thought that we were each other's best friend ever.

I decided I had to act. She was starting to make me nervous; she was so jumpy all the time. There seemed to be a real desperation to the way she felt about this relationship, and so I decided to talk to Dave about it. First thing he said was, "How did you find out about that?" I just said, "Look, Dave, I know, okay. She told me. And because she's my friend, I want you to know I don't think she's ready for marriage." And he just stared at me like I was from Mars. He told me he'd seen her a couple of times but it was not a big deal.

Now I was really scared, so I told her what happened. She got so mad at me, screeching over the phone: "You ruined everything. We were taking it slow, but I know he wanted to marry me, and you ruined it! I hate you, I hate you!" She hung up on me and wouldn't talk to me for months. At work, her behaviors kept getting stranger and stranger, more and more outrageous. Needless to say, Dave wanted

Bipolar disorders are equally common among people of all socioeconomic classes and ethnic groups.

nothing more to do with her, and quite truthfully, after awhile, I began to feel the same way. I mean she was so bizarre and frightening. By then, of course, I realized that she was terribly troubled. Yet for a long while I couldn't shake the thought that I had done something terribly wrong. Now that I know about her problem, it makes more sense. We're still friends, kind of, but not nearly like before. I went on one of those rides with her for several months, and I'll never forget it. On the other hand, what must it be like for her to live through them again and again?

Gina in Treatment: One More Time

In 1983, as she approached the age of 32, Gina decided to seek treatment with a new psychiatrist. Her emotions were stable at the time, due largely to a combination of the medications lithium and chlorpromazine. Nevertheless, she knew from experience that this stability would eventually change unpredictably, due either to changes in her reactions to the medications or to a change of heart about taking them. She had grown ever so weary of the roller-coaster ride, weary of gaining and losing friends, weary of all the unpredictability and pain, and she hoped that perhaps a new psychiatrist could help her gain better control over her symptoms.

Various genetic studies have linked bipolar disorders to possible gene abnormalities on chromosomes 4, 6, 11, 12, 13, 15, 18, 22, and X (Berrettini, 2000).

She contacted Dr. Shara Rabb. She had heard of Dr. Rabb from a friend, a man whom Gina had first met 2 years before at a group for people with mood disorders. The friend was himself seeing Dr. Rabb, and had been doing so for 4 years. He said that the psychiatrist had been able to help him settle down, where others had failed. He couldn't have been more positive, and so Gina, feeling that she was running out of time to live a normal life, decided to see Dr. Rabb. It was certainly worth a try. Thus began a doctor–patient relationship that was to continue for 17 years.

A Psychiatrist Prepares for Treatment:
A Delicate Balance

Experience had taught Dr. Rabb that medicating mood disorders, especially bipolar disorder, is complex and can involve a certain amount of trial and error. The stereotype of the bipolar patient who simply takes lithium, a mood stabilizer, in order to be free of symptoms was, unfortunately, more the exception than the rule. Most such patients require other medications at different phases of their disorder. Many need *antidepressants,* and some, in addition, require *antipsychotic drugs* for both their major tranquilizing and antipsychotic effects.

Dr. Rabb knew that when prescribing lithium, it was necessary to achieve a balance between the drug's therapeutic efficacy and its unpleasant side effects—side effects that often would lead patients to just stop using it. In addition, a special problem in the case of bipolar disorder was the pleasure that patients often would experience from their manic symptoms. Even with minimal side effects from lithium, the patients might be tempted to discontinue the drug in order to regain some of the highs that they had previously experienced.

Added to this was the issue of helping patients with bipolar disorder to accept the reality that they in fact have a lifelong disorder and that they probably will need to be on medications for most of their lives. Dr. Rabb had come to appreciate that the psychological management of patients was as critical as medication management. A psychiatrist had to be very sensitive both to the patient's concerns about medication side effects and to the changes in emotional life brought about by the medication. Additionally, treatment often had to include *behavioral strategies* to help patients recognize and seek help for their manic episodes before the episodes fully blossomed, as well as psychotherapy for unresolved conflicts about having a chronic illness.

The First Session After gathering a description of Gina's symptoms and history, Dr. Rabb was certain that the patient's condition met the DSM-IV diagnostic criteria for *Bipolar I Disorder*. Gina had experienced both manic and depressive episodes. Her manic episodes were characterized by inflated self-esteem (sometimes called *grandiosity*), decreased need for sleep, increased talkativeness, increase in goal-directed activity, and excessive involvement in pleasurable activities with a high potential for painful consequences (especially, sexual indiscretions and buying sprees). Conversely, her depressive episodes were marked by severely depressed mood, loss of interest in nearly all activities, excessive sleep, fatigue, feelings of worthlessness, and loss of appetite. Moreover, the episodes brought significant distress and impairment.

The psychiatrist explained to Gina her basic plan for treating bipolar disorder. She noted, first of all, that Gina was encountering a common problem for people with bipolar disorder, namely, difficulty in adhering to the medication regimen. In discussing this problem, Dr. Rabb felt it was important not to convey this observation in a critical fashion. Given Gina's somewhat girlish self-presentation and her involvement with her parents even at this stage of her life, the psychiatrist concluded that there might have been an adolescent-type rebellion in Gina's problems with medication compliance, in addition to the usual reasons patients fail to take their medications.

Since Dr. Rabb would now be assuming the role of an authority figure, she worried that Gina might decide to resist her recommendations as another way of demonstrating rebellion. Thus, Dr. Rabb's first tactic was to empathize with Gina's spotty record of medication compliance. She remarked that the medications used to control manic episodes often had the effect of reducing even a normal sense

---

Possible side effects of lithium include gastrointestinal irritation, tremor, metallic taste, cognitive dulling, weight gain, excessive thirst, and muscular weakness (Bowden, 1995).

Gina typically experienced full manic episodes. In contrast, a hypomanic episode is an abnormally elevated mood state that is not as severe as a manic episode. It produces little impairment for the sufferer.

of high spirits, and as a result, many patients were tempted to omit their medications occasionally.

Gina readily agreed, and she began to open up about the dilemma posed by medications. The feelings that resulted from omitting the medication were indeed pleasurable; moreover, once her feelings progressed to a manic phase, she was no longer capable of rationally considering the advisability of taking medication or of getting medical help. Gina wondered out loud how she could ever be helped out of this dilemma—it seemed she had to choose between a chemical straitjacket and destructive bipolar episodes.

The psychiatrist explained that the first step was to see if there was anything that could be done to maximize the anti-manic benefit of medication, while permitting a greater range of emotional feeling. She remarked that there had been considerable inconsistency in Gina's care to date, as her different hospitalizations had led to involvement with a variety of mental health professionals, none of whom had been able to follow her for any length of time. The psychiatrist stated that she would like to set matters on a different course, and asked for Gina's commitment to remain in treatment with her for the next year. Gina agreed, and the first stage of treatment was devoted to finding a medication regimen with which Gina could comply.

The First Year of Treatment

Dr. Rabb's goal during the first months of treatment was to determine the lowest therapeutic dose of lithium for Gina—specifically, a dose that would keep the patients's moods stabilized, but which was not so powerful as to flatten Gina's mood completely or create intolerable side effects.

When Gina first consulted the psychiatrist, she was taking 900 milligrams of lithium daily and 50 milligrams of chlorpromazine for sleep. Blood tests ordered by the psychiatrist at first seemed to indicate that this dose of lithium was operating at a therapeutic level. However, after listening carefully to Gina, the psychiatrist suspected that the patient's medication compliance problems in the past year might have been due not so much to her search for emotional highs, but to impaired judgment brought on by her repeated manic episodes. That is, as Gina declared again and again that she had really been trying in the past year to take the medication properly, the psychiatrist came to believe that the main problem might be that her dose of lithium was in fact too low.

Dr. Rabb discussed this impression with Gina and suggested that, as long as she was taking medication, she might as well be taking enough to get some of the intended benefits. The psychiatrist proposed increasing Gina's dose gradually, with the goal of raising the patient's blood level to the higher end of the therapeutic

In Bipolar I disorder, full manic episodes alternate or intermix with major depressive episodes. In Bipolar II disorder, hypomanic episodes alternate or intermix with major depressive episodes.

range. Gina agreed to this proposal and, over the course of the next couple of weeks, the daily dose was gradually raised.

Months 2–3 Unfortunately, even this higher dose did not bring about the desired results over the next few months. The first sign was Gina's arrival at a treatment session dressed more strikingly than Dr. Rabb had yet seen her. There was nothing outlandish in her appearance; she was simply wearing more jewelry and makeup than usual. Gina said she had decided to start dressing up a little in order to present a more professional image. She noted that colleagues seemed to treat her more professionally when she attended more to her appearance. In fact, she thought she might be considered for a promotion soon and wanted to "look the part" in case there was any chance of her influencing things favorably.

Dr. Rabb asked Gina if she was continuing to take the lithium at the prescribed dose, and she replied that she was. In fact, she said she was very satisfied with the medicine. She took it regularly, and felt that it was controlling her moods and helping her get back on the road to recovery. To be on the safe side, the psychiatrist had Gina visit the lab for another test of her lithium blood level.

A few days later the lab report came back indicating that Gina's blood level was the same as before—the lithium blood level had not increased despite the increase in medication. In the meantime, it soon became clear that something was indeed amiss behaviorally, as Gina failed to appear for the next scheduled session with the psychiatrist. It turned out that she was in the midst of a 10-day manic episode, marked by increasing euphoria and flirtatiousness, which culminated in a one-night stand with a participant from one of her medical conferences. When Gina's sexual partner informed her the next morning that he was headed home to his wife, Gina grew furious and began hurling hotel furnishings around the room, smashing lamps and ashtrays. Finally, the hotel manager was called, and Gina was ejected, along with her companion, who was grateful to have someone intervene on his behalf.

Gina descended on her parents' apartment, where she encountered her mother. Recognizing a manic episode, Gina's mother asked her daughter when she had last seen her psychiatrist and insisted that the young woman get in touch with Dr. Rabb right away. Gina said she didn't want to bother. Her mother then made the call herself, which made Gina furious. As her mother spoke on the phone, Dr. Rabb could hear Gina shrieking in the background. Eventually, the volatile woman came to the phone and agreed to come to the psychiatrist's office that evening.

Gina arrived in the company of both parents, who wanted to insure that their daughter kept the appointment. During the session, she was petulant and pouty. She berated her parents for treating her like a child but, at the same time, was very much acting the part. On their side, Gina's parents—her mother in particular—made snide references to Gina's "inability to keep her pants on" and her

---

Because lithium and other mood-stabilizing drugs help *prevent* bipolar mood episodes, clinicians usually continue patients on some dosage of these drugs even after a mood episode subsides (Baldessarini et al., 1999).

Identical twins of persons with a bipolar disorder have a 40% likelihood of developing a similar disorder, whereas fraternal twins and other siblings have a 5 to 10% likelihood (Craddock & Jones, 1999).

general failure to live up to their expectations. Throughout it all, Gina was extremely agitated; she spoke rapidly, in a shrill voice, and periodically rose from her seat and gestured wildly to emphasize a point.

After listening to everyone, Dr. Rabb asked to speak with Gina alone. After making sure that her patient was in fact still taking her medication, the psychiatrist concluded that the dose was inadequate. Gina at first resented this pronouncement, complaining that "everything good that I do is called an illness." Dr. Rabb was wary of confronting Gina with the facts of the past 10 days, and elected instead to focus on her current state, asking her how she felt and whether she was up to going to work. With this shift, Gina acknowledged that she needed help in order to return to work. The psychiatrist, therefore, advised her to increase her dose of lithium yet more; and at the same time, she gave her chlorpromazine to calm her right away.

The next evening, Gina called the psychiatrist, obviously in a much calmer state due to the chlorpromazine. She had gone back to her own apartment and had made arrangements to resume her work appointments on the Monday of the following week.

Early that week, Dr. Rabb met with Gina once again, and determined that her mood had indeed stabilized. The psychiatrist ordered blood tests, and this time her lithium blood level came back at the high end of the therapeutic range. The plan was to taper off the chlorpromazine, with the hope that the higher dose of lithium, if taken properly, would prevent further bipolar episodes.

> If people with bipolar disorder experience four or more mood episodes within a 1-year period, their disorder is further classified as *rapid cycling*.

Months 4–8 The new medication regimen appeared to control Gina's mood swings. In fact, she led a calm existence for the next 4 months, meeting all her work demands and leading a quiet personal life. During this period she practically went out of her way to avoid men.

After about 4 months of this existence, Gina began to grow increasingly more cynical about her "boring" life. Finally, she decided to stop taking her lithium. She called Dr. Rabb and told her that she just couldn't see herself living this way indefinitely. She had grown up with enough "domination" from her parents, and now she was being dominated chemically; she felt she was being deprived of her freedom. Furthermore, the new level of lithium seemed to produce enormous thirst, which led her to gulp water constantly, leading in turn to constant trips to the bathroom. She stated she just couldn't take it any more. The psychiatrist strongly advised Gina to keep to the medication, reminding her of her last manic episode. But all that Dr. Rabb could really do at this point was urge the patient to keep her informed about how she was doing and to call her at the earliest sign of either a manic or depressive episode.

Months 9–12 For the next couple of months Gina felt fine. She was happy to be off the lithium and feeling more like her "normal" self. As the weeks progressed, however, her feelings of contentment progressed to a state of euphoria, and then mania, which led to one of the most traumatic experiences of her life.

It began at a society fund-raising function where Gina, in her manic state, began flirting with a philanthropist from Mexico. As the evening progressed, the man suggested that Gina fly back with him to his country that very night. Gina, in high spirits and needing little encouragement to do almost anything, readily agreed, and the two headed for the airport directly from the party. On the plane, Gina was in a boisterous mood, feeling she was the life of the party and adored by everyone. Her companion was so taken with her vivacity that, upon arriving at their destination, he hired a limousine to take them to a hotel in grand style.

At the hotel, Gina and her companion settled in for a high time of fine dining, alcohol, and later, sex. After 3 full days of a wanton existence, Gina's companion raised the idea of Gina's "entertaining" a couple of his friends. Gina was shocked by the suggestion, but ultimately agreed, and there followed what she later described as "the most degrading week of my life." It all came to an abrupt end when her companion, tiring of the arrangement, checked out of the hotel, leaving Gina on the curb with mere cab fare back to the airport. Alone in a strange country, and with only a few dollars, Gina called her parents and explained her predicament. Her father immediately made travel plans to retrieve his daughter. Gina spent the next 24 hours awaiting her father's arrival, sitting on a lonely seat in the airport, fuming to herself, and kicking at any objects within reach.

Once home, the young woman spent 2 weeks in her parents' apartment, now overcome with depression. She felt she was a complete misfit who would never succeed in life or love, and all she wanted to do was die. In view of her condition, her parents begged her to get back in touch with Dr. Rabb. Gina agreed to schedule a visit, and she tearfully related the Mexican episode to the psychiatrist.

Dr. Rabb prescribed the antidepressant *amitryptiline* (Elavil) to treat Gina's acute depression, and reinstated the previous high level of lithium. Gina's depression lifted 2 weeks later. After a couple of months, the psychiatrist gradually tapered the antidepressant to avoid any chance of producing a manic episode.

Gina had thus come full circle. She was back on the lithium that she so detested, and her mood swings were under control once again. As one might predict by now, before long, she was expressing the same old complaints: She couldn't stand the side effects, she felt like she was wearing a straitjacket, and so on. She began omitting the lithium for a few days at a time, saying that she deserved a "couple of days of freedom" now and then.

Dr. Rabb felt that Gina was not facing up to the reality of her situation. Like a rebellious adolescent, she continued to see taking the medicine as something imposed on her, rather than something that she was doing for herself in order to avoid alternatives that were even worse. Thus, the psychiatrist suggested that Gina might benefit from some psychotherapy to help sort out her feelings.

Antidepressant drugs can trigger a manic episode for some people who suffer from bipolar disorder (Barak et al., 2000). Thus, clinicians must carefully monitor the impact of these drugs when prescribing them for people with such a disorder.

Psychotherapy, she explained, might also be helpful with some of Gina's other concerns, her problems with relationships, for example. The patient agreed to see a psychologist, Dr. Michael Kohl, for a consultation.

Second Year of Treatment

Gina saw the psychologist, Dr. Kohl, for intensive insight-oriented therapy during the next 12 months. For the first 3 months of therapy, they focused on Gina's relations with her parents. Gina complained that her parents devalued her and her problems. Specifically, she believed that they saw her mainly as a disruption to their otherwise tidy lives and fancy social concerns. Sometimes it seemed they resented her very existence and held Gina responsible for her manic and depressive episodes, as though somehow she was causing them deliberately.

Further discussions helped Gina recognize how extensive her resentment of her parents had grown. Time and again, she seemed bent on retaliation, by keeping her parents continually informed of her suffering through constant phone calls. Also, she often would try to "rub their noses" in her problems by creating crisis states—for example, by omitting medication—that forced them to come to her assistance. Dr. Kohl pointed out this pattern to Gina, suggesting that she was running her life much like an adolescent whose main goal was rebellion against her parents. The obvious conclusion was that she needed to stop making rebellion against her parents the primary guiding force of her life.

Armed with these insights, Gina spent the next 3 months of therapy trying to make some important changes. For example, she found a new apartment, further from her parents' home, which would cut down on the frequent, impromptu visits from both sides. In addition, the patient decided to cut down on her frequent calls to her parents, in which she would seek their advice on even minor matters. At times, the telephone calls were hard to resist, but as Gina got more used to handling simple things on her own, or talking them over with her friends or Dr. Kohl instead, her parents became less enmeshed in the details of her daily life, and they became less of a factor in her thoughts and actions.

The next step was for Gina to begin thinking about her own goals in life. Previously, she now realized, her parents' reactions had been such a powerful motivating factor for her behaviors that she had seldom considered her own needs and desires. Over the next 3 months of therapy, Gina decided that what she wanted most was a "normal" life—a life uninterrupted by the manic and depressive episodes that now checkered her past. As discussions on this theme progressed, the patient acknowledged that the medication she was now taking had been the one guarantee of control over these horrifying episodes. As therapy continued, Gina came to view the medication as the guarantor of her hopes to be a normal person, rather than an instrument of parental control. Furthermore, she recognized

The cause of bipolar disorders is not clear. However, some theorists point to improper transportation of sodium and potassium ions back and forth between the inside and the outside of a person's neuron membranes.

> Many bipolar treatment programs now include individual, group, or family therapy as an adjunct to medication. The adjunctive therapies focus on the need for proper management of medications, psychoeducation, improving social and relationship skills, and solving disorder-related problems (George et al., 2000).

that the medication helped her to live a truly independent life. The question was whether she could accept the trade-off that the medication required, including the loss of certain pleasures and excitement that manic periods initially produced.

Intellectually, Gina said she felt prepared to accept this trade-off, holding out for herself the hope that one day a better medication might be found or, at some point in the future, that she might no longer require medication. In the meantime, she felt that the advantages of the lithium outweighed its disadvantages.

The remainder of the year in psychotherapy was spent helping Gina achieve a more gratifying existence without manic episodes. The focus was on her relations with the opposite sex which, up to now, had been restricted to picking up men for casual sex while in a manic state. With Dr. Kohl's encouragement and coaching, Gina began to date men in a more conventional fashion, typically holding off sexual activity until the relationships progressed to the point where some true feeling developed.

The 3rd Through 7th Years

By the 3rd year of treatment, Gina's life truly began to stabilize. She developed independence from her parents and acquired a steady boyfriend for the first time.

She remained in psychotherapy with Dr. Kohl for the next 5 years, and continued to see the psychiatrist, Dr. Rabb, once a month. Throughout these years, there were occasions when Gina would omit her medication, but it usually involved skipping only a dose or two rather than stopping completely. Whenever she was tempted to discontinue, she would recall the painful episode in Mexico.

With greater emotional stability and a more mature self-concept, Gina was able to make greater progress in her professional life. She started applying herself more seriously to her work, took business courses, and was eventually promoted to regional manager. As she experienced the pride of professional success, the pleasures derived from manic episodes seemed less necessary to her. This helped her to take her medications even more reliably as time progressed.

> More than 60% of patients with bipolar disorder improve on lithium or another mood stabilizer.

After 7 years of treatment with Dr. Rabb, Gina reduced her visits to the psychiatrist to just a few times per year, while continuing to consult with Dr. Kohl, the psychologist, periodically.

Epilogue

A few years later, during one of her visits to Dr. Rabb, Gina raised the idea of taking some lithium "holidays." She told the psychiatrist that she still missed some of the "normal" highs that she used to experience when not taking the drug, and wanted to see if she could function without the lithium at least a few days out of the week. She pointed out that, as it was, she was sometimes skipping a day here and there—against medical advice—without any bad consequences. She thought it made sense to try to do this in a more regulated fashion, with the psychiatrist's supervision. Dr. Rabb was persuaded, and worked out a plan for Gina to begin omitting her lithium one weekend day each week.

This plan proceeded without any problems for a full 6 months, and the decision was then made to omit the lithium for the entire weekend. Once again, Gina appeared to tolerate the omission without any difficulty. She continued to lead her stable, productive existence.

Over the next 10 years, Gina stopped seeing Dr. Kohl but continued to see Dr. Rabb for her medication needs. In a sense they were growing older, and wiser, together. As the clinical field came to learn more about bipolar disorders and to develop some alternative treatments, Dr. Rabb was able to cut back on lithium and offer Gina some other medications, including *valproate* (Depakote), a new mood stabilizer. The new combination of medications allowed some of the emotional richness that she longed for back into her life—yet without heightening the risk of new bipolar episodes.

These changes were all done through a slow process of trial and error. The key to their success was that Gina had become a wise and attentive watchdog. She always knew to call Dr. Rabb as soon as the short, red dress in her closet—which she hadn't worn for years—started to look appealing again. Over the years, she obtained a business degree, advanced further in her profession, and developed a long-term romance. At last, her emotions—and her life—had indeed calmed down.

Two anticonvulsant drugs, *carbamazepine* (Tegretol) and *valproate* (Depakote), have been discovered in recent years to be effective mood stabilizers. They are about as effective as lithium, and often have fewer side effects.

CASE **6**

Hypochondriasis

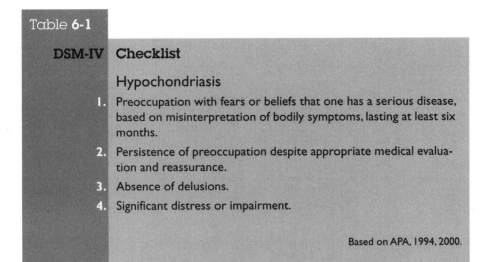

Table 6-1

DSM-IV Checklist

Hypochondriasis

1. Preoccupation with fears or beliefs that one has a serious disease, based on misinterpretation of bodily symptoms, lasting at least six months.
2. Persistence of preoccupation despite appropriate medical evaluation and reassurance.
3. Absence of delusions.
4. Significant distress or impairment.

Based on APA, 1994, 2000.

Looking back, 37-year-old Andrea Hilgard felt that she first began to worry about her health at about the age of 10, when she was playing with some friends after school. At that time, she was seized with "a sudden awareness of my own mortality." She was in the midst of a kickball game, and the emotional pall that came over her at that moment grabbed her attention for the rest of the game. While her friends were enjoying themselves and were completely caught up in the fun, Andrea could not shake her feeling. Afterward, she went home, where she found her mother doing her usual household activities, and the feeling gradually subsided.

Since that "awakening," Andrea felt that her emotional life was never quite the same. Although a basically happy, well-adjusted child, she was now sensitive to life's negative possibilities in a way that others did not seem to be. Occasionally, she would be at school or playing at a friend's house, and she would be seized by the thought that her parents or sisters could have been in a car accident without her knowing. The thought would keep her distracted and worried for the remainder of the day, at least until she could go home and make sure that the worry was unfounded.

People with hypochondriasis often have had serious illnesses during childhood or past experiences with disease of a family member (APA, 2000).

Despite their upsetting impact, such episodes did not dominate Andrea's childhood. In fact, her childhood was generally positive and the family environment loving. Her father was a salesman, who made a comfortable middle-class living, and her mother was a full-time homemaker. Andrea excelled in school; after graduation from high school, she attended an exclusive Ivy League college and then law school. After graduation, she moved to a major metropolitan area where she worked for a few years as an associate in a law firm. At the age of 30, she took a job as house counsel in a brokerage house.

Andrea had dated a number of men during her 20s. At age 32, however, she "panicked" at the thought of not finding a husband, and ended up marrying a man whom her better judgment was telling her to avoid. He was a self-described musician, who obtained occasional gigs with his rock band at underground clubs. His lifestyle seemed exciting to her, but a more reasoned analysis of his situation would have told her that he was immature and self-absorbed, with no real means of support. In addition, he had a cocaine habit that Andrea was at first willing to overlook.

Soon after marrying this man, over her family's objections, Andrea was struck by the stark reality of their life together: she had assumed the responsibility of supporting a self-indulgent parasite who showed no prospect of ever becoming a full partner. She would leave for work in the morning with her husband still in bed; when she returned after a long day's labor, the apartment would be awash with dirty dishes and beer bottles. In addition, as time passed, it was clear that he was using large portions of her salary to support his cocaine habit.

Although Andrea was a successful lawyer, she felt paralyzed by her marital distress, both personally and legally. Eventually, she swallowed her pride and asked her family to help her escape from this situation. They swiftly came to her assistance and helped her obtain the necessary legal firepower to annul the marriage and get this man out of her life.

Following the annulment, Andrea went through a period of despondency and entered counseling for about a year. Among the important insights that she gained in therapy was the realization that, in her dating, she had been favoring men who were "interesting, offbeat, or unpredictable." However, these attributes were not usually consistent with her long-term goals: children, financial security, and a stable home life. Over the course of counseling, she began dating men whom she previously would have overlooked as too "boring," and she discovered that in many instances the boredom had been of her own creation. Eventually, at 33 years of age, she met Paul, a high school science teacher, and they were married 6 months later. Her son, Jimmy, was born a year after that.

Andrea: Bodily Concerns Take a Serious Turn

Although hypochondriasis can begin at any age, it starts most often in early adulthood (APA, 1994, 2000).

For the first 34 years of Andrea's life, her tendency to worry had remained in check. True, she was always capable of becoming suddenly concerned about the safety or health of her parents, sisters, or husband, but such worries were usually mild and infrequent. It was not until she became pregnant that her occasional anxieties became more frequent, and focused specifically on the medical area. During her pregnancy, she made the usual visits to the obstetrician and loaded up on various pregnancy-related medical books. She also underwent the usual blood tests, sonograms, and other procedures that a modern-day pregnancy entails. As she moved deeper and deeper into the process, however, she became aware of the many potential threats to her health and to the baby's. With each passing month, the various tests and changes in her body produced increasing levels of anxiety that could be reduced only with the doctor's strenuous reassurance or a favorable test result.

When her son, Jimmy, was born, Andrea actually went through a period of calm, as she could see that he was healthy and strong. Before long, however, she returned to the focus on her own health. Her bodily concerns increased in intensity and frequency over the next 2½ years. Although she did not find them a constant problem, the young lawyer had more and more episodes in which she would become consumed with the belief that she had a serious, possibly fatal, illness.

Andrea: Bodily Concerns Take Over

Most of the time, Andrea felt fine. However, once one of her health fears struck, she could not rest until she got medical reassurance. Sometimes a single visit to the doctor was enough to put her mind at ease; but other times she required several visits, and to several doctors. Due to her persistence—with telephone calls, follow-up visits, and more telephone calls—doctors soon became exasperated with the worried woman, and some had even refused to see her. These medical visits were not enjoyable for Andrea, either. Indeed, they were among the least pleasant activities she could imagine. She sought the visits only because she had no other method of coping with her terrible fears.

A typical crisis unfolded one weekday morning in November when Andrea awoke with a curious sensation of numbness in her right arm. Concerned, she tried prodding her skin at various locations to determine how much sensation she had lost. While there was no doubt she had some feeling, it was obviously blunted.

Andrea thought of rousing Paul, her husband, to get his opinion. However, she hesitated, as just the day before she had asked him to feel the back of her skull, to get his opinion on whether a bony projection there had always been present. At that time, she had even insisted on feeling his skull to see if he had a similar projection—he did not—and she was only reassured upon feeling her son's skull and discovering that it resembled hers. And the day before that, she had asked Paul to comment on the appearance of a pimple on her neck. He had responded that it seemed like a typical pimple, and he begged her to wait just one day to see if it would disappear before concluding that it was cancer or smallpox, or some other dread disease. Andrea took his advice and, happily, found that the pimple was almost gone the next day.

The numbness in the arm, however, really worried her. She recalled having read an article in the newspaper a few weeks prior, entitled "Multiple Sclerosis: The Stalker of Young Adults." The article noted that MS typically strikes between the ages of 20 and 40. Andrea was horrified to learn that she was in the prime risk

Hypochondriasis is one of the *somatoform disorders*, physical illnesses or ailments that are explained largely by psychosocial causes. Other somatoform disorders are somatization disorder, conversion disorder, pain disorder, and body dysmorphic disorder.

period. Still, when reading the article, she was at least thankful that she didn't have any of the symptoms listed: weakness, vision problems, numbness. Now, however, she awoke with what was undeniably a sensation of numbness.

Andrea could not resist eventually rousing her husband and describing her fear. As she spoke, she could tell that Paul viewed her problem with a skepticism born of many false alarms in the past. He tried to get her to see reason, asking her to consider logically how seriously ill she could be if she could still move her arm normally and still had feeling in it. As in the past, he suggested that Andrea let the problem ride for a day before calling the doctor.

Paul's opinion did not hold her for long, however. The article had explicitly stated, Andrea recalled, that the initial symptoms of MS could indeed be minor, but the illness to follow could be devastating. If the disease were to progress rapidly, she could be reduced to a wheelchair within a few years.

Andrea decided to see her doctor that very day. She raced to get herself and her son dressed and on their way. The first stop was the nursery school, where she exchanged the usual morning pleasantries with the teachers and other parents. However, while there, all she could think about was how lucky they were to be in good health, whereas she might now be gravely ill. The young lawyer then gave Jimmy a sentimental kiss good-bye, and raced to her office.

Andrea called the doctor and was relieved to learn that she could get an appointment at 11:00 a.m. She left immediately and, when she arrived at the doctor's office, settled down in the waiting room, nervously flipping through a magazine. While she waited, anxiously anticipating the verdict on her symptoms, Andrea thought about her predicament. Why was it, she wondered, that she was subject to these alarming symptoms? How ironic, she thought, that she should be plagued in this fashion. Other people took their good health for granted—foolishly so, in her estimation. She recalled once reading a story about people who had survived various disasters, such as airplane hijackings. These people reported that, prior to their harrowing ordeal, they had had all the wrong notions about what mattered in life: careers, income, a nice house or car. Afterward, they emerged with a new appreciation of life's true gifts: the health and well-being of their family and friends.

In recalling the article, she thought:

> I already know this without the benefit of a disaster striking. The only thing I've ever cared about is my family and their health. So why should I, of all people, be singled out for this kind of treatment? Why can't an illness strike somebody who needs a little shaking up—someone who smokes, or who thinks her career is such a big deal, or who doesn't pay any attention to her kids? . . .

The doctor came into the waiting room and took Andrea into the office. She explained her symptom of numbness, and the physician performed a standard neurological exam. All findings were normal. When Andrea raised the question of

> Actually, the health habits (for example, healthful diet or regular exercise) of people with hypochondriasis are generally no better than those of people without the disorder (APA, 2000).

MS, the doctor replied that it couldn't be discounted completely—a statement that visibly alarmed her. Seeing Andrea's distress, the physician hastened to remind her that the results of the neurological exam were normal; therefore, it was unlikely that her numbness was serious. The physician suggested that they wait a few days to see whether the symptom subsided before conducting any further investigations.

Andrea left the office feeling not at all reassured. She wanted a definitive answer. Almost immediately, she made another appointment, this time with a neurologist, who might be better able to assess her condition. By the time she got to see the neurologist, a week later, the symptom had already disappeared. Still, she kept the appointment, just to hear what the neurologist would say. After an exam and several tests, the specialist, too, concluded that the numbness had not been a serious problem, perhaps a temporary muscle ache that had created the feeling of numbness.

The symptom did not reappear and, about a week later, Andrea's concern with MS had more or less subsided. She got back into her regular routine of work and family, and felt happy and content that she had no symptoms to worry her. Indeed, under these conditions, she was at complete peace with the world. The way she saw it, she had a wonderful husband and son, two loving parents, and a job that provided a reasonable living and a sense of doing something worthwhile. If only things could just stay this way, with no more symptoms or illnesses to worry about.

Things did stay that way for about 2 weeks, during which time Andrea maintained her sunny outlook. Then, one morning she awoke with blurry vision, and became frantic that it might be another sign of MS. The young lawyer asked her husband to take Jimmy to school, and then called in sick, determined to find an ophthalmologist who would see her that very day.

She was finally able to obtain an appointment for that afternoon. Over the course of the morning, the symptom actually disappeared. Still, she was deeply concerned because she had learned, during a morning reading of her home medical books, that the symptoms of MS can come and go.

The ophthalmologist examined Andrea's eyes, paying particular attention to the state of the optic nerve, since she had raised the MS question. He soon informed Andrea that everything appeared normal and, inasmuch as the blurring had vanished, he assumed it had just been a transient disturbance due to some eye irritation or a minor infection. He gave her eyedrops to counter the possible infection. Andrea thanked him and left the office feeling more reassured.

When she arrived home, she had time to consider her experiences of the past 3 years. She was very unhappy with the contrast between the secure adult image that she wanted to project in front of her young son, and the utterly helpless creature she seemed to become whenever preoccupied with a medical concern. Also, she could tell that Paul was getting more and more exasperated with her.

Between 1 and 5% of all people experience hypochondriasis (APA, 2000).

Not too long ago, after a particularly frenzied period of medical fears, he had even told her that he was at a loss as to what to do for her. Perhaps, he suggested, she should get "some professional help" for the problem. That evening, Andrea told Paul that she was indeed ready to seek some therapy. With his encouragement, she soon made an appointment with a psychologist, Dr. Frances Lloyd, through the referral service of her managed care network.

A Spouse's View: Living With Imagined Illness

When Andrea informed Paul that she was ready to seek therapy, he felt as if he were being given a "new life." He had just about given up all hope of his wife ever improving—or of her taking the steps needed to improve. For the most part, he had kept his exasperation to himself. He loved Andrea, and thought it would be cruel to belittle her or threaten her. Besides, when he did express upset or anger, things always seemed to get worse. She seemed to become even more convinced that a terrible illness was overtaking her. No, it was usually better to just calmly reassure her and make gentle suggestions that she might be overreacting.

On the outside, Paul tried to be calm and understanding. But on the inside he was boiling. He was able to hide his feelings—at least some of them—from Andrea, but he would periodically open up to a close friend or family member. Indeed, he felt he had to open up or else he would explode. Just a week ago, in the middle of his wife's MS scare, he had confided to his brother that he was, for the first time, considering seeking a separation.

> Her behavior is truly unbearable. I mean, I'm not sure I can continue in the marriage. You know, she never gave any indication that she had problems this serious when we first met. We fell in love, everything seemed wonderful. I guess that's what comes from marrying someone you only know for 6 months. I knew we were rushing things, but I was so sure. I never thought there could be any reason I wouldn't want to spend the rest of my life with her.
>
> Everything was great for about a year. Then she started in with her ridiculous "medical problems." It started with "The baby's going to be deformed. . . . He's going to be stillborn. . . . He's going to die within 6 months." At first I worried right along with her because she seemed so sure that something was going to be wrong. I thought it just might happen. But then the doctors told us everything was going to be fine, and her attitude was only "What if they're wrong? What if he dies?"
>
> Then I thought, well, she's just nervous about becoming a mother. But the sheer strength of her worries finally convinced me that her thinking was really disturbed. Then again, I told myself that the pregnancy must be wreaking havoc on her entire system and that she'd soon be back to normal. But after Jimmy was born and he was fine, I realized that she wasn't going to get any better.

It was cancer one week and tuberculosis the next. She might have a brain tumor during the day and a curvature of the spine by nighttime. Do you know how hard it is to repeatedly explain that the world isn't going to collapse, to repeatedly remind your wife that she's not gravely ill? It's been like living with Chicken Little, constantly screaming that the sky is falling. When she panics, even though I realize that she's not right and that there's no real problem, I can't help but get caught up in her emotion at first. Sometimes she's even able to convince me that this time it's for real—it's a problem that will change everything. But then it soon becomes obvious that it's the same old story—another false alarm—and I'm back to my usual job of trying to convince her that everything's going to be fine.

I guess what upsets me the most is that the woman I married no longer seems to be an adult. Here we are trying to raise a child, and she's behaving like a child herself. It's both surreal and depressing when you have to hold your wife while she cries in your arms because she has a headache or a cold that won't go away. I also get really nervous when I think about what this may do to Jimmy if it continues. When she tucks him in at night or drops him off at school, she sometimes gets teary, and even says things like, "Remember that Mommy always loves you, even if I go away!" I mean, for heaven's sake. When I think about what she's starting to put him through, and how he may feel when he really starts to understand what she's saying, well that frankly makes me mad. It's got to harm him, maybe seriously. How anxious, nervous, or all-around screwed up is he going to be?

After 3 years of this nonsense, I think I've had enough. I don't need this nightmare, and I certainly don't want my son exposed to it. But then again, I love her, and I don't want to hurt her. And, really, I don't want to leave her. I just want her to change, and for our lives to become normal. But then I come back to the fact that I'm running out of steam. I don't know how much longer I can be the patient, understanding husband, especially when I don't understand anything about this.

> **Men and women are equally likely to experience hypochondriasis.**

Fortunately, Paul didn't have to act on his thoughts of separation. It was as if he and Andrea had reached bottom at the same time. When she came to him, saying that she was ready for therapy, he knew that this was the right direction—not separation or arguments or accusations. Of course, even as Andrea made her appointment with the psychologist, Paul realized that there were no guarantees that everything would turn out all right. But at least she—and he—now had a chance.

Andrea in Treatment: Achieving a "Healthy" Perspective

Upon listening to Andrea's tale of suspected illnesses and repeated anxieties, Dr. Lloyd concluded that the young woman's condition met the DSM-IV criteria for a diagnosis of *hypochondriasis*. She had been preoccupied with fears of serious illness (based on misinterpretations of symptoms) for the past 3 years; this preoccupation persisted (or resurfaced in new forms) despite appropriate medical evaluation; and the preoccupation caused significant distress.

Dr. Lloyd's reading of clinical studies had convinced her of the parallels between hypochondriasis and obsessive-compulsive disorder. A hypochondriacal patient's anxious and intrusive focus on bodily sensations and physical symptoms is often equivalent to the obsessions with germs or disaster displayed by patients with obsessive-compulsive disorder. Similarly, the efforts of hypochondriacal patients to cope with fears of illness—repeatedly seeking reassurance, making doctors' visits, reviewing medical texts, and monitoring their physical states—are reminiscent of compulsions.

To many clinicians, such parallels suggest that the treatment for hypochondriasis should take its lead from that for obsessive-compulsive disorder. Thus, psychiatrists who specialize in drug therapy often give hypochondriacal patients medications that benefit obsessive-compulsive patients, particularly *fluoxetine* (Prozac). Similarly, psychotherapists often offer a treatment program of exposure-and-response-prevention for hypochrondriacal patients, similar to the behavioral treatment used in cases of obsessive-compulsive disorder. Many such psychotherapists also include cognitive interventions similar to the cognitive approaches used for anxiety or depression.

In Andrea's case, Dr. Lloyd decided to use the psychological approach first, and to refer the client for drug therapy only if psychotherapy were to fail. *Exposure* in the treatment of hypochondriasis involves bringing the person into contact with the stimuli—sensations, thoughts, or images—that provoke illness anxieties, with the goal of extinguishing those anxieties. In the *response-prevention component* of treatment, clients with hypochondriasis are prevented from performing the behaviors—for example, reading medical books or seeking reassurances—that they usually turn to when they experience fears about illness.

> People with hypochondriasis receive an additional (that is, *comorbid*) diagnosis of obsessive-compulsive disorder only when their obsessions or compulsions are not restricted to concerns about illness (APA, 1994, 2000).

Session 1 At the first session with Dr. Lloyd, Andrea related her history. Not currently experiencing one of her "crises," she was in good humor as she discussed her difficulties. She told the psychologist that in between the crises she had no real complaints. She enjoyed her work, loved her family, and was generally an upbeat and enthusiastic person. Still, she always felt mildly apprehensive, as she knew the slightest thing could set her off and plunge her into an acute, and terribly painful, anxiety.

As the first step in the treatment, Dr. Lloyd explained to Andrea the theoretical treatment model. To start, she cited the role that Andrea's self-scrutiny, reassurance seeking, reading of medical material, and doctor visits were playing in maintaining her problem. The psychologist explained that it was completely understandable that Andrea should engage in these behaviors as a means of coping with her fears; indeed, most people with hypochondriasis responded in the very same way. The problem was that while these behaviors often provided a certain measure of relief, in the long run they maintained the fear. Thus, the first step in the treatment, Dr. Lloyd explained, was to begin limiting some of these "coping behaviors" (the prevention component of the treatment).

Andrea: Don't I need to go to the doctor's to make sure I'm OK? I mean, what if there was something seriously wrong with me and I neglected it? What harm is there in going?

Dr. Lloyd: From a medical standpoint, there is no harm in going. From a psychological standpoint, however, the visits fuel the feeling that something is wrong, and rob you of any opportunity to learn to cope with the illness fears in another way. For our purposes, you will need to limit the doctor visits that are psychologically harmful.

Andrea: How do I tell one from the other?

Dr. Lloyd: I admit it's not always easy, but we will need to devise some guidelines. What is your impression concerning the necessity of the doctor visits you now make?

Andrea: At the time I make them they seem absolutely necessary. I mean, I get a symptom and I just have to know what it represents, or that it's not serious. But I know that what I'm doing is not normal, because the doctors usually get fed up. Often they start out being nice and understanding, but then things go to pot when I start calling too much.

Dr. Lloyd: So it would appear that some of these visits are unnecessary.

Andrea: Yes, but how do I tell which ones?

Dr. Lloyd said she would like to put the question of specific guidelines for medical visits on hold for now, and concentrate first on Andrea's other problematic coping behaviors. To begin, she wanted Andrea to start recording her illness concerns, using a written log containing the following elements: (a) the eliciting symptom or sensation, (b) her immediate concern about the symptom, (c) how she coped with her concern, and (d) the result of her coping efforts.

Next, Dr. Lloyd explained the exposure component of the treatment. She said that, generally, it would be a good idea for Andrea to limit her coping behaviors (for example, asking Paul for constant reassurance) whenever she was in the midst of a crisis; this resistance would help lessen her anxiety over time. In addition, rather than just wait around for crises to occur, therapy could speed along the process by *creating* conditions that produced illness anxiety and regularly exposing Andrea to such conditions. At the same time, the psychologist noted that creating such conditions presents logistical problems—one cannot readily manufacture unexplained physical symptoms—so the two of them would have to develop some type of substitute, such as a *visualization exercise,* in which Andrea would visualize in detail having such symptoms.

Hypochondriasis can present a clinical picture very similar to that of *somatization disorder,* the somatoform disorder that is marked by numerous recurring physical ailments that have no organic basis.

If a person experiences great anxiety over his or her numerous bodily symptoms, and the symptoms are relatively minor, a diagnosis of hypochondriasis is probably indicated. If, however, the numerous bodily symptoms overshadow the person's anxiety, a diagnosis of somatization disorder may be in order.

Andrea said she could see the value in exposure exercises, even remarking, "I guess it's the same as what you do if you're afraid of snakes—have greater and greater contact with snakes until the fear diminishes." At the same time, she expressed doubt that just visualizing herself ill would have any emotional impact. She assumed that there would be no therapeutic benefit in an exposure exercise unless there was some real anxiety to extinguish.

Dr. Lloyd and Andrea agreed to give this question some thought for the coming week. In the meantime, Andrea would keep the log according to the specifications described in earlier instructions.

Session 2 Andrea returned with blank record forms, saying she simply had not been troubled by any symptoms during the week. She noted that this was not unusual for her. She could go for a couple of weeks without a crisis occurring.

Dr. Lloyd said she would like to devote the session to two main matters. First, she wanted to devise some specific guidelines for limiting Andrea's coping behaviors, should any be provoked in her real life. Second, she would like to work out an exposure procedure, especially since Andrea was not currently experiencing any spontaneous disease fears that might be used for therapeutic purposes.

Regarding the guidelines for limiting coping behaviors, the psychologist suggested the following:

1. Stop consulting medical books, whether provoked by symptoms or not.

2. Stop taking blood pressure at home.

3. Refrain from seeking verbal reassurance from family or friends if a symptom arises.

4. Refrain from calling the doctor for at least 2 days when faced with symptoms that cause only minor discomfort.

Andrea agreed to try to observe these guidelines if any symptoms arose.

Next, she and Dr. Lloyd discussed an exposure procedure. The client remained firm in her belief that visualizing herself suffering an illness would not be compelling enough to produce anxiety. She stated that her fears just didn't seem to have a "visual component." She even tried closing her eyes in the session and imagining herself on a sickbed, but she had trouble conjuring up any image. She said it just seemed "artificial."

Accordingly, to help develop an appropriate exposure procedure, Dr. Lloyd asked Andrea to explain the exact sequence of events when a spontaneous illness fear arose. Andrea replied that the process usually began with her noting a particular abnormality in her appearance or an abnormal sensation; next, she thought of a dreaded illness that might be implied by the abnormality; and then she frantically sought reassurance, usually first by approaching her husband and then by calling or visiting the doctor.

Dr. Lloyd devised an exposure procedure modeled on this natural sequence. She suggested a written exercise, as follows: Three times a day, for the next week, Andrea was to take time out from her normal activities and briefly survey her body's appearance and sensations; then, based on a particular attribute that she identified, she was to manufacture a particular illness fear (a different one each time) and write it down in a notebook. In doing this three times a day, she would have produced 21 different illness fears by the end of the week. Should the fear be great enough to provoke a desire to engage in any coping behaviors, Andrea was to follow the guidelines described earlier in the session for limiting the behaviors.

To test the exercise, Dr. Lloyd asked Andrea to carry it out at that very moment. Andrea focused on her body for a few seconds and then remarked that she had a slight tingling sensation in her right foot, due, most likely, to the way she had been crossing her legs for the past ½ hour. Dr. Lloyd then asked Andrea to proceed to the next step, namely to think of a dire illness that the symptom might signify. Andrea was very hesitant, saying it would cause her great anxiety actually to verbalize an illness. The psychologist persevered, however, encouraging Andrea to proceed. Finally, in a soft voice, Andrea speculated that the tingling could be a sign of multiple sclerosis.

Dr. Lloyd praised Andrea for this effort and suggested that the client next carry out the exercise on paper, following the procedure outlined for the coming week's assignment. Accordingly, Andrea wrote down: "(a) My foot is tingling." Next, the client should have written: "(b) I have multiple sclerosis." But once again, Andrea hesitated; she said that she was seized with the fear that writing down the words might become a self-fulfilling prophecy. Dr. Lloyd empathized with Andrea's concern, but then led the client in a rational discussion of whether writing down an illness could actually have any role in producing it. Andrea replied that intellectually she knew it was nonsense, but somehow writing it down filled her with fright. Yet, at the same time, she felt intuitively that writing down the sentence—"I have multiple sclerosis"—would be therapeutic for her. All of a sudden, Andrea said that she wanted to go ahead and do the written exercise; she thought that if somehow she could accomplish it, she would feel like she was defying her fears. She took the pen in her hand, and wrote the sentence down.

Dr. Lloyd and the client agreed that Andrea would continue to carry out the exercise three times a day in the coming week, each time trying to think of a new illness, or, at the very least, not using the same illness more than once in a day.

Hypochondriasis and other somatoform disorders are among the least-researched mental disorders. One computerized search found around 300 literature selections for hypochondriasis over the past decade, compared to 3,000 for specific phobia, 7,700 for alcohol abuse, and 16,000 for depression.

Session 3 Andrea reported that she had carried out the exercise faithfully each day. The first few days, it was quite stressful. Each time she wrote down an illness, she almost felt as if she had doomed herself to the disease. However, as the week progressed, she noticed a shift in her feelings. She felt less and less threatened by the writing, and she seemed to become bolder and bolder in her thoughts. Furthermore, the more she wrote, the less threatened she felt.

Dr. Lloyd reviewed the entries that Andrea had made, one by one, and noted the increasing detail and daring as the week progressed. A typical entry for the first couple of days read: "(a) I had poor posture in sitting at a meeting at work," and "(b) I am getting osteoporosis." By the end of the week she had written: "(a) I have a slight headache," and "(b) It is a brain tumor, which will invade my brain, rob me of my senses, and leave me a vegetable in a hospital bed."

Andrea said she was amazed at what she was eventually able to write. The illnesses were still unpleasant to write about, but the utter fear was drastically weakened.

As to the general effect of the exercise on her hypochondriasis, the client said this was difficult to assess. She had not been subject to any spontaneous illness fears this week, but this was not necessarily a sign of improvement because, even in the past, she could go for weeks without an incident. Still, this was her 3rd consecutive week without a problem, and it was getting close to the longest time in the past years that she had ever gone without a medical concern. She wondered if the deliberate focus on symptoms had replaced her usual fears.

Dr. Lloyd said she would also like to discuss the cognitive component of Andrea's fears. To begin, she asked Andrea to consider her worst-case scenario should she become ill:

> **In addition to their illness concerns, people with hypochondriasis often have fears of aging and death (APA, 2000).**

Andrea: It's funny you should ask. When all this started about 3 years ago—when I got pregnant—I was focused mainly on my own fear of dying. I was just thinking: I don't want to die. But since Jimmy was born, dying itself doesn't seem like such a big deal. I mean, I still don't want to die, but it seems that my main reason now for not wanting to die is the impact it would have on my husband and son.

Dr. Lloyd: My next question may seem a little strange, but in overcoming a preoccupation with illness and death it is usually helpful to think things through completely. So my question is: Why would your dying be so bad for them?

Andrea: It seems obvious. Their lives would be ruined. Isn't it terrible to lose your wife or mother?

Dr. Lloyd: Yes, it is terrible. Did you ever know anyone who lost a parent at a young age?

Andrea: I had a childhood friend whose father died.

Dr. Lloyd: What happened?

Andrea: Well, he died suddenly. I think it was a heart attack. Afterward, my friend Sheila had to leave school for a month. She was really upset. And, of course, she really missed her dad.

Dr. Lloyd: What happened to her eventually?

Andrea: Her mom got remarried after a few years to a really great guy. But it wasn't like having her own dad back. She had a very hard time.

Dr. Lloyd: Was her life ruined?

Andrea: She's married now and has two kids. I guess you couldn't say her life was ruined. Still, I wouldn't want anything like that to happen to Jimmy.

Dr. Lloyd: If something did happen to you, if you did die, what do you think the effect would be?

Andrea: Oh, boy. This is hard. I can't believe we're talking about this. But I think I know what you're driving at. If I can learn to see it just a little less hysterically, I might be a little less hysterical about the whole illness thing.

Dr. Lloyd: Possibly.

Andrea: (sighing) Well, if I died, everyone in my family would be sad, and I know I would be missed. I think Jimmy would take it very hard. But on the other hand, I think Paul is the type to remarry, and I think that would help. I just hope he would choose a woman who would be a good mother to Jimmy. I think he would. I also hope Jimmy would remember me, but mainly I would just want him to be happy. (long pause) I hope my family never has to face my early death, but I guess they would eventually handle it.

Dr. Lloyd: I know that was hard to think through. What you just did was something known in psychotherapy as *decatastrophizing*, taking an event that you assumed you couldn't bear even in your thoughts, and figuring out a way that it could be faced and accepted. Having done this with an event as extreme as your own death, you may find it easier to do the same with lesser events, such as serious illnesses.

Dr. Lloyd then went on to explain the other aspect of thinking that produces anxiety, namely, *overestimating* the likelihood that a particular symptom signifies something serious. The psychologist reviewed with Andrea several of her most recent illness fears, noting how none of them came to pass. For example, her numb arm turned out just to be a muscle ache, not MS; her eye problem turned out to be a minor infection, not MS; and the bump on her skull was just a normal bony projection, not a tumor. The psychologist suggested that Andrea would benefit from learning to identify and correct her overestimation sooner rather than later.

Thus, she suggested an expanded exercise for the coming week. First, as before, Andrea would survey her body three times a day, identify a symptom, and create a disease thought on the basis of the symptom. Now, however, in addition, she was to describe the catastrophic aftermath of the disease—as she imagined it—so as to increase the intensity of the exposure.

The new exercise included a cognitive component as well. After having formed her disease thought, Andrea was to produce a more reasonable interpretation of the symptom. In so doing, she could draw on her past experience. Thus, for example, if she were to note numbness in a finger, in addition to forming the thought that it could represent MS, she was to produce a more rational alternative, such as that it probably represented a mere muscle ache or some other less dire condition.

In a bizarre coincidence, on February 17, 1673, the French actor-playwright Molière collapsed on stage and died while performing in *Le Malade imaginaire* [*The Hypochondriac*] (Ash, 1999).

Session 4 Andrea reported that she had carried out the exercise more or less as prescribed. She did find, however, that on some days she had difficulty identifying three different symptoms and three different disease thoughts. She said she didn't know whether this was a sign of progress or just an indication that she was running out of ideas. She thought it could be sign of progress, for she could never imagine herself at a loss for illness ideas in the past. She also noted that her attempts at decatastrophizing the aftermath felt very artificial at the beginning of the exercise, but that toward the end of the week her renditions seemed more believable.

Andrea also reported that she had experienced her first spontaneous disease fear since treatment began. One night, when entertaining guests, she noticed an abnormal swelling in her armpit. It was quite a noticeable lump, and the thought of a tumor arose. In a departure from her previous habits, she did not excuse herself to consult her medical books, although she was tempted. Instead, she tried to apply her new cognitive skills by forming a more likely disease thought ("It's just a boil"). This held her until the guests left, but then she felt compelled to ask her husband for his opinion. She didn't think that this represented a violation of the prohibition on requests for reassurance, as she didn't feel she was seeking reassurance, just "an unbiased opinion." Paul, for his part, didn't know what to think.

The next day, Andrea was in a quandary as to whether to call the doctor or not, in view of Dr. Lloyd's guideline concerning waiting 2 days for symptoms that caused only minor discomfort. The symptom did seem quite unusual—even her husband eventually recommended calling the doctor—so Andrea decided to call, although without actively seeking an appointment (another departure from her usual habit).

She followed her usual routine that morning, taking Jimmy to school and going directly to work. She then placed a call to the doctor without conveying any sense of urgency, just requesting that the doctor return her call when he was free. The doctor called back about an hour later, and Andrea described the swelling. After a few questions, the doctor concluded that the swelling was probably an infected hair follicle that would clear up in a few days. Andrea felt immediately reassured, which was a distinct departure from the past. Previously, she would have insisted on an appointment.

Andrea felt this experience represented a sign of improvement. Not only had she conducted herself differently, in order to honor the guidelines, but she also felt different in the process, as she did not experience the usual sense of fear or hysteria. She was pleased with her reaction.

Dr. Lloyd agreed that the client was showing signs of improvement. She advised her to continue her exercises and adherence to the coping rules for the coming week.

People with hypochondriasis often also experience an anxiety disorder, depression, or another somatoform disorder (APA, 2000).

Session 5 Andrea said she thought she had reached the limits of her imagination, as the entries in her writing exercises seemed to be getting more and more far-fetched. For example, by the end of this week, one of her selected symptoms was: "The hair on my arm looks slightly blonder than usual." The corresponding disease fear was: "My hair is turning white because I'm getting one of those accelerated aging diseases—advanced senescence!" The psychologist agreed that the exercise had probably outlived its usefulness.

In the realm of natural disease fears during the week, Andrea revealed that she had experienced only some brief concern with a cough that she developed. Consistent with the guidelines, Andrea did not ask Paul for reassurance and she refrained from calling the doctor for 48 hours; her impulse to call was not strong, in any event. By the end of the 48 hours, the cough had subsided somewhat and the impulse to call had gone. Andrea expressed delight, not only at her rather minimal fear, but also at being spared the burden of leaving work, arranging a doctor's visit, traveling to the doctor's office, and suffering the humiliation of the doctor's annoyance.

Reviewing her experiences of the past several weeks, Andrea felt that there had indeed been some basic change in her feelings. She believed that if she just continued to observe the behavioral guidelines, she might eventually be able to return to her normal self of 3 years ago.

The plan for the next week was for Andrea to stop the written exercises. If she experienced a spontaneous disease fear, she was to cope with it using the behavioral guidelines and cognitive reinterpretations. Dr. Lloyd also suggested that if the week proved uneventful, and Andrea was able to continue observing the guidelines, future sessions would be scheduled less often.

Sessions 6–8 Andrea returned for the sixth session, once again reporting an uneventful week. She said she was starting to grow more confident that she might have overcome the problem. A review of the week's events indicated that the client had experienced some appropriate concern over a high fever that her son had developed, but otherwise she had been anxiety free and not preoccupied with her own health.

At Session 7, held 2 weeks later, Andrea offered basically the same report; and at Session 8, held a month after that, she still had not experienced any new illness fears. She and Dr. Lloyd agreed to stop therapy at that point, with the understanding that the client would call if any difficulties arose.

Epilogue

Dr. Lloyd called Andrea 6 months after the last session, and the young lawyer reported she had more or less maintained her progress. There had been a couple of

> Most cases of hypochondriasis are chronic, but complete recovery does occur in some cases (APA, 1994, 2000).

isolated instances when she experienced unreasonable anxiety, but by using cognitive reinterpretations and following the behavioral guidelines, she had managed them pretty well. Generally, she continued to be aware—too aware—that life always carried a potential for tragedy, but her day-to-day feelings and behavior were not adversely affected by this awareness. Moreover, she found that she was also able to hold onto the flip side of this awareness, that is, an appreciation of the blessings of life and good health. The positive view more than counterbalanced the negative view. In a way, she felt that she had returned to two kinds of health—physical and psychological. She considered treatment a roaring success.

CASE 7

Psychological Factors Affecting Medical Condition: Type A Behavior Pattern

Table 7-1

DSM-IV Checklist

Psychological Factors Affecting General Medical Condition

1. The presence of a general medical condition.
2. Psychological factors adversely affecting the general medical condition in one of the following ways:
   (a) Influencing the course of the general medical condition.
   (b) Interfering with the treatment of the general medical condition.
   (c) Posing additional health risks.
   (d) Stress-related physiological responses precipitating or exacerbating the general medical condition.

Based on APA, 1994, 2000.

The main thing that Spencer, a 62-year-old married pharmacist, could recall about his childhood was that his father, a high school basketball coach, was a perfectionist and often angry. Spencer vividly recalled endless homework sessions in the evening with his father. Shortly after each session began, his father could not contain his frustration at Spencer's occasional inability to grasp what seemed like a simple concept. Sometimes his father would repeat the problem in a progressively louder voice, as though screaming the words would inspire Spencer with the answer. If the boy made a guess at the answer, but guessed wrong, his father would stalk out of the room, only to reenter a few minutes later, calmer but likely to react in the same way at the next roadblock.

Spencer: The Seeds of Anger

As Spencer got older, he assumed more independence in his schoolwork and the unpleasant interactions with his father lessened. Still, his father's tendency to perfectionism—as applied to Spencer—occasionally took other forms. For example, when Spencer was a varsity basketball player in high school his father would attend games and occasionally become overzealous. During one game, after Spencer had made a blunder, his father came down to the team huddle during a time-out, grabbed him by the shirttail, and began berating him in front of the other players.

In retrospect, Spencer didn't resent his father for these actions; he knew the man was motivated by a desire to see his son succeed. However, he did wonder what effect this behavior had on his own personality development, which eventually came to mirror his father's intolerant, perfectionist style.

Spencer: A Life of Anger

At the age of 31, Spencer earned a degree in pharmacy; he spent the next 31 years working continuously in the field. He started out employed in a retail store, but after a few years sought a hospital job. Careerwise, his perfectionist nature worked to his advantage; he was considered reliable and diligent, someone who could be counted on to come through and rarely make a mistake. Over the years, he moved to positions of greater and greater responsibility, until he was supervising the entire pharmacy operation of a large hospital. At the same time, his perfectionism could also work against him. He fretted constantly over potential lapses: errors that either he or his staff might commit, deliveries that might not arrive on time, even prescriptions that the doctors might have written inaccurately. As a result, he could not enjoy his work, nor did others like working with him. In his late 50s, Spencer took his pension and decided to return to the retail trade.

He found a new job that paid him more, but what it did not change was his lifelong pattern of reacting to situations with irritation and even anger. Over the years, the pattern had been evident in almost any situation: work, recreation, social occasions, even driving on the highway. Indeed, the drive to and from work was one of the most stressful periods of his day, as he always felt irritation with other drivers; occasionally, he even got into fights.

No sooner would he pull onto the highway than he became preoccupied with how the other drivers were conducting themselves. What particularly irked him were tailgaters. While driving, Spencer would glance up at his mirror constantly to keep tabs on the action behind him and, if he saw a tailgater, he could feel his anger start to rise. He would keep his eyes glued to the mirror, "staring holes in the head of the s.o.b." who was menacing him so. Sometimes, to teach the other driver a lesson, Spencer would slow his car down so as to interfere with the progress of the driver behind him. Once the tailgater passed, if he looked like the jerk that Spencer expected, Spencer might "flip him the bird."

Another pet peeve was drivers who would not maintain their place in line when two lanes of traffic had to merge. Spencer would closely observe the process and, inevitably, identify another driver who seemed to be getting ahead, trying to merge in front of him when he had defined the other driver's place as behind him. The angry pharmacist would deal with this by playing a game of chicken, deliberately trying to edge the other car out until the driver was forced to choose between colliding with Spencer or backing off.

The other regular source of stress in Spencer's day was his work. When he left the hospital and reentered retail pharmacy work, he found new stresses that he hadn't envisioned, particularly in the form of pressure from customers. It seemed

> Studies suggest that people who generally respond to life with optimism, constructive coping strategies, and resilience experience better immune system functioning and are better prepared to fight off medical illnesses (Taylor et al., 2000).

that almost every customer had a gripe or complaint. When the customers handed in their prescriptions, they usually asked how long they would have to wait. And when he handed them the medicine, they would usually look dissatisfied and, occasionally, would ask him why it had taken so long. To Spencer, the customers were implying that he didn't know what he was doing. To deal with the customers' impatience, Spencer sometimes rattled off the list of steps involved in filling the prescription. Curiously, customers rarely seemed to appreciate hearing this list, nor did it lessen their impatience.

He came to look at customers as the enemy. And unfortunately, as matters stood in the retail business, there was no hope of things easing up. What with managed care and prescription drug plans, the profit margin had dwindled, so Spencer's pharmacy relied on attracting ever greater numbers of customers. As the number of customers grew, the toll taken on Spencer's nerves seemed to increase correspondingly.

> According to research, men who hold an enduring sense of hopelessness die at above-average rates from heart disease, cancer, and other causes (Everson et al., 1996).

At home, he felt that his problems with anger and irritation were less pronounced. He lived alone with his wife, and their relationship was a good one in his opinion. Their two grown children, a son and a daughter, were both married and out of the house. The only problem that Spencer experienced at home was a tendency to brood. He found that he had difficulty putting the irritations and frustrations of the day behind him. He would spend a good portion of the evening apparently watching television but actually mulling over upsetting events of the day, trying to decide who had gotten the best of whom, and whether he had succeeded in teaching a particular character a lesson.

During his brooding, his wife, Sheila, might try to draw him out, asking what he was thinking about. Usually, he would try to minimize his concerns, telling her it wasn't important. If she persisted, he might make some comment about the "idiots" he had to deal with at work, but generally he did not want to go into details.

In their social life, Spencer and Sheila had a circle of friends, many of whom were retirees who would join them for dinner or for a round of golf on the weekends. In general, Spencer believed he was looked on as a good fellow and friend by their acquaintances. Still, there were occasional incidents when his emotional explosions would break through, usually during competitive sports. If he missed a tennis shot or a putt during golf, there was the occasional outburst of self-criticism, cursing out loud, or banging his racquet or club against the ground. Also, he had a tendency to argue or question close calls in tennis matches. It seemed to him that his wife was occasionally embarrassed by these displays—she sometimes begged Spencer to "tone it down"—but he couldn't avoid the outbursts entirely.

And so it went for him. Despite a comfortable life, successful job, and good family, he spent most of his time boiling underneath. He did not really see that he had a choice about his feelings or reactions. He didn't even realize that they were all that unusual. He suspected that anyone faced with his pressures and upsets would react the same way. He would not even have given it all a second thought had he not had what he termed "the ultimate wake-up call" at the age of 61.

Sheila: Life With an Angry Man

Sheila truly loved her husband, but over three decades of marriage, she could never understand why life with him had to be so difficult. And difficult it was, despite Spencer's contention that their relationship was solid and his belief that he was successfully hiding his anger from her. As Sheila told her sister-in-law in a candid moment:

> It's like I always have to walk on eggshells around Spencer. I never know at any given moment, on any given day, what the problem is going to be, but I can usually be pretty sure there's going to be a problem.
>
> It can come out of nowhere—an innocent remark, a playful tone, or a mild complaint from me—and he will turn his "death stare" on me. That look usually means that I've said the worst possible thing and I am going to have to explain myself, perhaps for several hours.
>
> And when he gets into his moods, absolutely nothing I do, nothing I say, is right. Nothing I cook is good enough. In fact, nothing I say or do can get me out of the hell that awaits me when he's like that. He starts breathing heavily and just lets me know with his body language how hard I am making his existence and how much easier things would be if I were as smart as him. At least that's how it seems to me. He just has a way of turning that rage on to me and making me feel like such an idiot, such a stupid little person. It's hard even to come up with an example of the things we fight about, because they're always so trivial. It's like he's just looking for things to be angry about.
>
> How I wish he would learn to calm down. He's always so agitated that he makes his life and mine nerve-racking. When he goes away on business to his pharmaceutical conventions, I actually feel relieved. He's usually gone for 3 days, and the first 2 are almost heavenly. Everything seems okay, nothing is too scary or burdensome, I feel I can be myself without being corrected. Then, the day before he returns, just thinking about it, I start to feel my heart racing. It's like I've only got 1 more day of freedom. I have to make the most of it so I don't waste it. That's not normal, to crave the times that your husband's away.
>
> But, you know, I wouldn't mind it so much if he didn't embarrass me in front of other people. That is truly unbearable. One of the most painful and embarrassing moments of my life was before we moved to the apartment. I had a friend from the school where I work and we used to have dinners and see each other socially: me and Spencer, she and her husband. One time, during a moment alone at the school Christmas party, she said, "Sheila, I know you must have a very difficult life with him." I said I didn't know what she was talking about, but she said, "Honey, you don't have to pretend to me." And I realized then that other people really didn't like him. I tried

During and after marital spats, women typically experience a greater release of stress hormones than men and, in turn, a greater weakening in immune system functioning (Kiecolt-Glaser et al., 1996).

to tell her that she just didn't know him, and she'd best not say anything else against him to me, but inside I was very upset because what she said had struck a nerve.

When we're in the car and he honks at other drivers and curses at them, I see the looks of anger and disgust on their faces. Sometimes I'm so embarrassed I wish I'd never met him. Years ago, at Jimmy's soccer game, Spencer got into such a screaming match with the referee that he actually shoved the guy and got us ejected from the game. Imagine that, a high school soccer game. I just stared at the ground as we walked away from the field, and didn't say anything. I guess I was afraid he'd turn that raging anger on to me. Too afraid to tell him what he was putting me, and the kids, through.

Of course, I know he's a good man, with a good heart. He would and does do anything for me and the kids. He loves us deeply, and that's why I love him, why I stay with him and put up with his difficult ways. And I do worry about him. He can't be very happy if he has that much anger in him. And having so much anger cannot be good for him. I'm afraid something's got to give, and then where will he be? And where will I be as well?

> The medical expenses of people who feel under constant stress are 46% higher than those of stress-free persons (Goetzel, 1998).

Spencer: The Ultimate Wake-Up Call

One Saturday morning, while shoveling snow in his driveway, Spencer suddenly found himself very short of breath; next, he broke out in a cold sweat, followed by a crushing pain in the center of his chest. It felt like an elephant had its foot on his thorax. Then he lost consciousness. His neighbor witnessed the collapse, and telephoned for an ambulance. Spencer was rushed to the hospital, where he was placed in the intensive care unit and diagnosed with a mild heart attack.

Fortunately, the damage was slight and Spencer spent the next several weeks convalescing. In the hospital, he attended classes on "behavioral risk factors in heart disease." Here he learned that certain forms of "stress," especially angry reactions, can be a risk factor for coronary heart disease. In particular, he learned that the "Type A" behavior pattern was considered to be a risk factor.

Noting that the Type A description—competitiveness, impatience, and hostility—seemed to fit him to a tee, Spencer decided that he must eliminate his Type A traits. He decided to be more easygoing, to avoid arguments, to stop criticizing people, and to cut down on his complaints about everything. Unfortunately, he was able to keep to his plan for only about a month. Before long, he was feeling as much anger and irritation as ever. Finding it impossible to manage his stress on his own, he contacted the Behavioral Medicine Program at the hospital and was referred to a psychologist, Dr. Thomas Lopez.

> The concept of a Type A behavior pattern was introduced in 1959 by two cardiologists, Meyer Friedman and Raymond Rosenman.

Spencer in Treatment: Calming Down

Dr. Lopez determined that Spencer's difficulties met the criteria for the DSM-IV category of *psychological factors affecting medical condition*. This is a broad category used to classify any problem in which psychological factors negatively affect a medical condition, either by having a direct causal role, by interfering with treatment, or by heightening the risk for illness. In Spencer's case, the psychological factors were heightening the risk for illness. Specifically, he exhibited a behavior pattern known to be a risk factor for cardiovascular disease.

The pattern that Spencer exhibited is typically called a *Type A* behavior pattern. Traditionally, researchers have described individuals with this pattern as having three main characteristics: excessive competitiveness, hostility, and impatience. Recent investigations have suggested, however, that it is largely the characteristic of *hostility* that increases the risk for coronary heart disease. Research has also demonstrated that anger and other Type A behaviors can be reduced through psychological treatment, and that heart attack victims who receive such treatment have a lower risk of experiencing a subsequent attack.

Dr. Lopez had been working with Type A heart attack victims for 12 years. In fact, what with the hospital referring so many patients to him, clients with this pattern represented at least 60% of his practice. He had gained a wide reputation for his expertise in this area.

The psychologist used a cognitive model of anger. According to this perspective, angry reactions are triggered not just by specific events, but by a person's interpretations of the events—particularly interpretations that one has been treated unfairly or improperly. Such interpretations lead to arousal of the autonomic nervous system and to a sense of anger. These reactions lead, in turn, to antagonistic behaviors by the individual—behaviors that further fuel the sense of anger and that trigger new upsetting events (Figure 7-1).

Thus, Dr. Lopez's treatment for anger was designed to change a person's interpretations and physical arousal as well as his or her antagonistic behaviors. If a pa-

> The cognitive view of anger used by Dr. Lopez, and his corresponding treatment program, were based on the influential work of R.W. Novaco (1975) and D. Meichenbaum (1977).

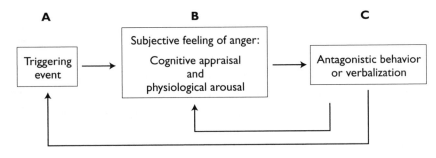

Figure **7-1**

Feedback model of anger

A specific event (A) triggers an internal reaction (B), comprising both cognitive and physiological components. The internal reaction, in turn, impels antagonistic behavior (C). The antagonistic behavior both heightens the internal reaction and produces additional triggering events.

tient can learn to react more calmly and think more flexibly, then many situations that previously evoked anger and antagonistic behavior may be dismissed as minor annoyances, or possibly disregarded entirely. And if antagonistic behaviors can be reduced, anger itself will be reduced, as will environmental triggers.

Dr. Lopez's treatment typically involved three stages. In the first stage, he educated patients about the cognitive model of anger. In the second stage, he taught them basic anger management skills. Finally, he guided them through a cognitive-behavioral approach called *stress inoculation*.

Session 1 Unlike many anger patients whom Dr. Lopez had treated, Spencer arrived with a certain degree of insight into his problem and a genuine desire to change. This can be contrasted with patients who are forced into treatment, cases of court-ordered treatment for domestic violence, for example.

At the same time, there was one element of coercion in Spencer's case. His seeking of treatment was triggered by his heart attack, and the psychologist wondered whether Spencer would otherwise have had any interest in working on his anger. The psychologist expressed this concern to his client:

> In a pioneering study, more than 3,000 healthy middle-aged men were followed over an 8-year period. More than twice as many of those with a Type A behavior pattern developed coronary heart disease as those with a Type B behavior pattern (Friedman & Rosenman, 1974).

Spencer: To tell you the truth, if it wasn't for the heart attack, I don't think I would be here. But by the same token, I wouldn't have quit smoking either. I think the heart attack made me look a little closer at some things that always bothered me. Still, I have to admit, it's hard for me to see how I can change.

Dr. Lopez: Why?

Spencer: Well, as I told you, I did try to turn over a new leaf. I tried not complaining about things or arguing with anyone for a month, but it was driving me crazy. To be honest, I think there *is* a lot to complain and argue about, and I felt like I was denying my basic nature.

Dr. Lopez: The therapy that I conduct is designed to accomplish two main goals. One goal is to keep you from feeling a lot of the anger in the first place; the second is to manage angry feelings, once they do arise, so that you can keep the feelings from escalating unnecessarily.

Spencer: How do you keep from feeling angry in the first place? I mean, I find that people do so many stupid, sloppy, and irresponsible things. Do you just ignore it?

Dr. Lopez: No. But you can make adjustments in the way you may be thinking about the people. The way you think about things can either fuel your anger or lessen it, depending on what you're thinking. Let me give you an example. Imagine you are walking down the street and you pass someone you know; and imagine you say "Hi" to the person and the person continues walking without responding . . .

Spencer: That's the kind of thing I see all the time! People have no manners or sense of courtesy anymore.

Dr. Lopez: Well, that's one interpretation.

Spencer: What other interpretation is there? What would you think of someone who deliberately ignores you?

Dr. Lopez: How do you know the person is ignoring you?

Spencer: Well, they're not answering. I suppose they could be deaf, and not answering for that reason.

Dr. Lopez: If you believed they were deaf, would you be less annoyed?

Spencer: Of course. If they were deaf then they wouldn't be ignoring you; they would just not realize you were talking to them.

Dr. Lopez: Is it possible someone could fail to realize you were talking to them and not be deaf?

Spencer: I suppose it's possible. Maybe the traffic was so noisy that they didn't hear.

Dr. Lopez: Any other possibilities?

Spencer: I see what you're driving at. I suppose they could also be upset or distracted. In that case, if they didn't answer, it would be unintentional.

Dr. Lopez: OK. Now let's take the worst-case scenario. Suppose it was intentional. Suppose they were actually saying to themselves, "There goes that guy Spencer, and I'll be damned if I'm going to pay any attention to him."

Spencer: I suppose you could say it doesn't matter that much when you get right down to it. I mean, what's the big deal if someone won't say "Good morning?"

Dr. Lopez: Now you see the role of what I call "cognitive" factors in emotional reactions. The way you interpret or think about events has a large effect on your emotional reaction to it. When your thinking is flexible, and you don't focus exclusively on the most negative interpretation, you don't feel so annoyed. For the coming week, I'd like you to keep track of angry feelings and at the next session I'd like us to look at the cognitive aspect of these emotions.

> In contrast to people with a Type A behavior pattern, those with a Type B pattern are thought to be generally more relaxed, less aggressive, and less concerned about time pressures.

The psychologist gave Spencer a form for keeping track of all angry emotions during the week. Using the form, the client was to record: (a) the triggering event, (b) his specific thoughts about the event, (c) how he handled the situation, and (d) the intensity of his anger reaction on a 1-to-10 scale.

For the remainder of the session, Dr. Lopez explained how the record keeping—including its emphasis on thought and behavior—fit into the overall model of anger, showing Spencer a version of Figure 7-1. He pointed in particular to the part of the figure that implied that antagonistic behavior actually increased the subjective sense of anger. Dr. Lopez noted that many people assumed that "getting it out

Only 23% of adults in the United States report expressing their anger openly (Kanner, 1998). Around 39% say they hide or contain their anger, and 23% walk away to try to collect themselves.

of their system" was the best strategy for dealing with anger. However, experience in treating angry feelings suggests otherwise, that angry behavior and speech increase one's sense of anger. At the same time, the psychologist emphasized that denying the feelings or suppressing them entirely is also not helpful. Often, the feelings reflect a true problem that requires a response. In such cases, it is helpful to identify what the true problem is and find a way of solving it without behaving in a confrontational manner.

Dr. Lopez went on to explain that treatment would include a focus on Spencer's behavioral reactions to problematic situations. On a case-by-case basis, they would be discussing how he might have handled various situations in light of the principles they had just discussed. Dr. Lopez noted that it might be useful to rehearse some of the situations in the office. Later in the treatment, it would be useful to find as many real-life opportunities as possible on which to practice the new cognitive and behavioral skills.

Session 2 Spencer returned, having kept the records of his emotional reactions. He had an entry for almost every day of the week, and the majority of these pertained to driving; others were tied to customers' impatience with his work.

Each day, he had been angry during a large portion of the drive to work as he observed other cars tailgating him. A typical entry in his diary was:

> Event: "Red car behind me is getting too close."
> Thought: "Why do people have to drive like that?"
> Behavior: "Nothing. Just keep watching in the mirror."
> Emotion: "Anger = 6" (1–10 point intensity scale)

Dr. Lopez: I see on your record sheet that you wrote down the thought: "Why do people have to drive like that?" What do you think is the answer to that question?

Spencer: It's a mystery. It's also stupid and reckless.

Dr. Lopez: But let's try to consider the question more closely, perhaps from the other driver's point of view. Why does *he* think he's driving like that?

Spencer: Well, sometimes it's obviously somebody who's trying to send me a message that I'm driving too slow and I better get out of their way.

Dr. Lopez: And the other times?

Spencer: The other times I don't know the reason.

Dr. Lopez: Try to think of something.

Spencer: Hmm. I guess that's just the way they drive. They don't recognize that it's a hazard.

Dr. Lopez: Why don't they recognize it?

Spencer: I never thought about it. Maybe they never had any problems driving like that. It never caused an accident.

Dr. Lopez:	Did you ever have an accident because someone was tailgating you?
Spencer:	No.
Dr. Lopez:	Given your experience, how great is the hazard, do you think?
Spencer:	I suppose when you come right down to it, it's not that great—but it's still not a good idea.

Dr. Lopez was seeking to: (a) have Spencer question whether the motives he attributed to other drivers were as evil as he assumed, and (b) have Spencer recognize that the practical results of the problem—whatever the drivers' motives—might be more minor than he was inclined to think.

With these new insights in mind, Spencer was asked to consider what this implied for his behavior. At first, the client could not see what behavioral adjustment might be warranted:

Dr. Lopez:	Let me put it this way. Suppose there was some feature of the traffic that you believed was fairly unimportant, like whether the car behind you was blue or not. How much attention would you pay to it?
Spencer:	I wouldn't pay any attention at all. There is no point. If the car is blue or not blue, it doesn't matter.
Dr. Lopez:	Can you transfer that reasoning to the situation with tailgaters? I mean, what does that imply for how you should deal with tailgaters?
Spencer:	Well, I'm not looking in the rearview mirror constantly to see if there is a blue car behind me. So I guess that means I should stop looking to see if there is a tailgater behind me. I can't stop them from tailgating anyway, so I guess the constant looking is just adding to my stress.
Dr. Lopez:	I think so. The rearview mirror is required occasionally for driving purposes, but not to keep assessing tailgating as you do.
Spencer:	I suppose this also means not slowing down to teach tailgaters a lesson, or giving them dirty looks as they pass.
Dr. Lopez:	Right.
Spencer:	But what if someone really is too close for safety's sake?
Dr. Lopez:	This is where it's important not to sweep things under the rug. Sometimes there is a real problem, and it will not help your anger to ignore it. If someone really is too close for safety's sake, you must do what safety requires—but no more than that.
Spencer:	Like just changing lanes without making any other kind of fuss, I suppose.
Dr. Lopez:	Yes. The point is to know when it's truly a safety issue, and when it's more of a "I-hate-it-when-people-do-that" issue.

For the coming week, Spencer agreed to remind himself of his new insight, or cognitive adjustments, whenever driving—that most tailgaters were not evildoers,

The field of treatment that combines psychological with physical interventions to treat or prevent medical problems is known as *behavioral medicine.*

and that the hazard was probably minor—and to avoid using the mirror continuously to check out possible tailgating. In addition, he was to avoid trying to "punish" other drivers or to teach them a lesson, for whatever reason. He was also to continue to observe and assess his stress reactions, using the record form.

Session 3 Spencer reported that he had drastically cut down looking in the rearview mirror for tailgaters. He told Dr. Lopez that at first the impulse to look was hard to resist, but he ultimately succeeded, and it had sharply reduced his stress while driving. By the end of the week, even the impulse to look was reduced, and he found himself hardly thinking about the issue of tailgaters. Spencer expressed amazement at this and said it inspired him to feel for the first time that his stress feelings were actually controllable.

Still, the other source of stress—conflicts with customers—was as bad as ever. He recounted one particular incident. A customer, an older man, had the "audacity" to ask if Spencer could "hurry it up" for him. When Spencer indicated that it would take at least half an hour, the man replied that that was "unacceptable." In reaction, Spencer launched into a long speech about why no one deserved special treatment, that the man had no idea of what a pharmacist does, and so on. The upshot, he explained to the customer, was that he would just have to wait it out like everyone else. The customer obviously didn't appreciate being lectured to, and finally told Spencer he wanted the prescription back so he could take it to a "real pharmacist." Spencer threw the prescription slip back at the man and told him to "be my guest."

Spencer was getting agitated and furious as he recalled the incident. Dr. Lopez felt two therapeutic goals should be set. The first was cognitive adjustment, and the second was learning some skills for dealing with someone who might be difficult.

> In one study, angry subjects acted much more aggressively after hitting a punching bag than did angry subjects who first sat quietly for a while (Bushman et al., 1999).

Dr. Lopez:	Why do you think that man wanted you to hurry it up?
Spencer:	Probably because he was a jerk.
Dr. Lopez:	Maybe he was. But if he wasn't a jerk—or even if he was—what might be another reason, from his perspective, for example.
Spencer:	I suppose he could have been in a hurry of some kind. But everybody's in a hurry. He's just got to wait his turn like everybody else.
Dr. Lopez:	But why would he be in a hurry?
Spencer:	I don't know. Maybe he's got an appointment.
Dr. Lopez:	What other reasons can you think of? What kind of prescription was he waiting for.
Spencer:	I think it was a blood pressure medication.
Dr. Lopez:	Do you think he might have been worried about getting his medicine? Maybe he needed it right away for medical reasons.

Spencer:	Look, if someone has an acute medical problem all they have to do is tell me and I'll help them out.
Dr. Lopez:	Is it possible he was too shy or embarrassed?
Spencer:	He wasn't shy. Like I said, he was just a jerk, with a capital J.

Spencer's perspective would not shift, so Dr. Lopez tried the other tack: getting him to focus on practical objectives. Specifically, he asked his client to identify the desired outcome from this encounter.

Dr. Lopez:	Let's say the guy was a jerk and had no right to do what he was doing. What would you like to happen in a situation such as this? What is the desired outcome?
Spencer:	I guess I just want the guy to give me the prescription, leave me alone, and wait like everybody else. Obviously that didn't happen in this case.
Dr. Lopez:	Do you think it could have happened in this case if you had handled it differently?
Spencer:	I don't know. What else could I have done?

Through discussion, the psychologist was able to get Spencer to recognize that the difficult customer's own objective in the situation was probably the same as Spencer's: to get the prescription filled with a minimum of fuss. Dr. Lopez then suggested that they revisit this incident, with Spencer playing the role of the difficult customer, and the psychologist taking the pharmacist's role. Dr. Lopez asked Spencer to respond in the way he thought the customer would respond, even using some of the customer's most troublesome comments.

> The upsetting cognitions of depressed people tend to focus on impressions of events ("I appeared stupid in my meeting with my boss"), which a therapist can often challenge by evidence; in contrast, the cognitions of angry people focus more on issues of fairness, propriety, or morality ("It is unfair that my boss made me wait for 10 minutes outside his office"), which cannot be settled factually. Thus, cognitive therapists typically direct angry clients away from fairness issues and toward the issue of *practical objectives*.

Dr. Lopez:	(assuming Spencer's role) "It will be about a half hour before it's ready."
Spencer:	(assuming customer's role) "That's not acceptable."
Dr. Lopez:	"I'm afraid I can't get it done any faster."
Spencer:	(inventing) "Why not?"
Dr. Lopez:	"It's just real busy here right now. I know a half hour is a long time to wait—I wish I could get it done faster—but that's the best I can do."
Spencer:	"Well, I need it sooner."
Dr. Lopez:	"I'm really sorry for the inconvenience. Maybe you'd want to leave the prescription and do some shopping in the meantime."
Spencer:	(stepping out of character) When you put it that way, I feel like the guy would probably give in. I just don't know if I could handle it as well as you did.

Dr. Lopez explained that sticking to one's practical objectives in an anger-provoking conflict was a skill that could be learned. The psychologist outlined what he considered to be the basic principles of the demonstration he had just made, in the form of a three-step procedure for handling conflicts:

1. Identify the desired outcome in the situation.

2. Express your belief that the desired outcome is proper for the situation, *but at the same time*

3. Recognize the other person's view about your desired outcome, and give that view dignity and respect.

Several studies have found that angry people display greater cardiovascular reactivity—for example, a greater rise in blood pressure—than less angry people, when they are antagonized or provoked in laboratory situations (Hardy & Smith, 1988).

In this incident, Spencer's desired outcome was to get the man to agree to wait for his prescription. Thus, Dr. Lopez, in demonstrating the technique, clearly expressed the need for the man to wait, while at the same time explicitly recognizing the man's point of view and giving it respect and dignity ("I know a half hour is a long time to wait—I wish I could get it done faster").

After listening to this, Spencer felt more confident that he could put the technique into practice, but expressed concern about his ability to control his initial impulse to respond angrily. Dr. Lopez explained that rehearsal of the strategy in future sessions should prove helpful for this. In addition, he suggested that relaxation training, which would give Spencer a means of controlling his physiological arousal, could also help dampen his initial angry response.

The psychologist concluded by giving Spencer an assignment for the coming week. As before, he was to continue keeping records of emotional reactions. However, in addition to recording his own immediate thoughts in response to the events, Spencer was to try recording an alternative perspective on the situation, one that looked for extenuating circumstances in the other person's behavior, or assessed more realistically the true extent of the practical problem posed. Dr. Lopez noted that Spencer might not find any of these alternative interpretations very convincing right now, but that he should try to form them anyway, as they might help him to adjust his thinking eventually. In addition, the psychologist urged Spencer to apply the three-step procedure for handling any conflicts that arose.

Session 4 Dr. Lopez began by inquiring about the written exercise. Spencer had recorded several incidents during the week, including his initial cognitive reaction and a cognitive reinterpretation. In one incident, he reported seeing some "fat cops" on the street and thinking, "Even the cops are getting lazy today." In another, Spencer fumed to himself while some "noisy kids" played in the school yard across the street; he was thinking, "Can't they find something more productive to do than bother the whole neighborhood?"

In these and other cases, Spencer had succeeded in identifying, to some extent, where his thinking might involve incorrect negative assumptions or exaggeration of the actual importance of the problem. He also had some success in forming alternative interpretations. For the "fat cops" incident, he considered later that the policemen might have been wearing bulletproof vests, in which case they would not have been as fat as they appeared. He also considered the possibility that some policemen might be hardworking and effective despite being overweight. Regarding the "noisy kids," he noted that he probably had been just as noisy as a kid—it was just part of being a child, and that the noise was not that disruptive. Spencer had also formed alternatives for several other situations and, with coaching from Dr. Lopez, succeeded in producing yet a few more alternatives.

A third matter involved an interchange between Spencer and a customer. The customer had handed him a prescription for a rare and expensive drug. Spencer explained that he didn't have the drug in stock and would have to make a special order from his supplier. The customer expressed what Spencer took to be skepticism. In his written records, he indicated that his immediate thoughts had been: "Uh, oh. Here we go again. Another jerk who thinks he knows everything and has to have his way." Spencer was, however, also able to produce an alternative interpretation: "Judging by the medicine this guy is taking, he must be pretty sick. I guess I'd be anxious too about getting my medicine."

Most important from a behavioral standpoint, Spencer had been able to save the situation this time. He had identified the desired outcome as "convincing the guy to leave the prescription in spite of the delay." Next, following the principles demonstrated in the last session, Spencer apologized to the man for the anticipated delay, expressed sympathy for the inconvenience, and explained that any pharmacy would have to make a special order for that particular drug, as it was too expensive to keep in stock. To Spencer's amazement, the man agreed to leave the prescription and, moreover, appeared to do so without any bitterness. Also to his amazement, Spencer found his anger lessening as he voiced the more caring statements.

He felt relieved of a tremendous burden knowing that he now had some skills to manage this type of conflict with customers. He began to appreciate that some of his anger at customers had been fueled by his resentment at being put in a situation that he could not handle effectively. Now that he felt he had some skills, there was less reason to resent the customers when they expressed complaints.

> "A cheerful heart is a good medicine, but a downcast spirit dries up the bones."
> —Proverbs 17:22

For the remainder of the session, Dr. Lopez taught Spencer a standard relaxation exercise (see page 26). The psychologist explained that this would provide an additional, physiological device for managing his stress reactions, in addition to the cognitive and behavioral skills he was learning and applying. The psychologist made a tape of the exercise instructions, as conducted in that session, and recommended that Spencer practice the relaxation exercise once a day for the coming week.

Next week or the week after, the psychologist explained, he would like to begin having Spencer carry out some *visualization rehearsal exercises,* which would provide a more systematic opportunity for Spencer to rehearse his skills and keep them at the forefront of his thinking.

Session 5 Spencer's daily records suggested he was becoming more effective at identifying his negative thinking and forming alternative thoughts, often in the heat of a situation. In general, he said, he was handling situations that used to provoke anger and annoyance in a more balanced fashion. On the other hand, he declared, there was one incident this week in which he felt he had "totally regressed." He had had an angry outburst while playing golf with his wife and another couple. After a disappointing shot, he threw his club to the ground, yelling to himself, "Damn it, Spencer!"

> It is not entirely clear how anger contributes to coronary heart disease. There is the possibility, for example, that hostile people have poorer health habits. Several studies find that hostile subjects tend to consume more alcohol, tobacco, and calories, and to be physically less active (Smith, 1992).

Dr. Lopez: What was it, exactly, that made you upset?

Spencer: I missed a simple putt. I don't know why I made such a big deal about it.

Dr. Lopez: Why do you play golf?

Spencer: It's a good game. Also, it gives me some exercise and gets me together with other people.

Dr. Lopez: How important is it to do well when you play?

Spencer: It's important.

Dr. Lopez: Why?

Spencer: I'm not sure what it is. Maybe I want to do well to prove myself or something.

Dr. Lopez: Prove yourself in what sense?

Spencer: Maybe to prove I'm worthy. It's like I'm not worthy of being there if I don't win.

Dr. Lopez: What do you think of that assumption?

Spencer: Well, now that I say it, it seems like a faulty assumption. I suppose it's better to win, but it has nothing to do with worthiness.

Dr. Lopez: Why not?

Spencer: Plenty of people have bad games. And even someone who isn't that good a player to begin with can still be worthy of playing. The main thing is enjoyment. It's funny, there is one player there who really *is* lousy, but he never seems to get upset, no matter how many bad shots he makes. Maybe I would feel less stress if I stopped focusing on the competitive aspect, like whether I'm going to win or lose.

Dr. Lopez: It seems like the issue of winning versus losing has taken on greater importance than you really intend. The next couple of times you play golf, why don't you try to concentrate on doing just a few things well, within your own limitations, and disregard the overall outcome for the time being. Consider this an experiment of sorts, and we'll discuss how it works out.

The therapist and client identified three aspects of Spencer's game that he would focus on during his next two golf outings, instead of a focus on competition: (a) keeping his eye on the ball, (b) making a smooth stroke on each shot, and

(c) exhibiting good sportsmanship. If he remained focused on these three objectives, then the outing was to be considered a success.

Beyond all this, Spencer reported that he had been practicing the relaxation exercise each day, and was finding it enjoyable. For the coming week, he was instructed to continue keeping records and carrying out all of the cognitive and behavioral strategies.

Session 6 Spencer reported that he had succeeded in focusing on the three aspects of his golf game identified in the previous session, and found that his tension level had dropped considerably. He said he even got some pleasure from complimenting others on their game. Normally, he said, he was so focused on his own game that he barely took notice of other players.

Spencer also reported that driving was producing much less stress now, as he was consistently resisting the impulse to keep track of tailgaters. He had even transferred this strategy to some of his other problematic driving habits: for example, observing who was cutting in and who was driving too fast. Now he was focusing on just getting to his destination, safely and on time, by tending to his own driving. Similarly, in the pharmacy, Spencer found that his new strategies were keeping angry feelings at bay and making him more successful in dealing with customers. Overall, the client felt that his stress had been reduced by 60 or 70%.

Next, Dr. Lopez began the visualization exercise, as part of the stress inoculation feature of treatment. He first helped Spencer devise a hierarchy of anger-provoking situations. The situations, from lowest to highest in stress value, were: (a) observing a speeder, (b) observing a tailgater, (c) observing someone cutting in front of him, (d) getting a complaint from a customer about having to wait, (e) getting a loud complaint from a customer about a medicine not being ready in the promised time, and (f) "getting the finger" from another driver on the road.

As a practice exercise, the psychologist had Spencer bring on deep muscle relaxation and then visualize a scene. If any sense of anger was provoked, Spencer was to induce relaxation once again, rehearse a cognitive coping mechanism, and then visualize himself coping behaviorally. Spencer first visualized a speeder. When he felt slightly annoyed, he reestablished the relaxation response and coped cognitively by telling himself, "The road is full of speeders and it's not my job to teach them a lesson—who knows, it might even be an undercover cop doing his duty." Spencer then visualized himself coping behaviorally, which, in this case, involved refocusing his attention on the road in front of him. He was advised to practice the visualization procedure once a day for the coming week.

Sessions 7–12 Over the course of the next 6 weeks, Spencer did the visualization exercises daily, progressing up the hierarchy. Along with the exercises, ses-

Stress inoculation—so named because it seems to parallel inoculations against medical diseases—involves progressive exposure to situations or stimuli that provoke anger, combined with the client's use of newly developed cognitive, physiological, and behavioral skills. Its techniques include exposure and rehearsal in the therapist's office and in vivo exposure (real-life practice exercises).

sions were devoted to stress inoculation through role-playing, with Dr. Lopez assuming the role of an angry customer and Spencer applying cognitive and behavioral coping skills in the face of the psychologist's (customer's) challenges.

In one case, for example, Dr. Lopez (in the role of customer) berated Spencer severely for not supplying the proper quantity of pills in a prescription. He said that Spencer didn't know what he was doing and shouldn't be allowed to practice. Spencer, keeping his composure, told the imagined customer, "I'm very sorry. You're absolutely right about the error. These things happen sometimes and I don't blame you for being annoyed. I'll fill the remainder of the prescription right away." With the role-playing concluded, Spencer remarked that, in the past, he would have grown defensive, told the customer how busy he was, accused the customer of overreacting, and generally avoided taking responsibility for the error. Now, however, he could see that the main thing was to get his business done as effectively as possible, and that defending himself or correcting other people were false issues. Not only did he find the new strategies more effective, he felt better about himself, and less stressed, in carrying them out.

At the same time, Spencer remarked that he still felt a lot of people were jerks. As is often the case with anger clients, he could not change his severe negative opinion of people who violated the rules of good citizenship, despite the psychologist's best efforts. Rather, what Spencer did succeed in doing was to shift his focus away from questions of morality or appropriateness, and onto the practical objective in a situation. This shift helped him to feel less anger in most situations, and also made him more effective behaviorally.

By session 12, Spencer had completed his stress-inoculation hierarchy, both through visualization and role-playing. By now, his day-to-day feelings of anger had lessened considerably, and his behavioral skills for managing conflicts were effective in meeting his objectives and avoiding outbursts of emotion.

Although therapy had not focused much on Spencer's angry feelings and behaviors toward his wife, Sheila, his therapy progress generalized to this very important realm as well. Increasingly, he was able to recognize that he did in fact regularly overreact and behave badly toward his wife. Second, applying the principles of anger management that he had learned in therapy, he came to better appreciate Sheila's perspective during their interactions and to significantly change his hurtful behaviors toward her. Over the course of treatment, the quality of their interactions genuinely changed, and they began to reestablish a level of closeness that had been missing from their relationship for many years.

Treatment was terminated at Session 12, with Spencer promising to continue applying all cognitive and behavioral procedures as consistently as possible. The client himself said he would like to come back in 1 month's time to report on his progress in "going it alone."

The Type A behavior pattern is not by itself a DSM-IV diagnostic category, nor is it considered to be a mental disorder.

Epilogue

A month later, Spencer reported that he had successfully maintained the gains he had made in therapy. The drive to work was becoming more and more stress-free, his interactions with customers likewise were less stressful, and his life with Sheila was getting better every day—for her as well as for him. In addition, he was enjoying recreational activities more, as he had shifted his focus from the competitive to the social aspect. Spencer knew that only time would tell whether such changes would help prevent further heart problems. Certainly, they would improve his chances for a healthy life. But in any event, he truly believed that the improved quality of life was its own reward. It might have taken a heart attack and months of psychotherapy, but he had finally begun to calm down.

In one study, heart attack victims who received a combination of Type A behavioral counseling and cardiological counseling showed a greater reduction of Type A behavior and had fewer second heart attacks than did subjects who received cardiological counseling alone (Friedman et al., 1984).

Psychological Intervention for a Medical Problem: Cancer Treatment for a Child

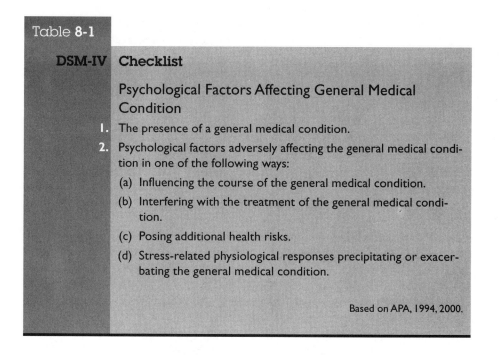

Table 8-1

DSM-IV Checklist

Psychological Factors Affecting General Medical Condition

1. The presence of a general medical condition.
2. Psychological factors adversely affecting the general medical condition in one of the following ways:
   (a) Influencing the course of the general medical condition.
   (b) Interfering with the treatment of the general medical condition.
   (c) Posing additional health risks.
   (d) Stress-related physiological responses precipitating or exacerbating the general medical condition.

Based on APA, 1994, 2000.

Victor Martinez was born in the Dominican Republic to a religious, Roman Catholic family. When he was 5 years old, his parents separated, and his mother emigrated with him to the United States. They settled in a large American city, in the heart of a community of Dominican immigrants. To support herself and her son, Victor's mother, Maria, obtained assembly line work in a glove factory, putting in long hours and just about managing to earn a living.

Despite growing up in a poor and often dangerous neighborhood, Victor attended school diligently and was considered a good student. In addition, he loved sports and he and his friends spent most of their time in athletic endeavors. One of his favorite activities was riding his bicycle up and down the steep hills of his neighborhood.

Victor's relationship with his mother was close and loving, but by the time he was 14, he had become almost an equal partner with her. Occasionally, he even felt like the head of the household. Due to the almost overwhelming Dominican presence in the neighborhood, his mother had failed to learn adequate English, even after 10 years in the United States. Victor, on the other hand, was fully fluent in English, and so by adolescence he assumed a certain leadership role at home.

Victor: The Unthinkable Happens

At the age of 14, Victor developed a set of medical symptoms that seemed innocent enough at first: fatigue, shortness of breath, fever, chills, and a mild cough.

When the symptoms lasted for 6 weeks, however, the doctor ordered a chest X-ray. To the horror of both Victor and Maria, the X-ray revealed a large mass, which the doctor suspected might be cancerous.

Pressure from the mass was increasingly interfering with Victor's ability to breathe. The boy first had to receive emergency radiation to reduce the size of the mass, so that his lungs would have greater room to function. Once this procedure had achieved its purpose, comprehensive diagnostic tests were begun, including *computerized tomography (CT) scans, blood tests, lumbar punctures* (withdrawing cerebrospinal fluid from the spinal column), and *bone marrow aspiration* (withdrawing fluid from inside the hipbone). Unfortunately, the tests confirmed the doctor's initial suspicion of *lymphoma,* a malignant tumor of the lymphoid tissue. Sadly, because of his fluency in English, it was Victor who had to receive this diagnosis from the doctor, and it was he who had to explain his diagnosis and its implications to his mother, rather than the other way around.

An aggressive course of chemotherapy was prescribed by the oncology team. Some of the treatment was provided on an outpatient basis, allowing Victor to live at home and attend school part-time. Other treatments involved hospital stays of 2 to 3 days, mainly to deal with the undesirable effects of chemotherapy, such as nausea and vomiting, loss of appetite, low blood counts (requiring transfusions), and infections (requiring intravenous antibiotics).

Throughout the teenager's treatment, he also had to undergo minor surgeries to implant and reimplant an *indwelling venous catheter,* a small plastic tube that permits intravenous administration of medicines or nutrients. Victor's catheter was implanted in the skin of his upper chest.

Victor: Too Much to Bear

Over 60% of people today believe that good psychological health plays a large role in maintaining good physical health. Only 2% believe it plays no role (APA, 2000).

Coping with a grave illness is very stressful for anyone, but Victor developed some special problems, common to children and adolescents. For example, he had great difficulty tolerating two of the critical, but more painful, treatment procedures. One, the lumbar puncture, involved insertion of a needle into the base of his spine to withdraw cerebrospinal fluid for laboratory analysis. The other procedure was the bone marrow aspiration, which involved inserting a large needle into the center of Victor's hip and withdrawing the soft material—the marrow—from the bone cavity.

At first, Victor seemed to accept these procedures rather well. He would follow the doctors' directions to the letter, and didn't even seem to flinch when the needle was inserted. When he arrived for the third lumbar puncture, however, the teenager could not sit still. He got up and started pacing around the waiting room, making tight circles. His mother begged him to sit down, and Victor tried, but within minutes he was pacing around once again.

The problem continued in the treatment room. Just as he was supposed to lie down on the treatment table, he balked. He stood at the edge and stared at the papered surface as though approaching a difficult horse that had to be mounted. Soon Victor was trembling, and tears were running down his cheeks. He told the doctors that he had barely been able to stand the first two punctures, and had hoped that he wouldn't have to have any more. Now it just seemed impossible. He asked them to delay the procedure for a day.

The medical staff realized they had little choice. The boy was obviously in no shape to attempt the procedure, so they let him go home, with the understanding that he would be back early the next day.

At home that evening, Victor was in a state of conflict. On the one hand, he was aware of the necessity of the procedure, but on the other, there was now something about it that he just couldn't face. Somehow the pain, combined with the absolute immobility required for the procedure, had taken him by surprise. Moreover, he realized that he actually felt worse physically than before all this treatment had begun. Due to the medicines, he was weak, nauseated, and losing weight. Now huge needles were going to be stuck into his spine and hipbone on a regular basis. "To hell with this," he concluded.

Later that evening, Victor told his mother that he couldn't go through with another lumbar puncture. Not understanding the seriousness of his intent, she suggested that they watch a movie on television together, and then get a good night's sleep. He'd feel different in the morning.

Upon awaking the next morning, however, Victor knew that he was never going back, and told his mother so. She pleaded with him to come to his senses, reminding him how important it was for him to have these tests. But there was no changing her son's mind. Maria had never seen him in such a state. Eventually, she called the oncologist to tell him that they would not be coming in. The oncologist asked to speak to Victor, but Maria could not even get him to come to the phone.

> "Pain is increased by attending to it." Charles Darwin, 1872.

A Parent's Perspective: "The Most Helpless Feeling in the World"

For Maria, Victor's refusal to undergo the lumbar puncture felt like the last straw. She had already been forced to stand by and watch helplessly as doctors tried to figure out what was wrong with her son. Then she was told that he had a terrible illness that could end his life. Now Victor was saying that he would not—could not—go through with the very procedures that were needed to make him well. How much more helpless could she be made to feel? What could she do to change this never-ending nightmare? How much more could she take? She called in sick to work, and decided to visit her Dominican priest later that morning.

Maria had tried to keep up a strong front throughout her son's illness, but now, as she was describing the current turn of events to her priest, she felt overwhelmed by her emotions, and the words came pouring out.

> Some studies suggest that the loss of a child is the single most stressful event that a person may experience in life.

I just couldn't believe that this was happening. Victor is my whole life. I can't even imagine what I would do if he were gone. I love him so much. And I depend on him for so much. If he were gone, I wouldn't even be able to shop, buy food, keep up with the bills, or speak to people in English. Victor takes care of me as much as I take care of him, and without him I would be alone in the world.

When he first got sick, I didn't think it was that serious, but of course I became worried sick when he didn't get any better. After a few weeks I became nearly hysterical. When the doctor told us that Victor had a tumor, I felt like I was about to lose everything. When the doctor talked to Victor about his illness, I could see from the look in my boy's eyes that the news was not good, even before he told me.

And then, finally, after all those tests, they told me my boy had cancer, and I felt like the whole world stopped. I was terrified, and I worried that maybe he was going to die. I cried every night. It only got worse as I saw him begin chemotherapy and look even sicker and more uncomfortable. I hated to see him suffering, and I couldn't stand the thought of life without him.

So when he went in for the lumbar puncture yesterday and refused to go into the treatment room, I didn't know what to do. The doctors told me to just let him go home for the night, so I guess I let myself relax. I told myself everything was going to be okay. But everything wasn't okay.

We spent a nice evening together last night, and I thought that he was feeling better. But this morning he wouldn't budge. He refused to go in for his procedure. He wouldn't even talk to the doctor on the phone. I just don't have the strength to face this. On top of everything else, to see him so upset, to see him give up, it makes me give up all hope too.

After unburdening herself to the priest, Maria felt calmer. The comforting man told her that she must keep her faith and get herself through the ordeal. He observed, "Often when things seem darkest, light is about to enter." Maria went home, resolved to think positively and to be strong for her son. She would wait for the light to enter.

Victor in Treatment: Psychological Interventions Enter

Just as Maria entered her apartment door, the phone began to ring. It was the oncologist, calling again to see if there was "any change." Maria put Victor on the phone, but his answer was still no. The oncologist told Victor he would not press the matter any further for the time being. At the same time, he added that he had an idea. He would like Victor to talk to another doctor on the phone, later in the day. This other doctor was, in fact, a psychologist, Dr. Moira Hoppe.

Victor grudgingly agreed to talk to the psychologist, thinking that he might finally be left alone if he just did this one more thing. When he told his mother about the psychologist, she became very excited. Although her son was doubtful that this could help in any way, Maria thought to herself that perhaps the light was about to enter—in the person of Dr. Hoppe.

When Dr. Hoppe called that evening, Victor answered the phone. The psychologist made no attempt to persuade the teenager to undergo further tests. Instead, she just asked what the previous tests had been like for him: what they felt like physically, how painful they had been, and how well Victor had been able to tolerate them. Victor began to relate his experiences and, once he started speaking, the words poured out. He talked about everything he had been through: the radiation, blood tests, and chemotherapy, as well as the two lumbar punctures and bone marrow aspirations.

Dr. Hoppe expressed admiration for all that Victor had accomplished. For the first time, he felt like he was speaking to someone who could appreciate his view. At the end of the conversation, the psychologist asked, "If a way could be found to make the lumbar punctures and bone marrow aspirations less painful, would you be open to trying them again?" Victor said he might consider it, and agreed to come see her in her office the next day, so they could talk about it some more.

By the time that Victor had hung up the phone, Dr. Hoppe knew that his difficulty met the criteria for the DSM-IV category of *psychological factors affecting medical condition.* This category is meant to include any problem in which psychological factors negatively affect a medical condition. The category can include any psychological problem that affects the medical domain: by having a direct causal role, by interfering with treatment, or by heightening the risk for illness. In Victor's case, the psychological factors were interfering with the treatment of his serious medical condition.

Dr. Hoppe specialized in the use of psychological techniques to help people deal with either acute or chronic pain. Some of these techniques are targeted specifically for pain in children who are undergoing unpleasant medical procedures. The techniques that she typically used to help children being treated for cancer included: positive motivation, behavioral rehearsal, emotive imagery, attentional distraction, hypnosis, and relaxation training.

Positive motivation means that the therapist provides positive reinforcement to the child for cooperating with a medical procedure. In *behavioral rehearsal,* the young patient practices various aspects of the unpleasant medical procedure. *Emotive imagery* is an imaginal procedure that is similar to *systematic desensitization,* tailored, however, to the mental capacities of children. *Attentional distraction* teaches the child to participate in an enjoyable activity or to employ an effective

Studies have found that patients with cancer who receive strong social support in their personal lives or supportive therapy often have better immune system functioning and, in turn, more successful recoveries then patients without such supports (Garssen & Goodkin, 1999; Spiegel & Classen, 2000).

People who experience more fear or stress before surgery tend to experience more complications after surgery and stay longer in the hospital (Kiecolt-Glaser et al., 1998).

Systematic desensitization is the behavioral treatment that uses relaxation training and exposure to a hierarchy of feared objects to help people with phobias react calmly to the objects or situations they dread.

mental strategy as a way of directing his or her attention away from the medical procedure. *Hypnosis* is one such mental strategy; by making use of the power of suggestibility, it can help patients distract themselves from the unpleasant procedure. And *relaxation training* teaches patients to relax their body muscles at will, thus providing them with a helpful technique for reducing anxiety, dampening the nausea associated with chemotherapy, or lessening the pain arising from medical procedures.

Session 1 The day after their telephone conversation, Victor met with Dr. Hoppe, and they continued the discussion of his reaction to the lumbar puncture. The young patient described his first two punctures, and how the second one had felt unbearably painful. Now the thought of going through another one filled him with still greater fear.

Dr. Hoppe sympathized with Victor's concerns and told him that she had worked with many kids who had to go through the same treatment as Victor, and that many of them had the same reactions. The psychologist explained that there are things that patients can learn, however, to help them manage these medical procedures so they are less threatening and painful. To give Victor a clearer idea of this, she asked him about his athletic interests, and whether he had ever gotten bruised or cut during a game while feeling hardly any pain at the time. Victor recalled one incident a year ago. He had just taken off his shirt to take a shower when his mother let out a gasp. She pointed to a spot just above his hip bone, where it turned out he had a gigantic dark bruise. Until that moment, Victor had not even been aware that he had the bruise; yet, when he pressed on the area, the bruise was extremely painful. The teenager then realized that he must have been injured the day before, during a baseball game, when he collided with a catcher who was blocking his path to home plate.

Dr. Hoppe asked Victor if he had ever gotten a comparable bruise, but one that *did* hurt at the time he received it. Victor recalled a time that an older boy in school punched him in the arm during an argument. That incident produced a similar bruise, but the pain was experienced by Victor at the moment of injury.

The psychologist used these contrasting examples to illustrate a basic principle of pain: that it is possible to experience either more or less pain from a particular injury, depending on one's circumstances, activities, thoughts, and emotions at the time. This same principle, Dr. Hoppe explained, can be used to *control* pain during medical procedures.

The psychologist explained that in the past she had helped many children, like Victor, undergo the lumbar puncture in a way that made it less threatening and painful. The children learned special relaxation procedures combined with imagination techniques to direct their focus away from the pain. With training, Victor

In many cases, professional athletes are removed from a game because *others* observe that they are bleeding, while the athletes themselves are oblivious to the injury.

could learn to do the same: to close his eyes and transport himself to another state of mind, one that would enable him to undergo the procedure with less pain and awareness. Victor asked if this was like hypnosis, and the psychologist replied that it was. "Gee," he remarked, "I've never been hypnotized before." She pointed out that actually Victor had experienced something similar: that time when he had barreled into home plate and collided with the catcher but had felt no pain from the injury he received. At that time, Victor was in a state of very focused concentration, similar to what happens with hypnosis.

Nevertheless, the boy still doubted that he would ever be willing or able to handle the lumbar puncture again. Dr. Hoppe replied, "No one can or will make you do that procedure if you are set against it. But you know how important it is for your treatment, and I'm sure you would want to do it if you could."

"Yes," Victor acknowledged.

"Why don't we do this: Let's do the training in relaxation and the imagination techniques—that will take several days—and then you can decide how you feel. If you feel like you can do the procedure, that will be great. If not, we'll look at our options at that point."

Session 2 The next day, during a 2-hour session, Dr. Hoppe instructed Victor in muscle relaxation. The exercise, about 20 minutes in duration, had the patient alternately tense and relax eight different muscle groups (see page 26). After that, the psychologist had him focus on his breathing, while trying to achieve a progressively deeper state of relaxation in his whole body. The instructions for the exercise were taped and, at the end of the training session, the teenager reported a definite relaxation effect.

Next, Dr. Hoppe discussed the visualization procedure that would form the basis of what Victor later came to call his "hypnosis." She explained that she and Victor needed to come up with a mental story—something from Victor's own experience—that included aspects of both touch and movement. The story should produce very intense images and sensations so that it would later be able to distract Victor from the pain of the lumbar puncture. Moreover, Victor should be able to bring the story and its images and sensations to their peak within a few minutes.

Victor described the sensations he felt when riding his bike up and down the bumpy roads of his neighborhood. He said he could easily "feel" the shock sensations traveling up his legs and into his back as he stood on the pedals while coasting down the hills. Dr. Hoppe asked him to provide a detailed 5-minute description, ending with an exciting ride down a hill.

Victor described a ride on an early Sunday morning, when hardly any cars were on the road:

Relaxation training, often in combination with medication, has also been used in the treatment of anxiety, high blood pressure, headaches, insomnia, asthma, pain after surgery, and Raynaud's disease, a disorder of the vascular system characterized by throbbing, aching, and pain.

In one study, children who underwent chemotherapy experienced less nausea and anxiety when they were allowed to play video games during particularly anxious periods of their procedures, than when they were idle (Redd et al., 1987).

It was a warm, sunny, breezy day. Victor bounced up and down as he went over the pavement, enjoying the sights, smells, and sounds of his home turf. After riding for a while, he came to the top of a huge hill. He paused and then headed over the edge, pedaling hard in order to pick up speed. The wind whipped across his face. Then, he steered the bike to a rough portion of the pavement, and felt the vibrations travel up his legs and into his back. He continued on and on, sometimes steering directly into breaks in the pavement, other times favoring the smooth areas. He felt in complete control.

Dr. Hoppe made a tape of herself telling the story in vivid detail. Victor listened with his eyes closed as she narrated, trying to get as deeply involved in the images as possible. Then the psychologist had the boy record the story in his own voice. Then they ran through the whole procedure.

Victor once again conducted the relaxation exercise, by listening to the taped instructions. Next, when deeply relaxed, he listened to the two consecutive biking descriptions (the psychologist's and his). He seemed truly engrossed. The boy was then instructed to take the tapes home and practice the complete procedure twice on his own.

Session 3 The next day, Victor said that the practice had gone well; he found that he became more relaxed with each practice, and that the imagined description was becoming stronger. He could practically feel himself riding the bike.

Next, the psychologist explained that she wanted to begin phasing out the tapes, so that Victor could achieve the same physical and mental states without the need for equipment. Thus, this session was devoted to teaching the boy a shorter version of the same relaxation exercise.

She had Victor alternately tense and relax four muscle groups: his arm, chest, leg, and forehead muscles. Then she had him relax any remaining muscle tension throughout his body. This was followed by a 2-minute period during which Victor was taught how to use his breathing to relax his body further.

Dr. Hoppe's use of a combination of various psychological techniques for children undergoing painful medical procedures was based on the work and research of a number of behavioral and cognitive clinicians (Gorfinkle & Redd, 1993; Jay, 1988; Manne et al, 1990).

With the young patient deeply relaxed, Dr. Hoppe began the bike riding description, mentioning the sights, sounds, and feel of a glorious ride down an enormous hill in the neighborhood. Victor seemed to be traveling with the description.

Next, after rousing the boy, Dr. Hoppe had him repeat the whole procedure on his own. Finally, she ended the session by asking Victor to practice the two-part exercise—relaxation plus imagery—three times at home without using the tape. In addition, she discussed what she had in mind for tomorrow's session. She would like him to accompany her to the hospital treatment room where the lumbar punctures were performed—and have Victor practice the relaxation and imagery exercises there. The boy agreed, though reluctantly, to hold tomorrow's session in the treatment room, after being assured by Dr. Hoppe that he would not be asked to undergo the procedure and that no other hospital personnel would be present.

Session 4 Victor accompanied Dr. Hoppe to the treatment room. Although nervous upon entering, he experienced nothing like the state of intense fear that possessed him the last time he had been there. Today, he was able to see features of the room that previously had escaped his notice. For one thing, in most respects it was just a plain room, not the horror chamber of his memory. Victor even remarked that if you took away the special lights and the treatment table, the room could almost be somebody's office or living room.

He was given permission to freely explore the room. He practiced turning the special lights on and off; he examined the counters and cabinets, and the medical supplies inside. He also looked at the treatment table. Without its stiff white paper, the table was "kind of just like a sofa." In all, he spent about 20 minutes going over every inch of the room.

Afterward, Victor sat down in one of the chairs and chatted with Dr. Hoppe for a few minutes. The next item on the agenda was to conduct the relaxation-plus-imagery exercise, this time using an even shorter version. Victor was guided to focus on relaxing the same four muscle groups—arm, chest, leg, and forehead—but this time without tensing them first. He was just to focus on the muscle groups, and then relax. After that, he did 1 minute of slow, deep breathing to increase his state of relaxation. Then, the psychologist guided him through the familiar bike riding imagery, using a shortened version, about 2 minutes in length. Next, Victor himself repeated the whole procedure, in silence.

After watching Victor silently go through everything for several minutes, Dr. Hoppe asked him to open his eyes, but Victor appeared transported to another world. When he did emerge, he said, "Wow, I was really out of it that time. I practically forgot where I was."

Dr. Hoppe:	The next step is for you to practice this shorter procedure a couple of times at home. Then tomorrow we should try something a little different, to see how good you really are.
Victor:	What do you mean?
Dr. Hoppe:	Well, the whole reason for doing this is to see if you can use it to help manage your reaction to the lumbar puncture. So, next time I'd like to have you try doing the story image, and practice staying with it while I make sounds or other sensations. What do you think of that?
Victor:	You know, for the first time I'm starting to wonder if I could go through with the lumbar puncture. Do you think I could do it? I feel so scared when I think about it.
Dr. Hoppe:	I know. It's natural to be scared. But you can do things now that you couldn't do before. Let's just take it one step at a time.

In addition to its very effective use in the control of pain, hypnosis has been employed successfully for such problems as skin diseases, asthma, insomnia, high blood pressure, and warts and other forms of infection.

Session 5 Once again, the session was held in the hospital treatment room. Dr. Hoppe explained that they would begin with Victor relaxing and then developing his imagery—which he could now bring to a peak within 3 minutes. However, this time Victor would do it on the treatment table, while assuming the reclining position used during the lumbar puncture. Then, Dr. Hoppe would make different noises in the room while Victor coordinated his imagery with the sounds in the room. After that, when the psychologist gave the signal ("Now"), Victor was to prepare for pressure to his back, which Dr. Hoppe would create by applying a stethoscope to Victor's lumbar area. Victor was to work that sensation into his mental story by steering his bike to a large bump in the road. He was to time the impact of the bump with the verbal signal ("Now") and the sensation of physical pressure on his back. He was to try to remain deeply relaxed and to focus hard on the scene. Any sensation or external stimulation was to be worked into the bike story.

Victor began relaxing and then moved on to the imagery. Dr. Hoppe then began opening and shutting cabinet doors, clanking instruments together, and the like. Victor seemed unbothered. Finally, she gave the signal ("Now") and pressed the stethoscope to Victor's lumbar area. The young patient shifted slightly, but seemed otherwise unaffected.

When the psychologist roused him from the hypnotic state, he remarked, "I was really into that." Some questioning made it clear that Victor had indeed achieved a deep hypnotic state, successfully working the external stimulation into his mental story narrative. He had, for example, been able to transform the sound of the cabinet door into that of a car door slamming. The clanking of the instruments had become the rattling of the bike's metal frame. Victor had given himself up completely to the imagery. The exercise was repeated.

> **Psychological interventions are of greatest help in the treatment of medical problems when they are combined with other psychological interventions and with medical treatments (Canty, 1996; Hermann et al., 1995).**

Dr. Hoppe: That was terrific. What do you think are the chances of your doing the real thing?

Victor: It's strange, but I actually feel like I might be able to do it. If I did agree to do it—I'm not saying I will—when would it be?

Dr. Hoppe: When would you want to do it—that is, if you were willing?

Victor: I guess the sooner the better. I'd kind of like to get it over with.

Dr. Hoppe: I'll talk to the oncologist to find out the scheduling possibilities.

Later that day, Dr. Hoppe contacted Victor and reported that the procedure could be done the next day at 10:00 a.m. The boy's first reaction was one of alarm; he hadn't expected it to happen so soon. Dr. Hoppe assured him, "Look, nothing is decided until you actually show up, and even then you don't have to go through with it. Let's tell the oncologist to go ahead and schedule you since you're feeling that it might be possible now. If you have to cancel, you cancel, and nothing is lost."

Victor agreed. Dr. Hoppe then said she would stop by his house that evening, just to review their procedure one more time. During the evening visit, the psychologist asked a nervous-looking Victor if he still wanted to proceed. The boy said he was very anxious but wanted to try. The practice confirmed that he was as skilled as ever.

Afterward, Dr. Hoppe went over the sequence of tomorrow's events. She suggested that Victor arrive with his mother at most 15 minutes early, so as to avoid a long period in the waiting room. The medical team understood that Victor was to be given time to do his exercises, so he should not feel rushed. In fact, the whole procedure would be paced according to Victor's wishes. Dr. Hoppe would of course be there, observing everything, and would allow the needle to be inserted only when Victor was prepared. At that moment, she would signal him, and he would adjust his mental story accordingly. Victor said he was ready.

Laboratory subjects who believe they have control over a painful stimulus report experiencing much less pain than do subjects without a sense of control (Hill et al., 1952).

Session 6 Victor and his mother arrived at the hospital at 9:45 a.m., meeting Dr. Hoppe in the waiting room. At 10:00 a.m., the boy, accompanied by the psychologist, entered the now familiar treatment room, disrobed, and lay down on the treatment table. Dr. Hoppe instructed Victor to begin his exercises. After 2 minutes of watching the young patient become increasingly relaxed, the psychologist signaled him to enter his bike riding imagery. The boy shifted uncomfortably, opened his eyes, and said, "I can't seem to do it." Dr. Hoppe came to his assistance by providing instructions for restarting the relaxation response. Once Victor was again deeply relaxed, the psychologist herself began describing the bike riding scene to him. Victor was now able to settle into the imagery.

The psychologist continued to narrate the story, taking Victor to the top of a steep hill. The oncologist verbally signaled each step in his preparations—palpating the area, applying the antiseptic, administering the local anesthetic—and Victor worked the events and sensations into his mental story. The psychologist then signaled the oncologist to get the needle ready. Next, she had Victor ride down the hill, picking up greater and greater speed. She told Victor to visualize a large bump in the road, and begin steering the bike in that direction. She then told the boy to be prepared to strike the bump and feel the shock waves at the moment she said "Now." The oncologist was standing ready to apply the needle at the same moment, verbally signaling the moment of insertion.

Sensing the right moment, Dr. Hoppe gave the word—"Now"—nodding to the oncologist at the same time. He then indicated that the needle was about to enter. As the needle punctured his lower back, Victor flinched slightly, but then appeared to settle back into Dr. Hoppe's spoken story. The needle remained in place as the oncologist withdrew the fluid. After about 5 minutes, he removed the needle and Dr. Hoppe continued to guide Victor down the hill in the mental story.

When subjects in one study had their hands placed in ice water and were given the opportunity to distract themselves with music, many spontaneously made efforts to make the music louder, tap their feet, sing, or otherwise increase their mental involvement in the music, as a way of controlling their sense of pain (Melzack et al., 1963).

When people are able to induce their own hypnotic state, the process is called *self-hypnosis*.

Soon, she gently told Victor to open his eyes. "Is it over?" Victor asked. "I can't believe I did it." The oncologist seemed amazed as well. "I can't believe it," he volunteered. "You were great. The difference between today and the last time we tried to do this is amazing."

Victor beamed.

Epilogue

A few weeks later, Dr. Hoppe conducted a less extensive training session to prepare Victor for the other painful procedure, the bone marrow aspiration. With the psychologist in attendance, the boy was able to master that procedure as well. Subsequent procedures were handled by Victor alone. In addition, the young patient learned to use his relaxation skills to help manage general anxiety arising from the stress of his illness.

Victor's training in managing the painful procedures not only enabled him to proceed with treatment, it actually enhanced his quality of life during this period. Eight months later, after repeated treatments and numerous diagnostic tests, including several lumbar punctures and bone marrow aspirations, Victor was pronounced "free of disease." Although the doctors would need to continue monitoring him closely for years to come, the outlook for his future was very bright indeed. The psychological techniques offered by Dr. Hoppe had played an enormous role in the return of his health. The techniques might not have directly made him better, but they had certainly helped him to get better. In his mother's mind, they had brought the light, just when everything had seemed to be at its darkest.

Bulimia Nervosa

Table **9-1**

DSM-IV **Checklist**

Bulimia Nervosa

1. Recurrent episodes of binge eating.
2. Recurrent inappropriate compensatory behavior in order to prevent weight gain.
3. Symptoms continuing, on average, at least twice a week for three months.
4. Undue influence of weight or shape on self-evaluation.

Based on APA, 1994, 2000.

As many as 3% of women develop bulimia nervosa. At least 90% of all cases of this disorder occur in females (Foreyt et al., 1996).

Rita, the 26-year-old manager of the women's dress department in a large department store, was born in 1975. Her childhood was not a happy one. Her parents divorced when she was about 5 years of age. She and her three older brothers remained with their mother, who often seemed overwhelmed with her situation and unable to run the household effectively. Rita would often refer to her childhood as utterly chaotic, as if no one were in charge.

She nevertheless "muddled through." When her brothers were finally all off to college or beyond, Rita entered high school, and the household seemed more manageable. Ultimately, she developed a close relationship with her mother, indeed "too close," Rita suspected. Her mother seemed like her closest friend, at times the entire focus of her social life. They were both "women alone," so to speak, and relied heavily on one another for comfort and support, preventing Rita from developing serious friendships.

Rita later attended college at a local public institution, majoring in business. However, she quit after 3 years to take a job in the department store. She had begun working in the store part-time while a sophomore and, after 1 year, was offered the position of manager of the dress department. It was a well-paying job and, since her interest was business anyway, Rita figured it made sense to seize an attractive business opportunity.

Just before leaving college, Rita began a serious relationship with a man whom she met at school. Their interest in each other blossomed, and they eventually became engaged. Everything seemed to be going well, when, out of the blue, tragedy struck. Her fiancé's mental state began to deteriorate. Ultimately, he manifested a pattern of schizophrenia and had to be hospitalized. As his impairment extended from days to months and then to more than a year, Rita was finally forced to end the engagement; she had to pick up the pieces and go on without him. She felt as if he had died.

A period of psychotherapy helped ease her grief and her adjustment following this tragedy, and eventually she was able to move on with her life and to resume dating again. However, a serious relationship eluded her. Rita knew that she was a moody person—she judged people harshly and displayed irritation easily—and, she believed, this discouraged potential suitors. She suspected that she was known as a "crank" at work, and she found it hard to make close friends.

Rita: Fundamental Concerns About Weight and Appearance

Throughout her adolescence and young adulthood, Rita had always been sensitive to people's opinions about her appearance and weight, particularly the opinions of other women. Socially, she always seemed to fall in with a group of women who were equally preoccupied with dieting and weight control. To Rita, their preoccupation seemed to be based not on vanity but on anxiety. They lived under a cloud of concern that their weight and eating might somehow grow out of control. Typically, her acquaintances did not have significant weight problems, nor were they unusually vain or intent on being popular. In fact, most of them had serious academic interests and career goals. Thus she found it almost ironic that they, in particular, were so focused on their physical image. But focused they were, and Rita was no exception.

Between the ages of 14 and 25, she always tried to keep her weight between 114 and 116 pounds, a standard that began in the ninth grade, after she experienced a slightly overweight period. She would rigidly follow what she called her "weight watchers" plan, although she had never actually gone to the program of the same name. The eating plan consisted, when she was being "good," of a breakfast of dry toast and juice, a lunch of turkey or dry tuna on diet bread, and a low-fat frozen meal at dinnertime. On some days, it also included, when she was being "bad," a couple of candy bars or two large "gourmet" chocolate chip cookies. She tried to keep bad days to a minimum, but there were probably three to four of them each week. Rita felt she could tolerate such days, however, as she was a regular exerciser, attending an aerobics class three evenings a week. During a particularly bad week, however, she might go to the gym a couple of extra times to exercise on her own.

In addition, she developed the habit of weighing herself several times a day, to reassure herself that the reading did not exceed 115 pounds. When the scale showed that her weight was at or below 115, the young woman felt enormous satisfaction, similar to what another person might feel if her or his bank statement showed a comfortable balance. Rita saw her 115 pounds as the well-earned reward for sustained and concentrated effort. And like a miser who

People with bulimia nervosa tend to be particularly concerned about pleasing others, being attractive to others, and having intimate relations (Striegel-Moore et al., 1993).

Surveys find that 5% of Americans may weigh themselves more than once per day, 8% once per day, 10% twice per week, and 36% twice per month (Kanner, 1995).

counts her money over and over, she would get on the scale frequently to recapture that feeling of satisfaction, especially when other aspects of her life felt less than satisfying. One evening at home, when she saw that her weight was 113, she returned to the scale a dozen times to experience the pleasure at seeing that number.

At the same time, the frequent weighing had its downside. Sometimes she would observe a reading of 116 or 117 pounds and have a very negative reaction: She would feel fat and bloated and would resolve to limit her eating to a much stricter version of her weight watcher's plan. In addition, she might throw in extra exercise sessions for good measure. In the meantime, to avoid anyone seeing her "fat" body, she would hide it under bulky sweaters and other concealing clothing. This way, other people would at least not gossip about her.

Rita: Caught in a Binge–Purge Cycle

Shortly after her 26th birthday, Rita's eating habits became much more troubled. First, she began to have eating binges, perhaps two to three times per week. Typically, she would become aware of the urge to binge sometime in the afternoon, while at work. As the afternoon progressed, the urge would build into a sense of inevitability, and by the end of the workday, she knew she would be spending her evening on a food binge. She would then start to fantasize about the foods she would be buying on the way home.

The foods that figured in Rita's binges were items that she had labeled as "bad"—foods that, in her mind, should never be eaten if she had any hopes of maintaining proper weight. On one binge day, for example, the young woman made three stops on the way home from work. The first was a pizzeria, where she picked up three large slices to go. The next stop was a gourmet cookie shop, where she bought three large "super chunk" chocolate chip cookies. The final stop was the grocery store, where she bought a half gallon of ice cream, which, as usual, was heavily laden with chocolate chips and nuts.

Once home, Rita locked the door behind her and unplugged the telephone. Something about the secrecy, the single-mindedness, and what Rita called the "depraved indifference" of her binges made her feel as if she were committing a crime. Yet, once the eating began, she felt powerless to stop it. After the first mouthful, the binge was destined to run its course.

On this particular evening, Rita tore into the pizza first, while she sat in her kitchen watching the evening news on the small television. She ate rapidly, without pause, taking little notice of the program's content. After the pizza came the cookies; these were eaten in a matter of minutes. After about a 20-minute break, during which Rita changed out of her work clothes, she proceeded to the ice cream. This she ate in her living room at a slower, more leisurely pace while she watched the larger television. Within about 1½ hours, she was scraping the bottom of the

Binges are usually preceded by feelings of great tension (Johnson et al., 1995).

carton. Spoonful by spoonful, she had devoured all of it. In fact, within a 3-hour period, Rita had consumed more than 4,000 calories.

The young woman often felt as though she were in a changed state of consciousness during such binges. Nothing else in the world seemed to matter when she was eating like this. She would avoid answering the phone or doorbell.

Although Rita viewed the binge overall with disgust, she couldn't deny there was some pleasure in it. It was the only situation in which she could eat foods that appealed to her. Under normal conditions, eating was not a source of pleasure, because she would restrict herself to unappetizing foods. For her, "normal eating" meant dieting—avoiding all foods that she enjoyed. She was convinced that if she regularly ate foods that she did like, she would set in motion a process that she couldn't stop. And now, indeed, her binges seemed to be bearing this theory out.

Once the binge was over, the next step, in Rita's mind, was to repair the damage. By the time she was through, she was left with feelings of both physical and psychological revulsion. Physically, she would feel bloated. The blow to her self-esteem was even more pronounced. Binge eating was so inconsistent with her usual style of behavior that she wondered if she was developing some sort of split personality: the competent, striving Rita versus the irresponsible, out-of-control Rita. She was becoming concerned for her mental health.

Most important, the binge posed a severe threat to the one area of life by which she measured most of her success and worth as a human being: her weight. After a binge, she felt that if she didn't do something about it, she might see a 5-pound weight gain on the scale the next morning. During her first 2 or 3 months of binge eating, she would attempt to avoid weight gains by trying to fast for a day or two. Then she saw a television show featuring women with bulimia, a show that examined purging behavior at length. The message of the show had been to avoid this fate at all costs. However, with her binges becoming more extreme and her weight reaching an all-time high of 122 pounds, Rita saw purging as the solution to her problem: a way of eating what she wanted while avoiding undesirable consequences.

She started to purge at home several times a week. She would stand over the toilet, touch her finger to the back of her throat, and throw up as much of the binge food as she could. The first time Rita tried this, it was not so easy. Indeed, she was surprised at how hard it was to stimulate a gag reflex strong enough to bring up the food. Eventually, however, she often didn't have to use her finger at all; the food would seem to come up almost automatically as she bent over the toilet.

In the early stages of her disorder, Rita's purging felt gratifying. It typically brought an immediate sense of release, as though some terrible wrong had been set right. The bloated feeling would go away, and Rita would avoid seeing a weight gain the next day. But over the next few months, the need to purge grew and grew. Even after eating normal meals, Rita would feel fat, and she couldn't get the thought of purging out of her mind.

> Typically, binges are followed by feelings of extreme self-blame, guilt, and depression, as well as fears of gaining weight and being discovered (APA, 2000).

Beyond purging, the young woman would try additional practices to undo the effects of binge eating. For example, she would try to go to a health club to exercise each day. Before going, however, she had to follow a particular ritual in front of the mirror. She had to convince herself that she looked slim enough to appear in a gym environment. She put on her exercise outfit and inspected herself in the mirror from every angle. Rita's weight was within the normal range: she was 5 feet, 5 inches tall and weighed 122 pounds. Anyone would have described her as "slim." However, there were aspects of her body that caused her repeated concern. She felt that her "center of gravity was too low," meaning she was heavy in her hips and thighs. If, after surveying herself in the mirror, she believed that she looked "dumpy," she would abandon her plan to go to the gym. She just couldn't face going there "looking fat."

Usually, however, if Rita spent enough time in front of the mirror, she was able to convince herself that her appearance was not entirely repulsive. Sometimes in order to do this she had to change outfits, moving to more concealing clothing. At the gym, she would spend at least 2 hours, alternating between jogging on the treadmill and baking in the sauna. Going to the gym achieved two things in her mind. It burned calories and it kept her away from food for a period of time. When she returned home, usually at about 9:30 p.m., she drank a couple of cans of diet soda and tried going to bed. Unfortunately, the long workout often left her ravenous, and frequently she found herself getting up again to binge and purge.

When she was not bingeing or skipping meals, Rita would try to follow her dieting plan: a breakfast of dry toast and juice, a lunch of a half sandwich of dry turkey or tuna on diet bread, and a dinner of a low-calorie frozen meal. Sometimes she would allow herself a snack of fat-free cookies or frozen vanilla yogurt. When eating in this way, she felt she was in an odd harmony with the universe. The restrictive eating gave her a sense of control, competence, and success. She felt more worthy as a human being, and more at peace.

Unfortunately, the controlled feeling could not be sustained. Eventually, she would give in to periodic binges. And, after bingeing, she felt compelled to begin the cycle—all over again.

A Coworker's Perspective: Piecing Things Together

Even as Rita's pattern of bingeing and purging at home was increasing month after month, she was able to keep it under control at her job. She sensed that allowing the pattern to enter her work life would mark the beginning of the end of her promising career. To be sure, there had been some slips. One afternoon, for example, she ate a whole tuna salad sandwich with mayonnaise in the staff cafeteria. The full feeling that resulted was so intolerable that Rita went to the employees' bathroom and purged. However, afterward, she felt horrified at the idea of someone observing or finding out about her purging, and she promised herself that she

---

People with bulimia nervosa often have numerous inaccurate and disturbed attitudes toward eating (DeSilva, 1995). In one study, they generally perceived their body size to be larger than did control subjects of similar size; and they believed that their body size became larger still after they ate a small snack (McKenzie et al., 1993).

would try with all her might to limit the practice to home. It was not easy to do, but for the most part, she was able to keep her bingeing and purging out of the workplace.

That is not to say that Rita's problems totally escaped the notice of people at work. Coworkers were increasingly able to tell that something was amiss, and some began to piece things together. Kate, a 22-year-old coworker and friend, was one such individual.

Working under Rita in the dress department for the past year, Kate had developed a cordial relationship with her manager. Although the two of them were not terribly close friends outside of work, they had gone to an occasional movie or out to a bar together. In recent months, however, Kate noticed that Rita had become more distant and withdrawn at work, and she became concerned for her coworker's well-being. "I always knew that she wasn't the happiest person in the world, and that she was certainly unhappy about not having any boyfriends," Kate later told another manager at the store.

Of course, that was true of a lot of people, so at first I didn't give it much thought. However, after awhile, I started to notice a troubling pattern in Rita. She would be very cheerful and friendly—for her—when I'd first arrive for my shift around 11:30 a.m., but as the day wore on her mood would turn distant and sour. From about 3:00 onwards, she would hardly talk to me, or anyone else, and she often seemed to be staring into space as though she was thinking about something far away.

Not long after this started, Rita stopped making plans to see me outside of work. Since we didn't get together all that often, at first it didn't seem that unusual. She was always "busy," too busy to spend time together outside of the store. A couple of times, I asked her what she was so busy with. Not that I was prying, but I was curious about what she was up to, since I really didn't think she had anything going on besides work. But when I would ask her, she would suddenly seem nervous and say something like, "Oh, just a few things I'm working on. Stuff for friends, you know." I didn't know, but her tone made it clear to me that I shouldn't pry further.

After about 2 months of this, it was apparent that she didn't want to spend any time with me outside of work. She *never* had any time to get together. And if I said, "Well, we really should find time to get together soon," she would brush the whole issue aside. He moodiness at work was getting worse, too, and I wasn't the only one who noticed it. Of course, we all knew that she's not the most jovial of managers, but now she seemed totally distant and nervous at work. And she always was in a tremendous hurry to get out of the store at the end of the day. I kept wondering what was going on in her personal life—what was she so desperate to get to after work—and why she wanted to shut me out of her life altogether.

Her appearance was also suffering. She seemed to be gaining some weight, nothing too alarming. But the way she carried the extra weight was a bit disturbing. Her

People with bulimia nervosa are more likely than other people to have histories of mood swings, to become easily frustrated or bored, and to have trouble coping effectively or controlling their impulses (APA, 2000). They also tend to be ruled by strong emotions and may change friends and relationships frequently (APA, 2000).

face, especially around the eyes, seemed kind of puffy, like she wasn't getting enough sleep. Her eyes were also red. It looked as if some extreme upset or unhappiness was showing in her face. She also seemed very tired at work. I knew something was terribly wrong, but I was wary of asking her what was going on.

Finally, I decided that I was worried enough about her to go ahead and ask what was going wrong, regardless of what her reaction was. It seemed more important than maintaining our friendship. So I just asked one day, "Rita, I can tell that you're very upset about something. You seem like you're very unhappy and secretive all the time, and frankly your appearance is starting to suffer. Is there something that I should know about? Or something you'd like to get off your chest? You know, I do consider you a friend, whatever you think of me, and I do care about you."

She just looked at me very coldly and said, "I don't know what you're talking about. You have some dresses to rehang." But her coldness led me to believe that she knew very well what I was talking about. Then I noticed that her weight, while generally on the increase, seemed to be going up and down every few days. I started to suspect that there was some kind of eating disorder going on. Of course, I'm no expert, but I had a feeling that maybe she was so depressed about something that she'd taken to binge eating or something. I knew that this was dangerous, but what could I do? She was uninterested in pursuing our friendship or in responding appreciatively to any offers of support. Eventually, her responses to me became downright nasty. So, finally, I decided that I had no choice but to wash my hands of the whole situation and stop trying to lend my hand. I had done what I could.

> Americans spend $31 billion each year on weight-reduction products and services, including $500 million on diet drugs (National Task Force on the Prevention and Treatment of Obesity).

Rita in Treatment: Gaining Real Control

After 6 months of bingeing, Rita found that she was falling further and further behind. As the binges and snacking had become more regular, she experienced a gradual 10-pound weight gain, "ballooning," as she called it, from 115 pounds to 125 pounds. She had never been this heavy before, and she felt desperate to lose the weight. All the purging, dieting, and exercise was adding up to naught.

Rita was also becoming increasingly worried that she might resort to more extreme measures, such as purging at work, in order to lose weight. Ironically, her only temporary relief from these anxieties was achieved through bingeing. But after the binge and purge were over, Rita would often find herself sobbing. Overwhelmed, she contacted a behavior therapy program for weight management at a nearby medical center. There she was directed to Dr. Francine Heston, a psychologist with expertise in the treatment of eating disorders.

During her first interview with Rita, Dr. Heston concluded that the 26-year-old woman's eating behavior and related attitudes about food and weight fit the DSM-IV criteria for a diagnosis of *bulimia nervosa*. First, the client had recurrent episodes of binge eating, over which she felt little or no control. Second, she engaged in inappropriate compensatory behavior in response to the binges—mainly purging and occasional fasting, but some inappropriate exercising as well. Finally, Rita's self-concept was largely influenced by her body shape and weight.

A growing number of therapists have come to use a combination of approaches—primarily behavioral and cognitive—to treat persons with this disorder, and Dr. Heston was no exception. Her treatment program had two main components: (a) changing the patient's bingeing and compensation behaviors; and (b) changing the patient's distorted attitudes about weight and shape, and any other thinking patterns that might cause distress and, hence, lead to bingeing. Her techniques included educating patients about their eating disorder; helping them perform more appropriate weighing and eating behaviors; teaching them how to control binges and eliminate purges; and leading them, through cognitive therapy, to identify dysfunctional ways of thinking and to develop more accurate cognitions.

> Dr. Heston's combination of cognitive and behavioral therapies for bulimia nervosa is similar to the successful approach developed by C. Fairburn and his colleagues (1993).

Session 1 Rita framed her problem mainly in terms of the bingeing. She stated that the binges were increasing in frequency and were causing her to gain weight. What was most upsetting, she didn't seem to have any control over the binges at this point. Her weight was inching up and she felt helpless to stop it.

Dr. Heston listened sympathetically and expressed optimism that Rita's problem could be solved. She then showed the client a diagram that depicted a functional model of bulimia nervosa (Figure 9-1), explaining to Rita that, although bingeing was her main complaint, it was really just one element in a system of interconnected parts. That is, the bingeing was the result of such elements as unpleasant emotions, concerns about shape and weight, and strict dieting. Furthermore, in a vicious cycle, the bingeing was also helping to intensify these other parts of the system. Similarly, it was both causing and being caused by purging, another element in the system. To stop a bingeing pattern, treatment had to bring about changes in all of the system's elements. It could not focus on bingeing alone.

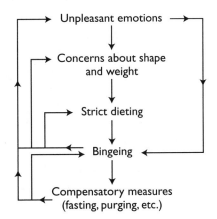

Figure 9-1

Functional model of bulimia nervosa (after Fairburn, Marcus, & Wilson, 1993).

Dr. Heston then outlined the treatment approach. First, she explained that in order to reduce the urge to binge, certain steps are usually helpful. Chief among these is structuring eating in a manner that keeps physical and behavioral deprivation to a minimum. In addition, the therapist noted, it is usually helpful to develop certain measures for heading off binges should the urge arise. Finally—and this is where Dr. Heston felt it advisable to tread lightly initially—it is usually helpful with this kind of problem to become "less preoccupied" with eating and weight matters. She explained that when people have a problem with binges, it is sometimes because such matters have assumed a greater role in the person's thinking than is desirable.

The psychologist also told Rita that she would like her to start keeping records of her eating and related stresses, using a special form. Rita expressed some reluctance about such record keeping. She explained that she had tried keeping records of her eating in the past and had not found it helpful. If anything, it had increased her focus on her eating. Dr. Heston acknowledged that Rita's past record keeping might not have been helpful, but suggested that it would be used more constructively now. Now the record keeping would be part of an overall strategy, and clinical experience showed that it was quite important. It would allow the therapist to understand Rita's eating better and help the young woman make appropriate changes.

Dr. Heston did acknowledge that, as Rita suspected, the record keeping might initially increase her preoccupation with her eating and weight, but said that such increases would be temporary. Over time, the client would become less focused on the whole problem. Rita agreed to keep the records for the coming week.

> Treatments that combine cognitive and behavioral therapies help as many as 65% of patients to stop bingeing and purging (Compas et al., 1998; Walsh et al., 1997). Other approaches that have proved helpful in some cases of bulimia nervosa, often in combination with cognitive-behavioral therapy, are interpersonal, psychodynamic, group, and antidepressant drug therapies.

Session 2 Rita's food records indicated that during the week, binges had occurred on 3 evenings after work. Each consisted of two to three slices of pizza, followed by some cookies or cake, then, later in the evening, a pint or two of ice cream. Rita purged afterward. During the day, the young woman's eating was severely restricted; on one of the days she was virtually fasting, consuming only no-calorie beverages (coffee, tea, diet soda) before surrendering to several large cookies in the late afternoon. On the 3 post-binge days, Rita reported skipping lunch and later having an apple and a couple of rice cakes, before once again surrendering to high-calorie snacks. On days when she followed her "normal" weight watching diet, her total calorie intake was around 800, about half the requirement for someone of Rita's weight and activity level. In contrast, on binge days, Rita was consuming 4,000 to 5,000 calories.

Dr. Heston did not discuss the specific calorie values with Rita, knowing that it can be counterproductive for patients with bulimia to monitor calories too closely. It creates a dieting mentality that the treatment is trying to discourage. Instead, the psychologist simply noted that soon they would begin the process of trying to fashion a more regular eating pattern for Rita, one that might lower some of her urges to binge.

Most of the session was spent reviewing basic facts about weight and eating. Dr. Heston explained that it would be important for Rita to recognize, first, that her current weight of 125 was not considered excessive according to standard criteria and, second, that the deprivation needed to maintain the very low weight of 115 could in fact lead to physically overpowering food cravings.

Rita said she understood that 115 was on the low side, but voiced strong reservations about accepting anything higher, particularly 125, as a weight for her. Dr. Heston suggested that there was no need to decide on an appropriate body weight for Rita now, only to recognize that her assumptions about proper body weight might call for some reexamination sooner or later.

The psychologist then recommended that the client stop weighing herself more than once per week, explaining that frequent weighing was fueling Rita's preoccupation with her weight. Moreover, frequent weighing gives false feedback, as day-to-day scale fluctuations often reflect water retention or a particular state of the excretion cycle, rather than true weight gain or loss based on body fat. Rita replied that this would be a big change for her; but on the other hand, she liked the idea of not being a slave to the scale.

Dr. Heston made one additional recommendation, that Rita stop skipping lunch at work, a habit that she had developed. The therapist said she understood Rita's motivation—concern about weight gain—but explained that skipping meals ultimately produces overeating.

Rita: I just don't see how I can do what you're proposing. If I don't skip some meals, I'll turn into a blimp. As it is, I've gained 10 pounds in the past 6 months. The only thing that is keeping me from gaining another 10 is skipping lunch now and then. Wouldn't it make more sense for you to tell me to stop bingeing?

Dr. Heston: Yes, I could tell you to stop bingeing. But bingeing is probably the thing that you have the least control over right now. Instead, it's better to focus on something that you have more control over, such as whether you eat lunch or not. I know you feel that skipping lunch is helping you to maintain your weight, but skipping meals actually produces the urge to snack or binge. Not skipping meals will eventually help you to stop overeating.

Rita: It makes me nervous to think of eating lunch every day.

Dr. Heston: I know this will take some getting used to. But let's try it out this week, and we'll review how you feel about it next time.

Rita: OK, I'll try it.

The weight of people with bulimia nervosa usually stays within a normal range, although it may fluctuate markedly within that range (APA, 1994, 2000).

Research has found that normal subjects placed on very restrictive diets develop a tendency to binge. For example, after participating in a very low-calorie weight-loss program, 62% of the subjects, who had not previously been binge eaters, reported binge-eating episodes (Telch & Agras, 1993).

Dr. Heston closed by giving Rita three main instructions for the week: (a) continue to keep the food records, (b) weigh herself only once, and (c) eat lunch every day.

Session 3 Rita's records indicated that she had had two binge nights during the preceding week. As instructed, she had made an effort to eat a lunch every day, which for her, was still the "diet" meal: for example, a half sandwich of dry tuna on diet bread. In addition, the client had limited weighing herself to only once during the week. Dr. Heston asked how Rita felt making these changes:

Rita: To tell you the truth, it's making me very nervous. I feel I must be gaining weight. Not only am I still snacking and bingeing, but I've added regular lunches.

Dr. Heston: What does the scale say?

Rita: 124 pounds.

Dr. Heston: So your weight is basically the same. Even if it were higher, it wouldn't mean that you were necessarily gaining weight. As we've discussed, one week's weight reading doesn't tell much about the overall trend.

Rita: Well, it just feels wrong not to skip lunch occasionally.

Dr. Heston: I know how difficult this must have been and I appreciate the effort you've made. However, you will eventually benefit from this change. I'm afraid, though, that what I'm going to ask you to do next will not be any easier, but I think you're ready for it and it's important that we keep moving forward.

Rita: Don't tell me you want me to start eating even more!

Dr. Heston: Yes. That's exactly it. As we discussed in the beginning, your calorie intake on your so-called normal days is too restricted and is therefore producing binges. You need to start consuming more calories in the course of your regular meals.

Rita: But how do I do it? I have no idea what else to eat. I've been eating this way for so long.

Dr. Heston: One way is to match your eating to what others eat, perhaps even take your cue from friends, coworkers, or even recipe books. Right now, you seem to be having a half sandwich for lunch. As you probably know, most people eat the whole sandwich; therefore, I'd encourage you to do the same. For breakfast, most people have some cereal, fruit, or eggs in addition to toast and juice, so you could add that as well.

Rita: I guess I could try it.

> Most cases of bulimia nervosa begin after a period of dieting.

Session 4 Rita reported having made the suggested meal changes, adding cereal to her breakfast and eating a whole sandwich for lunch, although complaining that eating the whole sandwich made her feel fat for the rest of the afternoon. Dr. Heston praised the client for these changes, and reminded her that there was a difference between feeling fat and actually gaining body fat. The psychologist suggested that Rita relabel the feeling that she got after a regular meal as "feeling full," which has nothing to do with a true weight gain.

Rita's food records during the week indicated two episodes that the client labeled as binges, each consisting of two slices of pizza and a pint of ice cream. The amount of food involved in these episodes was less than in her past binges, yet she still described them this way because of the frame of mind she had been in at the time: She was focused only on the eating, and experienced the usual feelings of guilt and shame. And, she purged afterward. Dr. Heston observed that, nevertheless, eating somewhat more during the day had seemed to promote less ravenous eating in the evening.

The psychologist now suggested a two-pronged approach, in which Rita would further normalize her meals and would also develop some strategies for eliminating binges at night. With respect to meals, Dr. Heston observed that Rita was still limiting herself to a diet frozen dinner in the evening. She suggested that instead she start to have a regular dinner: meat with rice or potatoes, plus a vegetable. It had been a while since Rita had prepared a regular dinner, and so the client was concerned that the sheer effort might force her back to the frozen meals. Thus the therapist suggested that she at least eat conventional frozen dinners, rather than the dietetic ones.

Next, Rita and Dr. Heston discussed some measures for avoiding binges, should the urge arise. First, the psychologist advised that she plan an evening activity at least 3 nights a week: a movie, a dinner out, or a moderate exercise class. Second, Rita should buy all the food for the week in one or two shopping trips, preferably on the weekend; she should shop from a list and go to the store on a full stomach. Third, Rita should change her route home from work so as to bypass the stores in which her binge foods were usually purchased.

Finally, Dr. Heston said she thought the time was right for Rita to start refraining from purging. The client's better eating habits had already reduced the severity of her binges, and so she was better off just accepting the full calorie consequences of those binges, as opposed to purging. The psychologist emphasized that purging was actually helping to produce bingeing by making Rita feel that she could protect herself from the consequences of a binge. In other words, knowing she could purge, she was feeling freer to binge. By rejecting purging, on the other hand, Rita would be more likely to try to control her bingeing. Dr. Heston also pointed out that, by retaining the calories from the binge, Rita would be less likely to feel deprived afterward, thus reducing the need to binge at a later point.

Rita expressed agreement with the goal of not purging, saying it made her feel "disgusting." But once again she was concerned about gaining weight. Dr. Heston reminded the client that the proposed measures did not, according to

> Individuals with bulimia nervosa are more likely than other people to experience symptoms of depression, including sadness, low self-esteem, shame, pessimism, and errors in logic (Burney & Irwin, 2000; Paxton & Diggens, 1997).

> Vomiting fails to prevent the absorption of at least half the calories consumed during a binge (Garner et al., 1985; Wooley & Wooley, 1985).

experience, cause people to gain weight. That is, the increased calories that might result occasionally from not purging would be offset over time by a reduction in overeating. This could be verified by keeping track of Rita's weight.

Rita said she would do her best not to purge.

Session 5 Rita reported that she had followed the new meal plan, eating a regular breakfast, a whole sandwich for lunch and, on most nights, a complete dinner—sometimes frozen, sometimes a meal prepared by her. Snacks consisted of fruit and rice cakes. Also, as advised, the client had scheduled activities for herself on several nights.

Still, there were two episodes that Rita described as binges: a pint of ice cream on one night, and a couple of large chocolate donuts on another night. The quantities of these "binges" were not really extraordinary—it now appeared that her more regular meals were holding down her cravings—but Rita considered them intolerable and, in fact, she purged on both occasions.

She said that she had decided to purge because she just felt "so fat" after eating those foods. Still, she asserted, "I really want to stop purging," and she asked for another chance to try during the coming week. Dr. Heston encouraged the client to try again, but asked that she bring some so-called bad foods to the next session. The psychologist explained that they could do a practice exercise in which Rita would eat the foods with Dr. Heston and then practice tolerating the feeling of fullness.

Most cases of bulimia nervosa begin between the ages of 15 and 21 years (APA, 2000).

Session 6 Rita reported having purged after two episodes of "overeating" at home in the evening. In one case, she purged two large chocolate chip cookies that she had bought in a gourmet shop; in another, she purged two pieces of chocolate cake. She had intended not to do any purging this week, but once she ate those foods and felt as if she had gained weight, she couldn't stand it.

Dr. Heston asked the client whether she had brought any "bad" foods, as advised. Rita at first stated that she had forgotten, but then admitted that she had deliberately not brought the foods in the hope of avoiding the eating exercise. The psychologist, having anticipated this complication, informed Rita that she had brought some chocolate donuts to the session herself. The client reluctantly agreed to do the eating-without-purging exercise during the session. She said she "might as well get it over with," as it appeared she could not do the exercise on her own right now.

Dr. Heston brought out four large chocolate donuts and suggested that they each eat two. Rita balked, saying she hadn't expected the donuts to be so large, and she asked whether she could just eat one. The psychologist explained that the exercise would be of no value if Rita restricted her eating to an amount that felt "safe." "I know," Rita replied, "but I'm afraid of gaining weight."

Dr. Heston then asked Rita to estimate how much weight she would gain by eating the two donuts. "I don't know; 2 pounds?" she guessed. In response, the psychologist gave Rita some factual information on eating and weight gain. First, the donuts themselves did not weigh more than 3 ounces each; so by ingesting both of them her weight could not increase by more than 6 ounces. Moreover, like all foods, some of the donuts' weight reflected their water content, which would be excreted eventually; most of the rest would be burned off in the natural course of events. Dr. Heston suggested they conduct an experiment in which the client would weigh herself on the office scale just prior to eating the donuts, and then immediately afterward.

Rita agreed to eat the donuts, first weighing herself on the office scale; her weight was 124. She then ate her donuts slowly, as if taking a bitter herb, but at the same time she admitted that she liked them. After finishing, the young woman remarked that she "felt really fat" and had a strong desire to purge. The psychologist suggested that she return to the scale. Rita discovered that her weight did not show any increase. Dr. Heston used the finding to make the point that feeling fat after eating and actually being fat or gaining weight are not the same. The therapist also noted that sometimes eating a large quantity of food will indeed produce a considerable weight gain immediately afterward, but most of this gain is water and will be excreted eventually. In order to get used to this, however, Rita would have to stop purging.

For the remainder of the session, Rita and Dr. Heston focused on other matters, reviewing Rita's meal plan, binge control strategies, and evening activities. All three areas seemed to be going smoothly. At the very end of the session, the psychologist asked Rita how she felt about having eaten the donuts. The client replied that she still felt fat, but not as much as before. She said it had been a long time since she had let such a feeling stand without purging afterward. Dr. Heston repeated the importance of Rita's not purging after she left the office, or undertaking any other compensatory measures. The young woman indicated she thought she could comply.

Finally, the psychologist asked Rita what the prospects were of her refraining from all purging during the coming week, should she get the "fat feeling" after eating. Rita replied that she thought the prospects were better now. If she could keep these two donuts down for the rest of the night, she thought the experience would help her resist purging on future occasions.

Session 7 Rita reported that she had gone the full week without purging. There were a couple of occasions when she had been sorely tempted—once after she ate a whole pint of ice cream at night, and another after eating a couple of large chocolate chip cookies. When she first selected those foods, she had in fact planned to purge afterward. However, she later "willed" herself not to do it, recalling her success in the therapist's office.

> The behavioral technique that requires clients to eat taboo foods and then prevents them from vomiting, in order to show that eating can be harmless and even constructive, is similar to the *exposure and response prevention therapy* used in cases of obsessive-compulsive disorder (Rosen & Leitenberg, 1982, 1985).

Dr. Heston praised Rita for this accomplishment, and said she wanted to help the client lock in these gains by once again eating some "bad" foods together. Today, the psychologist explained, she had brought some large chocolate chip cookies. "I was afraid of that," Rita replied, but she was clearly more willing to conduct the exercise this week.

Once again, they ate the foods together, and Rita agreed not to purge either these cookies or any other foods in the coming week. As usual, she was to continue eating regular meals, observing the binge control strategies, and scheduling activities at night.

Sessions 8–11 During the next four sessions, Dr. Heston and Rita continued to eat foods that the young woman would normally have avoided—potato chips, pizza, and cake—and again Rita refrained from purging. In fact, she succeeded in not purging throughout the 3-week period, despite several occasions when she ate "bad" foods at home.

During this period, the combination of regular meals plus the lack of purging seemed to be naturally reducing the client's desire to binge. By the 11th session, she reported bingeing only occasionally, and the quantities eaten were actually rather modest.

Also during this period, Dr. Heston had Rita add some taboo foods into her diet. By the 11th session, the client was deliberately eating such items as pizza or a sausage-and-peppers hero for lunch, chips or candy bars for afternoon snacks, and barbecued chicken for dinner.

Throughout this whole period, Rita worried about gaining weight, but the scale indicated that her weight was remaining the same—from 123 to 126 pounds. Still, she complained that this eating pattern made her feel fat.

Rita: I know the scale says my weight is the same. But when I eat such large meals during the day I feel fat and bloated. My clothes are tight, I feel that people can tell that I'm fat. Before, I didn't have this feeling. I miss that feeling of being in control.

Dr. Heston: How were you in control before?

Rita: By dieting, by following my "weight watchers" plan.

Dr. Heston: But what about the binges?

Rita: Well, except for the binges I was in control.

Dr. Heston: I don't think you can separate one from the other. Your dieting was causing binges. Besides, the term *control* doesn't really describe what you were doing when you dieted. You weren't controlling your food, you were *being* controlled by a vicious cycle of dieting, bingeing, and purging.

Rita: Well, I had a *feeling* of control when I dieted. It made me feel good—like I was accomplishing something.

Dr. Heston:	You seem to be equating control over food—or what you thought was control—with accomplishment. Does that stand up?
Rita:	Well, maybe it's not the control part. I mean, I can see that the idea of controlling food is sort of dumb by itself. It doesn't make you accomplished or anything. It's more my *weight* that matters. Maybe I wasn't going about it in the best way, but 125 pounds is fat as far as I'm concerned and nothing in the world is going to convince me not to lose that weight.
Dr. Heston:	What's wrong with 125 pounds?
Rita:	It's more than I should be weighing.
Dr. Heston:	But we've seen that 125 is normal for your height.
Rita:	I don't care. *I am* fat at 125.
Dr. Heston:	I'd like you to consider the possibility that your thinking on this matter is really groundless. For example, what evidence do you have to support the idea that you're fat?
Rita:	I feel fat.
Dr. Heston:	That's just a feeling. We're trying to see if the feeling is justified. What evidence do you have?
Rita:	Well, I used to weigh less—that's evidence—but I suppose you would say I used to be too thin. How about the fact that my love life is zilch? I haven't had a date in months.
Dr. Heston:	What was your love life like when you weighed 115 pounds?
Rita:	Not that great either, I suppose. People don't want to go out with me because I'm such a crank more than because I'm fat.
Dr. Heston:	But you still believe you're fat.
Rita:	Well, I guess I'm not actually obese. I just look heavy at this weight.

This discussion seemed to shift Rita's view of her weight slightly: She moved from declaring she was fat to thinking that maybe she just "looked heavy." Still, Dr. Heston felt that her client's thoughts had not yet shifted far enough. It was critical that she arrive at a more neutral view of her weight.

Thus, the psychologist asked Rita to consider all the ways in which her current behavior differed from the way she had behaved at 115 pounds. Rita noted that at her current weight she tended to: (a) wear a bulky sweater or jacket at the office, (b) check her body shape for extended periods in a full-length mirror before leaving the apartment, (c) wear concealing clothing at her gym, (d) avoid swimming, (e) spend most of her time alone in her office at work, and (f) rarely accept dates.

Dr. Heston explained that these actions were actually all serving to strengthen Rita's belief that her weight was terrible. The therapist thus suggested behavioral exercises to help Rita change such behaviors, and they agreed to devise the first set of exercises at the next session.

As many as half of elementary school girls have tried to lose weight, and 61% of middle school girls are currently dieting (Hunnicut & Newman, 1993; Shisslak et al., 1998).

Sessions 12–15 The next four sessions were devoted to planning and carrying out behavioral "exposure" exercises and cognitive reinterpretation exercises to help eliminate Rita's fear and avoidance of various activities. In these exercises, Dr. Heston systematically guided her client to perform and reinterpret those activities that, according to the previous week's list, Rita had been avoiding or eliminating from her life.

The first exercise was for the young woman to remove her jacket at work and venture onto the shop floor for a minimum of 1 hour—later 2 hours—each day. When she carried out the plan initially, Rita felt enormous anxiety. As instructed, the client recorded her negative thoughts and then tried to refute them in writing. In one instance, for example, Terry, a "slim" coworker, had seen Rita and had given her a critical look. Rita's first impression was that Terry must be thinking that she had grown fat. As part of her written exercise, Rita also considered contrary evidence—for example, that Terry had not actually said anything about her appearance. Rita then produced an alternative interpretation of her interaction with the coworker—namely, that Terry's so-called critical look could just as easily have been a meaningless glance or a reflection of some other concern.

At first, such counterarguments didn't feel very convincing to Rita. But after continued written thought exercises, coupled with the behavioral exposure, her thinking and feelings started to shift. In fact, after 2 weeks of going out onto the shop floor without concealing her shape, Rita was no longer feeling self-conscious in this activity.

The client also experienced reductions in anxiety following repeated exposure to other activities, coupled with the thought exercise. By the 15th session, she no longer felt the need to wear concealing clothing at work or at the gym, and she was leaving her apartment with just a quick glance at the mirror. Rita had even gone swimming several times at her gym, and felt pretty comfortable doing so by the fourth venture.

Rita:	By doing these things over and over I'm getting used to them. I'm back to doing normal things in spite of my weight. People don't really seem to view me any differently. More likely, they simply don't care one way or the other. I guess I need to consider why *I* care so much.
Dr. Heston:	What thoughts do you have?
Rita:	I guess I've been equating my weight with some sense of worthiness, like I don't deserve anything unless I'm thin. Where do you think I got that?
Dr. Heston:	I don't know, but obviously our culture promotes that concept to some extent. In any case, the important thing is to recognize you've fallen prey to that idea and need to counteract it.
Rita:	I think these exercises have helped to some extent. But I can't help feeling that being successful or worthwhile is tied to being thinner.

Research indicates that individuals with bulimia nervosa are extremely focused on weight matters, and virtually define their self-worth in these terms (Fairburn et al., 1986).

Dr. Heston had Rita consider arguments both for and against the belief that thinness is a sign of success. Rita concluded that being thinner might be desirable from an appearance standpoint, but that it did not represent any form of merit. To further this, the psychologist had Rita carry out a new exercise. The client agreed to survey the appearance of women whom she considered attractive or successful, particularly at the gym and the swimming pool. Rita was to attend specifically to the flaws in body shape they might each possess. Such observations would help her recognize that she might have given her own flaws in body shape unfair emphasis.

Sessions 16–17 By the 16th session, Rita had been almost binge-free and purge-free for 8 weeks. She was continuing to eat regular meals, including formerly forbidden foods. And she had eliminated most of the behaviors that had been inspired by anxiety over her weight and shape.

By the 17th session, the client had spent 2 weeks carrying out the exercise of noticing other women's body shapes. She noted that the exercise was very different from the way she normally directed her attention to other women. Usually, she would focus on their most flattering attributes. If one had a slim waist, she would focus on that; if another had slender legs, she would look at them, all the while making unfavorable comparisons with herself. With this new exercise, she was forcing herself to do the opposite, and it was quite an eye-opener. She learned, for example, that Terry, the coworker Rita had always considered the epitome of slimness, was actually quite thick in the calves and had large feet. Similarly, she noted that a woman at the pool, one Rita had consistently admired, had dimpled thighs. These observations, in combination with the ongoing behavioral exposure exercises, were helping her to see her own situation in a different light. She was starting to consider that maybe her dissatisfaction with 125 pounds was overblown. Although still preferring to weigh 115, she was now thinking of postponing any further weight loss; the effort might not justify the result.

Dr. Heston was very supportive, suggesting that it would be best to put the whole weight loss question on hold for at least several months. This would give Rita time to lock in her more realistic views on weight and body shape. Then the client could consider the question of weight reduction objectively.

Sessions 18–22 The next five sessions were devoted to the consolidation of Rita's behavior and attitude changes and to relapse prevention. During this period, she had been instructed to stop her daily food records and behavioral exercises. In addition, the sessions were spread more and more apart, to give the client practice in functioning for longer periods of time without supervision. All continued to go very well, and treatment ended after the 22nd session. In the final session, Dr. Heston advised Rita to keep on the lookout for any signs of slipping into

Treatments for bulimia nervosa produce immediate significant improvement in 40% of clients (greatly reduce or stop bingeing and purging) and moderate improvement in another 40% of clients (partially reduce bingeing and purging) (Button, 1993; Keel & Mitchell, 1997).

old habits: for example, skipping meals, avoiding many foods, excessive weighing, and, of course, purging. If she were to detect any such signs, she was to counteract them right away; if this proved too hard to do on her own, she was to contact Dr. Heston for "booster" sessions.

Epilogue

Six months after the final session, Rita contacted Dr. Heston by telephone. She said that she had successfully maintained her progress, although there had been one occasion, about a month after the treatment had ended, when she purged. Rita said she regretted the purging immediately afterward, and had now been purge-free for the past 5 months. She continued to follow a regular meal plan, although she had to admit that her old dieting habits were often tempting. Her weight remained about the same throughout this period.

Her main reason for calling, she told Dr. Heston, was that she was not doing well in her dating relationships: on more than a few occasions, she had driven off guys by being too critical and cranky. She asked Dr. Heston for the name of a therapist who was experienced in interpersonal problems. The psychologist suggested a colleague, and asked Rita to continue to keep in touch. The therapist was of course not pleased that her former client had these new problems, but she was very pleased indeed with her continued success in the realm of eating and appearance. With those problems under control, Rita's chances of addressing her interpersonal problems, or any other problems for that matter, were greatly improved.

Follow-up studies indicate that by 10 years after treatment, 89% of clients with bulimia nervosa have recovered either fully (70%) or partially (19%).

Alcohol Dependence and Marital Distress

Table **10-1**		
DSM-IV	**Checklist**	
	Substance Dependence	
	1.	A maladaptive pattern of substance use leading to significant impairment or distress
	2.	At least three of the following:
		(a) Tolerance
		(b) Withdrawal
		(c) Substance often taken in larger amounts over a longer period than was intended
		(d) Persistent desire for substance or unsuccessful efforts to control substance use
		(e) Considerable time spent trying to obtain, use, or recover from the substance
		(f) Substance use in place of important activities
		(g) Substance use that continues despite its causing or increasing persistent physical or psychological problems

Based on APA, 1994, 2000.

Half of all American high school seniors drink alcohol each month, most of them to the point of intoxication, and 3.5% report drinking every day (Johnston et al., 1993, 1999).

Kirk was never a moderate drinker. He began drinking in high school and, right from the start, consumed large amounts of alcohol. Throughout high school, he limited his drinking to weekends. He and his friends would get a case of beer and a couple of bottles of scotch or rum, and then drive to a wooded parking area in the suburbs. There they would turn on the radio, open the car doors, sit out in the open, and get what Kirk described as "blissfully buzzed."

Kirk generally returned home from these parties after his parents had fallen asleep, so they never fully appreciated the extent of his drinking. They themselves were just social drinkers, and it never occurred to them that their son's drinking might deserve attention. Moreover, Kirk and his friends never got into any trouble as a result of their drinking.

Kirk: Drinking on the Rise

In college, Kirk joined an off-campus fraternity and he continued his high school drinking pattern, only it became more regular. Almost every Friday and Saturday night, the fraternity brothers would get together for free-flowing beer and liquor.

At least a couple of other fraternity brothers equaled or exceeded Kirk's sizable capacity for alcohol, so the young man felt more and more at home with his own drinking.

Upon graduation, Kirk married Michelle, whom he had been dating since high school. Michelle herself enjoyed an occasional drink, but always stopped at one since she did not like feeling light-headed. She was aware that Kirk drank heavily, but she assumed that all college men drank as he did and she expected his pattern would change when he later took on the responsibilities of a family and a career. The pattern did later change. But rather than drinking less, Kirk began drinking more.

Soon after graduation, he obtained a good job in a prestigious telecommunications corporation. His new job afforded him an opportunity to drink almost every day, both at lunches and at parties with colleagues and clients. In addition, the young man would "reward" himself after each workday by pouring himself expensive scotch and rum at home. Within a few months of joining the work world, he was averaging 12 drinks daily. This pattern continued for the next 17 years.

In spite of his high level of drinking, Kirk received positive work evaluations and promotions throughout the 17 years. Nor did he experience any legal problems due to drinking. Although he regularly drove with a blood alcohol level over the legal limit, he had not had any accidents or arrests.

> Each year, American college students spend $5.5 billion on alcohol, mostly beer (Eigan, 1991).

Michelle: Awareness on the Rise

What Kirk could not ultimately avoid was the toll his drinking took on his marriage. For the first several years, Michelle tolerated her husband's drinking, not recognizing it as a problem. A man with a drinking problem, to her way of thinking, was someone who couldn't hold a job, got into fights, stayed out all night in bars, or beat his wife while drunk. Kirk, however, came home every night, enjoying a quiet dinner with her either at home or at a restaurant.

This was the pattern for the first 8 years of their marriage. During this time, Michelle worked as a secretary. However, when she gave birth to their daughter, she quit her job to become a full-time mother and homemaker. Four years after that, their son was born.

When their daughter entered school full-time and their son was a toddler, Michelle began to do child care at home, 5 days a week, for several preschoolers. Although it was demanding, she enjoyed the work, and the extra money helped. However, after a while, she began to feel a need for more adult contact. In addition, she began to feel the effects of Kirk's drinking, as he was unable to provide much companionship or assistance in the evenings. To compensate, Michelle began joining volunteer organizations in her community. Before long, she was going out every weeknight to attend one volunteer function or another. Kirk responded by withdrawing into his drinking even more.

Alcoholism and Marriage Don't Mix

At the age of 40, Kirk seemed to be the picture of success—on the surface. The father of a 9-year-old daughter and a 5-year-old son, he held a responsible position as vice president in charge of sales for his company, earning a high salary and regular bonuses. He supervised 20 individuals and was respected for his business acumen. He arrived at work consistently at 9:00 a.m., rarely missed an important meeting, and usually met his deadlines and sales quotas. Moreover, he was providing comfortably for his family.

At the same time, Kirk was continuing his long-term pattern of having 12 drinks a day, mostly scotch or rum, along with a few beers. His first drink of the day usually occurred at lunch, when he went out to eat with colleagues or clients. To start off, the businessman would have a couple of scotches while waiting for his meal. When his food arrived, he would order a couple of beers to go with the meal. Kirk was under the impression that he was drinking no more than his lunch companions. However, he was actually doubling their consumption—not that they took special notice of his drinking. Although outgoing and gregarious at these lunches, Kirk's general behavior didn't differ much from that of the others. His heavy drinking practices over the years had caused him to develop a *tolerance* to alcohol, so his four drinks affected him no more than one or two drinks might affect someone else.

At least 2 days a week, Kirk had another work-related drinking opportunity. This was at a private club where important clients were entertained by his company. The club had an open bar, with waiters who took drink orders and automatically brought refills as soon as an empty glass was detected. It would be hard not to drink in such a place, Kirk once reflected. And, of course, he had no intention of making any such effort.

The purpose of the parties was to entertain visiting clients. The idea was to build relations with them on a personal as well as business basis. Kirk's company was looking for every edge possible, and if this meant spending several hundred dollars on a party that would help to secure accounts worth millions, it was considered well worth the investment.

Kirk was acutely aware of the pressure to be friendly, jovial, and well-liked at these parties. In fact, inwardly the parties were a trial for him. There were high expectations for him to be entertaining, and each time he was doubtful of his ability to carry it off. The alcohol took an edge off his anxiety, loosening him up, and allowing him to mix freely. It took at least three drinks for him to reach this point, and at least another two to keep the feeling going for the rest of the party.

Once home from work, whether on a party night or not, Kirk felt the need to unwind. One Tuesday evening was typical. He came home and had a couple of scotches before having dinner with his wife and their two children. He had planned to drink nothing more, aside from two beers with dinner, for the rest of the evening. But, as usual, things went well beyond that. After dinner, Michelle had

---

Around 6% of all adults in the United States are heavy drinkers, consuming at least five drinks on at least five occasions each month (NHSDA, 1998). Among heavy drinkers, men outnumber women by more than 4 to 1 (Wilsnak et al., 2000).

When the concentration of alcohol reaches 0.09% of the blood volume, the drinker usually crosses the line into intoxication.

to go to a PTA meeting, and when she left, Kirk felt neglected and bored. He knew that his wife would like him to do the dishes or entertain the kids while she was gone, but looking at the pile of pots and pans in the kitchen did not inspire him. Anyway, the kids seemed perfectly satisfied watching television in the living room. He made a half-hearted effort to ask them if they wanted to play a game or listen to a story, but they barely looked up from their show.

Feeling he had done his duty, Kirk poured himself a drink and retired to the den to watch television. He sat there watching sports for the next hour and a half, pouring himself another couple of scotches along the way.

When Michelle returned, she found a quiet house with two television sets glowing—one with cartoons, the other with a basketball game—and felt her usual resentment. The dishes in the kitchen were untouched and the kids were still dressed and nowhere near ready for bed. And, as usual, Kirk was drinking. Some nights, Michelle would just ignore the situation, get the kids ready for bed herself, and do the dishes. But that night she tore into her husband, telling him he was lazy, irresponsible, and self-centered. Kirk seized on the "self-centered" part, and told his wife she should try applying the label to herself. She was the one who was out every night pursuing personal interests, not he. Michelle asked what point there was in staying home to watch television with a "drunk." For his part, Kirk denied he was drunk, saying he had every right to have a couple of drinks to unwind. What did she care anyway, since she wasn't even home?

Then the phone rang and Michelle went to answer it. It was one of Kirk's colleagues. Michelle didn't even consider turning the phone over to her husband; she carried out her usual policy of shielding him whenever he got calls this late in the evening and this deep into his drinking. She simply told the caller that he was "out visiting a friend." After hanging up, she decided just to drop the whole matter and get on with things. Why waste any more time banging her head against a wall.

Arguments such as these left Michelle feeling increasingly unhappy with their life together. Indeed, she and Kirk now barely had any life together. In the evenings, they went their separate ways. On weekends, they—mainly Michelle—did household errands. For recreation, she would attend activities tied to her volunteer work; he would watch sports on television while drinking himself into isolation. The children would either tag along on Michelle's errands or hang around the house, receiving only limited supervision from Kirk. Over time, Michelle began to consider leaving him.

> Spouses and other family members often shield problem drinkers from some of the negative consequences of their drinking. The spouses may, for example, make excuses for the drinker or fulfill the drinker's social or business obligations. This is sometimes called "enabling."

The Incident

Kirk and Michelle sat down one evening to do some paperwork for their taxes. As usual, Kirk had been drinking throughout the evening, but he was still quite alert and had no problem in sorting receipts, organizing records, and carrying out calculations. It was a 2-hour project and the couple actually worked effectively together, chatting and even joking throughout the task. It was one of their rare periods of togetherness; how ironic, Michelle thought, that it should come over an activity like taxes. They got the whole job done that night and both went to bed in good humor.

The next morning, however, Kirk said something that floored his wife. He asked her when she wanted to get together to do the taxes. She stared at her husband in disbelief, but soon realized he was absolutely serious; he had no recollection of having completed the paperwork the night before. Michelle told Kirk that they had already done the taxes, and he didn't believe her. "How could I forget doing taxes?" he asked. At this, Michelle ran to get the evidence, bringing her husband the paperwork from the night before. Kirk was shaken. Michelle was right. He had done the taxes, but for the life of him he could not remember it. It was as if somebody else had done the whole thing for him.

Truly upset, Kirk decided that from then on he would have no more than a couple of beers in the evening. However, after a few days, his determination broke down and he returned to his usual pattern of drinking.

After the incident with the taxes, Michelle took to quizzing Kirk routinely about events from the day before, and it soon became clear that the tax affair was not an isolated event. There were many mornings when he could not recall details from the night before. Michelle finally persuaded her husband to seek professional help with his drinking problem. She had seen an advertisement describing a community clinic that specialized in treating alcohol dependence and related marital problems through the use of marital therapy. Michelle called for information and then, with Kirk's agreement, arranged an appointment for them.

Kirk and Michelle in Treatment: A Marital Approach

While interviewing Kirk and Michelle, it became clear to Dr. Daniel Aronson, a psychologist who had been in practice for over 20 years, that Kirk was suffering from *alcohol dependence*. The client had developed a tolerance to alcohol. He often drank larger amounts than he intended; he had a persistent desire for alcohol; he drank to intoxication on a daily basis and had done so for many years; he neglected household obligations due to his drinking; and he continued his drinking, despite realizing that it was possibly causing memory difficulties.

Dr. Aronson used a behavioral model, the so-called *SORC model*, in his work with drinking problems. The acronym SORC stands for the chain of events—*stimulus, organism, response, consequences*—that lead to a given pattern of behavior. In the SORC model of alcoholism, the stimulus refers to external situations that prompt drinking, such as being at a bar, being with certain friends, or having an argument with one's spouse. Organism denotes events that take place within the

> Over a 1-year period, as many as 10% of all adults in the United States exhibit a pattern of alcohol abuse or alcohol dependence, either of which is known in popular terms as alcoholism (Kessler & Zhao, 1999). As many as 18% display one of the patterns at some time in their lives.

> When people develop tolerance to a substance, they need increasing amounts of it in order to keep getting the desired effect.

individual, such as thoughts, emotions, or withdrawal symptoms. Response refers to the specific drinking behaviors prompted by stimulus events and organismic states. And consequence refers to the results of drinking behavior, such as the reduction of anxiety or reduction of productivity.

According to the SORC model, each instance of drinking is a response to stimulus events or organismic states, and drinking is maintained because the consequences are in some way reinforcing. Correspondingly, in order to eliminate excessive drinking behavior and to help people develop more adaptive behaviors, therapists must try to change each element in the SORC chain.

Whenever a client's drinking was destroying his or her marriage, Dr. Aronson would conduct treatment within a couple therapy format, in which he would use a combination of cognitive and behavioral techniques, applying them in three stages. In the first stage, he would teach the drinker skills for reducing and eliminating excessive drinking. In the second stage, he would help the spouse to see his or her role in the partner's drinking, both as a trigger and as a consequence. In the third stage, he would offer communication and problem-solving training to help improve marital functioning. Throughout treatment, he would use the language and principles of the SORC model.

Research suggests that including the spouse in the treatment of people who abuse alcohol increases the probability of a successful outcome (McCrady, 1990).

Session 1 After gathering a complete picture of Kirk's problems and of Kirk and Michelle's marital difficulties, Dr. Aronson explained to them the logic behind his treatment approach. Specifically, he presented the SORC model, noting that drinking can be viewed as a behavior that an individual carries out in response to certain situations or feelings, which the psychologist labeled *triggers*. Sometimes the drinking may occur out of habit, other times it may be a means of coping with the triggers themselves. For example, the drinking may be a way of coping with feelings of anxiety, loneliness, or the need to be sociable. The psychologist explained that the goal of treatment was for Kirk to develop alternative ways of responding to these triggers.

Dr. Aronson also noted that sometimes the triggers themselves need to be changed. That is, certain situations, be they marital or work situations, may have some undesirable features, in addition to promoting drinking. The psychologist pointed out that, although it would be important for Kirk to learn to respond to such circumstances without drinking, it might be equally important to eliminate or reduce some of the undesirable features themselves. For example, if Kirk was drinking because he was lonely, it might be helpful to see what could be done to decrease his loneliness.

At this, Michelle voiced concern that she was being blamed for Kirk's drinking. She stated that if her husband was lonely, he had only himself to blame. It was hard enough dealing with Kirk's drinking—and for her to be considered responsible was the last straw.

Dr. Aronson clarified his point, explaining that, from a treatment vantage point, the person with the drinking problem should be viewed as entirely responsible for his or her drinking. At the same time, the psychologist noted, it would be important for both Kirk and Michelle to examine the changes that each was willing to make to help him avoid alcohol. Under no circumstances, however, would Michelle be asked to make changes that she felt were unfair.

Next, the psychologist explained the *behavioral monitoring* that would be used throughout treatment. Both Michelle and Kirk would fill out cards each day. On his card, Kirk was to record any urges to drink, the intensity of the urges (on a 1-to-7 scale), the type and amount of drinks consumed, and his marital satisfaction that day (also on a 1-to-7 scale). On her card, Michelle would record her perception of Kirk's urges to drink, the level of drinking she perceived that day, and her level of marital satisfaction.

Also, Dr. Aronson instructed Kirk to fill out a "trigger sheet" (Figure 10-1) during this first week, both to assess his drinking in SORC terms and to help him see the triggers and consequences of his drinking.

Because Kirk was so shaken by his memory lapses and concerned about his health in general, Aronson felt that his motivation to stop drinking was strong. Nevertheless, he gave the client an additional homework assignment that involved listing both the advantages and disadvantages, as Kirk saw them, of continued drinking versus abstinence.

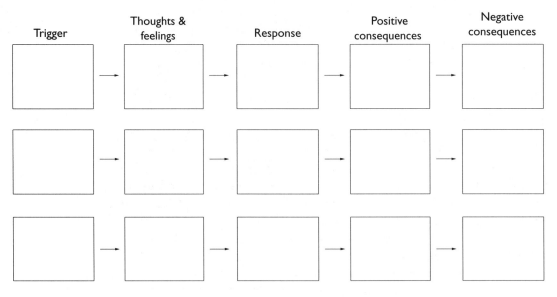

Figure **10-1**

"Triggers" sheet used by Kirk (from McCrady, 1993)

Session 2 Dr. Aronson, Kirk, and Michelle examined Kirk's drinking in detail, based on the records of the past week. The client's trigger sheet indicated that there were three main circumstances in which his drinking occurred: business lunches, business parties, and watching television in the evening. During the business situations, the following thoughts often occurred:

"They expect me to drink."

"I need to drink to be part of the crowd."

"I can't be jovial enough with the clients if I don't drink."

According to the trigger sheets, his drinking in these situations had two positive consequences: the feeling that he was doing what was expected of him, and the ability to be more outgoing with the clients. Although Kirk was unable to cite any negative consequences, Dr. Aronson noted one that he could see: By drinking consistently in business situations, Kirk kept himself from ever learning whether his assumptions about the need to drink were valid. Perhaps Kirk was overestimating the external pressure to drink at business functions. Dr. Aronson suggested that he test this possibility by observing the drinking of others—not just the heavy drinkers—to see if everyone was drinking as much as he.

According to the trigger sheets, two thoughts often occurred in the other major drinking situation, watching television at home when Michelle would go out: "There's nothing else to do" and "I need a drink to unwind." Kirk also noted that a positive consequence of drinking at home was a feeling of comfort and relaxation, while negative consequences included his failure to do anything constructive with his time, distancing himself from his children, and upsetting Michelle.

Dr. Aronson suggested that, for the coming week, Kirk begin reducing his drinking in either the business or home circumstances. Kirk volunteered to reduce it at home. He agreed to try to limit his home drinking to one scotch before dinner. In fact, he stated that he felt bad about neglecting his household responsibilities, and he hoped that cutting back his drinking at home would bring him and Michelle closer together. Michelle was clearly touched by her husband's wish to improve their relationship. She volunteered to stay home every evening if this would help him in his effort. It was decided that she would still go to one monthly PTA meeting.

Dr. Aronson noted that with these changes in the home, some consideration should be given to the evening's structure. If Kirk were simply to follow his usual pattern of watching television by himself, Michelle would feel neglected and become resentful, leading him back to alcohol in short order. Thus, it was decided that Kirk would not watch any television on his own during the coming week. Instead, after dinner, the couple would do the dishes together. Then, Kirk would help their daughter with her homework. After that, Michelle would give the kids their baths and Kirk would read them bedtime stories. With the kids in bed, the

People who begin drinking before age 15 are twice as likely to develop alcohol abuse and 4 times as likely to develop alcohol dependence as those who begin drinking at age 21 (Grant & Dawson 1997).

couple would do any remaining household tasks or read or watch television together until bedtime.

Session 3 The couple reported that Kirk had successfully limited his drinking at home to the one scotch before dinner. In addition, the two of them had followed the new evening schedule. Michelle was very pleased with her husband's progress, and especially with the renewed sense of togetherness that the new evening routine was producing.

At the same time, Kirk expressed some areas of concern. Although his drinking had decreased, his urges to drink remained frequent and intense, perhaps more intense than ever. Indeed, his records showed that, on most days, he was rating the intensity of his urges as 5 to 7 on a 7-point scale. He was worried that he would not be able to keep up the new pattern.

Dr. Aronson explained to Kirk that the intense urges he was now experiencing were a common and predictable result of his reductions in drinking. The psychologist pointed out that when people habitually use a drug under certain circumstances, they can develop a craving for the drug whenever those circumstances arise. If the craving is not satisfied with drug intake—in this case, having a drink—then the craving will rise and may become intense. This is what Kirk was now experiencing in the evenings. On the other hand, Dr. Aronson emphasized that if Kirk continued to resist drinking, the urges would gradually weaken.

Toward the end of the session, Kirk also mentioned that he had decreased on his own the amount of drinking during business lunches. As directed, he had observed the drinking behavior of his colleagues at lunch and was surprised to see that he was drinking much more than the others. He was above all surprised to learn that one of his most respected colleagues abstained from alcohol entirely during lunch. In turn, he decided to start having only one scotch before lunch and only one beer with the meal.

Between home and the business lunches, Kirk had lowered his daily average from 12 drinks to 4. Since the change was so large, Dr. Aronson did not press for any further reductions for the coming week.

Session 4 The couple reported that things were continuing to go well with the evening routine. Kirk continued to limit himself to the one drink before dinner, and the couple was dividing up the household and child-care tasks. With Michelle continuing to stay home each evening, Kirk was starting to feel that he had his wife back; with Kirk remaining sober and sharing household responsibilities, Michelle was starting to feel that she had her husband back. The rewards produced by the new routine seemed to be locking in the couple's commitment.

> The term *alcohol abuse* denotes a somewhat less severe pattern than the term *alcohol dependence*. People who manifest alcohol abuse experience significant and recurrent problems at home, at work, and socially, but without the compulsive usage, tolerance, or withdrawal effects seen in alcohol dependence.

Kirk also reported that he had reduced his drinking even more. He was now going without beer at lunch. With this reduction, he was now averaging only about two to three drinks per day.

The client expressed concern, however, about his ability to reduce the drinking further. So far, he had made no attempt to change his drinking at business-related dinners and cocktail parties, which would occur 2 to 3 days a week. He continued to have four or five drinks at each. Reducing his drinking in these circumstances seemed like an impossible task, he said. Kirk noted that his colleagues and clients drank heavily at these functions and expected him to join them. If he didn't drink, they might perceive him as less friendly—he might truly be less friendly without alcohol.

Dr. Aronson encouraged Kirk and Michelle to work together to develop a solution to this dilemma. He suggested that they draw on their experience in treatment so far, as well as on ways in which each had coped with other difficult situations in the past. Kirk noted that he usually favored a logical approach, breaking a problem down into specific goals and then proposing individual steps to help achieve those goals. Michelle noted the importance of emotional support from friends and family.

Thus, Kirk first identified the goal at hand: to attend his business functions without drinking, but remaining friendly. He considered that perhaps he could hold a glass of club soda in his hand throughout the evening, but he seriously doubted whether he could socialize effectively without alcohol. He just knew it wouldn't be the same.

> Alcohol plays a role in more than one third of all suicides, homicides, assaults, rapes, and accidental deaths, including 41% of all fatal automobile accidents in the United States.

Dr. Aronson:	How do you know it wouldn't be the same?
Kirk:	I just know. I need the alcohol to get loose. There's a lot of pressure on me to be a regular guy; you know, to glad-hand the clients and keep them amused.
Dr. Aronson:	Did you ever go to one of these functions without drinking?
Kirk:	No.
Dr. Aronson:	Then there's no way of knowing for sure whether your sociability would suffer if you didn't drink.
Kirk:	I suppose that's true.
Dr. Aronson:	Also, you seem to be assuming that the mood you achieve through drinking is the only acceptable mood at these parties. Is it possible that you don't have to be as outgoing as you think?
Kirk:	It's very important to be outgoing.
Dr. Aronson:	Is everyone as outgoing as you?
Kirk:	No, not everyone. My boss is kind of a quiet guy. He's the relaxed, confident type.
Dr. Aronson:	Do you think that clients are put off or offended by his behavior?

Kirk: No. In fact, I think he puts the clients at ease. I could never be that way, though. I'm just too hyper by nature.

Dr. Aronson: Perhaps there is some middle ground between your boss's quiet style and the high-pressure style you usually display.

Kirk agreed to conduct an experiment of sorts. He would try keeping a glass of club soda in his hand and observe whether abstaining from alcohol hurt his behavior at business functions. If he did experience strong urges to drink, he would deal with them by reminding himself of the experiment.

Michelle added that, in the past, she had rarely attended these business functions, as she had long since decided not to link her social life with Kirk's. However, in listening to Kirk's plans, she felt that carrying them out successfully would be a tall order for him without some support. Accordingly, she thought she should start accompanying him to these functions. Her husband welcomed this offer.

Dr. Aronson complimented them on having arrived at a strategy on their own. He made one additional recommendation, that, before each party, Kirk and Michelle decide the specific length of time that they would spend there. This would help keep their task more limited and manageable.

Session 5 Kirk reported that he had remained abstinent for the two business parties he and Michelle had attended this week. He said that the urge to drink had been intense at both parties, but with Michelle distracting him and reminding him of his goals, he had been able to keep on track.

Kirk noted that carrying the club soda around had relieved him of any awkwardness. Also, contrary to his expectation, he found that he was as outgoing without the alcohol as he had been with it. All this time, he had been assuming that his social skill at these parties was due to the alcohol. Now he realized that he was a good mixer whether drinking or not.

With all the reductions Kirk had made—at home, at lunch, and at these two business parties—his total intake for the week was only 10 drinks, an average of about 1.5 drinks per day. Also, he was experiencing urges to drink less frequently, although the intensity of those urges remained high. Finally, he and Michelle felt that things were continuing to go well at home, as they had developed a regular routine for sharing household responsibilities.

Based on this success, Dr. Aronson asked whether Kirk was ready to consider total abstinence. The client responded, "I don't know, it seems like too big a step." Michelle, however, pointed out that, in numerical terms, her husband wasn't that far from abstinence, especially considering how far he had come. Kirk said he realized it was just a matter of eliminating the remaining drink or two each day, but somehow taking that added measure seemed too extreme; he said he'd feel like he was losing his "safety valve."

The self-help program Alcoholics Anonymous has more than 2 million members in 98,000 groups across the United States and 150 other countries (AA World Services, 1998, 2000).

Michelle replied that she felt Kirk was still not facing up to the full seriousness of his drinking problem. She appreciated all the effort he had made thus far, but she thought he was kidding himself if he thought he could maintain a safety valve. What he was describing was not a safety valve, but an "open pit."

After some thought, Kirk said that what really bothered him was the personal statement he would be making by becoming totally abstinent: practically "branding [himself] an alcoholic." Michelle responded that he was getting too hung up on terminology. If it made things any easier, she suggested, why not view himself as having an allergy to alcohol: Alcohol simply didn't agree with him, in the same way that some people can't tolerate dairy products. In the tradition of Dr. Aronson, she even suggested that Kirk view abstinence as an experiment. Why didn't he just try it out? He could then find out through experience whether complete abstinence was as difficult or stigmatizing as he feared.

Her suggestion seemed to strike a chord with Kirk. Once again, viewing a new step as an experiment seemed to enable him to move forward; it no longer seemed like such a leap. Thus, he devised a plan. He was scheduled for a knee operation in the next week, which would force him to spend a week at home recuperating. This, he felt, would be an ideal time to see what it was like to stop drinking entirely.

Under Dr. Aronson's guidance, the couple worked out the details. First, they would remove all the alcohol from the house the day before the operation. In addition, Kirk would buy some spy novels to keep him entertained during his recuperation. And Michelle volunteered to cut down on her child-care work that week so she could spend more time with her husband.

Dr. Aronson further recommended that Kirk treat himself to a special reward during this period, since complete abstinence would represent a major loss of gratification. The client decided to buy some new furniture that he and his wife had been wanting.

> One of the most debated areas in the clinical field is whether persons with alcoholism must become abstinent in order to overcome their disorder, or whether they can simply learn to keep their alcohol use under better control. Research has not settled the debate.

Session 6   Kirk reported that he had remained abstinent during the entire period. He found that total abstinence was less difficult than he would ever have imagined 6 weeks ago, when he started treatment. Of course, the skills that he had been learning for managing his urges and cutting down on his drinking had set the stage for this accomplishment. At the same time, he recognized that the triggers encountered during this 1-week abstinent period had been limited, and that the challenges would increase when he returned to his regular routine at home and at work.

Dr. Aronson agreed. However, he repeated the principle that Kirk's urges to drink would continue to weaken—"extinguish"—as long as the client continued to resist drinking in various situations. The psychologist explained that treatment from now on would follow a "relapse prevention" mode, meaning that Kirk must always be looking for ways to maintain abstinence. Whenever urges to drink occurred, he was to view them as signals to devise alternative ways of coping with a situation, not as signs of weakness. In addition, Dr. Aronson cautioned both Kirk and Michelle not to react with alarm if a slip occurred. They should simply view such slips as indications of a need to be more watchful under certain circumstances and to develop better coping skills.

Sessions 7–9 At Session 7, Kirk reported on his 1st week of normal activities as a nondrinker. As expected, his urges to drink had increased, but not as much as he had anticipated. One bit of welcome relief had occurred during lunchtime, when he had his first business lunch without drinking. He had been concerned that ordering a club soda would be ridiculed by his colleagues. Instead, no one seemed to notice. The others just ordered their drinks as usual, without paying attention to Kirk. The second time that he ordered a club soda, one colleague did ask him if he had given up drinking. Kirk replied, "I've decided alcohol really doesn't agree with me." The colleague accepted this as perfectly reasonable, although to Kirk it felt like a momentous revelation.

By Sessions 8 and 9, he reported that both the frequency and intensity of his urges to drink had declined quite a bit. He was now experiencing only about two distinct urges to drink per day, and these were only moderately strong. In addition, he was continuing to devise new methods of coping with urges. He found, for example, that urges to drink often arose at parties when there was a lull in the social action. Previously, he would go refill his drink under such circumstances; now, however, he was using the urge as a signal to go talk to Michelle or someone else, and he was finding that this allowed the urge to disappear. Another strategy he found helpful was avoiding excessive hunger; if he ate more evenly during the day, he was less likely to experience strong urges to drink.

> About half of all treated couples say they are "happily married" at the end of couple therapy.

Sessions 7 through 9 were also devoted to a more direct focus on Kirk and Michelle's relationship. Over the course of treatment, Dr. Aronson had concluded that the relationship was basically loving and supportive, but because of Kirk's drinking, they had little positive interaction. To help reestablish more positive feelings, the psychologist recommended that they set aside a couple of periods each week to do fun activities together, such as play a game, go for a walk, or go out to dinner. The couple agreed to do this. At first, the activities seemed forced to them, but after doing them a few times, they started to look forward to them and sought out additional opportunities to do things together.

The next exercise that Dr. Aronson proposed seemed even more artificial to the couple at first. He had them designate specific days on which they would go out of their way to please each other. For example, if Kirk thought that Michelle would be particularly pleased by his making the bed, he was to make the bed; if Michelle thought that Kirk would be pleased by her making him a cup of coffee, she was to make the coffee. The goal of this exercise was to lead each spouse to focus more on the needs or perspective of the partner, as well as to increase the number of positive interactions between them.

Sessions 10–15 The final 6 weeks of treatment took three main directions: (a) cognitive therapy to help Kirk manage his negative emotions more effectively, (b) communication training to help Kirk and Michelle become better at resolving marital difficulties on their own, and (c) relapse prevention.

Cognitive strategies Periodically, Kirk would brood about failings or mistakes he believed he had made at work. For example, he might become excessively worried about a client's long delay in returning a phone call. Typically, he would think that he had somehow bungled the original phone call and offended the client, and he would consider the dire consequences of losing the client. Before long, he would also be worrying about losing additional clients, as well as his job and his income.

When Kirk brought up one such incident, Dr. Aronson guided him to recognizing the errors in his thinking. First, the psychologist encouraged the client to consider the evidence both for and against his negative conclusions. He also encouraged Kirk to consider alternative interpretations of the troubling event. Upon carrying out this exercise, Kirk recognized that he had done nothing deliberate that could have offended this client. He also allowed that the client might have been delayed in returning his phone call because he (the client) had been busy, sick, moody, or just plain slow. Finally, Kirk recognized that it wouldn't make much difference in the overall scheme of things even if the client were to take his business elsewhere. Cognitive reviews of similar incidents brought similar results.

Dr. Aronson also had Kirk regularly write down the irrational thoughts that he had when alone and produce alternative, more balanced interpretations of the events in question. Kirk found that this exercise suited his logical way of thinking and improved his moods.

Communication training for marital difficulties Although making good progress, Kirk and Michelle still had a few basic issues to settle in their marriage. One of these was the question of the day-care work Michelle was doing in their home. She had started doing this when her younger child, Danny, had entered nursery school. Currently, she was taking in three to four toddlers every morning, and the work was starting to wear on her. She was constantly busy from morning to night. Even with Kirk's help, she barely had time to read the newspaper, let alone do something relaxing or enjoyable, such as visit a friend or attend an exercise class.

> The biological children—particularly males—of parents with alcoholism are more likely to themselves develop this problem than the biological children of nonalcoholic parents (Cloninger et al., 1981).

Both spouses are employed in 60% of today's American families, more than double the percentage of several decades ago (Kate, 1998).

Kirk had become much more aware of the burden his wife was under since he had taken over more responsibilities in the evening, so the couple was able to come to a quick agreement that 2 days a week of child care should be the limit for Michelle. Certainly their budget did not require any more. However, Michelle's desire to go back to some of her volunteer activities was not so easily worked out. She said that, in spite of being much happier with Kirk's companionship, she needed a periodic change of scenery and wanted to explore some "more meaningful interests."

Kirk: What do you mean "more meaningful interests"? What could be more meaningful than your family?

Michelle: Well, I just need to get out. You spend 10 hours a day away from the house at your job. I need an outside interest, too.

Kirk: My job is not an "outside interest." I work that job to support us. Somebody's got to be the breadwinner around here. How far do you think we'd get on the child care you do?

Michelle: I suppose you'd have me go back to work as a secretary.

Kirk: The money you'd make as a secretary would be almost nothing after taxes and baby-sitting costs are taken out.

Michelle: Well, we're not exactly living in the lap of luxury with your job.

Kirk: So what are you saying, that I should get another job?

Dr. Aronson pointed out how far the two of them had strayed from the issue. They had begun with the question of Michelle's doing more volunteer work and had ended up questioning the suitability of Kirk's job.

The psychologist pointed out that each of them had a tendency to view any statement of dissatisfaction from the other as an attack, an attack that required a counterattack. When, for example, Michelle seemed to compare Kirk's work to having outside interests, he quickly defended his role as breadwinner and pointed out Michelle's limited earning capacity. She then viewed the debate as a contest over the amount of money each earned. This led her to propose something— going back to work as a secretary—that neither of them really wanted.

Dr. Aronson proceeded to teach them a communication strategy that might help avoid such misunderstandings and conflicts. Before expressing their own feelings, Kirk and Michelle were to try summarizing the meaning of the other person's previous statement, allowing the partner to verify or deny the accuracy of the summary. So, the psychologist explained, when Michelle said, "You've got your job...I need an outside interest too," Kirk could first try to summarize Michelle's meaning before responding.

Kirk: I guess your main message is that you find it harder to be tied down to the house than I realize. You feel that my job involves certain social opportunities that I take for granted. I guess that could be true. When I was at home all week recovering from the knee operation, I was practically climbing the walls after a while.

The psychologist then asked Michelle to summarize the meaning of Kirk's statement, "I work that job to support us. Somebody's got to be the breadwinner." She replied:

Michelle: I guess you seem to feel that I'm not recognizing the importance of your job to our survival. I didn't mean to imply it's not important. I know you work hard and it's not for your entertainment.... But your work also gives you meaning apart from the breadwinning aspects. I want the same meaning.

Kirk: You feel that your family is not meaningful enough?

Michelle: My family *is* the most meaningful thing. I think it is for you, too. But that doesn't mean we can't have additional interests. You like to watch sports, for example. I wouldn't ask you to stop doing that just because it's not family related.

Kirk: I guess you're saying that nobody can have a single purpose in life. I suppose I do get satisfaction from my job and I suppose you're looking for similar satisfaction.

The couple eventually agreed that Michelle would spend one night out a week doing volunteer work. They continued to practice summarizing each other's meaning whenever they found they were starting to argue. They also learned additional strategies, such as avoiding complaints or criticisms that the other person could do nothing about (for example, "Your mother is so annoying").

Relapse prevention In preparation for the end of treatment, Dr. Aronson placed special emphasis on relapse prevention. The most important task was for both Kirk and Michelle to be alert to *warning signs* of relapse, in particular, indications that Kirk might be at risk of taking a drink. The psychologist divided the warning signs into behaviors, cognitions, and moods. An example of a *behavioral sign* was Kirk's taking a long business lunch; a *cognitive sign* was Kirk's thinking that his drinking had not been a serious problem in the past; a *mood sign* was Kirk's becoming increasingly anxious or depressed. For each of these warning signs, the psychologist had the couple discuss strategies for managing the situation. They also agreed to call and arrange for a therapy session if Kirk ended up actually taking a drink. In addition, Dr. Aronson scheduled four follow-up sessions: for 1 month, 3 months, 6 months, and 1 year after the final treatment session.

Finally, toward the end of treatment, the psychologist had Kirk and Michelle enroll in a group for couples who had completed the same type of therapy. This was not a treatment group, but a group where couples with a history of drinking problems could meet and discuss ongoing concerns and support one another. It

According to surveys, almost two thirds of all adults believe that it should be harder than it is now for married couples with young children to get a divorce (Kirn, 1997).

was led by a couple who themselves had once had drinking problems, but who had been abstinent for over 10 years and had undergone training as lay counselors.

Epilogue

By the end of 15 sessions, Kirk had not had a drink for more than 2 months, and he remained committed to abstinence. In addition, he and Michelle reported they were communicating better and working out their problems more effectively.

Dr. Aronson saw them four times over the next year. Kirk continued to be abstinent throughout the year, and reported experiencing only a few urges to drink each week. Moreover, the couple's marital satisfaction remained high. They continued to attend the couples group once a week as part of Kirk's relapse prevention strategy. Overall, life without alcohol was good. As Kirk would often say, he had put the "monster" back in the bottle, and along the way had rediscovered his wife, his children, and the many pleasures that life could bring.

CASE 11

**Sexual Dysfunction:
Male Erectile Disorder**

Table 11-1

DSM-IV Checklist

Male Erectile Disorder

1. Persistent or recurrent inability to attain, or to maintain until completion of the sexual activity, an adequate erection.
2. Significant distress or interpersonal difficulty.
3. The erectile dysfunction is not better accounted for by another psychological disorder and is not due exclusively to the direct physiological effects of a substance or a general medical condition.

Based on APA, 1994, 2000.

Sexual dysfunctions are disorders in which persons are persistently unable to perform normally in some area of the human sexual response cycle.

Walter, a 59-year-old married man, the financial editor of a large city newspaper, had been raised on the West Coast. Throughout his childhood he always found his father, a local politician known for strong-arm tactics, distant and unapproachable. His mother, a traditional homemaker, in contrast, was warm, although a bit smothering.

Walter did not have much sexual interest during adolescence, although he did masturbate some. He was raised in a conservative small-town community, where teenagers' sexual behaviors were tame by today's standards. After high school he was drafted into the army. His first sexual experience was with a prostitute at a brothel visited by soldiers on the base. He found this encounter pleasurable, if awkward, and he continued to go to the brothel a couple of times each month.

Walter and Cynthia

After serving in the army, Walter went to college, majoring in economics. There he met his first wife, Lisa, whom he would later describe as a "hot number" and a "flirt." Their relationship was based largely on sex, and after about 4 years it became all too apparent that neither of them wanted to spend the rest of their lives together. Eventually, they divorced. After this marriage, Walter decided to pursue an interest in journalism, securing positions of greater and greater responsibility in the newspaper business. Because of his knowledge of economics he eventually covered financial news.

During this time, he dated around for several years and had a few affairs, until he met Cynthia; he was 35, she 28. Cynthia was different from the other women Walter had been dating, who tended to be, in his words, "more the wild and crazy type." She was "demure and serious," with her own career as a registered nurse in a suburban hospital. They met when she was caring for Walter's mother during a hospital stay for gall bladder surgery. After dating for a few months, Walter proposed marriage, and Cynthia accepted. Their first child, a boy, was born about 3 years later; a girl followed a couple of years after that, and 2 years later another girl.

As Walter later remembered it, he and Cynthia did not have significant sexual problems during the first 24 years of their marriage. True, when they first began sleeping together, he did go through a temporary period of premature ejaculation, but this was typical for him in adjusting to a new partner. As with prior partners, after a few weeks this difficulty passed. Granted, Walter found Cynthia less adventuresome sexually than his earlier partners—she rarely initiated sex or attempted something new on her own—but he accepted this as part of her personality.

> Around one fourth of men in the United States experience premature ejaculation at times in their lives (Laumann et al., 1999).

For her part, Cynthia had been raised in a religious (Catholic) household consisting of her parents and five siblings. Her relations with both parents were warm and loving, though it was often hard not to get lost in the large family. Cynthia was one of the younger children and, as such, her older siblings did a lot of the caring for her. Both parents worked in a grocery store that they owned.

Cynthia attended parochial school through high school. Upon graduation, she entered nursing school, earning her bachelor's degree. Her first sexual encounter was with a medical resident she began dating in nursing school, and to whom she became engaged at age 24. The engagement did not last, however, as Cynthia became increasingly dissatisfied with her fiancé's total focus on his work and his unwillingness to make any compromises for the relationship. Ultimately, he chose to make a cross-country move to accept a prestigious fellowship, and Cynthia stayed behind. She dated a few men after that, without any sexual involvement, until she met Walter. Cynthia did not consider sex to be a key element of their marriage, or of her life for that matter. Although she enjoyed sex with Walter, she had to admit that most of the time it was not something she cared to initiate on her own.

The Unfolding of a Sexual Dysfunction

During his 59th year, Walter was experiencing extra pressure at the newspaper where he worked, due to the downsizing of the editorial staff in his department. Although he was not affected directly, some of his junior colleagues had been laid off and Walter now had to work hours that he had not put in since he was a night reporter on the city beat. He was feeling more tired than he had in years, and he also felt some degree of job apprehension. Although told that his own job was safe, he had been in the newspaper business long enough to know the real score.

On top of all that, his financial responsibilities had increased, with two children in college, and a third to be entering in 2 years.

Partly due to Walter's concern about his job, Walter and Cynthia began to have sex less frequently—perhaps once a month. However, one night in February, Cynthia was decidedly in the mood, and she was uncharacteristically unwilling to take "no" for an answer. As she made sexual overtures, Walter tried to dissuade her, telling her he was really too preoccupied with work. However, she became extremely insistent. To help him "relax," she poured him a large glass of wine, which he accepted. He still did not want to pursue things, but then accepted a second glass, as the first did seem to ease his concerns somewhat. After drinking the second glass of wine, Walter was prepared to put his preoccupations aside and attend to Cynthia. She had completely disrobed in front of him and was now stroking him in a provocative manner. Walter was starting to get aroused.

Usually, sex with Cynthia had followed a formula. They would watch the evening news in bed on Saturday night and Walter, if feeling amorous, would turn toward Cynthia and start kissing and fondling her. If Cynthia was similarly inclined, she would respond by relaxing her limbs and returning Walter's kisses. After a few minutes of foreplay, Walter would assume the superior position and complete intercourse.

That night, however, Cynthia was acting much more aggressively. As Walter sat on the edge of their bed, she pulled down his pants and undid his shirt. She continued stimulating him, both manually and orally for a few minutes. Then she lay back on the bed and urged Walter to initiate intercourse. Now he was very interested.

As Walter positioned himself to enter his wife, he found, unbelievably, that his erection was starting to go soft. Completely bewildered, he tried and tried, but could not get firm enough to proceed. All the while, Cynthia continued to urge Walter on in a manner that he found indescribably enticing. However, the more he tried, the more he became aware of the flaccid state of his penis, and the less he succeeded. Finally, Cynthia asked Walter what was wrong, and he explained the difficulty he was having. He stimulated Cynthia to orgasm manually, and they both fell asleep.

At work the next day, Walter was in a state of confusion. True, his interest in sex had not been high in recent times; but now he was consumed with the question of why he had failed to achieve an erection with Cynthia the night before, especially as she had been so enthusiastic and sexy. He wondered whether he would be able to perform the next time, and finally decided to end his suspense by initiating sex with Cynthia at the next available opportunity.

That night, their evening followed the usual routine and they headed upstairs to watch the late news. As they watched television, Cynthia gave no evidence of the desire she had displayed the night before. Just as well, Walter thought, as he

Half of all men experience erectile difficulty during intercourse at least some of the time (Feldman et al., 1994).

didn't need any additional pressure in what he was about to attempt. As the news concluded, he leaned over toward his wife and began stroking her in the usual fashion. She relaxed her limbs, and Walter continued fondling her. He was pleased that this encounter seemed to be following their familiar pattern, but there was nothing familiar in his thoughts. The whole time, he was keeping track of the condition of his penis and whether he seemed to be showing enough responsiveness. About 5 minutes into the encounter, he realized he was only semierect, and for the life of him he couldn't remember whether or not this was normal for him during foreplay. He decided to end his suspense by proceeding to the main event. However, in doing so, his erection only got softer, and within a minute he concluded that all efforts at penetration were hopeless. Once again, he "salvaged" the situation by stimulating Cynthia to orgasm manually, all the while turning over in his mind the question of why he had failed once again.

Cynthia, sensing his upset afterward, tried her best to be understanding and to take the pressure off Walter. She told him to let the issue rest for a while. Maybe he *was* too stressed during this period to be interested in sex, and she had been wrong to force the issue the other night. By the same token, he should avoid forcing the issue now.

But Walter could not let the issue rest. Each night in the coming week he tried initiating sex with Cynthia, always with more or less the same results. He would become semierect during foreplay, but at the moment of penetration he would be acutely aware of any sign of difficulty, and this very awareness seemed to deflate him further.

Finally, he took Cynthia's advice and did try to let the matter rest for a while. Curiously, he found he could get normal erections when masturbating alone. He wondered to himself whether this meant that he and Cynthia were "sexually incompatible," but then dismissed the idea as absurd, noting that they had had a good marriage and sex life for over 20 years.

In the next couple of months, things became only slightly better. Walter attempted intercourse with Cynthia on the average of about once a week. On a couple of occasions he succeeded in getting hard enough to enter her, but his frantic efforts to achieve an orgasm before getting soft seemed almost to guarantee that he could not maintain the erection. Moreover, each new attempt at intercourse had become an unbearable trial. After each disappointment, Walter brooded over the experience and its implications.

Throughout this period, Cynthia tried to soothe Walter, telling him that it wasn't important and that things would get better. However, Walter could tell that she herself was beginning to wonder what was happening. Once she hinted that maybe he needed to "take a vacation—or see a doctor."

What Cynthia had little inkling of was how much this sexual problem was beginning to carry over into the rest of her husband's life. At work, Walter had be-

Most cases of erectile disorder result from an interaction of biological and psychosocial factors (LoPiccolo, 1991).

Erectile problems account for more than 400,000 visits to physicians in the United States each year (Ackerman & Carey, 1995).

come painfully self-conscious about his predicament. He felt like a weakling, less than a normal man, and also felt certain that others, if they knew about his difficulties, would mock him or think of him as a pitiful specimen. In meetings with male colleagues, he now felt a sense of distance and inferiority that he hadn't known since his days as a college intern, when he was awed to be in the presence of the gruff, competitive newspaper types. He felt like a fraud who didn't belong with the grownups.

After 3 months of disappointing results, Walter decided to seek medical assistance. As it happened, the radio airwaves were being flooded at the time with a persuasive advertising campaign promoting "new, effective treatments for impotence." He soon found his way to a physician who specialized in this sexual dysfunction.

The physician interviewed Walter about his difficulty and inquired about his medical and sexual history. He also gave Walter a standard physical exam, and conducted some tests to assess the possible roles of neurological, endocrine, and vascular dysfunction, all of which are known physical factors in erectile difficulties.

The physician could find nothing physical to account for Walter's difficulty, although he noted that an undetectable physical component could never be ruled out completely. He outlined for Walter three main medical treatment options. One, a *penile implant,* was considered by the physician to be a far too radical solution in Walter's case. The second was a *vacuum pump,* a device that draws blood mechanically into the penis, producing an erection; the erection is then maintained by the use of constricting rubber bands placed at the base of the penis. The third option was medication, specifically *sildenafil (Viagra).* Walter had certainly heard of this drug. Who in this society hadn't? The physician explained that a pill of Viagra increases blood flow to the penis within 1 hour of taking it, enabling a man to attain an erection during sexual activity. Given that Walter had no signs of coronary heart disease, the physician recommended this approach as a simple and safe way to solve his difficulties.

At the same time, the doctor allowed that Walter might want to consider psychological therapy. After all, the patient was able to achieve satisfactory erections with masturbation, which would suggest there was a situational component to his problem. Psychological treatment might assist him in expanding this existing capability to sexual situations with his wife.

Walter said he would have to think about it. He was very tempted by the Viagra option. It seemed so simple and was likely to bring immediate improvement. On the other hand, he was hoping to avoid an artificial solution. He didn't want to take pills for the rest of his life in order to have sex. He later explained the various options to Cynthia. After a few days, they both decided that it was preferable to start with the psychological therapy. The next day, Walter called Dr. Sandra Rostow, a psychologist who had been recommended by the physician, and made an appointment for him and his wife.

Physicians wrote 120,000 prescriptions for Viagra during its first month on the market in 1998, making it the fastest-selling new prescription drug in history (Adler, 1998).

A Spouse's Perspective: "Concerned, Yet Kind of Relieved"

When Walter first told Cynthia that he had consulted a physician for his problem, she felt a strange combination of concern and relief. Concern because the doctor visit confirmed that her husband's problem was very real and in need of solution, rather than a difficulty that would pass on its own. Relief because, in one sweep, the news of the visit had put to rest a whole slew of suspicions and worries that had been building within her for months. Later that week, Cynthia called her older sister and unburdened herself:

At first, I thought he was having an affair. It was the lowest I've ever felt in my entire life. "Fool," I would say to myself, "you should have seen it coming." He was always such a sex fiend. Well, maybe not a fiend but he was certainly always interested in sex. I loved him, but I could never keep up with him. And he always seemed to want more. So I thought that he'd eventually gotten tired of me.

I thought, "What am I doing wrong?" I tried to be sexier for him, but more often than not it seemed to backfire. I kept picturing him with some 20-year-old fact checker or intern or secretary. I imagined the things they might do together, all the things he's tried to get me to do—things I would never do. I came to hate this perfect, blond girl he was sleeping with, this girl who didn't exist.

I dressed up for him. I tried to say the things I thought he wanted me to say. But he just couldn't be excited about me. I would figure that he must be thinking about her. But then he would seem so genuinely upset when he couldn't have sex with me. He would get so upset about it, I couldn't be mad at him. I wanted to believe that he really had a problem, that he loved and wanted me but just had a problem. Much of the time, I did believe that. And, of course, I was concerned about him. So I told him to not worry about it.

Meanwhile, I myself had trouble thinking about anything else. I started going back to the gym, which I hadn't done in a few years. I bought a few new outfits, not that he noticed. But he just kept on being unable to perform. Other woman or no other woman, I kept thinking that I was just a failure, that my own husband would never desire me sexually again, that I was ugly and boring. I started to dread lying in bed at night, because he would so bravely start to be physical with me, and then he would try so hard, but he would lose his arousal and I would know that my husband wasn't being satisfied.

It was so hard to face the idea that I was disappointing him, or that he had found someone else who was more exciting, but I didn't let him know how upset I was. I also missed the feeling of being close to him, of having him make love to me. I really—and I know this will sound crazy—I really thought I was going to lose Walter. I tried to be as reassuring and understanding as I could, and all the while I was a wreck inside. I told him everything was fine and that it was normal, when I knew in

In an extensive survey of people in the United States, respondents estimated that their average sexual experience lasts 39 minutes, including foreplay (Kanner, 1995).

my heart that everything wasn't fine and that something was dreadfully wrong. I told him that maybe all he needed was a little rest, maybe a vacation, maybe a doctor even.

And then, Monday, Walter told me that he *had* gone to see a doctor. And I saw how scared he looked and I knew, in an instant, that there had never been another woman. That I had been a fool even to think such a thing. I felt relieved, but more than that I felt stupid. Stupid for being so jealous. Stupid for not knowing my husband. And stupid for not fully recognizing the fear and pain he must have been going through. Hopefully, this therapist—her name is Dr. Rostow—will make a difference. To be sure, it's better than doing nothing, or, worse, imagining things that aren't true.

Walter and Cynthia in Sex Therapy: Giving and Receiving Pleasure

Dr. Rostow spent two sessions obtaining background information from Walter and Cynthia. In the first session, she interviewed them together. In the second session, held a week later, she met with Walter and Cynthia separately for about half an hour each.

By the close of these sessions, Dr. Rostow had determined that Walter's sexual difficulty fit the DSM-IV criteria for *male erectile disorder,* a type of sexual dysfunction. That is, his difficulty had three key features: (a) a recurrent inability to attain an adequate erection or maintain it until completion of sexual activity, (b) significant distress over that inability, and (c) absence of a physical condition that would completely account for the inability.

Studies on male erectile disorder had convinced Dr. Rostow that, in many cases, a sequence of psychological factors helps produce the problem. Initially, the man may experience an instance of erectile failure due to stress, fatigue, mild physical impairment, alcohol intake, discomfort with his partner, or another such reason. Once such a failure occurs, he places extra demands on himself to perform in a productive manner. Given the recent failure, however, such demands tend to provoke negative expectancies for the man: He may, for example, anticipate failure, disappointment, or ridicule. With such negative expectancies going through his mind, he focuses intensely on his performance during the sex act, searching for indications that he is not functioning adequately. This extra focus, in turn, produces an actual or perceived decrement in erection. The continued concern and focus on performance eventually leads to an actual decrement in erection, and the man becomes even more acutely focused on his performance. The cycle continues until the erection is lost entirely.

As a result of this episode of failure, the individual is primed to experience a similar result in the next encounter. Each encounter sets the stage for the next, causing negative expectancies, performance scrutiny, and erectile failure to become further and further entrenched. Dr. Rostow believed that this psychological

---

A revolution in the treatment of sexual dysfunctions occurred in 1970 with the publication of William Masters and Virginia Johnson's book *Human Sexual Inadequacy.* The combination of cognitive, behavioral, couple, and family interventions that they used to treat sexual dysfunctions is the foundation for today's sex therapy programs.

People with *performance anxiety* during a sexual encounter worry that they will fail to perform adequately. In turn, they take a *spectator role* during the encounter; that is, they keep observing how they are performing, rather than relaxing and enjoying the sensations of sexual pleasure.

process must be reversed if an erectile problem was to be overcome. Sex therapy, as she conducted it, included a combination of cognitive and behavioral techniques, all of which were intended to accomplish a fundamental goal: shift the man's focus from his performance to the sex act itself. As part of therapy, the psychologist also sought to reeducate clients about sexual matters and disprove any maladaptive attitudes about sex that they might have.

Sessions 1–2 The first two sessions were spent gathering both current and background information from Walter and Cynthia. Toward the end of the second session, Dr. Rostow explained the treatment plan to the couple. In practical terms, Walter and Cynthia would undertake certain exercises that would minimize performance anxiety in sexual situations. At first, the exercises would involve different types of massage and sexual touching, but later they would progress to more explicit sexual activities.

In the meantime, it was important, the sex therapist explained, that Walter and Cynthia refrain from any "unauthorized" sexual activity. In fact, for the present, sexual contact should be limited to the specific exercises designed to further the treatment process. Both Walter and Cynthia expressed a sense of relief. As matters now stood, all attempts at sexual relations had become a trial for them; indeed, the sense of obligation to keep trying to have sex, combined with the disappointing results, was turning into an unbearable burden. With Dr. Rostow's recommendation that they stop making these attempts, that responsibility was taken off their shoulders. Walter, particularly, seemed to welcome the idea of simply following instructions, especially as, from the sound of it, the types of things the psychologist would require of him were far less demanding than what he was currently requiring of himself.

Dr. Rostow then explained what would be required of Walter and Cynthia during the coming week. They would perform an exercise called *sensate focus,* in which the goal was to engage in pleasurable touching and caressing while undressed, but avoid any genital touching. The point of the exercise, the therapist explained, was for them to recapture a state of physical intimacy without any sense of demand. When conducting the exercise, they were just to immerse themselves in the sensations each received during the caresses, and also to note the pleasure they were giving while administering caresses. Dr. Rostow gave Walter and Cynthia each a copy of written guidelines, including a suggested sequence of body areas to caress, as well as some pictorial supplements. The therapist recommended that the couple perform the exercise at least three times in the coming week.

Sensate focus exercises **are sometimes called** *nondemand pleasuring,* **or** *petting exercises.*

Session 3 Walter and Cynthia reported that, as instructed, they had refrained from sexual activity. In addition, they had carried out the sensate focus exercise three times. Cynthia volunteered that she found the exercises enjoyable. Walter echoed this, but also observed that he had been tense during the first exercise, as it reminded him of his deficiencies. By the later two exercises, he had set aside his concerns and was giving himself up to the process; then he also found the exercises enjoyable.

Dr. Rostow explained the next exercise, which involved a procedure similar to the sensate focus, but with the inclusion of genital touching. Cynthia and Walter were to take turns caressing one another as before, but now were to include caressing each other's genitals as part of the sequence. The therapist noted that the inclusion of genital touching should not distract Cynthia and Walter from the goal of the exercise, which was the same as before: just to enjoy the sensations.

The psychologist, as before, gave Walter and Cynthia written guidelines for suggested approaches. For example, for Cynthia, part of the guidelines was as follows:

> Do as much of the general body caressing as you like initially. Then play with his penis. Play with the tip and the shaft and the testicles for a while. Then go to another part of his body. One that he likes. Caress his belly or his ears or his thighs, for example. Then go back to his penis. Use your fingers or lips as you and he please. (adapted from Kaplan, 1987, p. 46)

For Walter, the written guidelines included the following:

> Play with her whole body first. Then when you feel she is ready, or when she tells you, play with her breasts. Gently kiss and massage the nipples. Play with the pubic hair around her clitoris. Play around the vagina. Do not put your finger all the way into the vagina. Touch the clitoris lightly. Go somewhere else. Go back to the clitoris. Be as gentle and sensitive as you can. (adapted from Kaplan, 1987, p. 49)

Dr. Rostow emphasized once again that, just as with the sensate focus exercise, the idea was simply to enjoy the sensations, no more and no less. Walter and Cynthia said, smilingly, that they would "do their duty."

Around 10% of men suffer from male erectile disorder (APA, 2000).

Session 4 Walter and Cynthia seemed upset when they returned. Walter told Dr. Rostow that they had tried the new exercises, but they "weren't working." The therapist asked Walter for details, and the client indicated that they had conducted the exercises as instructed—including genital caressing—but that Walter had "failed" to get an erection. "What was wrong?" he wanted to know.

Dr. Rostow explained that there was nothing at all wrong. She had urged Walter in the previous session not to focus on the erection issue. However, as often happens, these words can lose their meaning once a man is introduced to the sexual situation. The sex therapist went on to acknowledge that Walter's situation in treatment was somewhat contradictory: He was being asked to avoid observing his erection during exercises, yet the whole point of the overall treatment was to promote erections.

Dr. Rostow advised repeating the same exercises for the coming week, emphasizing that the question of erections should be set aside entirely. She recommended that Walter (and Cynthia) just focus on giving and receiving pleasure, the same as they did with the nonsexual caresses. She also suggested that closing their eyes while receiving pleasure might help to keep it a purely touching experience. The therapist further suggested to Walter that if he found he could not rid himself of the erection preoccupation, he should think of his goal as deliberately trying to avoid getting an erection during the exercise.

> Most men with erectile disorder are over the age of 50. The disorder is experienced by 5 to 9% of all 40-year-old men, and by at least 15% of all 60-year-old men (Laumann et al., 1999).

Session 5 Cynthia and Walter returned in good spirits. Once again they reported a "failure" of sorts, only in this case, it was Walter's failure to avoid an erection during the genital caressing exercise. Apparently, Dr. Rostow's paradoxical instruction had its effect. Walter found that the strategy of deliberately trying to avoid an erection allowed him to refocus his attention on the sensations of touching. By the second exercise, when adopting the same strategy, he found that he could not avoid the erection. During the third exercise, he was erect most of the time.

Clearly pleased with these results, Walter said he was ready to "go for broke," meaning skip the intervening stages and proceed directly to intercourse. The sex therapist did not want to dampen Walter's enthusiasm or rob him of his newfound sense of capability; but on other the other hand, she knew from experience that jumping prematurely to later stages can become a problem if the results prove disappointing, as the patient's anxieties will then resurface. She explained:

> I understand your desire to move things along. It's very possible that you and Cynthia could go ahead and have intercourse, and it would work out fine, but I'd prefer to stick to the original game plan. We only have a few weeks longer at the current rate, and jumping ahead, in case it doesn't work out, can sometimes make things take longer overall.

Dr. Rostow then explained the next step in the sequence. In the coming week, Walter and Cynthia would perform an exercise similar to the one they were already conducting, but one that would now include genital-genital contact. Specifically, first Walter would give Cynthia the full body and genital caresses, and then Cynthia was to do the same for Walter. This time, however, part of Cynthia's task would include sitting astride Walter as he lay on his back, and stimulating his penis by rubbing it against the exterior of her vagina. During this exercise, Walter was to remain completely passive, as before, just thinking of himself as receiving a massage, paying no attention to whether he got an erection or not. As before, the goal was simply to immerse himself in the sensations and, if trying to avoid getting an erection assisted him in this endeavor, he could use that device, too. The therapist emphasized that this exercise really differed from the previous week's only in that Cynthia would be using her genitals in addition to her hands. Cynthia and Walter agreed to conduct the exercise at least three times in the coming week.

Session 6 Cynthia and Walter reported that they had carried out the prescribed exercise four times. The first time, Walter found that he became tense when Cynthia performed the genital-genital contact, and this seemed to prevent the involuntary erection that he had been getting from Cynthia's manual caresses. The second time that they tried the exercise, however, Walter felt more relaxed, and Cynthia's stimulating his penis with the exterior of her vagina did not evoke anxiety, nor did it prevent an erection. The third and fourth exercises similarly brought positive results. After each exercise, Walter and Cynthia stimulated one another manually to orgasm, which was now permitted under the guidelines.

Dr. Rostow: You two have been doing wonderfully with the exercises so far. The next step is only slightly different, in physical terms, from what you have been doing up to this point. Technically, it is sometimes called *vaginal containment*. It means that you essentially do the same exercise as before, but now Cynthia is using the inside of her vagina to stimulate Walter's penis, instead of just the outside. Once again, she sits astride, and she is in charge of the stimulation. She controls the insertion, and moves her body just a little bit—without Walter thrusting on his own—in order to maintain the stimulation. After a few minutes she then withdraws your penis and resumes manual stimulation.

Walter: (pause) Well, I guess we've finally made it to the real thing.

Dr. Rostow: Meaning?

Walter: You know. We're finally "doing it." I just hope it goes OK.

Dr. Rostow: "OK" in what sense?

Walter: I mean, I hope I can keep the erection. I guess this will be the real test of all that we've been doing.

Dr. Roslow: I understand your feeling. It's often hard not to look at this as a test of sorts, but in my view, it is no such thing. I'm looking at it as simply the next step in a progression. It's best if you can adopt the same frame of mind that you did with the other exercises. In other words, the idea is not to see if you are maintaining your erection but, once again, simply to immerse yourself in the sensations. The exercises should be considered a success if you can maintain that focus.

Walter: I see what you mean. I guess I'm just anxious to get this over with, but I'll do my best.

After this exchange, the sex therapist was not entirely confident about Walter's ability to approach the exercises in the proper frame of mind. However, there was little else to be said, and she felt it best just to wait and see how Walter fared.

Session 7 Unfortunately, the intervening week had borne out Dr. Rostow's concerns. Walter and Cynthia reported that they had abandoned the exercises out of frustration. They explained that they had begun the exercise as before, but that soon after Cynthia inserted Walter's erect penis into her vagina, he started to grow soft; he then tried thrusting on his own to revive the erection, but to no avail. They then stopped the exercise. After experiencing a similar "failure" when trying the exercise the next day, they again stopped, and did not attempt any more exercises for the remainder of the week. Once again, they were very upset, particularly Walter. He was wondering if this was a sign that his problem would not respond to treatment after all. The therapist felt it important to normalize Walter and Cynthia's experience.

Dr. Rostow:	What you experienced is very common at this stage of the treatment, and you shouldn't place too much importance on it. It's hard not to think of the moment of insertion as a momentous event, and to avoid examining how you're reacting, but that's what happened this time. As a result, your ability to immerse yourself in the sensations was probably undermined, your erection was reduced, and you became overly discouraged, causing you to end the exercise prematurely.
Cynthia:	What should we have done?
Dr. Rostow:	In general, it's always best to follow the exercise to its conclusion, regardless of what happens. As you may recall, I recommended that you resume manual caressing of Walter's penis after vaginal insertion was ended. In this case, even though the vaginal insertion ended sooner than expected—because Walter became too soft to remain inside— you still could have resumed the manual caressing.
Cynthia:	That's what I wanted to do, but Walter was so discouraged. The idea just seemed to annoy him.
Walter:	Yes. I guess it wasn't the best reaction on my part. But as soon as I realized my erection was going down and I couldn't stay inside, I lost all interest in continuing.

The therapist felt that Walter might benefit by increasing his psychological tolerance for the loss of an erection. The experience was becoming far too loaded for him, and unless he could get used to the idea that erections can come and go, and then come back again, he would remain overly attentive to any decline in performance.

> If a man is able to have an erection in certain circumstances—for example, when masturbating, or with certain partners, or when asleep—then it is generally concluded that psychological factors are at least partially responsible for his erectile disorder.

Dr. Rostow:	In the past, before this whole problem developed, how did you handle it when your erection went down during sex?
Walter:	I never had an erection go down before...
Cynthia:	(interrupting) Actually... I beg to differ.
Walter:	What? What do you mean?
Cynthia:	Well, I don't think you ever paid much attention to it before, but there have been plenty of times during foreplay, when we've been taking turns on each other, that you've gone soft for a time. I just stroked you for a little while, and you'd come back.
Walter:	Really?
Cynthia:	Yes. It happened all the time. You just never seemed to notice or care about it, so it never became a problem.
Dr. Rostow:	I think Cynthia has just made an important observation. It sounds like the critical aspect is not whether you lose an erection, but how you interpret it once it happens. I gather in the past you never gave it any thought, so its very occurrence didn't trigger any alarms. I think it would be useful to do some exercises to promote that mindset again.

The therapist explained a new set of exercises that she wanted the couple to try for the coming week. They would return to the earlier exercise, involving manual caressing and genital stroking. This time, however, there would be a new feature. During the time that Cynthia was stroking Walter, if he was to achieve an erection, she was to stop stroking for a while, in a deliberate attempt to have him lose the erection. Then after Walter lost the erection, he was to focus on stroking and caressing Cynthia for while; after that, Cynthia would resume stroking Walter. Walter's guideline, as usual, was to immerse himself in the sensations, giving no mind to the question of whether he got an erection at any given stage. The point of the exercise was for Walter to learn to tolerate the loss of an erection and not see it as a signal to end the sexual episode, but, rather, as a typical part of the experience.

> The sex therapy technique in which a man's partner stops caressing him whenever he gets an erection, and does not resume caressing until the man loses the erection, is sometimes called the *tease* technique.

Session 8 The couple returned in a happy mood. They reported carrying out the exercise to the letter. During each of four attempts at the exercise, Walter deliberately allowed himself to lose his erection after Cynthia stopped stroking him; he then turned his attention to caressing and stroking Cynthia. After that she returned to stroking him, and he found that his erection could gradually be regained. The exercise seemed to energize him. By the fourth exercise, he had developed a complete confidence in his ability to regain the erection and, in fact, he and Cynthia decided to resume the previous week's vaginal containment procedure. As before, Walter began to go a little soft soon after insertion. He then withdrew and took his turn at caressing Cynthia. After that, Cynthia returned to stroking Walter and, with his erection revived, she once again tried vaginal containment. This time, his erection remained hard as Cynthia continued moving on top of him. He ended up ejaculating inside her vagina. The following day, Cynthia and Walter repeated this activity with similar results. And the next day, they had regular intercourse without any difficulty.

The experiences were empowering. Now Walter and Cynthia wanted to resume normal—free-form—intercourse. Feeling that the couple was ready, the therapist agreed to this plan. She requested, however, that Cynthia and Walter stick to a few basic guidelines: (a) Intercourse should never be initiated as a "test" of sexual performance adequacy, but only out of a genuine desire for lovemaking; (b) if Walter should experience any loss of erection during lovemaking, he should not stop but switch to an alternative lovemaking activity, for example, manual stimulation instead of intercourse; (c) after switching to an alternative activity under such circumstances, intercourse could be started again, if desired, but only when a sense of comfort was restored; (d) if comfort was not restored, remain with alternative activities to complete the lovemaking.

Sessions 9–11 Walter and Cynthia reported making love twice in the previous week. Walter had pressed for a third encounter, but Cynthia resisted, sensing that Walter was doing it mainly to test his responsiveness. On the two lovemaking occasions, Walter was able to complete intercourse both times, although the second time he appeared to become soft as he was trying to penetrate. In this case, switching back to foreplay for a while restored his comfort level, and in turn his erection, for another penetration.

At the 10th and 11th sessions, held 2 weeks apart, Walter and Cynthia reported similar experiences: They completed intercourse four times, although there was one instance when Walter did not attempt penetration again after first losing his erection, because, as he put it, "the desire did not return." On the whole, however, the couple felt that their sex life had been restored to a very satisfactory level and that, by observing the guidelines, Walter could avoid the type of performance anxiety that had been hurting him previously. They wanted to discontinue their visits to the sex therapist and just "go it alone" for the time being.

Dr. Rostow agreed to the plan, with the strong suggestion that they call her if any difficulties arose and that, either way, they speak on the phone in 1 month's time for follow-up.

Epilogue

A telephone conversation 1 month later confirmed that Walter and Cynthia had maintained their progress. They were making love about two times each week, and were completing intercourse almost every time. As before, there had been one occasion when Walter's erection softened too much for penetration, and

Viagra was discovered by accident. Testing it as a possible heart medication, researchers found that the drug increased blood flow to subjects' penises more effectively than to their hearts.

switching to an alternative lovemaking activity had created a satisfactory ending to the sexual encounter. The key point, they noted, was that Walter did not get anxious or upset by the experience, so it had no carryover to the next encounter. Overall, they were both back in the "pleasure business," as Walter described their progress.

About 10 months after this conversation, Walter telephoned Dr. Rostow to say that he was planning to visit his physician because his problems in maintaining erections had become more pronounced in recent weeks. He was choosing a medical route because there didn't seem to be any anxiety component to his problem and, also, because he had noticed that maintaining an erection, even when masturbating, was proving difficult on occasion.

Any physical problem that reduces blood flow into the penis can contribute to erectile difficulties. Common biological causes of such difficulties are vascular problems (problems with the body's blood vessels), nervous system damage (resulting from such conditions as diabetes, spinal cord injuries, or kidney failure), the use of certain medications, and various forms of substance abuse (including cigarette smoking and alcohol abuse).

Walter's physician reevaluated him with a complete battery of medical tests that revealed that he was experiencing a mild "venous leakage," which could account for his recent difficulty in maintaining erections. In this condition, which often occurs with age, blood flow to the penis is sufficient to produce an erection initially, but some of the blood then leaks out of the vessels and the erection softens. The physician noted that Walter could continue dealing with the problem as he had been doing—that is, engaging in manual and oral stimulation with Cynthia rather than intercourse during some sexual encounters—or he could try one of the available medical remedies. Given that Walter was still in excellent health, the physician recommended the use of Viagra on occasion, as a kind of boost or insurance. This time Walter agreed to Viagra.

Over the following months, both Walter and Cynthia were very pleased with the medication. It almost always helped Walter to achieve an erection that was satisfactory for intercourse. At the same time, Walter noted that he really did not need the drug at least half of the time, and he preferred to do without it whenever possible. Overall, he felt that the current combination of psychological and medical methods offered a perfectly fine solution for his periodic problem. Cynthia and he were once again back in the "pleasure business."

CASE **12**

Schizophrenia

Table **12-1**	

DSM-IV Checklist

Schizophrenia

1. At least two of the following symptoms, each present for a significant portion of time during a one-month period:
   a. Delusions.
   b. Hallucinations.
   c. Disorganized speech.
   d. Grossly disorganized or catatonic behavior.
   e. Negative symptoms such as flat affect.
2. Functioning markedly below the level achieved prior to onset.
3. Continuous signs of the disturbance for at least six months, at least one month of which includes symptoms in full and active form (as opposed to attenuated form).
4. Disturbance is not due to the direct physiological effects of a substance or general medical condition.

Based on APA, 1994, 2000.

Approximately 1 of every 100 people in the world suffers from schizophrenia during his or her lifetime (APA, 2000).

Jim, born in 1973, was the third of four brothers. His parents had both been born and raised in Argentina. They met when his father was 38 and his mother 19, and decided to marry soon after his mother became pregnant. They then emigrated to the United States where they hoped to make a better life for themselves. Their first few years on American soil were happy, but difficult financially. The couple had several business failures before Jim's father started a clothing manufacturing company that did well.

After arriving in the United States, Jim's mother, Consuela, gave birth to three healthy baby boys in close succession. Her fourth child was stillborn when Jim was 13 months old. Devastated by the tragedy, Consuela soon stopped eating, and began drinking heavily. She eventually became so depressed that she could not function and had to be hospitalized briefly. The notion of being hospitalized for a mental disorder particularly concerned Consuela because her own mother was, at that very time, also a patient at a mental hospital back in Argentina—a hospitalization from which she was never to be discharged, as it turned out. During Consuela's hospitalization, care of the children fell to a series of nannies, as Jim's father was required to work long hours.

Two years after her hospitalization, Jim's mother became pregnant again. This lifted her out of her depression, and she was able to stop drinking. By the time the new baby was born, she seemed restored to her former self. She later told family members that the birth of this child had been her "salvation."

Jim: Unfulfilled Promise

Throughout childhood, Jim and his younger brother were the better students of the four boys and, as such, received most of the attention from their parents. Jim was considered a prize pupil by his teachers as well. He was enthusiastic, motivated, and typically finished at the top of his class. As head of the chess club in high school, he led the school's team to victory in several tournaments. He was also among the top scorers on the state-wide scholastic achievement test. Everyone who knew him had high hopes for his future.

However, things began to change for Jim toward the end of high school when his father, Roberto, suffered a heart attack. Jim could no longer concentrate on his studies, and spent almost all his time praying for his father's recovery. His father did recover eventually, and Jim became convinced that it was due to his prayers.

Despite poor grades in his final semester, Jim graduated from high school; however, he seemed to have lost his bearings. He registered at a community college in the fall, but after a few weeks became lax about attending classes. Eventually, he stopped going to classes altogether and spent more and more time in front of a television set in his room at home. The extended television time, however, was not due to laziness, or lack of ambition, or lack of interest in people. Rather, Jim was coming to believe that he had "special powers." He would closely observe the movements of every character on the screen, trying to determine the extent of his influence. The more he watched, the more his suspicions were confirmed. His effect on the characters was just too obvious to deny.

At first, this belief was just a feeling, but eventually Jim concluded that a specific change had occurred: He had acquired the capacity to control other people's emotions and behavior. He discovered this by going into restaurants and observing the patrons. He noticed that if he looked at people long enough, he could cause them to rub their eyes, scratch their noses, or make other simple gestures. At first, he thought he had to be within close range to have this effect. However, as time went on, he concluded that he could project this influence over great distances. He found this out one day as he watched the news on television. While watching, Jim observed that the reporter glanced down at her notes periodically. Suddenly, Jim "realized" that he himself was directing these movements. From that moment on, he believed that he could guide characters on television to move in ways that they ordinarily would not. Gradually, he became convinced that not only people but objects such as traffic signals and automobiles were responding to his

If one identical twin develops schizophrenia, there is a 48% chance that the other twin will do the same (APA, 2000; Gottesman, 1991). If the twins are fraternal, the second twin has a 17% chance of developing the disorder.

Delusions are strange, false beliefs that are firmly held despite evidence to the contrary. *Delusions of persecution* are the kind most commonly held by people with schizophrenia.

influence. If he stood on a street corner, for example, and observed the flow of traffic, he found he could direct the cars' movements.

In the beginning, Jim was not sure how he controlled people and things, but one day, while pondering his situation, he had a flash of insight. He concluded that he, like God, must have a "life force" in his breath. In effect, he influenced people and objects through his breathing.

This was a momentous revelation for him. It meant that his power was not just "your garden variety black magic or wizardry." Rather, he had been selected for some sort of holy mission. This suspicion seemed confirmed soon afterward when Jim heard God's angels whispering that he had been chosen to be the Messiah.

With this discovery, Jim also became increasingly convinced that people were talking about him behind his back. One day, for example, he got on a bus and believed that some of the passengers were engaged in conversation about him, while others were glancing at him and pointing. This, he presumed, meant they knew about his power.

After the bus experience, Jim became extremely anxious. He was afraid that other people, particularly those with evil intent, might somehow gain control of his power and use it for destructive purposes. The best solution, as he saw it, was to stay home as much as possible. He also began to use greater and greater amounts of marijuana because, he believed, "it reduces the oxygen in the breath and that reduces its effect."

As Jim's discovery of his special powers evolved into the hearing of voices, then into his understanding that he would be the Messiah, and, finally, into his realization that others were talking about him, he became more and more confused. One day, as he emerged from his room after an intense session before the television, his mother asked him how he was feeling and he could only respond by babbling incoherently about "angels" and a "life force" in his breath. His parents, who previously had seen their son as merely withdrawn and somewhat depressed, were alarmed, and arranged the first of what turned out to be several hospitalizations.

At the hospital, Jim was diagnosed with *schizophrenia, paranoid type,* a label that initially meant nothing to his family but which they would eventually know all too well and hear all too often. At this hospital, Jim was treated with *thorazine,* an antipsychotic medication. Within a week, his speech became coherent again and he stopped hearing voices. He continued to believe in his special powers, but he became less preoccupied with them. After a 4-week hospital stay, he had improved considerably and was discharged.

At home, Jim continued to take the thorazine for a while and, as a result, was less troubled by symptoms. However, he lapsed into his previous lifestyle. Most of the time he still watched television or slept, emerging periodically for meals. He had no interest in returning to school or doing anything else constructive, in spite of his parents' urgings.

Hallucinations are sights, sounds, and other perceptions that are experienced in the absence of external stimuli. Auditory hallucinations—hearing sounds or voices—are the kind most commonly experienced by people with schizophrenia (APA, 2000).

As the weeks passed, he decided to stop taking the medication because it made him "tired and dizzy." Within a couple of weeks, his hallucinations, intense anxiety, and confusion returned. Once more he had to be hospitalized.

This pattern was, unfortunately, to be repeated again and again over the next decade. Jim would be hospitalized periodically with a major flare-up of symptoms; he would be stabilized on anti-psychotic medication; and, after a period of relief—sometimes just a few weeks, other times as long a year—he would either stop taking his medication or the medication would stop being effective. Even when his medication did "work," only some of his symptoms disappeared: his hallucinations and incoherent speech. The delusion that he could control people and objects with his breath was only mildly lessened, and he remained isolated from normal events and activities.

At the age of 27, after 10 years of treatment disappointments, Jim was still spending most of his time in his room at home, not having done any productive work for several years. He had one friend, someone he had known since grade school, whom he believed was immune to his breath's effect. Their interactions consisted largely of smoking marijuana together. Otherwise, Jim socialized only with his immediate family.

Jim's Mother: Unfulfilled Dreams

Jim's parents were at first devastated and then, over the years, drained by his schizophrenic condition. Particularly hard-hit was his mother, Consuela. Having lived through difficult times at a very young age, she found her son's deterioration to be a last straw, of sorts. Occasionally, she would attend a support group for members of the families of people with severe mental disorders. The people in the group were nice, and the discussions sometimes helped her cope with Jim's condition. During one session, the focus was on her and she reflected on her reactions over the years to Jim's disorder.

> At first, I just didn't want to let myself believe that his problem was serious. I'd been through so much, and I basically didn't want to think about anything. Jim was one of the only things in my life that seemed truly fine. He was my hope that some day I would be able to look back on my life with a sense of pride and accomplishment.
>
> Then, there was Roberto's heart attack. When Jim kept talking about how he had saved his father's life, I indulged him. For one thing, I sort of believed it. We were all terribly upset and anxious, and I really did believe that Roberto survived through our love and our prayers to God. Even when Jim started to insist that *he* and he alone had saved his father through prayer—a direct line of communication with God—I figured simply that he was being overly emotional about the situation. I thought that he had been overwhelmed by the horror of not knowing whether his

Psychosis is a loss of contact with reality. Various disorders or conditions (for example, substance misuse) can produce psychosis; schizophrenia is one of the most common causes.

father would die, and so he was now experiencing an unusual kind of relief and joy that Roberto had pulled through.

That was also when I first became aware of Jim's problems with marijuana. But, again, I didn't think that was too bad. I'd experimented with it myself when I was young. Then the problem with his room started. He would spend more and more of his time alone there. I guess I really didn't look into that closely enough. I never tried to stop his withdrawal, and I never really saw just how big his problems were. I think I was afraid of what I might find if I looked too closely.

Suddenly, my shining honor student was in his own world. I had wanted him to become someone important, to change the world. It sounds silly, but I thought he could one day be president, or a famous scientist. But he just seemed to give up, and nothing Roberto or I did could awaken him. At dinner, he would pull away from the conversation and stare at his food, mumbling when we asked questions, otherwise not talking or even acknowledging us. He was so moody, no longer the boy I had known. I didn't know what to think, but in our hearts we knew something was terribly wrong. It wasn't just that he was ignoring us; that would have been hard enough. But he actually seemed to be paying attention to something else, something we could not sense.

Finally, one night he came out of his room muttering gibberish about talking to the angels in the television set, or something like that. He said he could make the people on the screen move, and that the voices were confirming this power. I was just petrified. I figured, it's just like my mother—he's insane! We rushed him to the hospital, thinking that they would fix whatever was wrong with him. But it wasn't that easy. They told us Jim had schizophrenia . . . paranoid schizophrenia. We didn't know exactly what it meant, but we knew it wasn't good. They told me that my precious little boy was seriously mentally ill and had to take anti-psychotic medications. I hoped so much that they were wrong. I just couldn't face the idea that they might be right. At the same time, I knew that it was the only possible explanation for what had been happening.

That was almost 10 years ago, and since then, our problems have been endless. For periods of time, Jim will take his medicines, but even then he basically seems depressed and slow; and he is still, I am certain, focused somewhere else. And sometimes he has flare-ups; he gets really bad and has terrible psychotic episodes. He hears voices and may even scream at them, which is terrifying.

We've had to spend so much money over the years, to put him in and out of hospitals, and to pay for his medications, that we've nearly gone into debt. We've never been able to get the kind of house we always wanted, or to travel to the places that we've always wanted to. We know now that it is unlikely that he, or our lives, will ever be normal again.

After the support group session, one of the members, a man Consuela had not seen at past sessions, approached her. He said that he and his family had

> Around 10% of the first-degree relatives of people with schizophrenia (parents, siblings, and children) manifest the same disorder (APA, 2000).

moved to the area around a year ago, and at that time he and his wife had sought a therapist for their 25-year-old daughter, whose severe problems sounded a lot like Jim's. They made numerous calls—to their physician, to a referral service for people with severe mental disorders, to the leader of a support group, and to a university professor. The name Dr. Brian Sorkin kept coming up during these calls. Apparently, this psychiatrist had built a reputation for his successful treatment of people with schizophrenia—even individuals who had previously shown little improvement. Dr. Sorkin believed strongly that psychological interventions must supplement anti-psychotic medications if people with this disorder were to make successful and lasting recoveries.

The man said that his daughter had now been seeing Dr. Sorkin for the past 6 months and had been making real progress for the first time in years. When he heard Consuela tell her story, it reminded him of his own situation, and he really believed that she should give Dr. Sorkin a try.

Consuela had just about run out of hope, and so she was inclined to ignore the man's suggestion. But something about his enthusiasm, his joy—perhaps it was his hope—called to her. That night, she discussed everything with Roberto, and they decided to gear up for yet one more try. The next day, they had a long talk with Jim, trying to persuade him to see Dr. Sorkin.

Jim was not interested in a new approach; he was certain it would be just another in a long list of disappointments. However, by now he tended to give in to his parents on such things. The disorder had worn him down quite a bit, and it was often easier, from his point of view, to go in whatever direction they pointed. He allowed his parents to make an appointment for him to see Dr. Brian Sorkin.

> It was once theorized that people with schizophrenia typically had mothers who were cold, domineering, and impervious to their children's needs—so-called *schizophrenogenic mothers*. Research does not, however, support this theory.

Jim in Treatment: The Journey Back

As Dr. Sorkin directed his questions to Jim, the new client gave only minimal replies. Most of the time, he averted his eyes, looking miserable and frightened. Finally, however, the young man showed a spark of interest when the psychiatrist changed his approach and asked him what he considered to be the "real problem." In reply, Jim stated that he had been seeing therapists since age 17, and this was the first time anyone had shown an interest in his view of the situation. "Usually, they only want to know about the voices."

Jim then proceeded to tell Dr. Sorkin, at length, about the special power that he possessed, and the problems that this had created for him. The client eventually stated that he didn't like secluding himself in his room at home, but felt it was his duty, given the overwhelming responsibility imposed by this special power. It was like having the power of God, but with none of the desire or wisdom to use it. To cope with his predicament, he could emerge only for occasional meals, bathroom visits, and synagogue services on Friday evenings. By restricting his activities in this way, Jim said he minimized the chance of doing anyone unintentional harm; also, it kept his power from falling into the hands of evil forces.

The client admitted to Dr. Sorkin that he continued to hear the voices of angels; he also remained anxious that others were talking about him. Most recently, he said, he had been trying to understand his situation by immersing himself in biblical study, looking for scriptural evidence that he had been chosen for a special mission. He began to spend more and more time at this endeavor and, as his parents described it, his room was now strewn with Hebrew texts that he would study until the early hours of the morning.

Although at first skeptical about seeing another therapist, Jim was grateful that Dr. Sorkin was interested in hearing him out on the subject of his religious concerns. Perhaps, he stated, the psychiatrist would help him explain to his parents why his recent biblical studies were his own business and not "craziness," as they believed.

After talking to Jim and his parents at length and reviewing Jim's history, Dr. Sorkin was certain that the young man's condition did indeed meet the DSM-IV criteria for a diagnosis of *schizophrenia, paranoid type*. He exhibited a *bizarre delusion*, namely the belief that he could control others with his breath; he experienced auditory hallucinations; and he suffered from *avolition*, the inability to initiate or persist in normal, goal-directed activities, such as work, education, or a social life. In addition, his social and occupational functioning were far below what might have been expected, based on his capabilities as a child and adolescent. Finally, Jim's symptoms were not transient, but had lasted for a number of years.

Like many clinicians and researchers, Dr. Sorkin believed that schizophrenia is best explained by a *diathesis–stress* model. That is, certain individuals may have a predisposing vulnerability (a diathesis) to schizophrenia, but the risk of developing the disorder is affected by the degree of stress in their environment. Theoretically, the diathesis must exist in some degree in order for a person actually to develop the disorder; however, the diathesis can vary in severity. People who have a severe diathesis would probably develop schizophrenia regardless of the environment in which they are placed. Those with a milder diathesis, in contrast, might develop the disorder only in a less favorable environment. And those without the diathesis—the majority of the population—are incapable of developing schizophrenia, no matter how severe their environmental stress.

Given this view of the disorder, Dr. Sorkin used an approach called *biobehavioral therapy*. This treatment introduces *protective factors* into the life of each client—factors that will, it is hoped, lessen the person's vulnerability to schizophrenia or lessen the effects of stress on the client. For example, medications can lessen the person's biological vulnerability; training in social and independent living skills can lower his or her behavioral vulnerability.

> "I shouldn't precisely have chosen madness if there had been any choice, but once such a thing has taken hold of you you can't very well get out of it."
> —Vincent van Gogh, 1889

> Research suggests that people with schizophrenia have excessive activity of the neurotransmitter *dopamine,* or some form of imbalance between this neurotransmitter and the neurotransmitter *serotonin.*

Similarly, the degree of stress in the individual's life can often be lowered by family counseling or supportive services, such as case management, special group housing, and a sheltered work setting.

Phase 1: Engaging Jim as a Collaborator

Dr. Sorkin educated Jim and his parents as thoroughly as possible about schizophrenia, including the diathesis–stress model. The psychiatrist also explained that symptoms would likely recur without continued medication and stress management.

The delicate part was in getting Jim to try a medication treatment once again. Currently, the young man was not taking any medication, nor was he interested in returning to an approach that he felt had had no benefit for him in the past, only unpleasant side effects. Thus, Dr. Sorkin suggested that they work together to eliminate his "special powers," which Jim was finding so burdensome:

Dr. Sorkin: I know this has been a tremendous problem for you, and I want to help in any way I can. As you know, I'm a psychiatrist, and I've told you, as others have before me, that you have schizophrenia. I believe that the power that you've noticed in your breath is a result of this illness. If we can treat your illness properly, I believe that this power will go away, or at least be weakened. Do you feel that this would be desirable?

Jim: Yes. But I've been taking that crap the doctors prescribe for years, and it hasn't done any good. The power is as strong as ever.

Dr. Sorkin: I understand your reluctance to try again, but I'm going to take somewhat of a different approach. I think it is important that you feel that the medicine I prescribe is helping, otherwise I wouldn't blame you for not taking it. Therefore, I'm going to seek your guidance on this question, rather than just telling you what to take.

Jim: What exactly do you want me to do?

Dr. Sorkin: I'm going to ask you to take some medicine, and then to keep track of the medicine's effect on specific symptoms, using a special record-keeping form. This way, we'll both be able to tell whether the medicine is producing any benefits.

Jim: What if I don't think the medicine is working?

Dr. Sorkin: I'm going to take your opinion very seriously, and if you don't feel the medicine is working I'll accept that fact, and we'll have to consider our options. However, in return, I'm going to ask you to give the medicine a fair trial. It's going to take a little bit of trial and error. But I'd like you to bear with the process until we've had a chance to figure out how much benefit we can get from the medicine. This will mean living through a period of time when the medicine is not yet working to the maximum, or not working at all. I will tell you when I think I've got the best possible

---

Dr. Sorkin's treatment for schizophrenia followed a biobehavioral program developed in the late 1980s (Psychiatric Rehabilitation Consultants, 1991). This program includes five behavioral training "modules" designed to teach basic skills in areas where patients with this disorder are often lacking: medication and symptom management; grooming and self-care; recreation; job finding; and basic conversational skills. The approach also engages the patient as a "collaborator" in the treatment program.

Brain scans indicate that many people with schizophrenia have smaller temporal lobes and frontal lobes, and larger ventricles—the brain cavities that contain cerebrospinal fluid (APA, 2000; Wright et al., 2000).

Dr. Sorkin: dose, and I'll seek your input about how much symptom reduction you've experienced each step of the way.

Jim: It sounds OK. But I'm warning you, I'm not going to take it if I don't notice any change.

Dr. Sorkin: OK. But we may need a month before we can tell whether the medicine has any benefit. How about bearing with this for a month, and then I'll accept your verdict.

Jim: OK. I'll give it a month.

Jim's parents, who were present during this early discussion, were heartened that their son had agreed to go back on medication, but his mother doubted that he could take the medication reliably. She asked if they could monitor his medication. After some discussion, Jim grudgingly agreed to let his father watch him take the medication at bedtime.

Phase 2: Attacking Jim's Symptoms This phase of treatment was devoted to finding a medication dosage that would relieve Jim's psychotic symptoms. There were three main kinds of symptoms that could be helped by the anti-psychotic drugs: hallucinations (hearing angels talking), delusional thinking (Jim's belief that his breath could control others), and suspiciousness (his concern that others were aware of his powers and were hostile toward him). In order to track Jim's improvement, Dr. Sorkin and the patient would each regularly measure the severity of his symptoms on rating scales.

The medication that the psychiatrist had Jim try was *risperidone* (Risperdol), one of the newer, so-called *atypical* anti-psychotic drugs. During the first 2 weeks, Dr. Sorkin slowly raised the dose of risperidone, while carefully monitoring symptoms and side effects in collaboration with Jim. By the end of this period, the client complained that not only were his powers unaffected, but he was experiencing some unpleasant side effects: dizziness and fatigue. He said he was ready to stop taking the medicine. Dr. Sorkin reminded Jim of their original plan to allow 4 weeks to find out whether it was producing any benefit. However, the psychiatrist also told Jim that he respected his concern about side effects, and would therefore slow the rate of drug increase, which should allow his body to get more accustomed to the drug.

By the 4th week, when Jim had reached the full target dose, the side effects were minimal. On the other hand, he had noticed only a slight change in his target symptoms. He pointed out that the 4-week mark had been reached, and he was leaning toward stopping the medicine.

Dr. Sorkin privately felt that the patient had not yet spent enough time at the target dose to determine whether that dosage might eventually prove helpful. Still, he knew that he had, in effect, given his word to Jim that he would respect

---

Among their various actions, conventional anti-psychotic drugs (also known as *neuroleptic drugs*) reduce the activity of dopamine in certain brain areas. This helps reduce the symptoms of schizophrenia but may also produce Parkinsonian symptoms (for example, uncontrollable shaking), symptoms known to be caused by low dopamine activity.

Risperidone and other so-called *atypical* anti-psychotic drugs—developed only in recent years—do not operate on the dopamine activity of people with schizophrenia in the same way as the conventional anti-psychotic drugs, and so do not produce as many Parkinsonian symptoms.

the client's decision to stop the medication after 4 weeks. A critical juncture had been reached.

Dr. Sorkin: I know we had discussed using 4 weeks as the trial period for the medicine. However, it took a couple of weeks longer than I anticipated to iron out the side effects. I'm going to ask a favor, and request that you maintain this dose for another 2 weeks. Often it takes this long to determine a medicine's full potential once the maintenance dose is reached. I wish that the medicine had taken effect sooner, but I hate to abandon it at the point when we can finally find out if it's going to do any good.

Jim considered Dr. Sorkin's request. Reflecting their growing relationship, the patient said to the psychiatrist, "I can tell you're trying your best to help me. I guess I can give it another 2 weeks."

Jim maintained the target dose 2 more weeks, and by the 2nd week, he noted a significant decrease in the symptoms on his rating scale. Correspondingly, he stated that although he believed he still had some power in his breath, it now seemed weaker, so he didn't have to think about it all the time. He also noted that the angels had stopped talking, and other people seemed to be talking less about him. Thus, he was willing to continue taking the medicine.

During this same period, Dr. Sorkin had Jim enroll in the psychosocial skills training program at a nearby mental health center. In particular, Jim was assigned to the *medication self-management group* and the *symptom self-management group*. In these groups, each of which met twice a week over a 3-month period, he learned (a) the importance of continuous medication regimens (that is, that medicine does not work from dose to dose but as a result of cumulative doses), (b) how to work out medication problems with a psychiatrist, (c) how to identify the warning signs of relapse, (d) how to intervene early to prevent relapse once these signs appear, (e) how to cope with psychotic symptoms that continue despite medication, and (f) how to avoid alcohol and drugs, which exacerbate the symptoms of the illness.

Jim was quite responsible in attending these groups, which provided the first real structure in his life in years. More important, he learned skills there that were directly relevant to his situation. For example, he had always assumed that smoking marijuana was beneficial, both because it had a place in his delusions and because he believed that it lowered anxiety. He learned in his training that drugs and alcohol usually increase the symptoms of schizophrenia, and also further lower motivation and interest in normal activities.

Over the course of meetings of these groups, Jim became more responsible about taking anti-psychotic medication. He increasingly seemed to recognize its purpose and benefits; eventually, his family no longer needed to keep a careful watch over his taking of the medication. Jim also stopped using marijuana.

A growing number of therapists now act as *case managers* when treating people with schizophrenia. Not only do they treat the patients, but they also try to coordinate available community services, guide patients through the complexities of community services, and protect patients' legal rights (Chan et al., 2000; Pickett et al., 1999).

Phase 3: Stabilization After 3 months of taking risperidone, the young man's symptoms persisted, but at a lower level. His delusion about having a power in his breath remained, but he was much less focused on it. As a result, he had stopped looking through religious texts for a sign that he was the Messiah, although he continued reading the Bible for a large portion of the day. Perhaps most important, he had successfully avoided hospitalization during this period.

The next aim was to help him set some longer-term goals and teach him the skills to achieve them. Potential goals included: employment, financial security, adequate housing, friendships, dating, and family support. When discussing these matters with Dr. Sorkin, Jim identified two priorities: improving his relations with his family and developing an ability to function independently. It was agreed that the psychiatrist would conduct *behavioral family management* sessions with Jim and his family, and that Jim would attend a separate *individual behavioral skills training group*.

Behavioral Family Management

During the early sessions devoted to behavioral family management—a set of procedures designed to improve family functioning—Dr. Sorkin had Jim and his parents discuss the problems they had been having. The parents started to discuss the problem of their son's remaining in his room continually, and things soon broke down into a shouting match. Jim explained that the time he spent in his room was necessary for his Bible reading, but Roberto was soon arguing that the main problem was his son's laziness. Consuela interrupted, saying that Roberto had no idea what went on most of the time because he was usually away at work. Roberto in turn replied that he was able to see enough to figure out that his son had become a "good-for-nothing slob" and that his wife was not doing anything to discourage it. Jim listened to most of this conversation with his eyes turned upward in the "Oh, brother!" mode. Eventually, however, he joined the fray, saying that a major reason he stayed in his room was so he didn't have to listen to "this kind of crap." Roberto yelled that "this crap" was due to their utter frustration in dealing with their son's problems. In short order, all of the family members were yelling.

Dr. Sorkin could see that family interactions were characterized by high levels of *expressed emotion*. Research has shown that individuals whose families display high levels of expressed emotion—frequent critical, hostile, or intrusive remarks during family communication—are more likely to suffer a relapse of schizophrenia than those whose families have lower levels.

Dr. Sorkin: I can see that you all have been experiencing a lot of frustration in connection with Jim's problems, which has led to a lot of arguing. Having a family member with an illness such as Jim's is stressful for most families. It would benefit everyone if we could reduce the general tension and bad

---

According to research, interventions that also address the social and personal difficulties of people with schizophrenia significantly improve their recovery rates and reduce their relapse rates (McGuire, 2000; Penn & Mueser, 1996). Such approaches offer practical advice; teach problem solving, decision making, and social skills; make sure patients are taking their medications properly; and help them find work, financial assistance, and proper housing.

feeling. One thing we have learned through studies is that this kind of bad feeling in the family may interfere with recovery from schizophrenia. I would like to hold several sessions devoted to showing you how to reduce the arguing and bad feeling.

The family agreed, and the next 12 sessions with the psychiatrist were devoted to behavioral family management.

Several of the first of these sessions concentrated on *education:* simply informing the family of the basic facts of schizophrenia. Dr. Sorkin gave the entire family some written material on the disorder, including descriptions of the deficits produced by it. The psychiatrist also had the family view a videotape that explained that most people with schizophrenia have difficulty performing routine activities. On the tape, a series of examples were given of patients who had stopped being able to work, go to school, or attend to even the most basic needs, such as eating or taking showers on a regular basis.

Jim's mother and father acknowledged their surprise at the resemblance between Jim and the cases shown in the tape. They had often assumed, they said, that Jim's limitations were due either to his not trying hard enough or to a downright refusal to face up to his responsibilities. Now they were feeling regret at having criticized him constantly for his failures, both large and small. Dr. Sorkin cautioned the couple not to blame themselves unfairly for their reactions or for Jim's illness. He reminded them of something else shown on the videotape, that families typically react with a certain degree of upset over the limitations of the disturbed family member, finding it difficult to understand how someone who once seemed so capable and full of promise had fallen to such a simple level. The task now, he said, was to put their new knowledge to good use, beginning with the next phase of family therapy, which would be devoted to *communication skills training*.

Among the communication skills that Dr. Sorkin attempted to teach the family members were: acknowledging positive actions in others, making positive requests of others, and expressing negative feelings constructively.

The psychiatrist explained that in many troubled families the simple art of *praising one another for positive actions* is lost. Criticism of a person's shortcomings or mistakes becomes the sole form of providing feedback, while the person's positive efforts are simply taken for granted or ignored. Jim's parents, for example, found it easy to point it out whenever Jim failed to pick up his clothes, forgot to take out the trash, or spent an entire day holed up in his room. But they had given up praising any positive efforts by Jim, such as his mowing the lawn or sticking to his medications. Similarly, for his part, Jim had gotten into the habit of noting only what his parents failed to do for him, while ignoring their positive efforts.

Thus, Dr. Sorkin had the family members perform an exercise. Each of them had to identify something positive that one of the others had done in the past

Dr. Sorkin's family approach was based on an approach called *behavioral family management,* in which families are taught to cope, in a practical fashion, with the difficulties arising from having a family member with schizophrenia (Falloon & Liberman, 1983; Liberman et al., 1994). The approach includes psychoeducation, communication skills training, and training in problem-solving skills.

few days. Each member was then to practice stating his or her appreciation in Dr. Sorkin's presence. Jim, in particular, was coached to make better eye contact and to make his statement of appreciation with more vocal emphasis: "Mom, when you made my favorite meal the other night, I really felt good. Thanks a lot." To keep up with this task on a daily basis, the family had to record, over the next 2 weeks, all occasions when this skill was successfully practiced. With time, this kind of communication increased in frequency, and became more natural.

To learn another skill, how to *make positive requests,* the family was asked to cite examples of things that irked them, and how they had specifically communicated that annoyance to each other. Jim's mother volunteered that just that morning she had gotten fed up with the pile of laundry in Jim's room. When asked what she had told her son, she replied that she had said: "The laundry in your room is a disgusting mess. You simply must start shaping up." Dr. Sorkin then used this example to explain to the family how to rephrase concerns or requests in *positive and specific* terms rather than negative and global terms. "Positive" statements indicate what the person *should do* under the circumstances, as opposed to what the person should not do or should stop doing. "Specific" statements clarify what should be done; they are not just some vague demand for better performance. Consuela was asked to restate her concern in line with these guidelines. Her new statement was: "Jim, please bring the laundry from your room down to the basement at the end of the week." Again, the family members were told to record each successful practice of this skill over the next few weeks.

Similar training was carried out for *expressing negative feelings constructively,* that is, effectively letting persons know how their actions upset you. Often, family members neglect this piece of the communication process, keeping feelings of dissatisfaction or disappointment to themselves and then moving directly to criticism and insults. Expressing a feeling is a way of telling a person that there is a problem, but without making incorrect assumptions or accusations. Thus, for example, Jim's father was guided to say to his son, "When you look away while I'm talking, it makes me feel that you don't care what I'm saying," rather than declaring, "You don't care about anything you're told."

Over the course of 6 sessions, the family members became more able to use the new communication skills, and the skills became a more natural part of their interactions.

Now the family was in a position to learn the final set of skills in behavioral family management: *problem solving.* To introduce these skills, Dr. Sorkin had Jim and his parents choose a concrete problem to solve. They decided to work on the problem of Jim's staying in his room continually. He acknowledged that it was not just his religious concerns that kept him there all day; he was also trying to avoid his parents' frequent arguments. If he left his room, he would usually get drawn into their quarrels. His parents agreed that there were many arguments in

Studies find that parents of people with schizophrenia often display more conflict, have greater communication difficulties, and are more critical and overinvolved with their children than other parents (Miklowitz et al., 1995). It may be that schizophrenia greatly disrupts family life and helps produce such family patterns.

According to some studies, family therapy—particularly when combined with drug therapy—helps reduce tensions within the families of people with schizophrenia and so helps relapse rates go down (Baucom et al., 1998; Cameron et al., 1999).

the home, but they believed that Jim's withdrawn behavior was the cause. If he could bring his activities more into line with those of the household in general, they felt that some of the arguing would be reduced.

Dr. Sorkin explained the principles of problem solving. All members would have a few minutes to reflect on solutions to the problem; then they would propose their specific ideas, with each member withholding judgment on any stated idea until all alternatives had been listed. Consuela suggested that Jim come down for meals three times a day. Roberto had the same suggestion, but also added that Jim might be allowed to leave the table if he felt anxious or uncomfortable. Jim proposed that he join the family for a dinner out once a week—he felt that his parents would be less likely to argue in public—and that he have some of his new friends (from his self-management groups at the mental health center) over for dinner on another night of the week. Several other possibilities were spun, and then the family members discussed the advantages and disadvantages of each alternative. Dr. Sorkin urged them to reach a solution by consensus. It was eventually decided that Jim would join the family every night for dinner, provided that the family would eat out on 1 night a week, and that Jim would have a friend come to the house for dinner on another night.

The family put this plan in action and it did eventually reduce the usual arguments about Jim's participation in household activities. Other sessions were devoted to similar problem-solving exercises following the same format. With time, the family members developed some skill at finding solutions to problems on their own.

Individual Behavioral Skills Training

As some of the stress in Jim's life became relieved through medication and behavioral family management, he developed a growing desire to function independently, inspired in part by the example of other patients he had met in his self-management classes. One friend there, David, had improved to the point where he got a paying job as a clerical assistant at a small social services agency called Helping Hands, which housed the homeless. Jim visited David at his job and was impressed to see that he had his own desk and was given respect and responsibility. Jim thought about developing his own work skills, with the hope that he could ultimately live independently. He raised this hope with Dr. Sorkin, who encouraged him and had him enroll in the mental health center's training group on *personal effectiveness for successful living.*

This group was set up along the same lines as the medication- and symptom-management groups that Jim had already attended, but was geared toward individual problems. Led by a social worker, the group used behavioral techniques, such as modeling, role-playing, corrective feedback, and behavioral

> "I feel cheated by having this illness."
> —Individual with schizophrenia, 1996

practice exercises, to train members in various skills needed for managing in the world.

After a few sessions, Jim told Ms. Simpson, the social worker, and other group members that his immediate goal was to go on interviews for jobs advertised in newspapers, something he had never done before and had no idea how to approach. The group broke the process down into separate skills: (a) scanning the newspaper for appropriate ads, (b) telephoning for further information and requesting an interview, (c) arriving at the appropriate time and place, and (d) being interviewed. First, the group focused on telephoning for an interview. One member, who had a fair amount of interview experience, played the prospective employer, while Jim acted out his own role as applicant. The pair went over the process repeatedly, while Ms. Simpson and group members gave Jim corrective feedback on his telephone conversation.

Jim's homework assignment was to make five telephone calls in response to ads and to report the results at the next group meeting. The point of the homework exercise was not for him to obtain actual interviews, just to practice his telephone behavior. In fact, to reduce pressure, it was understood that he would not be going on any interviews that he actually obtained. He would simply cancel them for now.

At the next session, Jim was excited to report that he had made the five phone calls. On three of them, he was told that the positions had been filled. On two others he was told he could come down and fill out an application. He felt he had gotten much more comfortable with the process by the fifth call, and he decided to make five calls each week.

During this time, Dr. Sorkin had been continuing to work with Jim in individual therapy to find a medication level that would make a further dent in the young man's belief that he had power over others. Although Jim had certainly improved on risperidone, he felt that his breath still had some power to affect people. Dr. Sorkin tried increases and then decreases in the level of risperidone and added and subtracted some additional drugs as well. Perhaps it was the medication changes or perhaps it was the impact of the personal effectiveness group, or perhaps it was both. But at one point, psychiatrist and patient hit on a medication combination that made a large difference. Jim began to notice a significant drop in the intensity and frequency of his main symptom. He told Dr. Sorkin that the medicine seemed to have "neutralized" his capacity to influence other people through his breath. The patient also noticed that other people had stopped talking about him when he went out in public.

Stabilization Phase This change produced a sense of confidence and optimism that Jim had not felt in years. For the first time, he seriously considered seeking paid employment. He discussed this ambition with the members of his

One study of people with schizophrenia revealed that 39% of them were receiving too low a dosage of their anti-psychotic drugs, 32% too high a dosage, and only 29% an appropriate dosage (PORT, 1998).

group, and eventually decided to try a volunteer position as a stepping stone. He chose to pursue a lead given to him by David, his friend who worked at Helping Hands. David told him about another agency that delivered hot meals to the homebound elderly. Despite all his years of disability, Jim was able to drive and had in fact maintained his driver's license in good standing.

Once again, the various components of obtaining the job—the initial call, the interview, the first day on the job—were practiced in the group, with group members playing the role of phone screener, interviewer, and fellow employees.

Jim made the initial call and was accepted for an interview. At the interview itself, he was rather well-prepared for the various questions and asked some good questions himself. The interviewer was impressed with his sincerity and motivation, and told him that they would be glad to accept him on a trial basis as a volunteer assistant to one of the paid drivers. He could begin the following Monday, working 3 half days a week.

The following Monday, at noon, Jim arrived at the agency to meet the driver for his assigned route. He was extremely nervous at first, but once he began working and saw how readily he took to the job, his confidence rose. Over the course of the next several weeks, he worked hard and, eventually, was offered a job as a paid driver.

Epilogue

Over the following years, Jim continued both to take medications and to attend his group on a weekly basis. It would not be accurate to say that he made it all the way back to a fully functioning and productive lifestyle. In fact, he had several periods in which his notion of having power over others and his belief that others were talking about him returned to some degree. On the other hand, those ideas never again took over his life as they had in the past, and they were always temporary: Adjustments in his medications were able to eliminate the ideas within days or, at most, weeks.

Similarly, Jim was not able to make it out of his parents' house and into his own apartment. Actually, he did try moving out once, but found life on his own too stressful. He had great difficulty keeping up with making his own meals, cleaning his clothes, and keeping things straight, and so he eventually concluded that he did indeed need the help of his parents. Furthermore, his job, while a huge improvement over years of unemployment, did not represent the level of work or responsibility that he had seemed destined for when he was young. No, he hadn't made it all the way back, but, on the other hand, a decade of repeated hospitalizations, full-blown delusions, isolation, and confusion had apparently come to an end. He was now leading a much more normal life—and for that Jim and his parents were grateful.

Conventional antipsychotic drugs reduce or even eliminate the symptoms of schizophrenia in 65% of cases. Atypical antipsychotic drugs reduce or eliminate symptoms in 85% of cases (Awad & Voruganti, 1999; Lieberman, 1998).

CASE **13**

Borderline Personality Disorder

Table 13-1

DSM-IV Checklist

Borderline Personality Disorder

A pervasive pattern of instability of interpersonal relationships, self-image, and affects, and marked impulsivity beginning by early adulthood and present in a variety of contexts, as indicated by at least five of the following:

1. Frantic efforts to avoid real or imagined abandonment.

2. A pattern of unstable and intense interpersonal relationships characterized by alternating between extremes of idealization and devaluation.

3. Identity disturbance: markedly and persistently unstable self-image or sense of self.

4. Impulsivity in at least two areas that are potentially self-damaging (for example, spending, sex, substance abuse, reckless driving, binge eating).

5. Recurrent suicidal behavior, gestures, or threats, or self-mutilating behavior.

6. Affective instability due to marked mood reactions.

7. Chronic feelings of emptiness.

8. Inappropriate, intense anger or difficulty controlling anger.

9. Transient, stress-related paranoid ideas or severe dissociative symptoms.

Based on APA, 1994, 2000.

Karen, a 36-year-old single, unemployed woman, was admitted to the West Raymond Medical Center after deliberately taking an overdose of sedatives combined with alcohol. She made this suicide attempt when the man she had been dating for 3 months told her he didn't want to see her any more. Karen lost consciousness from the overdose, and spent the next 3 days in West Raymond's intensive care unit.

Because doctors at the hospital were reluctant to discharge her until they were certain that she would receive follow-up counseling, Karen called her psychotherapist and asked him to tell the hospital staff that she was indeed in counseling. The therapist, however, did not respond as Karen expected. He pointed out that this was her third suicide attempt in the past 2 years and, as a result, he was not prepared to vouch for anything. In fact, the therapist did not think that he should continue treating Karen. He described her suicide attempts as "manipulation," and said that she was using the attempts and other forms of "self-harm" to draw attention to herself and to avoid confronting her underlying disturbance.

Karen had been giving herself minor injuries several times a week for years. She inflicted the injuries in a slow, deliberate fashion, typically when alone and feeling rejected or abandoned. She would sit down with a razor blade in hand and watch closely as she dragged the blade across the flesh of her arm or leg. The cuts were relatively superficial, but deep enough to draw a thin line of blood that she observed with fascination as the droplets trickled down. For a brief moment, she felt reassured of her own existence. The pain was physical, real, and deserved—quite unlike the feelings of emptiness or depression she tended to experience much of the time.

Karen's efforts to cut herself, or to use drugs and alcohol to deaden emotional pain, varied according to her relationships with men. When she had a steady boyfriend, she generally felt more positive, as though life had meaning and focus. On the other hand, the slightest hint of problems in the relationship could trigger deep emotional distress.

> A personality disorder is a very rigid pattern of inner experience and outer behavior that differs from the expectations of one's culture and leads to dysfunctioning.

Karen: A Typical Relationship

Karen's relationship with Gary, a 32-year-old construction worker, was in many ways typical. They met in a bar and for the next 2 weeks were together almost every night in a torrid love affair. Karen felt happy and on top of the world; after only a week, she started to fantasize about their life together, even to the point of naming their children. She stopped drinking alone in the evenings, or doing any of the cutting that accompanied her darker moods.

As time passed, Karen and Gary stopped seeing each other every day, but her focus on him was still complete. While at work, she would call her answering machine several times an hour to see if he had left any messages. If she was home in the evening and she hadn't heard from him, she would frantically try to locate and call him, even if he had told her earlier in the week that he couldn't come over.

With time, Karen grew more and more sensitive to signs that Gary might be pulling away. She would keep asking him about his feelings for her, and she became irritated if he seemed evasive. At first, he told her he "liked her a lot"; but after a while he said he didn't understand why they had to talk about their "relationship" and their "feelings" all the time. He began calling her less and less, and Karen started feeling rejected.

On nights when she had no contact with Gary, she would sit alone in a darkened room just cradling the telephone in her lap. Sometimes she would dial his number over and over, hanging up as the answering machine clicked on, hoping that he might just be coming in the door and would pick up the phone. When she did reach him, Gary sometimes would sound distant and strained. When Karen would try to pin him down as to when they could get together, he would just reply, "I'll call you." And if Gary did call, he rarely asked her to do anything special anymore. His interest in seeing her seemed physical at best.

One night, Karen and Gary went to the movies together and, just as they were taking their seats, he said he wanted to get some popcorn. Karen immediately became suspicious, as she recalled seeing a cute-looking young woman working at the concession stand. Karen demanded that Gary stay with her. He left his seat anyway, explaining that he would be right back. Karen then reached out, grabbed his arm, and yanked him back in his seat with surprising force. Gary was momentarily shaken but, after collecting himself, he rose again and stalked out of the theater. Karen followed him onto the sidewalk; by the time she reached the curb, he was already across the street and moving briskly. She just stood on the curb screaming, "Come back, you bastard!" and finally, "I hate you!"

The woman returned home feeling miserable. She tried to call Gary but there was no answer. She got out a razor blade and did some of her first cutting in weeks, making two superficial cuts on her left thigh. She tried Gary's number one more time, but still no one picked up.

When Karen finally reached Gary the following evening, she tried apologizing, but he told her he didn't want to see her any more. She pleaded with him, declaring that she loved him and couldn't live without him. She promised to be more considerate of his need for "space." Gary replied that he just didn't think it was working out and that they should part company as friends. At this, Karen became furious and slammed down the phone. She found a bottle of wine to ease her misery, but even after drinking it all, she still couldn't bear the pain of separation. It was then that she decided to end it all. She went to her night table, reached for a bottle of sedatives, looked at them for a few seconds, and then swallowed about 30 pills.

When Karen's roommate, Cecily, came home, she found Karen unconscious on the floor of her bedroom. Cecily phoned for an ambulance and Karen was rushed to the emergency room where her stomach was pumped.

In some ways, Karen's stormy affair with Gary had actually been more positive than many of her relationships. Gary, for example, did not take advantage of her, whereas some of her past boyfriends were happy to maintain a sexual relationship long after losing interest in her. Several even abused her physically. She was so desperate for the sense of worth she received from being in a relationship—any relationship—that she would put up with a great deal. When a relationship did end, it was almost always at the man's instigation, and Karen always felt a profound sense of emptiness, abandonment, and despair.

Unrewarding though her relationships were, she considered almost all of them preferable to being alone. When not in a relationship, she practically felt as if she

Approximately 70% of people with borderline personality disorder attempt suicide at least once; about 6 to 9% actually commit suicide (Davis et al., 1999; Zisook et al., 1994).

didn't exist. She never really developed any personal interests or work ambitions, and seemed to go from low-level job to low-level job.

A Roommate's Perspective: "Two Years of Hell"

After finding Karen near death and finally getting her to the hospital, her roommate was shaken and drained. At first, she thought that she would feel better within a few days, but a week later she took stock and realized that she was feeling, if anything, worse. Cecily's family persuaded her to make an appointment with a counselor to discuss the ordeal and her reactions. During her session, the shaken woman declared that finding Karen on the bedroom floor was, in fact, the culmination of "2 years of hell."

Cecily explained to her therapist that she had met Karen two years earlier, after placing an ad in the newspaper for a new roommate. At the time, Karen did not really confide in Cecily about her emotional problems. She did say that she was "in therapy" and "I'm really crazy, totally neurotic." However, since Cecily herself had been in therapy, she thought little of it, and even believed that their common neurotic tendencies might be a bonding issue. As it turned out, the 2 years that followed were far from a bonding experience.

As Cecily told the therapist:

> At first Karen was a lot of fun, but then she would become really depressed off and on, and ... well, weird. For the first month, I thought that we were having fun living together, discovering that we liked a lot of the same movies and music and things. Then one night, about 2 months after she moved in, I was getting ready to go out with a friend, and Karen demanded to know where I was going. I told her I was going out. That wasn't good enough for her. Where was I going? Who was I seeing? What was I doing?
>
> Then she tried to make me feel guilty for going. "Fine, just leave," she pouted. She complained that we were no longer spending any time together, which was ridiculous because we had just spent a whole day at an art museum together. When I pointed that out to her, she got hysterical, yelling at me, telling me that I only cared about myself and that I was leaving her with nothing to do. By then, I was mad, and I told her in no uncertain terms that I did not plan to spend every waking moment of my life with her just because we were roommates. I stormed out.
>
> When I came home that night, it was really scary. There was a little blood on the floor, and it made a trail that led to her bedroom door. When I banged on the door to see if she was all right, she said that she'd accidentally cut herself making a sandwich and everything was fine. I wasn't sure I believed her, but I preferred to go along with that, rather than consider the possibility that she might be seriously disturbed.
>
> After that evening, she was distant from me for awhile. She seemed very angry, and I must admit that I was really put off. The last thing I needed was to be living

About 2% of the general population are thought to suffer from borderline personality disorder.

with someone who wanted all my attention, who was so high-maintenance. I wasn't so much scared as annoyed. Dealing with her was starting to take a lot out of me. Eventually, she got over being angry with me and went back to her old ways: constantly draining my attention and making me feel guilty about not spending more time with her. No matter how much time I did give her, it was never enough.

Then she started dating this guy, Eric, and I thought that things were getting better. I didn't know much about him, but Karen was spending almost no time at home and that was just fine with me. When I did see her, she would gush about how incredibly happy she was—I mean, this was just weeks after she met him—how deep their relationship was and how perfect everything was. She was sure he was "the one." Of course, by now I knew how unbalanced she was and I suspected she was probably being crazy like always, but I didn't want to look a gift horse in the mouth. She was no longer my problem for the moment.

I should have seen what was coming next but, like an idiot, I didn't. Eric left her, and she was totally my problem again. She stayed home and cried for days at a time. She made me take care of her, telling me she was too depressed to do anything for herself. She even fantasized about the violent things she would do to Eric when she felt up to it, and cursed a blue streak while talking about him. And that's pretty much how it's been ever since.

After Eric, there was Ahmad, then James, then Stefán. Always the same story, always the same ending. And always with me in the middle—having to smile while she gushed endlessly about the latest relationship, or having to pick up the pieces when the relationship would end. But nothing prepared me for the other night, seeing her lying there after her breakup with Gary.

Karen: The Early Years

Karen grew up in a family that seemed stable and loving on the outside. Her father was a prominent local businessman who was also the lay minister of a church. Her mother was a homemaker. Karen also had two older brothers who were considered model students.

In private, however, the family was violent and abusive. Even as a toddler, Karen was frequently beaten with a belt by both parents. Some of the beatings were inspired by misbehavior. Others were carried out on general principle, to "keep the devil out of her," in her father's words.

Her parents were extremely unpredictable. Her father might hold her on his lap and tell her she was a "darling girl" and how much he loved her, but minutes later he would once again be "beating the devil out of her." Nor was the abuse Karen suffered at the hands of her family limited to beatings or words. Beginning at about age 6, her father began abusing her sexually, by fondling her genitals and engaging in oral–genital contact. This occurred about a dozen times and continued until Karen reached the age of 12. After molesting her, her father would call

> Studies have often found instances of great trauma in the early lives of people who develop borderline personality disorder (Atlas, 1995; Spoont, 1996).

her a "cheap whore" who was "going to hell." Then he would beat her severely and make her kneel in prayer to confess her "sins."

Starting at age 6, she was also sexually abused on a weekly basis by her oldest brother, John, who was 13 years old and favored by her parents. This abuse involved both oral–genital contact and intercourse. When she was 9 years old, two of John's friends also participated in the abuse. When the young victim told her mother what was happening, the woman responded by beating her daughter for using "sexual language" and for being "seduced by the devil."

Even after John left for college, he would continue to abuse Karen during visits back home. Finally, when she was 16 years old, she told her other brother, Ted—who was 18 years old at the time and a senior in high school—what was happening. Ted, who had been Karen's only source of comfort throughout her childhood, confronted John and said he would kill him if he ever touched their sister again. This put an end to the abuse.

Two years later, on the day Karen graduated from high school, she left her family and moved to a rooming house in the next county. She found work as a waitress in a local diner, started dating a man whom she met there, and married him just a few weeks later. Her new husband, George, a car salesman who was 15 years older than she, began dominating Karen in short order. In many respects, their life together was a replay of Karen's upbringing.

George generally suspected, without basis, that Karen was flirting with other men and carrying on affairs behind his back. He made her quit her waitressing job and kept her a prisoner in their home. He demanded that his wife leave the house only with him or to do necessary food shopping; he also forbade her to buy any new clothes. On one occasion, Karen visited her former coworkers at the diner, despite George's "house rules." When word got back to her husband, he confronted her with her "deceitfulness" and beat her when she defended her visit.

When not in a jealous mood, George could be very nice to Karen. Often, he would take her out to dinner or dancing, tell her she was "the prettiest girl in town," and apologize for any unkindnesses. He would describe his hopes of making "a pile of money" someday and his desire to then treat Karen "like a queen." Such affection was typically short-lived, however. The next day he might very well return home from work drunk and beat her for cheating on him.

Karen's family background made it extremely difficult for her to accurately assess her life with George. Of course, she hated the beatings, but she could not judge whether they were undeserved or whether she might be able to find better treatment elsewhere. As it happened, she never had to confront the question of leaving George, because he was killed in a car accident 3 years into their marriage.

With George's death, Karen went through a period of utter confusion, in which feelings of both devastation and relief rose to the surface. She was now free of his cruelty, but Karen had nevertheless become completely dependent on him. She felt lost and went into a clinical depression, leading to a psychiatric hospitalization.

Karen underwent at least 10 more psychiatric hospitalizations over the next 15 years. She received a wide range of diagnoses during this period, and dozens of different drugs were prescribed for her without much benefit. When not hospitalized, she would support herself with waitressing or secretarial positions. Work was of little importance to her, however. It was relationships with men that filled her thoughts or her dreams, as she moved from one intense and unrealistic attachment to another.

Karen feared *abandonment* more than anything else in life. She tried to kill herself three times during this period, and indeed, all three of the attempts were direct responses to being jilted by men to whom she had formed passionate attachments.

During those 15 years, in addition to her hospitalizations, she saw at least nine different psychotherapists—psychiatrists, psychologists, and social workers—on an outpatient basis. She even had a sexual relationship with one of her male therapists, who later lost his license after two other women filed charges against him for sexual misconduct.

> Close to 75% of the people who receive a diagnosis of borderline personality disorder are women (APA, 2000; Grilo et al., 1996).

Karen in Treatment: "The Break of a Lifetime"

After Karen's third suicide attempt and her therapist's refusal to continue working with her, the hospital discharged the troubled woman to the local community mental health system, where she received once-a-month medication management and weekly group therapy. After awhile, she concluded that her treatment there was only "maintaining [her] misery"; and she was about to stop when, without warning, her life took a very positive turn. In what she would later describe as "the break of a lifetime," a staff member at the mental health center recognized Karen's broad pattern for what it was, and referred her to Dr. Dierdra Banks, a psychologist specializing in *dialectical behavior therapy*.

During a lengthy initial session, in which Karen described her problems and history, Dr. Banks grew confident that the woman's condition met the DSM-IV criteria for a diagnosis of *borderline personality disorder*. Karen repeatedly engaged in frantic efforts to avoid abandonment; she exhibited a pattern of unstable and intense interpersonal relationships; she had a markedly unstable self-image, or sense of herself; she engaged in recurrent suicidal behavior and self-mutilation; her moods were unstable; she had chronic feelings of emptiness; and she frequently displayed inappropriate anger.

For years, borderline personality disorder seemed almost untreatable, as various approaches brought little or no change to the emotional turmoil and self-destructive lifestyles of sufferers. However, by the early 1990s, an increasing

Research indicates that individuals with borderline personality disorder often improve markedly during treatment with dialectical behavior therapy (Linehan et al., 1991, 1993).

number of therapists were applying dialectical behavior therapy (DBT) in cases of borderline personality disorder. Dr. Banks was one such therapist.

Karen in Treatment: Dialectical Behavior Therapy

Like other practitioners of DBT, Dr. Banks believed that people with borderline personality disorder suffer primarily from *emotional dysregulation,* a reduced capacity to regulate their emotions, particularly negative emotions such as sadness, anger, and anxiety. Because of a *biological vulnerability,* the individuals have a high sensitivity to emotional stimuli, an intense response to such stimuli, and a slow rate of recovery from their emotional arousal. And because of a *skills deficit,* the individuals cannot hold back inappropriate behaviors or consider constructive behaviors when they experience strong emotions. In short, people with borderline personality disorder have a dual handicap. Not only are their emotions stronger than the average person's, their skills for managing emotion are deficient. The result is a lifelong pattern of emotional and behavioral instability.

According to dialectical behavior theory, the failure to acquire adequate skills for managing emotions arises from an *invalidating environment* during childhood. In such an environment, a child's thoughts and feelings are not taken seriously or supported. One of the most harmful kinds of invalidating environments is one in which a child is repeatedly victimized. Children who grow up in this situation may learn to not trust their own feelings or thoughts. In addition, they may develop little sense of who they are. They must depend on other people for direction, support, and meaning.

Like other dialectical behavior therapists, Dr. Banks would typically address such problems in stages throughout treatment. During a pretreatment stage, she would explain the principles of DBT and ask clients with borderline personality disorder to commit themselves to the treatment program for a minimum period of time. Then she would move on to three treatment stages. In the first stage, she would try to address issues fundamental to survival and functioning, such as decreasing suicidal behaviors, decreasing therapy-interfering behaviors, decreasing behaviors that were interfering with the quality of a client's life, and increasing behavioral skills. In the second stage, the psychologist would work to reduce distress due to past trauma, such as sexual abuse. And in the final stage, she would address longer-term issues, such as increasing self-respect and achieving career, social, and interpersonal goals.

The theory and techniques followed by Dr. Banks and other dialectical behavior therapists are based largely on the work of Marsha Linehan (1993).

Also, like other dialectical behavior therapists, Dr. Banks would typically conduct treatment on two fronts. She would have clients participate in *behavioral skills training groups,* where they would develop needed behavioral skills. At the same time, she would conduct *individual psychotherapy sessions* with her clients, focusing on what was happening at the moment. The goal of individual therapy was to soothe clients, help them through crises, and guide them in the application of their new behavioral skills. The relationship between client and therapist was a key part of treatment; Dr. Banks would try mightily to create a *validating environment* that had been, according to the DBT model, missing in the client's past.

In addition, Dr. Banks would encourage clients with borderline personality disorder to make telephone contacts between visits. She considered such contacts opportunities for her to provide immediate help in a crisis; to guide clients in problem solving at the time the problem arose; and to deal with any strong, negative emotions that the clients might develop about therapy between sessions. The active use of telephone consultations in DBT differs from most other approaches in treating this disorder. In fact, other approaches typically view between-session calls from borderline clients as attention-seeking, manipulative, or maladaptive, and most therapists discourage such efforts.

Pretreatment Stage Dr. Banks's primary goal during the pretreatment sessions was to obtain a commitment from Karen to stay with therapy for a minimum period of time. She considered such a commitment essential in cases of borderline personality disorder, in light of most such clients' disappointing past experiences in therapy and their explosive reactions, which could lead to impulsive, premature terminations of therapy.

At the same time, Dr. Banks recognized that, prior to obtaining any sort of commitment, it was important first to discuss Karen's past fully and gain a proper appreciation of her experiences, both in therapy and out. Only then could Karen feel that the therapist's recommendations were well considered. Accordingly, Dr. Banks spent two full sessions with Karen before asking for a commitment to treatment. During these sessions, she empathized with how much fear and mistrust of the treatment process Karen must have developed due to her unsuccessful past therapies. She also expressed empathy for Karen's own attempts to handle her feelings, through the use of self-harm, dependent relationships, and, occasionally, alcohol. Finally, the psychologist expressed admiration for Karen's persistence in trying to improve her situation, despite a long history of invalidation and abuse.

The client expressed surprise at the psychologist's recognition of her strengths, noting that more typically therapists would shake their heads over how "messed up" she was. Dr. Banks replied that she recognized Karen indeed had problems, but that she also recognized Karen was probably coping with them in the best way she knew how.

To help her client decide whether to commit herself to this therapy, the psychologist described the principles and techniques of DBT. To begin, she explained that Karen's problems fit a pattern known as borderline personality disorder, a term that Karen said she recognized from some of her previous treatments. The therapist explained that the term "borderline" was unfortunate, being a holdover from days when clinicians mistakenly thought that people with the condition were

The term *dialectical* is meant to suggest that the goals and methods in dialectical behavior therapy often involve achieving a balance between two opposing forces, especially a balance between self-acceptance and making changes for the better.

"on the border" between neurosis and schizophrenia. She said that current thinking on this disorder was that it primarily involved difficulty in managing strong emotional feelings; many of the behavior problems—self-harm, impulsive behavior, interpersonal difficulties—were now seen as stemming from the individual's understandable need to cope with these feelings. The treatment, Dr. Banks explained, would involve learning more effective ways of coping with emotions. She then described the various stages of treatment and the two formats of treatment: group behavioral skills training and individual psychotherapy.

Karen said she was impressed with the organization of the treatment approach. In all her previous therapies, a systematic plan had never been laid out for her. She said the approach made sense to her, but she was wary of her ability to succeed. Dr. Banks expressed sympathy for her wariness, and also tried to shift some of the burden of success, explaining that success was dependent not only on Karen's efforts but on the psychologist's ability to apply the treatment appropriately. Moreover, she suggested that Karen define treatment success by how well she was sticking to the treatment plan, and let the symptom improvements take care of themselves.

The psychologist and Karen agreed to work together for at least 6 months. Dr. Banks estimated that the total treatment time might be 2 years.

First-Stage Treatment: Addressing Issues of Survival and Basic Functioning
In the first stage of treatment, Dr. Banks focused on issues critical to survival and functioning: increasing behavioral skills, decreasing suicidal behaviors, decreasing behaviors that interfered with therapy, and decreasing behaviors that reduced the quality of one's life.

> Although termed *behavioral,* the techniques of dialectical behavior therapy also draw from such sources as psychodynamic therapy, meditation practices, Zen Buddhism, and feminism.

Increasing behavioral skills (group training) Karen began attending a weekly DBT behavioral skills training group, designed to teach behavioral skills in a systematic fashion, using lecture material, group practice exercises, and homework assignments. Five specific skill areas were covered: (a) mindfulness skills, (b) interpersonal effectiveness skills, (c) emotion regulation skills, (d) distress tolerance skills, and (e) self-management skills.

Mindfulness skills refer to the ability to step back from and look at one's emotions, while at the same time not being judgmental about them. *Interpersonal effectiveness skills* involve being able to make and decline requests, while at the same time maintaining self-respect and sound interpersonal relationships. Training in these skills resembles the social skills or assertiveness training techniques used with other patients who have social skills deficits. *Emotion regulation skills* involve being aware of intense and inappropriate emotional arousal, and behaving rationally in spite of inappropriate arousal. *Distress tolerance skills* refer to the ability to cope with negative emotional arousal, by employing such techniques as distracting oneself during a crisis, soothing oneself, or considering various responses. Finally, clients in the group were taught *self-management skills,* including how to set and achieve realistic goals.

At first, Karen was reluctant to participate in the behavioral skills training group, asking why she couldn't just see Dr. Banks for the individual sessions and forget about the "group thing." The psychologist, however, explained the importance of learning the skills; she also pointed out that if the individual sessions were spent entirely on skills training, there would be no time to deal with Karen's day-to-day concerns. The client agreed to attend as part of her commitment, and, after a few weeks, began to feel that the group training was worthwhile. In addition to gaining mastery in certain skill areas, she came to feel comfort in the emotional support supplied by the group, and a sense of gratification in providing support to others. She continued to attend the group for close to a year.

Decreasing suicidal behaviors   In the first individual therapy session, Dr. Banks explained that she would like to focus on Karen's tendency to harm herself. She began by having the client keep a daily diary detailing her level of suicidal thinking, her misery level, her self-harm urges, her self-harm actions, what she did to cope with any self-harm urges, and her use of new skills.

At the second session, Karen and the psychologist reviewed the diary of the past week. The records revealed that the client was cutting her upper arms or inner thighs with a razor blade approximately five times a week. The injuries, which she bandaged herself, were visible to others only if she wore shorts or a tank top.

Unlike Karen's previous therapists, Dr. Banks was careful not to criticize her for creating these injuries, label them as "manipulation," or threaten to stop treatment if the behavior continued. Instead, she responded to each instance with a behavioral analysis, trying to get Karen to see how the cutting was serving a function. In one case during the week, a man whom Karen had met at a party took her phone number, then failed to call her the next day as promised. Karen's misery level rose as the hours passed without a phone call, and she eventually made two superficial cuts on her upper thigh, which briefly reduced her emotional pain. At that point in time, Karen in fact called Dr. Banks to tell her what she had done and to receive support.

During the next session, when reviewing the incident and Karen's reactions, the psychologist validated the woman's sense of disappointment, but also recommended that she start coping differently with her urges to cut. Dr. Banks explained that she wanted Karen to begin managing her emotions with a different device, by calling the therapist and discussing her feelings *prior* to doing any cutting. In fact, they put a "24-hour rule" into effect: Karen would be prohibited from calling the therapist for at least 24 hours following any cutting. The rationale was two-fold. First, phone calls to the therapist immediately after cutting have no

Because people with borderline personality disorder are more emotional than analytic, dialectical behavior therapists teach clients how to make a *behavioral analysis* of problems. The therapists help them to see that problems— emotional, behavioral, or interpersonal—are usually just one element in a chain of events, a larger context.

problem-solving value, because cutting has already taken place by then. Second, not being able to speak with Dr. Banks until 24 hours after cutting behavior would create an incentive to use the new problem-solving procedure of calling the therapist beforehand.

On the night following this session, at about 3:00 a.m., Karen called Dr. Banks at home. Breathing heavily and almost sobbing, the client said that she had not yet cut herself, but desperately wanted to do so. She was afraid, on the one hand, that the therapist would reject her if she carried out the cutting and, on the other, that Dr. Banks would be angered by her calling so late at night.

> According to dialectical behavior theorists, the self-mutilation of people with borderline personality disorder serves to produce physical pain that competes with—and, hence, partially reduces—the much more painful experience of negative emotions. Other impulsive behaviors, such as gambling, substance abuse, irresponsible spending, reckless driving, binge eating, or unsafe sex, may similarly help reduce negative emotions.

Though desperately tired, Dr. Banks made it clear to Karen that it was "absolutely wonderful" that she had taken this step, and was glad she had taken the risk of calling rather than doing the cutting. These words alone had a very calming effect on the client. The psychologist reminded Karen of some of the distraction, self-soothing, and distress tolerance strategies she had learned at the behavioral skills-training group. The client, in turn, decided to make herself a cup of hot cocoa, take a warm bath, and read her favorite magazine.

Karen made a similar call two days later, and the day after that. In both cases, Dr. Banks guided her to use distress tolerance strategies, and Karen was able to resist the urge to cut herself.

At the next session, her diary revealed no instances of self-harm for the week. Dr. Banks devoted most of the session to analyzing this achievement, noting how Karen had successfully replaced cutting with more constructive coping strategies. Still, Karen's misery level had remained high during the week: a "10" on most days.

Over the next 3 months, she called the therapist an average of three times a week and succeeded in avoiding all self-harm during this period. Correspondingly, her misery level began to improve. Then she started dating a man to whom she was strongly attracted. On the second date, they slept together. At her therapy session the next day, Karen announced that she had found the perfect man and felt certain she was in love. She was brimming with enthusiasm—more than Dr. Banks had ever seen in her. The psychologist supported her feelings, noting how wonderful it was to be in love.

Unfortunately, the man didn't share Karen's enthusiasm and failed to call the following evening as promised. When Karen finally reached him and suggested they make plans for the weekend, he said he really didn't feel like "getting involved." Karen was devastated and, over the next several days, cut herself multiple times before calling Dr. Banks. When she did call to tell the therapist what had ·happened, she felt certain that Dr. Banks would reject her for having "regressed." She begged her not to end the treatment.

Dr. Banks: Why would I want to end treatment?

Karen: I started cutting again, and I didn't even try to call you to get help.

Dr. Banks: What kept you from calling?

Karen:	I just felt so ashamed.
Dr. Banks:	But you're calling now, and that's great. I understand your reluctance to call. It's perfectly natural. No one likes to bring bad news. But try not to think of this as such bad news. You were under a lot of stress for the first time since our therapy began; it's understandable that you might not be able to manage it perfectly. But look at what you did do. You did stop the cutting eventually, and you did call me. I think it's best to look at this as a temporary slip, as opposed to a complete relapse. I think you'll find that you can get back on track again and avoid the cutting once the distress from this experience subsides.
Karen:	I think I can stop cutting now. Just hearing you tell me that it was natural to get upset helps. But I feel so miserable.
Dr. Banks:	I know. Let's discuss some concrete things you can do now to cope with that feeling.

Dr. Banks then reviewed some concrete problem-solving strategies. Karen agreed to make out a schedule of things to do for the rest of the day, including three errands and one recreational activity, so as to reduce her thoughts about being rejected. In the evening, she would go to a movie rather than waiting around in her apartment to see if anyone else would call her.

At the next session, Karen said she had carried out the scheduled activities the day before, and this had helped reduce her focus on the dating situation. However, now she was feeling "completely hopeless" about the progress of therapy itself. She said there was no point in continuing with something that just didn't work. She demanded that the psychologist admit that she was a hopeless case who could never live a normal life.

Dr. Banks was momentarily at a loss for words. But before she could speak, Karen herself came to her assistance. "Don't be upset," the client said, smiling. "Sometimes I say these things. If you don't overreact, if you believe in me, it's easier for me to believe in myself, and not in the hopeless part." The psychologist replied that she certainly did believe in Karen, and then offered the client a parable. She said that the way out of misery is like finding your way out of the desert; you walk and walk, and often things look just the same: dirt, sagebrush, rocks, no water, no shade, no relief. However, if you follow a fairly straight path for a long time, even though things look and feel the same, you're in a very different place, much closer to getting out of the desert.

A number of times after this exchange, Karen expressed the same kind of hopelessness and claimed to be giving up. However, such claims were typically followed by her working even harder, and achieving new goals the next day or week. She gradually came to appreciate that she had a tendency to experience hopelessness, and that she should not literally believe the thoughts that often ensued.

Psychotropic medications have helped calm the emotional and aggressive reactions of some people with borderline personality disorder (L. L. Davis et al., 2000; T. Davis et al., 1999). However, given the heightened risk of suicide by these individuals, the use of drugs on an outpatient basis is quite risky.

Over the next year, Karen had only two episodes of self-injury, which she described as mainly due to "habit." She then remained injury-free for the remainder of treatment.

Decreasing therapy-interfering behaviors   Karen frequently displayed two kinds of therapy-interfering behavior: She would (a) repeatedly express extreme hopelessness and insist that she could not follow the treatment plan any longer; and (b) she would experience extreme anger toward the therapist.

Although Karen seemed, overall, to have warm feelings toward Dr. Banks, there were many occasions when feelings of fear, hopelessness, shame, or depression caused her to lash out. She would turn bright red and criticize the psychologist or call her names. For example, on one occasion, she said, "Thanks for your brilliant suggestion. You know, other therapists I've had were stupid, too, but at least they cared about me."

Although at first taken aback by comments such as this, Dr. Banks recognized that they were signs that she had unwittingly invalidated some aspect of Karen's experience. Unlike her client's friends, the psychologist knew that it was important not to respond defensively to an attack or an insulting remark from her. Indeed, the most therapeutic reaction, for Karen's sake, was for Dr. Banks to admit right away that she might indeed have said something unwise. During the initial stages of therapy, for example, she would respond to Karen's outbursts by saying something like, "Boy, I must have really messed up for you to be this angry. What am I missing? I really want to know what's going on." As therapy progressed, Karen was able to exercise more and more self-restraint in her angry reactions. Instead of criticizing or attacking the psychologist, she would say something like, "Hey, I don't think you're understanding me."

Other times, the anger that Karen expressed toward Dr. Banks actually had more to do with people whom she had encountered and had been upset by outside of therapy. With time, she was able to distinguish between these outside feelings and feelings produced by Dr. Banks's actions. At later points in therapy, she was able to simply tell the psychologist, "I'm in a bad mood. It has nothing to do with you, just some idiot in the parking lot. It's OK. I'll get over it." Ultimately, Karen was able to apply such skills to her interactions with friends as well.

Decreasing behaviors interfering with quality of life   When Karen began therapy with Dr. Banks, she was unemployed and dependent on disability benefits. Moreover, she resided in a one-room apartment in a decrepit building in a dangerous part of town. However, as therapy progressed and Karen developed greater control over her feelings and actions, she was in a position to consider improving the quality of her life. Accordingly, about 9 months into therapy, she de-

Because therapists are continually confronted with the emotional crises, self-destructive acts, and intense anger of, and even insults from, clients with borderline personality disorder, treatment is emotionally demanding for the practitioners. Thus, dialectical behavior therapists often consult with other therapists: to help them remain professional and stay on track with the principles of DBT.

cided to obtain some job training, and enrolled in a training program for medical assistants at a local college. The specific job skills that were taught included answering doctors' phone calls, making appointments, retrieving and filing medical records, and filling out insurance forms.

Karen did not find the training easy. Although a perfectly bright woman, it had been 18 years since she had been in school, and sticking to a curriculum was an unfamiliar experience. The skills training that she had already received in the DBT group helped her to keep up with the course work. At one point in the training, Karen did temporarily stop attending classes after becoming depressed over a broken date. However, when faced with the prospect of not obtaining her certificate and remaining stuck in her current living situation, she eventually pulled herself together and resumed the work, making up for the missed classes.

During this stage of therapy, Dr. Banks also helped Karen to see that sometimes her difficulties in relationships were not due to her own interpersonal ineffectiveness, but to a lack of compatibility between herself and the people she chose. Accordingly, Karen worked hard not only on increasing her personal effectiveness but also on choosing more stable and trustworthy friends, including romantic partners.

In spite of her efforts, she endured several failed relationships over the course of her treatment, which often brought back suicidal feelings. As she and Dr. Banks worked on managing these feelings, they became less intense. The process was helped along by a truly supportive and mutual friendship that Karen developed with another trainee in her medical assistants' training program. This friend, Ann, was a divorcee who lived not far from Karen. In response to a suggestion from Dr. Banks, Karen asked Ann to join her for coffee one day after class, and it soon became a regular event. In the past, the client had been so single-mindedly focused on her relations with men that she sometimes entirely overlooked friendships with women. And the relationships that she did develop with women were often one-sided, with Karen so completely absorbed in her own problems that other women viewed her as unbearably self-centered. With Ann, however, she showed some of the consideration and emotional restraint that she had developed in her relationship with the therapist. Ultimately, they became close friends.

> During their 30s and 40s, most individuals with borderline personality disorder obtain somewhat greater stability in their relationships and jobs (APA, 1994, 2000).

Second-Stage Treatment: Reducing Distress Due to Past Traumas

The focus of the second treatment stage was to help Karen overcome lingering feelings of distress due to past traumas, such as her sexual abuse. In fact, her abuse history had been addressed to some degree from the beginning of treatment. Indeed, in the first stage of therapy, Karen had developed skills to help her tolerate her abuse memories. She had learned, for example, to *soothe* herself—to do especially nice things for herself, such as eat favorite foods, dress in favorite clothes, or go for a walk in her favorite park; and to *distract* herself, which involved finding constructive and engaging projects to work on, such as repairing her bicycle.

At the second stage of treatment, however, the goal was not only to manage the emotional distress that would result from abuse memories, but to reduce the capacity of the memories to produce distress. Dr. Banks used *exposure* techniques similar to those used in the treatment of posttraumatic stress disorder, in which clients undergo repeated, controlled exposures to stimuli—external or internal—that have been linked to past traumas.

Initially, the psychologist asked Karen to describe her past abuse experiences in general terms only. As the client described the same experiences over and over again as a regular exercise, the exposure seemed to result in reductions in her distress levels. Thus, after repeatedly describing her father's molestation of her in general terms—three times per session for three sessions—Karen's distress level was relatively mild by the ninth description. The procedure was then repeated using greater and greater levels of detail, until even the most detailed descriptions of her traumatic experiences produced only moderate distress. The same procedure was applied to Karen's other traumatic memories, with similar results.

> People with borderline personality disorder often suffer from another mental disorder as well. Common ones are mood disorders, substance-related disorders, bulimia nervosa, posttraumatic stress disorder, attention-deficit/hyperactivity disorder, and other personality disorders (APA, 2000).

Third-Stage Treatment: Addressing Longer-Term Issues

The focus of the third stage of treatment was to help Karen gain greater self-respect and achieve career, social, and interpersonal goals. In fact, in her case, the achievement of these goals had been occurring naturally, as a result of the gains she had been making during the first and second stages of treatment. As Karen had stopped injuring herself, developed stable behavior patterns, increased her interpersonal effectiveness, and pursued career training, she was in fact valuing herself increasingly and providing a more dignified existence for herself. Thus, sessions with the therapist at this stage of treatment tended to solidify a process that was already well under way.

Epilogue

Karen remained in weekly individual therapy for a total of 2 years, and now continues with periodic follow-up sessions or phone calls every month or two. Overall, her life has improved greatly, especially compared to what it was prior to entering dialectical behavior therapy with Dr. Banks.

Above all, she no longer hurts herself, even when extremely upset. She also rarely uses alcohol to deal with feelings of distress, and has not been hospitalized since the month before her therapy began. She works part-time as an assistant in the medical records department of a local hospital, and takes courses at a nearby college, with the goal of obtaining a bachelor's degree. Once a week, she coleads a DBT support group.

Most important, Karen has regained control over her mental and emotional life. As she puts it, "I get to have my feelings, and nobody has the right to control me anymore." In addition, she feels that a major achievement of therapy has been "my recognition, deep down inside, that, like other people, I am an acceptable human being and that life can be safe. My life is my own now."

Antisocial Personality Disorder

Table 14-1

DSM-IV Checklist

Antisocial Personality Disorder

1. Pervasive pattern of disregard for and violation of the rights of others occurring since age 15 years, as indicated by at least three of the following:

   a. Failure to conform to social norms with respect to lawful behaviors.

   b. Deceitfulness.

   c. Impulsivity or failure to plan ahead.

   d. Irritability and aggressiveness.

   e. Reckless disregard for safety of self or others.

   f. Consistent irresponsibility.

   g. Lack of remorse.

2. Individual is at least age 18 years.

3. There was evidence of conduct disorder if onset was before age 15 years.

Based on APA, 1994, 2000.

Jack was a 22-year-old single man, admitted to a state psychiatric hospital in a large midwestern city with complaints of depression and thoughts of suicide. He was admitted to the hospital after arriving there one evening appearing completely distraught. He told the psychiatrist on call that he could not bear life any longer and was thinking of ending it all. Jack said he had spent the past hour standing on the overpass of a nearby highway, staring down at the traffic and trying to gather enough courage to jump. He eventually decided he could not bear to do it and, realizing he was near a hospital, pulled himself together enough to "get some help instead of running away from my problems."

In relating these events, Jack seemed deeply upset. Occasionally he would stop speaking and bury his face in his hands. When the psychiatrist asked what sort of difficulty he was experiencing, Jack replied, "You name it, I've got it." He said that he had recently lost both his job and his girlfriend, and now his mother was gravely ill, among other things. He feared that unless he got some help, he was going to "go off the deep end."

Most of the individuals with *antisocial personality disorder* who receive treatment have been forced to participate by an employer, their school, or the law; or they are seeking treatment for another psychological disorder (Fulwiler & Pope, 1987).

Jack: Disturbed or Disturbing?

Concerned about suicide, the psychiatrist decided to admit Jack, and ordered that he be placed on suicide precautions for the next 24 hours. An orderly escorted the young man to the admitting desk, where the clerk took down pertinent information. After that, Jack surrendered his valuables—a wallet with no ID, $3 in cash, and an earring—and was escorted to a locked ward. When they arrived at the door to the ward, the orderly took out an enormous skeleton key, opened the large metal door, and escorted Jack inside.

The orderly brought him to the nurses' station, a large semicircular area enclosed in safety glass, where a half dozen staff members were busily writing notes on patients' charts. Upon seeing Jack, a nurse exited the station, introduced herself, and took him to his room, one of 15 down a long, bare corridor reserved for male patients (female patients occupied an identical corridor on the other side of the floor). At the room, the nurse gave Jack some pajamas for sleeping and a hospital suit for daytime wear; she informed him that a relative could bring his own clothes tomorrow, if he preferred. She also told Jack that she would have to take his shoelaces, since the admitting physician had ordered suicide precautions, and she gave him a pair of slippers to use as footwear.

After the nurse left, Jack flopped down on his bed and buried his face in his pillow. An hour later, a house physician came by to give the patient a routine physical examination, which seemed to perk him up a little. Jack greeted the physician with a friendly, "Hi, Doc, " and the doctor proceeded to examine the young man's heart, lungs, blood pressure, and other vital signs. To make conversation, he remarked on an "interesting" tattoo that Jack had on his chest, a crude picture of a nude woman striking a pose that left nothing to the imagination. With obvious pride, the patient explained: "Yeah, I got it in honor of my girlfriend." After the physician left, Jack donned his hospital pajamas, got into bed, and slept soundly through the night.

The next morning, he joined the other patients in the day area, where breakfast was being served. As he took his place at the table, he announced that he was "hungry as a horse," and began chowing down with abandon. After he finished his own food, he glanced over at a patient across the table and noticed that the man, a patient with schizophrenia, had only nibbled at his eggs and toast. "Hey, old-timer," Jack called out, "you don't mind if I take some of your grub, do you?" The man just stared, glassy-eyed, while Jack, without waiting for a response, took his plate and started scraping its contents onto his own dish.

Another patient sitting at the table reprimanded Jack for having taken the first patient's food. "We're not supposed to share food. It's against regulations. Besides, that fellow is pretty sick. He's been throwing up for days. You wouldn't want to eat anything he's touched."

The terms *sociopathy* and *psychopathy* denote a psychological pattern similar to *antisocial personality disorder,* although some distinctions have been drawn between these disorders.

Jack was unimpressed by the patient's disapproval. "Who appointed you hall monitor?" he asked. "I guess you want all the food for yourself. Well, sorry, pal, I beat you to it."

Jack in Treatment: Not

Later that morning, Dr. Selina Harris, a staff psychiatrist, arrived to conduct an evaluation of Jack. Dr. Harris found the young man standing at a pool table in the day area, playing a game of eight-ball with another patient. As soon as the psychiatrist approached, Jack looked up and smiled. He had an appealing, cheerful quality, and at first Dr. Harris wasn't sure she had the right patient. She was expecting someone deeply depressed, as specified in the admitting note. This patient, however, was extending the warmest, happiest greeting.

"Hey, Doc. Good to see ya," he said. "I'm just shooting a little game of pool here."

Dr. Harris explained that she would be Jack's doctor while he was hospitalized, and had him accompany her to her office on the unit floor. Once inside, she had Jack take a seat and told him that she wanted to know all about the troubles he had been having and why he had been contemplating suicide. Jack confirmed that he was "real depressed" and didn't know if life was worth living. When the psychiatrist asked what he was depressed about, the patient replied, "Everything and anything." He went on to explain that it was mainly his girlfriend but, basically, he "just felt like giving up." "Frankly, Doc," he said, "it's too painful to talk about." Jack didn't look particularly pained, however.

Dr. Harris told him that they would have to discuss these matters eventually, if he was to get any help. At this, Jack said he didn't think that talking would do any good. "Don't they have meds for depression?" he asked. "What's there to talk about when all you got to do is take a pill? How about giving me some Prozac?"

"Did you ever take Prozac?" Dr. Harris asked.

"Me? Oh, no."

"Did you ever take any psychiatric drugs?" she asked.

"No," Jack insisted, "This is my first time in the loony bin, or even talking to a shrink."

"How about street drugs. Did you ever try those?" the psychiatrist asked.

"To be perfectly honest with you, I have tried marijuana—but who hasn't? I stay away from the harder stuff, though."

Since Jack would not discuss his depression, Dr. Harris tried a different tack, asking the young man about his living situation, his work, and his family. Jack replied simply that he had been living with his girlfriend, but "she's real sore at me now." He explained that he had recently lost his job at a loading dock after another employee had stolen some goods and then blamed the theft on Jack. Dr. Harris tried

Antisocial personality disorder is as much as four times more common among men than women (Kessler & Zhao, 1999).

People with antisocial personality disorder have higher rates of alcoholism and substance-related disorders than do the rest of the population (Myers et al., 1998).

to inquire more about that matter, but Jack said he was getting tired and wanted to go lie down.

Before he departed, the psychiatrist asked him whether he was still having thoughts of suicide. Jack replied that he was feeling more secure now that he was in the hospital, and he was hopeful that Dr. Harris could help him. The psychiatrist explained that, in order for her to help him, he would have to talk more about his feelings. The patient promised that, in time, he would. He just had to develop "a little rapport" with Dr. Harris first.

Jack got up and opened the door to leave, but then paused in the doorway as if having second thoughts. He said he really appreciated the time that the psychiatrist had given him, and hoped that they could talk more. As the young man spoke, Dr. Harris observed his hand slip down the edge of the door, and push the button that unlocked the door handle, allowing entry from the outside. For a moment, she considered confronting Jack with what she had just seen, but decided to let the matter ride.

Jack said goodbye, and after he had rounded the corner, Dr. Harris pushed the button to lock the door once again. As it was getting late, she packed up her briefcase and left for the day.

The next morning she sought Jack for another interview. This time she found him seated in the television viewing area. He apparently was enjoying himself immensely, laughing loudly at a situation comedy, while the other patients stared glumly at the same set. As Dr. Harris approached, the young man looked up and greeted her with a cheery, "Hey, Doc! I'll be ready in a minute, as soon as this show is over." The psychiatrist waited for Jack in her office.

A few minutes later he ambled in, closed the door, and sat down. Then he began telling Dr. Harris that she had upset him, that she had hurt his feelings by locking her door after he had unlocked it; it showed she didn't trust him. Going even further, he told her that it was underhanded and dishonest of her. The psychiatrist was momentarily dumbstruck. Here Jack was accusing her of dishonesty for relocking her own door!

"What were you doing, trying to unlock my door?" she asked.

Jack replied that he just didn't like locked doors. "Speaking of which," he added, "I can't take it being cooped up in here all day and night. I know I was suicidal before, but I think I'm coming out of it. Can't I have grounds privileges?" Then he went on: "Look, I'm sorry about the lock thing. It was a stupid prank I pulled. I've just been upset about having to be in a hospital—even though I know I need to be here," he quickly added.

Dr. Harris explained that in order for anything to change in Jack's hospital status—lifting of suicide precautions, grounds privileges, or whatever—he would have to discuss his situation more openly.

Jack's attitude then changed and he said he was ready to speak frankly. First, he apologized profusely for any trouble he had caused. He said that if he was sometimes crude, it was a front he had developed out of fear that others might take advantage of him if he didn't act like he could take care of himself. He admitted to Dr. Harris that he had spent 6 months in prison for a "stupid petty theft"; while in prison, he was bullied constantly because of his small stature. That experience had hardened him, he said, and now he sometimes "acted like a jerk," even among people who had his best interests at heart.

Jack went on to admit that he hadn't really considered suicide; he had simply claimed that in order to gain admission to the hospital. On the other hand, in his opinion it was no exaggeration to say that he was at the end of his rope. He said that since being paroled, he had had tremendous difficulty finding and keeping a job. He had tried everything, from mechanic to electrician to drill press operator, at various auto plants, but in each case he was laid off within a few weeks due to his low seniority in the union.

In addition, he explained, his mother's heart condition had worsened considerably, forcing her hospitalization and the loss of their apartment. And his girlfriend, with whom he sometimes lived, had gotten fed up with his losing jobs and his inability to contribute to the rent, and had demanded that he leave. After being kicked out, he had even gone to a homeless shelter before being hounded out of there by "ruthless thugs" who stole whatever money he had left. Feeling that he was losing this daily struggle for survival, he had come to the hospital.

Jack said he was sorry if he had offended anyone by his charade for getting admitted, but he felt he was suffering as much as any patient, and his false claim of suicidal thoughts showed just how desperate he was. He said he felt he was experiencing a "crisis of confidence" and he needed some intensive therapy to help him through this period. "Look," he concluded, "I could tell you that I still want to commit suicide, but I'm trying to be honest with you now in the hope that I'll get the right kind of help."

Dr. Harris listened to Jack's story with an open mind. Although skeptical about his claims, she decided against recommending immediate discharge. Instead, she decided to proceed with a complete pretreatment evaluation, which included a mental status exam, an EEG, psychometric testing, and an occupational evaluation. His case conference would be held in 5 days, at which point the treatment team would decide whether to discharge him or proceed with treatment. In the meantime, the psychiatrist removed Jack's suicide precautions, but reminded him that he would still be restricted to the locked unit for at least the next several days.

Jack thanked her profusely for "understanding" and said he would cooperate with the evaluation procedures and make less of a pest of himself generally.

During the next several days, the patient seemed true to his word. He behaved almost perfectly and cooperated fully with all the evaluation procedures. But then, the day before his case conference, he disappeared. The building was searched, but there was no sign of Jack. A few hours later, Dr. Harris received a call from the

In one study, clinical psychologists viewed videotapes of statements made by individuals, and evaluated their truth or falsehood. The clinicians were able to identify only 62% of the lies, a performance similar to that of federal judges (Ekman et al., 1999). Police were successful at identifying only 51% of such lies.

A mental status exam is a structured interview in which the clinician asks about specific symptoms, such as anxiety or hallucinations; observes other symptoms, such as emotional expression or motor activity; and tests certain cognitive capacities, such as memory or abstract reasoning.

state police saying they had picked up a patient—obviously Jack—for possession of a stolen vehicle, her's. Jack had also been charged with driving without a license, driving while intoxicated, speeding, and failure to heed a stop signal. The police said they were calling to investigate Jack's claim that the psychiatrist had lent him the car. Dr. Harris explained that she certainly had not done this, but was nevertheless willing to drop any charges. The police replied that they already had enough outstanding warrants on Jack to hold him "from here to doomsday"; and he was arraigned on the other charges.

With Jack unable to return to the hospital, his next of kin—his mother—was contacted to pick up his personal articles. As it turned out, his mother was in perfect health, in spite of Jack's dramatic story of her grave heart condition and recent hospitalization. After picking up her son's belongings, she spoke with Dr. Harris and supplied some details about his background.

A Parent's Tale: Watching Antisocial Behavior Unfold

> "In most of us, by the age of thirty, the character has set like plaster, and will never soften again."
> —William James (1890)

Jack's mother, Marlene, told Dr. Harris that everyone who encountered him as a toddler immediately fell in love with him. He was such a sweet child, and he had a smile that could win over anyone. However, "as soon as he was old enough to go to school, the trouble started."

At about the time that Jack entered first grade, he seemed to develop a "thing" for jewelry or, more accurately, for stealing it. For example, he would take items from Marlene's jewelry case and sell them one by one to classmates or to older boys in the neighborhood, often for no more than pocket change, which he would spend on candy or trading cards. Marlene and her husband learned what Jack was doing after he tried to sell a pair of genuine pearl earrings to his 2nd-grade teacher for 50¢. At first, his parents just scolded him. When the behavior continued, the scoldings turned into beatings. Eventually, they decided that the only way to deal with the situation was to keep their valuables—bills, coins, jewelry—under lock and key.

Jack's parents provided him with a generous allowance in an effort to reduce his desire for spending money. However, this desire could never be satisfied. By the age of 8, the boy began breaking into neighbors' houses to steal items, again to sell to others. In many ways, he became quite ingenious in these break-ins: He learned to pick locks, disable alarms, and slip into small openings. At the same time, however, the way in which he would dispose of the stolen items often seemed remarkably stupid, according to his mother. His most spectacular bungle occurred when he tried to sell jewelry to members of the very same household from which it was stolen.

This triggered his first arrest, at age 10, but he was remanded to the custody of his parents, who told the judge that they would figure out a way to control him.

They did indeed try to control his antisocial ways by keeping a more careful eye on him. When they sent Jack off to school, for example, they would actually escort him into the building in order to make sure that he was attending classes. But the boy was not beyond slipping out in the middle of the day, inevitably to get into some kind of trouble.

Jack's stealing soon took a more serious turn. He joined up with a group of teenagers who made a profession of shoplifting. They saw in Jack an opportunity to steal with reduced risk of detection, since he was much younger and less likely to be suspected. Typically, one of the teenagers would case a store, locate items of interest, and then send Jack inside to remove the items according to their instructions. The gang would then sell the items to a regular fence who paid them in cash, drugs, and alcohol.

Associating with these older boys led Jack to develop more varied and sophisticated interests, including a precocious sexual awareness. The turning point in his antisocial career came when, at age 12, he lured a 10-year-old neighborhood girl into some woods behind her house, undressed her, and tried to perform sex acts with her. When she started screaming, her mother came running and was confronted with the horrifying scene. Jack at first claimed that the girl had lured *him* into the woods. When that didn't work, he offered the girl's mother $5 "to keep her mouth shut." As it became apparent that the woman was not warming to the negotiations, Jack finally tried threats, telling the mother she had better take the money or she would get the same treatment.

With this incident, Jack entered the world of serious legal trouble and was sentenced to a year in reform school. There he learned more advanced methods of taking advantage of others. As soon as he was released, he embarked on a career of auto theft. He could now hot-wire a car in 30 seconds, and would do so whenever he needed ready cash or even just transportation. Why take the bus, he reasoned, when there were cars all around to take him wherever he wanted to go. Jack's mother estimated that he hot-wired 50 cars before finally getting caught in the act, leading to another sentence in reform school, this time for 2 years.

When he was released, at around age 15, his parents tried to persuade him to return to school and pay enough attention to his studies to get a high school diploma. The teenager agreed to attend a trade school to learn how to repair electrical systems and electronic components. His mother now realized that her son had probably favored this route because he had hoped to become more skilled at disabling alarm systems; also, with electronics training, he thought he might get jobs that would bring him into contact with equipment worth stealing.

Jack actually stayed with his electrical studies, and after receiving his certificate at age 17 found employment at an auto plant, assisting in the installation of electrical systems. He seemed to work hard for several months, and Marlene

Antisocial personality disorder was called "moral insanity" during the 19th century.

marveled at his capacity to apply himself. But it all came to an end when he was later caught stealing electrical supplies on a massive scale. Somehow, he had gained access to the plant's supply depot, where he had been removing switches, wiring, batteries, and other electrical supplies for sales to competing auto plants. He eventually got caught when, in a manner reminiscent of his childhood error, he tried selling some of these supplies back to his own plant.

Thus, at age 18, Jack was sentenced to 3 years in a state penitentiary. Not being the violent sort, he was paroled after 1½ years for good behavior. Upon his release, he stunned his former colleagues by applying for employment at the very same auto plant where he had been caught stealing. He expressed outrage and hurt, seemingly sincere, when they refused to take him back. For the next several months, Jack hitchhiked around the country, bouncing from one job to the next.

As for his love life, such as it was, Jack's mother reported that he had been married at least twice, although she doubted he had ever been divorced. He met his first wife at age 21, while hitchhiking around the country after his release from prison. Marlene had never met the woman, but learned from Jack that she was a 45-year-old divorcee who had picked the young man up as he was hitchhiking through her town. Jack later told his mother that this woman completely repulsed him: She was dull and unattractive, according to his description. Nevertheless, he felt a sexual stirring while riding in the car with her and proposed sexual intercourse. The woman replied, half teasingly, that he would have to marry her first. Viewing this as but a small problem, Jack immediately agreed, and they drove non-stop to a western state where they found a justice of the peace to perform the ceremony. Then they paid for a motel room where they retired for the night.

The next morning, the couple drove back to the bride's hometown, and Jack moved into her house. He resided there for a few weeks, until she started nagging him about finding work. At this, he decided he had hung around long enough, and he departed for home, hitchhiking and hot-wiring his way there.

Once back in his home state, Jack acquired several girlfriends, one of whom he married under similar circumstances. In each such involvement, Jack showed no concern about the age, appearance, or character of the woman. Rather, his interest in women seemed largely a matter of housing and, to a lesser extent, sex. No sense of love or attachment was ever involved.

At the time that Jack had sought admission to the psychiatric hospital, he was, according to his mother, in truly desperate straits. She and Jack's father—fed up with having to hide their valuables constantly—had refused to allow him entry into their home; also, his latest girlfriend had locked him out. Marlene suspected that, in seeking hospital admission, her son was simply looking for a place to stay, although he may also have considered the prospect of obtaining psychiatric drugs, either to use or sell, as an added bonus. Typically, Jack would become bored with his plots when they could not be executed immediately; and this was probably why he ran off with Dr. Harris's car rather than see what he could accomplish at the hospital. Marlene, an old hand at Jack's behaviors, encouraged the psychiatrist not to take the car theft personally, explaining that he probably chose her vehicle only because her name on the reserved space had caught his eye.

Jack's mother then signed for her son's belongings—the wallet, the $3, and the earring—and departed.

Jack: A Failure of Therapy

Marlene's departure marked the end of Dr. Harris's involvement with Jack. The young man had left the psychiatrist's professional life as suddenly as he had entered it. And, the therapist was certain, she had made little or no impact on him. This failure of treatment did not surprise her, although it did cause her disappointment. During her short time working with him, she had come to suspect that Jack manifested *antisocial personality disorder,* a pattern that is notoriously unresponsive to treatment. Based on her talks with Jack and with his mother, Dr. Harris felt that he clearly met the DSM-IV criteria for a diagnosis of this disorder. That is, he failed to conform to social norms; also, he was deceitful, impulsive, reckless, irresponsible, and remorseless. And, as the DSM-IV criteria stipulate, his antisocial behavior dated from well before the age of 15.

Although many people with this personality disorder exhibit criminal behavior, their brand of criminality is often marked by idiosyncratic qualities. For one, their criminal acts often seem to be inadequately motivated. The individual may, for example, commit a major crime for very small stakes. In this regard, Dr. Harris recalled that Jack tried to sell his mother's pearl earrings for 50¢. Also, the criminal acts of these individuals often seem to be committed without much sense of self-preservation. They may fail, for example, to take obvious precautions against detection when carrying out their crimes. Here, again, Dr. Harris recalled Jack's attempts to sell items to the very source from which they were stolen.

In short, Jack showed the disorder's classic overall pattern of long-standing antisocial behavior, dating from childhood, aimed at nothing higher than the immediate gratification of transient desires. His behavior did not seem to be deterred by any sense of shame, remorse, or even plain self-interest.

Clinicians have generally despaired of devising an effective treatment for antisocial personality disorder. Perhaps the main reason for this is that people with the disorder, by definition, have no recognition that their behavior pattern is problematic. They usually reject the need for or value of psychological treatment, and so they are unlikely to initiate it or adhere to it for very long. Still other factors may also be at work, but the sad reality remains that the mental health field is currently unable to help most people with this personality disorder.

> Approximately one fourth of all people with antisocial personality disorder receive treatment for it, yet no treatment appears to be particularly effective (Regier et al., 1993).

Unfortunately, the single greatest hope for improvement may lie with the simple passage of time. It appears that adults with this pattern, who often begin a criminal career as teenagers, significantly reduce their level of criminal activity after age 40. That is, they experience fewer convictions and serve less time in prison as they grow older. The reason for this shift remains unclear, but, for now, it is the one optimistic note in an otherwise bleak affair. On that note, Dr. Harris decided that it was time to leave her office and visit her newest admission on the psychiatric ward.

CASE **15**

Autism

Table 15-1

DSM-IV Checklist

Autistic Disorder

1. A total of at least six items from the following groups of symptoms:

   A. *Impairment in social interaction,* as manifested by at least two of the following:

      1. Marked impairment in the use of multiple nonverbal behaviors such as eye-to-eye gaze, facial expression, body postures, and gestures to regulate social interaction.
      2. Failure to develop peer relationships appropriately.
      3. Lack of spontaneous seeking to share enjoyment, interests, or achievements with other people.
      4. Lack of social or emotional reciprocity.

   B. *Impairment in communication,* as manifested by at least one of the following:

      1. Delay in, or total lack of, the development of spoken language.
      2. In individuals with adequate speech, marked impairment in the ability to start or sustain a conversation with others.
      3. Stereotyped and repetitive use of language, or idiosyncratic language.
      4. Lack of varied, spontaneous make-believe play or social imitative play.

   C. *Restricted repetitive and stereotyped patterns of behavior, interests, and activities,* as manifested by at least one of the following:

      1. Abnormal preoccupation with one or more stereotyped and restricted patterns of interest.
      2. Inflexible adherence to specific nonfunctional routines or rituals.
      3. Stereotyped and repetitive motor mannerisms (e.g., hand or finger flapping or twisting).
      4. Persistent preoccupation with parts of objects.

2. Prior to 3 years of age, delay or abnormal functioning in either social interaction, language, or symbolic or imaginative play.

Based on APA, 1994, 2000.

Adam was born on August 11, 1997, to Michelle, age 32, and Joe, age 39. Michelle's pregnancy was full-term, delivery was normal, and the baby weighed in at 7 pounds, 15 ounces. Michelle and Joe also had another child, Jarrod, who was 6 years older than Adam. With his brown hair and brown eyes, Adam was handsome, and his smile was beautiful. The family looked forward to an exciting future, filled with the dreams that having two children can inspire.

Adam's development over the first year of his life was normal. He was able to sit without support by 7 months, crawl at 10 months, and stand alone by 12 months. He took his first independent step at 15 months, and was walking everywhere within a week. All visits to the pediatrician went well, and immunizations were given at the appropriate times.

Adam: Clues During the Second Year

After Adam's first birthday party, to which several young children were invited, Michelle began to pay attention to some characteristics of her son's personality that just didn't seem to match those of the other children. Unlike the other toddlers, or even his brother when he had been 1 year old, Adam was not babbling or forming any specific word sounds. Michelle thought that her son should have mastered at least a couple of words by then, especially after hearing other 1-year-olds say "mama" and "cake" and "cookie." Adam could only produce a few noises, which he would utter randomly throughout the day. Michelle also noticed that these sounds were rarely directed toward anyone or anything. The child made no attempt to label people or objects; he would just make those noises.

At first, Michelle and Joe attributed Adam's language delay to the fact that he had an older brother who would speak for him and fulfill many of his needs without Adam's even having to ask. But they soon became suspicious that a language delay was only part of the problem. At the birthday party and in other situations, Adam seemed uninterested in playing with the other children or even being around them socially. He seemed to enjoy everyone singing "Happy Birthday" to him, but he made no attempt to blow out the candles on the cake, even after others modeled this tradition for him. He was only 1 year old, but his indifference bothered Michelle and Joe.

Upon closer examination, his parents also noticed that Adam in fact had very few interests. He would seek out only two or three Disney figurines and their corresponding videotapes, and that was it. All other games, activities, and toy characters were rejected. And if pushed to play with something new, he would sometimes throw intense, inconsolable tantrums. Even the figurines that he did enjoy were typically not played with in an appropriate manner. Often he would line them up in a row, in the same order, and would not allow them to be removed until he decided he was finished with them. If someone attempted to rearrange or clear away the figurines, he would again have a tantrum.

Autism affects 5 of every 10,000 children (APA, 2000).

About half of all people with autism fail to speak or develop language skills (Dawson & Castelloe, 1992).

As her concern grew, Michelle decided to monitor her son's play habits more closely. She was both frightened and amazed at the meticulous way in which he manipulated the Disney characters. On a few occasions, she realized that the order in which he aligned the figurines matched the order in which the characters appeared on one of his favorite Disney videotapes. Similarly, if Adam's figurines had movable arms and legs, he would arrange their body stances to match that videotape.

He also had a marked preference for being with his mother. He had less of an interest in Joe, Jarrod, or other people. In fact, Adam might cry for hours if Michelle had to go out without him. Upon her return, he would stop crying but would not necessarily want to be with her. Content knowing that she was home, he would then go back to playing with his Disney toys by himself. In addition, when called by either parent, Adam often failed to respond to his name, and he displayed odd food preferences: He could not seem to get enough of some foods, and he simply could not tolerate the textures of others.

As the months went by and he remained unable to express his wants and needs, Adam's tantrums became more frequent. If his mother did not understand his noises and gestures, he would grow angry at not receiving a desired object. The intensity of these episodes was also growing; Adam was even beginning to hit his ears with his hands and cry for longer and longer periods of time. One of the most frightening aspects of this for Michelle was the fact that her misinterpretations of the episodes might sometimes endanger Adam's health; she had no way of knowing if he had an upset stomach, a headache, or some other ailment.

Finally, when Adam was 19 months old, Michelle took him to his pediatrician for some answers once and for all. The doctor agreed that there were some significant "delays" in Adam's development, and he referred the child to a neurologist for a complete evaluation. The recommendation of a neurologist greatly upset Michelle and Joe. They were now forced to confront their deepest fears. They found it extremely difficult to wait for the neurological evaluation, repeatedly dwelling on all of the terrible scenarios that the word "delay" evoked.

Prior to the appointment with the neurologist, they also followed up on the pediatrician's recommendation that they have Adam's hearing formally tested. His hearing was found to be within normal range, and this news caused a mixed reaction in his parents. On the one hand, they were happy that serious hearing deficits could be ruled out; but, on the other hand, where did that leave them? The results left many questions in their minds. Also prior to the neurological evaluation, Michelle and Joe began to research the term "developmental delays" on the Internet; there, for the first time, they saw the word "disability." When the time for Adam's appointment with the neurologist finally arrived, they were extremely frightened, but they also still held out hope that everything might prove to be a mistake of some kind—just skills that were a little late in coming.

Some individuals with autism who do learn to speak show peculiarities in their speech, including *echolalia,* the exact echoing of phrases spoken by others; *pronominal reversal,* the confusion of pronouns, such as the use of "you" instead of "I"; or difficulties naming objects, employing a proper tone, or speaking spontaneously.

Adam: Confirming His Parents' Worst Fears

The neurologist was pleasant, and very thorough. She reviewed Adam's history from pregnancy through birth, and then his milestone achievements. She also completed physical, neurological, and motor examinations. Finally, she addressed his language delays and maladaptive behaviors, by observing his lack of speech and his limited play skills. For all the weeks of waiting for this examination, it seemed to pass very quickly—almost too quickly, the parents believed, for the doctor really to get to know Adam. Actually, however, she was able to gather a great deal of information and she proceeded to tell Joe and Michelle that Adam seemed to be manifesting *pervasive developmental disorder/autistic spectrum disorder,* or *autism,* as it is known to the public.

Autism is a severe developmental disability, with a range of symptoms that can occur at various levels of severity. The neurologist cited several factors that led to her tentative diagnosis of Adam: his severely delayed receptive and expressive language skills, his nonverbal communication, his lack of imaginative play with toys, his social perceptual difficulties, and his history of repeated and rigid behaviors. In short, everything Michelle, Joe, and several other family members had noticed were symptoms of this disorder.

A diagnosis of autism had been his parents' worst fear, after having read so much about its different forms during their Internet research. From their gathering of information, they had formed a mental image of an aggressive or self-injurious child, locked in his own world and unable to communicate. Joe began to tune out as the doctor described the typical features of the disorder. Too many questions were pounding inside his head: Should they get a second opinion? Could it possibly be as bad as she was describing? Whose fault was it? Why hadn't the pediatrician said something sooner? How would Michelle handle this? What would the rest of the family say? What was the cure?

By the time Joe was able to focus again, the visit was over, and the neurologist was talking about her forthcoming report and discussing her recommendations. He heard her explain that, with appropriate early interventions and services, the disorder was "workable," and that because Adam was starting treatment at such a young age, he had a great deal of potential for progress. Joe couldn't imagine how this devastating problem might be workable. He knew that on the long car ride home he would have to be filled in on the missing pieces of the doctor's conversation with Michelle.

> Several other disorders have similarities to autism but differ to some degree in symptoms or time of onset. These different disorders are, collectively, called *pervasive developmental disorders.*

Adam: Seeking an Early Start

Michelle took charge and played a more active role than Joe in following up on the recommendations of the neurologist. In part, this was because she worked from home in order to be with her children. However, it was also because she felt

Four of every five persons with autism are male.

she needed to keep busy in order to keep negative thoughts and mounting questions out of her mind. Joe, who was feeling overwhelmed by the weight of the diagnosis, followed his wife's lead.

The first course of action was to have Adam more fully and precisely evaluated and to have him begin *early intervention services*. And it was important that these services be provided by clinicians who specialized in the field of autism. After consulting an advocacy group for individuals with developmental disabilities, Michelle learned of several prominent early intervention centers. She scheduled an evaluation with the one that would be available the soonest. Six weeks after seeing the neurologist, Adam received a comprehensive evaluation and began treatment at the Manning Child Development Center.

From this point forward, the family's lifestyle became a whirlwind of doctors' visits and an introduction to a variety of therapies. The initial diagnostic evaluation itself was completed in 1½ hours. One clinician interviewed the parents, while a second took Adam to a separate room for an individual assessment. Diagnostic and rating scales were explained to the parents, including the DSM-IV criteria and *The Childhood Autism Rating Scale (CARS)*. All of Adam's delays and behaviors were specifically categorized and totaled to arrive at a detailed clinical picture and diagnosis.

Consistent with the DSM-IV criteria for autism, Adam showed (a) impairment in social interaction, including marked impairment in the use of nonverbal behaviors such as eye-to-eye gaze, failure to develop peer relationships appropriate to his developmental level, and lack of social or emotional reciprocity; (b) impairment in communication—in his case, a total lack of spoken language—and a lack of varied, spontaneous, make-believe play or social imitative play; and (c) restricted, repetitive, and stereotyped patterns of behavior, interests, and activities, including abnormal preoccupations and inflexible adherence to specific, nonfunctional routines or rituals. His developmental delays also had begun before age 3, and could not be accounted for by any other disorder.

The pattern of autism was first identified by the American psychiatrist Leo Kanner in 1943.

Based on the CARS assessment, Adam's autism was rated in the *mild* to *moderate* range. He displayed a number of symptoms from the rating scale's 15 areas of assessment, including areas such as relating to people, imitation, emotional response, object use, visual and listening response, adaptation to change, verbal and nonverbal communication, and intellectual response. Slowly, these terms were starting to have more meaning to Michelle and Joe. The diagnostic team at the center concluded that early intervention was certainly the treatment of choice at this point, and they helped the parents set up a variety of therapies for their son.

Adam was enrolled in the center's early intervention program, which provided 3 hours of behavioral therapy each week: 2 hours at the center itself and 1 hour at home. The goal of these behavioral sessions was to help the child develop *learning readiness skills*—basic skills that one needs in order to be able to learn and acquire broader knowledge, behaviors, or skills. Adam was to be taught skills such as making eye contact, sitting appropriately, and following simple directions. Again and again, in trial after trial, he would be rewarded whenever he performed these target behaviors or some approximation of them, and not rewarded if he failed to perform them. It was expected that, through such efforts, the child would become increasingly able and willing to perform the behaviors across a wide range of situations and, in turn, be more ready to learn broader behaviors and skills. The sessions were to follow the principles of the *Applied Behavior Analysis (ABA)* model—a strict behavioral strategy that, according to research, helps many persons with autism and other developmental delays. Adam was also signed up for speech therapy 2 days a week and for occupational therapy 1 day a week. Ultimately, the three therapies would all be seeking to increase his ability to engage new people.

The child's life was turned upside down by the early intervention program. Strangers were now being thrown into his world on a rotating basis, and these people were placing demands on him and changing his routines. He was also being separated from his mother in a strange place for the first time ever. During the first few therapy sessions, Michelle wanted to run from the observation room into the treatment room and "rescue" him from the therapist. Adam cried and threw tantrums throughout those sessions. The therapist continually had to reassure Michelle that the child would become less resistant as long as the sessions were carried out consistently. Otherwise, the distraught mother would have withdrawn him from the program and tried teaching him herself.

Slowly, Adam's tears and tantrums lessened as his therapy sessions became a regular part of his weekly schedule. Michelle and Joe began to notice, after 2 months, a slight increase in his eye contact and less resistance when they asked him to complete specific tasks within the home, such as clearing away his figurines after he was finished playing. Nevertheless, his progress felt unbearably slow to them, and they noticed no developments in the area of language, despite the speech therapist's positive reports. Adam also remained unreceptive to all new toys, and his play skills continued to be very limited.

Thus, Michelle and Joe decided to supplement the center's early intervention sessions by hiring therapists on a private basis to provide more learning trials at home, as well as scheduling speech therapy sessions. In fact, it was the speech therapy that was of most interest to the couple. They believed that if they could just help their son talk, they could better understand what he was feeling and, in turn, could more effectively resolve his other issues.

The in-home private therapy was difficult at first, as Adam could not bear having his home routine disrupted even more than it already had been. But the home therapists persevered and tried to apply their services consistently. Like the center's program, the supplemental learning trials focused on learning readiness and

In order to help children with autism to speak, teachers often supplement their speech therapy with another form of communication, including *sign language* and *simultaneous communication,* a method combining sign language and speech.

on teaching Adam to identify and manipulate various objects. In their work, the therapists selected objects that were particularly relevant to the child's home environment: chairs, eating utensils, light switches. When they incorporated Disney characters into the sessions, the learning tended to go even better. Nevertheless, progress continued to be slow.

The speech therapists—both those from the clinic and the in-home practitioners—worked together on several aspects of Adam's speech. First, they did exercises with his mouth (open the mouth wide) and tongue (stick out the tongue) to strengthen muscles that are typically needed in speech. Second, they used imitation training to help Adam mouth verbal sounds, for example, the sounds "mmm" or "bababababa." Finally, they sought to develop a working communication system that would enable him to convey his wants and needs. Everyone agreed that establishing a communication system for Adam was the number one goal, for if he could communicate better, his needs could be better met and his tantrums would likely decrease. The speech therapists decided that it would be best to introduce a basic *Picture Exchange Communication System*—a system in which Adam could point to or select pictures to help express himself.

> Speech teachers may also turn to *augmentative communication systems* for individuals with autism, systems in which they are taught to point to pictures, symbols, letters, or words on a communication board or computer.

At first, his parents were opposed to this system. Joe, in particular, feared that Adam would come to rely solely on these pictures. He believed that unless his son were required to speak or at least make sounds in order to receive items, he would have little chance of learning to speak. The therapists explained, however, that many children with language processing problems like Adam's initially learn better with a visual representation of the desired items. Eventually, the children come to appreciate that pictures of items can bring about the items themselves, and they grasp that there is a connection between their thoughts and their environment. Moreover, by helping the children to communicate their needs, the use of pictures reduces their frustrations and tantrums, thus creating a more positive environment for learning verbal skills. Although hesitant, Michelle and Joe agreed to give the picture system a try.

At the same time, though, their worries continued to grow. Adam was now 2 years old and continuing to grow physically, but was without language and cognitive understanding. Their other son had called for "mama" and "dada" long before his 2nd birthday, and Adam could not even imitate the "m" sound. Privately, they questioned how hard the therapists were really working, and whether Adam was being given enough hours of therapy. Maybe there was more that they could do with him at home. Before long, he would be 3; and if this trend continued, they would have to seek placement in a specialized full-day program.

Michelle and Joe: Trying Everything

After Adam reached the age of 2, Michelle also began to investigate other interventions that she had heard about, just to see if anything out there could make a difference. One of the most talked about treatments that she came across was *diet change*—eliminating certain foods from Adam's menu, foods with ingredients that some autistic children have trouble tolerating. In particular, Michelle read on the Internet that a gluten-free, wheat-free diet was helpful in many cases of autism. Apparently some autistic children are unable to properly digest gluten (an ingredient in flour) and wheat, leading many clinicians to speculate that such ingredients may contribute to the inappropriate behaviors of autism, perhaps by causing great discomfort. Michelle read that autistic children who were put on diets eliminating most breads, pastries, crackers, snacks, and the like, sometimes showed significant improvements in their behavior. Although she knew that the outcome of this approach would be uncertain—many children with autism failed to respond to such diet changes—she felt that she must try everything in her power to reverse Adam's delays. Otherwise, she would be failing him and perhaps missing the one intervention that could make a difference. Michelle and Joe found a nutritionist familiar with the diet. Wanting to be as objective as possible, they decided to give the dietary changes a year, with an assessment of his skills both before and after that year's time.

The whirlwind that their lives had become was continuing. In addition, Adam's older brother, Jarrod, now 8 years old, was beginning to show signs of resentment for the amount of attention that his brother was receiving. Michelle and Joe did their best to create special activities for Jarrod, but, in fact, Adam's therapies did take most of their time and energy. Time was passing, still with none of the vast improvements Michelle and Joe were hoping for.

When Adam reached the age of 2½, the couple decided to sign him up for *auditory integration training*. They suspected that Adam, like a number of children with autism, might be *hypersensitive* in the auditory sphere. That is, he might have sensory-perceptual difficulties that cause certain sounds or tones to feel particularly unpleasant, making it difficult for him to listen to and process the words and noises within his environment. Auditory integration training is a procedure in which individuals wear headphones that actually alter (for example, soften) certain auditory inputs, making sounds more comfortable and, theoretically, improving the individuals' capacity to process what they are hearing. Although some children with autism do greatly improve their language capabilities with this training, Adam showed no such improvement. Once again, his parents were faced with disappointment.

Growing Child, Growing Problems

Even with all of his interventions at the child development center and at home, Adam continued to develop into a mystifying little boy. His fascination with the Disney characters remained strong, and was now joined by an added interest in Legos. If he was left alone, these items would occupy him for hours, but, again, he didn't play with them in the appropriate manner. The lining up of the Disney characters continued, and the new-found Legos had to be carefully stacked according

Some people with autism seem *overstimulated* by sights and sounds and try to block them out, while others seem *understimulated* and perform behaviors that may add to their stimulation, such as flapping their arms, cupping their hands so that they can scream in their ears, or rapidly moving their fingers before their eyes.

to color and then in rows—with the pattern always identical (first red, then green, then yellow, and so on). His preference for certain routines and patterns became even stronger as he grew older; increasingly, these routines were dominating the family's schedule.

For example, Adam was now in the habit of having his bath before going to sleep, and it had to be given by Michelle. For his first 2 years, this set procedure had been easy enough to carry out. But as Adam's brother, Jarrod, grew older, he often needed his mother's help with homework. Moreover, Michelle had to attend more and more parent groups or conferences regarding Adam. When someone other than Michelle had to give Adam his bath, or if a bath had to be skipped altogether, he would throw a major tantrum, followed by poor sleep throughout the night. To avoid this situation, Michelle and Joe found themselves scheduling as many activities, meetings, and outings as possible around the daily bath ritual. Recognizing that they were becoming slaves to the child's rigid routines, the couple came to realize that they needed help with their son's home behaviors every bit as much as with his educational goals.

As Adam grew older still, and encountered new milestones, he revealed delays in yet other areas—producing further difficulties at home. Michelle was uncertain how to begin him on toilet training, for example, since he showed no inclination to go to the bathroom or understanding regarding how and where to go. She was also unsuccessful in teaching him to brush his teeth. The first, and last, time that she tried this, he became extremely upset and resistant, as his oral sensitivities to certain textures made the activity particularly uncomfortable for him. As his frustrations grew, Adam's tantrums also seemed to be getting worse, both in intensity and in duration. Some days he would hit his ears so very hard that Michelle feared he might be damaging them.

Still another difficulty for the family was their inability to manage their growing son's behaviors out in the community. They were unsure from one outing to the next how he would behave in a grocery store, mall, or restaurant. Sometimes, accidentally leaving a Disney figurine at home would spark a tantrum so loud, upsetting, and embarrassing that Michelle and Joe would be afraid ever to return to the store or restaurant. Family outings kept decreasing, and eventually became a rarity—the very opposite of the family lifestyle the couple had always hoped for.

Adam at 3: Fully Entering the System

As Adam approached 3 years of age, his parents knew that a *full-day program* was the way to go. Once again, it fell on Michelle's shoulders to find the best such program. Joe was feeling depressed by his son's slow progress and by the position in which his family now found itself. This was not how he had envisioned his future. Since his wife seemed better able to handle everything, he decided that his role should be limited to that of breadwinner—working very hard to earn the extra

---

In the 1940s and 1950s, it was believed that autism was the result of "refrigerator parents." However, research has totally failed to support a picture of rigid, cold, rejecting, or disturbed parents (Roazen, 1992).

income needed for all of Adam's therapies. Throwing himself into work also helped him to deny, at least partially, that his son had a disability that would probably affect the rest of his life.

Michelle insisted, however, that Joe accompany her on her tours of full-day school programs for children with autism. While they focused primarily on preschool programs, they were also provided with information about how such programs would set the stage for Adam's later years—if he were still to need services 5 years down the road. The more Joe and Michelle spoke with professionals, the better equipped they became for Adam's next few years. They started to see how the various early intervention services they had been providing would now come into play for their child as he entered a full-day program, and how the full-day services would help with later educational and vocational programs. They also learned about behavior management strategies that the family might be able to use to help deal with Adam's increasing demands and routines. In fact, the discussions with professionals at the prospective schools helped Joe emerge from his depressive state and take a few more steps toward acceptance of his son's disability.

The search for the best full-day program eventually led Joe and Michelle to two schools in two different counties. At each school, they were given a tour, an application form, and an appointment for an intake interview. The intake process was similar at each school: The director of the program interviewed the parents, while three or four other professionals took Adam into a separate area to assess his skills and behaviors.

By this point, Michelle had already contacted her school district about Adam's diagnosis and his need for specialized instruction. In fact, the district's officials had set up an appointment as well, completed their own assessment of Adam, and assigned him a case manager and a child study team. The school district's involvement was necessary because it was they who would have to provide, or pay for, any special educational services that Adam might need during his school years. The officials were supportive of Michelle's search for an appropriate outside program, as they themselves had a minimal number of preschool classrooms equipped for the special needs of students with autism or other pervasive developmental disorders.

The school district's psychological and social profiles were added to the evaluations by the neurologist and the early intervention therapists to form a referral packet that Michelle took with her to her interviews at the special preschool programs. She was pleased, and relieved, that this part of the process had gone so well, as she had heard many other parents describe the enormous difficulties they had encountered trying to convince their school districts' child study teams to find special programming.

The first school at which Michelle and Joe made an appointment had been highly recommended by several other parents they had grown close to. Enrollment was small—a total of 30 students—and its teaching strategies followed the

Today's behavioral programs for individuals with autism often train parents so that they can apply behavioral techniques at home. Such programs typically include instruction manuals and home visits by teachers.

ABA principles they had come to know so well from Adam's early intervention therapists. Days at this school were very structured, and there was an ongoing effort to *mainstream* students into less restrictive environments.

This first interview was also the most difficult, since his parents had to convey all of their hopes and dreams for Adam to a complete stranger. It was also painful for them to observe Adam have a tantrum when he was separated from his parents for skill assessment during the interview. The director asked questions about Adam's history, the family's history, and how the young child was responding to the early intervention services he was receiving. Michelle and Joe tried to fit every piece of relevant information they could think of into the short hour of the interview, feeling as if there was much more to say.

For Adam, this was yet another set of strangers placing demands on him, in a completely new environment. The people assessing his skills included a special education teacher, a speech therapist, and an occupational therapist. They completed a checklist of his skills, as well as of his maladaptive behaviors. Their assessment agreed with previous findings that the absence of language or a formal communication system, along with Adam's problematic behaviors, would necessitate a preschool program with very special teaching techniques, including a continuation of the slow, trial-by-trial teaching program that Adam had slowly been responding to with his early intervention therapists. One opening would be available at this first school in September, and Michelle and Joe were told that Adam was among several candidates applying for this opening. The parents would be contacted within the next 3 weeks.

The second interview went much like the first, except that this school was run by the Manning Child Development Center and so was closely affiliated with the early intervention program that Adam had been attending for almost a year. Michelle and Joe felt a bit more comfortable on this interview because they knew that Adam's behavioral therapist at the center would be stopping in to check on his assessment; and they had previously met the director at one of the parent training sessions offered by the center a few months earlier.

Again, the interview seemed too short to convey all of Adam's needs; but Michelle and Joe made sure to express their interest in a behaviorally based program that would address every aspect of Adam's learning potential. By now, they recognized the value of learning programs in which tasks—all tasks, from toilet training to speaking—were broken down into the simplest possible steps to be learned one at a time. The consistent application of such learning programs over the past year had in fact produced some results. Adam could now maintain eye contact and sit appropriately for longer periods of time, as opposed to the fleeting glances and constant movements of past times. He could wave hello and good-bye on command, a skill that helped bring him closer to his family. And his skill with the Picture Exchange Communication System was beginning to emerge;

Mainstreaming is the placement of children with special needs and disorders in regular school classes with children who do not have those special needs.

he was using pictures to convey five of his most desired items. Although the progress seemed a long time in coming, and was far behind what Michelle and Joe had expected of Adam by the age of 3, the fact remained that it had occurred, and they wanted to see it continue.

When asked about Adam's diet, the couple had mixed feelings. In Joe's opinion, Adam's special foods had not really brought about much change, and it was hard to keep him on these foods now that he was aware that his older brother was eating, and enjoying, different—often very enjoyable—foods. Food stealing, and even vomiting, had become mealtime issues at home, and Joe wondered whether they might be a problem at school lunches as well. On the opposite side, Michelle speculated that Adam's steady, if slow, progress might be due, in part, to this special diet, and so she wanted to give it more time. The school was familiar with the gluten-free, wheat-free diet, as several students were currently following it. Thus, Michelle and Joe's ultimate decision regarding the diet would not affect his placement at the school.

At this school, there would be two openings available in September, with four candidates applying. Three of the four applicants in fact had been receiving early intervention services at the center's associated program, and all had individual needs warranting specialized services. This decision would also be made within a few weeks, and once again Michelle and Joe were forced to wait.

While awaiting the letters of acceptance or rejection, they reviewed the various scenarios they might be facing. They actually preferred the second school—the one run by the Manning Child Development Center—because they were already familiar with the school's policies and staff members. They believed that the transition there would be the easiest for Adam, as well as for them. On the other hand, they felt that if he were accepted at the first school as well, they would almost have to accept that placement, given the sterling reputation of that program. With either school, Joe and Michelle knew that they would have to continue at least some of Adam's in-home therapy. They were prepared to do whatever it took to help their son reach his potential during these early years. At the same time, they understood the risk of overloading a child once full-day programming started.

They didn't even want to think of the possibility of rejections from both schools. If Adam were not accepted by either program, the school district child study team, by law, would be responsible for finding an appropriate placement for him. Michelle and Joe feared that the team might place him in a preschool program that was designed for children less disabled than Adam. Although at the earlier meetings and evaluations, the team's case manager had seemed caring and aware of Adam's severe limitations, Michelle remained on the alert, having heard so many horror stories from other parents.

The letters from both schools came within a day of each other, a rejection from the first school and then an acceptance from the Manning school. Michelle

Most of today's theorists believe that autism is caused by biological factors, although the precise biological causes are not yet known. One line of research has linked the disorder to abnormal development very early in life of the *cerebellum*, a brain area that helps to control shifts in attention (Courchesne & Courchesne, 1997).

and Joe were overwhelmed by the emotional roller-coaster ride that they experienced within a 24-hour period. If asked 5 years before how rejection from one preschool program and acceptance at another would make them feel, they would completely have underestimated the sheer effect that those letters had. They found it impossible to sleep during the night in between their receipt. But now, with Adam's enrollment in the school that had links to his early intervention services, a school that already knew him, his parents felt a weight lifted off their shoulders.

For the first time in quite a while, they felt a sense of hope. They focused less on the many things that Adam could not do and felt more empowered by the things that he might be able to do with a proper program. With full-day, trial-by-trial learning, behavioral management strategies, and one-to-one student-to-teacher ratios, Adam was going to be given an opportunity to work through his disorder to reach his fullest potential. While Michelle and Joe were still far from fully accepting Adam's disability, especially its lifelong implications, they were a step closer to understanding Adam and enhancing his life.

His enrollment in the new program was only 2 months away, and a number of decisions had to be made. Michelle had some transportation concerns, but was told that that responsibility fell to Adam's case manager. That is, it was the responsibility of the school district to arrange Adam's transportation to and from this school. She and Joe decided to continue with Adam's special diet for another 6 months, and to then make a further decision about it after seeing how the new school was progressing. Finally, they decided to discontinue the behavioral therapy at home, also for the first 6 months of the new school program. The behavioral program at the school would be intense, and additional behavioral therapy at home might create burnout and hinder Adam's progress. On the other hand, they did decide to continue his home speech therapy program, even though he would be receiving individual speech sessions four times a week at the new full-day program.

The month prior to enrollment, the school's *home program coordinator* put together a parent information and training session for Michelle and Joe. This meeting provided them with an introduction to the school's executive director, a review of the school's policies and procedures, and a chance to meet their son's classroom teacher and teaching assistants. There would be five other students in the class, all between the ages of 3 and 6 years old. Michelle and Joe learned that, in fact, a series of parent training sessions would be following, and that at least one of the parents would be required to attend. The family would also be assigned a *home program consultant*—a staff member who would visit their home on a regular basis to help them identify, prioritize, and work on home issues one at a time.

Adam's enrollment in this school program also had an important advantage that Joe and Michelle really didn't want to think much about at this point: the opportunity for *life span services*. Although students with autism graduate from school at age 21, they typically have needs that last a lifetime. Recognizing these potential needs, Adam's new school had expanded its services. They offered workshop training and placement for adults with autism. They also ran several group homes in which persons with autism live in a house under the supervision of staff members. Their typical group home had eight residents and four supervisors. The needs of an adult Adam were a long way off, and his parents decided that they would cross that bridge when they came to it. Nevertheless, it was reassuring to know that such services would be there when the time came.

Adam's first day of school came, and off he went on a school van. He always enjoyed car rides, so Michelle hoped that that enjoyment would overcome his anxiety at being separated from her. She had also provided him with a new set of his favorite Disney figurines to keep him occupied during the ride. She decided to follow the van on its 40-minute journey to the school, taking care to keep her distance so that Adam would not spot her car. Once he arrived safely at the school, Michelle watched as his teacher took him off the bus and escorted him into the building. She knew that he was on his own.

All day she expected a phone call that she would have to come pick him up because his tantrums were inconsolable or because he was too disruptive in the class. But no phone call came, and the van dropped Adam off at the end of the day. The note from his teacher described a typical first day—with some tears and some smiles. The note also indicated that Adam had been able to successfully carry over some of the behaviors and skills that he had acquired in the early intervention program. Michelle felt very reassured that she had underestimated her son's coping abilities; at least the first day of school was a positive experience.

The next few months were ones of transition. Adam's sleep pattern was disrupted for awhile. He had to rise for school an hour earlier than he was used to; this caused him to nap on the bus ride home, making it hard for him to fall asleep at the proper time later in the evening. But with the consistent application of his new schedule, and the assistance of the home program consultant assigned to the family, he came to accept his new routine, and the family was able to move on to other issues.

The first few months of Adam's full-day school program were devoted primarily to helping him carry over gains that he had made previously in the early intervention program. The new school program also introduced several self-care skills during the early months. Adam's teacher even introduced toilet training within 2 weeks of his starting at the school, wanting to establish this skill as early as possible. He started on what the school called a "5-minute schedule." He was directed to sit on a potty seat for 1 to 2 minutes, then was returned to a regular session of activity for 5 minutes, then directed back to the potty seat, and so on. Throughout the procedure, he was given extra fluids, which meant that he would have many

The number of *sheltered workshops* and *group homes* available for teenagers and adults with autism is currently on the rise (Van Bourgondien & Schopler, 1990).

opportunities to go to the bathroom. Whenever Adam successfully used the potty, he was rewarded with his favorite cookie. Over time, the number of toilet successes increased and the number of accidents decreased, and the teacher was able to slowly expand the length of the intervals between potty sittings. Adam was on his way to being toilet trained.

In October, Michelle and Joe met with all of the key persons in Adam's school program to discuss the goals and objectives for the coming year. The participants at the meeting included Adam's case manager, the psychologist from his school district, his special education teacher, his speech therapist, his occupational therapist, and the director of the school. All programs and goals were reviewed, and questions from all parties were discussed. The teacher indicated that the program for the following year would center on developing a consistent communication system for Adam and on teaching him learning readiness skills and self-care skills, including maintaining eye contact; appropriate sitting; imitation skills; following simple one- and two-step directions; matching colors, shapes, and letters; pre-handwriting; waiting; appropriate play skills; handwashing; brushing his teeth; and getting dressed.

> Individual therapy and support groups for parents of children with autism are now becoming more available. A number of parent associations and lobbies also offer emotional support and practical help.

Joe asked whether mainstreaming would be included in Adam's program. The teacher indicated that at this point it was important for the child to spend a great deal of his time in school increasing his beginning skills through the behavioral therapy. Throughout the year there would be several community experiences and field trips for Adam's class, where there would be potential to play with other children; but mainstreaming would not be a central part of his school program for this first year. At the same time, she noted, there were extracurricular activities that other parents often enrolled their children in, which could also provide mainstreaming experiences. Examples included toddler gymnastics sessions, music and movement classes, and specialized horseback riding lessons. More and more disciplines were becoming sensitive to working with children with special needs, and offered special sessions devoted to enhancing the socialization skills of these children.

Epilogue

As the school personnel laid out their plans and hopes for Adam, Michelle and Joe felt reassured. They sensed that he, and they, were in good hands. It was comforting to know that they were no longer in this alone, and that Adam would have the opportunity to work every day, all day, with people who knew something about this horrible and pervasive problem.

At the same time, they knew, and the staff members reminded them, that they were at the beginning, not the end, of a long and difficult and confusing journey. While school programs such as this one were considered state-of-the-art, they rarely helped children with autism to reach normalcy. Nor could such programs guarantee particular gains or achievements. They could, at best, help children with autism reach their full potential, a potential that remained limited and somewhat unpredictable. Thus, Michelle and Joe settled in for the continued journey—with feelings of fear, depression, and also anger that this fate had befallen their child and their family. They prepared for a journey in which their son would continue to grow and learn in his own way, with everyone involved—his teachers, his parents, and his other relatives—working to find the techniques and reinforcements that would challenge him and move him forward, step by step. Surely, Adam's life, and the lives of his parents, did not have to be devoid of joy, satisfaction, or accomplishment. But, just as surely, the satisfactions and accomplishments that awaited them would be very different from the ones that Michelle and Joe had envisioned just a few years ago. It was now time for Adam to become Adam.

"No two people with autism are the same. Its precise form of expression is different in every case."
—Oliver Sacks (2000)

Attention-Deficit/Hyperactivity Disorder

Table **16-1**

DSM-IV Checklist

Attention-Deficit/Hyperactivity Disorder

1. Either of the following groups:

   A. At least six of the following symptoms of *inattention*, persisting for at least six months to a degree that is maladaptive and inconsistent with development level:

      1. Frequent failure to give close attention to details, or making careless mistakes.
      2. Frequent difficulty in sustaining attention.
      3. Frequent failure to listen when spoken to directly.
      4. Frequent failure to follow through on instructions and failure to finish work.
      5. Difficulty organizing tasks and activities.
      6. Avoidance of, dislike of, and reluctance to engage in tasks that require sustained mental effort.
      7. Frequent loss of items necessary for tasks or activities.
      8. Easy distraction by irrelevant stimuli.
      9. Forgetfulness in daily activities.

   B. At least six of the following symptoms of *hyperactivity-impulsivity,* persisting for at least six months to a degree that is maladaptive and inconsistent with developmental level:

      1. Fidgeting with hands or feet, or squirming in seat.
      2. Frequent wandering from seat in classroom or similar situation.
      3. Frequent running about or climbing excessively in situations in which it is inappropriate.
      4. Frequent difficulty playing or engaging in leisure activities quietly.
      5. Frequent "on the go" activity or acting as if "driven by a motor."
      6. Frequent excessive talking.
      7. Frequent blurting out of answers before questions have been completed.
      8. Frequent difficulty awaiting turn.
      9. Frequent interrupting of or intruding on others.

2. The presence of some symptoms before the age of 7.

3. Impairment from the symptoms in at least two settings.

4. Significant impairment.

Based on APA, 1994, 2000.

Although low birth weight can sometimes be associated with ADHD, most children with low birth weight do not develop the disorder, and most children with ADHD do not have a history of low birth weight (APA, 2000).

Billy was his parents' first child. He was born after a normal, uncomplicated pregnancy, an especially healthy baby who grew rapidly and reached the standard developmental milestones—sitting, crawling, standing walking, etc.—either at or before the expected age. His parents marveled at his exuberance and his drive to be independent at an early age. He was sitting by the age of 5 months and walking at 11 months. Once mobile, he was a veritable dynamo (in fact, they called him "the Dynamo") who raced around the house, filled with a curiosity that led him to grab, examine, and frequently destroy almost anything that wasn't nailed down.

Billy—From "Dynamo" to "Dynamite"

During his toddler period, Billy's parents had no inkling that his activity level was at all unusual and, in truth, in many ways it was just an exaggeration of tendencies that most toddlers exhibit. Still, his parents found it exhausting to cope with his behavior. Just watching over him was a full-time job. Billy's mother, Marie, had at one point contemplated doing some freelance accounting at home to earn extra money. However, with her very first project she quickly realized that this was completely unrealistic. Marie had hoped that she could contain Billy by keeping him in a playpen while she worked, but she found that he wouldn't tolerate such confinement for more than 2 minutes before he was yelling to get out. Once out, he was a roving accident scene. Within minutes, Marie would hear a crash or some other noise that demanded investigation.

When Billy's mother became pregnant with his sister, Billy was well into the "terrible twos" and his mother and his father, Stan, were beginning to doubt their suitability as parents. Of course, other new parents whom they met remarked on how demanding children were, but Marie and Stan could tell that the other parents felt nowhere near the same sense of desperation.

With the arrival of Billy's sister, Jennifer, Marie and Stan developed a budding awareness that their problems in handling their son might not be due entirely to their inadequacy. As an infant, Jennifer—unlike Billy—did not try to squirm and break free every time she was held. Later, there were other differences. As a toddler, she was content to sit quietly for long periods just playing with her toys, and she listened until the end of the entire story when someone read to her, whereas Billy would get restless and run off within a couple of minutes.

When Billy reached school age, and Marie and Stan received more objective feedback about his situation, their sense of his difficulties became more defined. After his first day of school, his kindergarten teacher described him as "quite a handful"; then, at the parent–teacher conference, she informed Billy's parents that his activity level was well above that of the other children. In the first and second grades, as the academic component of the curriculum increased and the demands on the children for behavioral control increased correspondingly, Marie and Stan started to get yet stronger complaints from his teachers. In addition, Billy's academic progress was slowed due to his attentional problems. Although he eventually learned to read, he didn't really begin to master the skill until the second grade. Now 8 years old and in the third grade, Billy was falling behind the other children in a wide range of academic tasks. With encouragement—actually, insistence—from his teacher, Mrs. Pease, his parents decided to seek help for him at the Child Development Center.

Billy at Home: A Parent's Perspective

By age 8, Billy rarely carried out his parents' requests or instructions, or he carried them out only partially before becoming caught up in some other activity. An evening in November was illustrative. Billy's mother had just finished preparing dinner when she went to her son's room and asked him to stop playing his video game, wash his hands, and take his place at the table. "OK, Mom," Billy answered.

"Thank you, Billy," Marie said as she went back down to the kitchen to do some final preparations. However, 5 minutes later she realized she still had seen no sign of Billy. She went back up to his room and found he had never left the video game.

"Billy, I mean it. Stop playing now!" she told him.

"Oh, all right," he said, and turned the game off.

Although this was Marie's second effort, for once Billy was coming without too much of a struggle, so his mother was relieved. "Go wash your hands," she reminded him.

"OK," Billy replied. He headed down the hall toward the bathroom, but caught a glimpse of his 5-year-old sister already seated at the table, holding a new doll. Jennifer was pulling a string that made the doll talk.

"Hey, neat!" Billy exclaimed. "Let me try." He ran over, grabbed the doll from Jennifer's hands and pulled the string. The doll spoke in a squeaky voice, while Billy's sister complained that she wanted her toy back. "Does the doll say anything else?" Billy asked, ignoring Jennifer's protests. He began to pull the string over and over in rapid succession until, finally, it broke off.

"Uh, oh," Billy observed.

"Mommy, he broke my doll!" Jennifer cried.

Billy's mother emerged from the kitchen to find him holding the broken doll while his sister wailed. What had begun as a simple attempt to get Billy to wash his hands and seat himself at the dinner table had ended in a tumultuous scene.

And so it would go. Unless Billy was escorted through every task of the day, he either got sidetracked or into some kind of trouble, and it usually ended with an argument or something getting broken. Consequently, his parents often found it easier just to do things for Billy—wash his hands, clean his room, get him dressed, and the like—because getting him to do the tasks himself was the greater effort.

Half of children with ADHD also have learning or communication problems, many perform poorly in school, a number have social difficulties, and about 80% misbehave (Mariani & Barkley, 1997).

As many as 90% of children with ADHD are boys (APA, 1994, 2000).

When left to his own devices, Billy's behavior was disruptive in other ways. He jumped on the beds, ran through the house, or played shrill games of hide-and-seek under the dinner table with his unwilling parents or sister. If his mother was on the phone, he would think nothing of yelling out demands for a drink, a snack, or help in finding some lost toy, despite Marie's numerous warnings not to interrupt her.

Even playing out in the yard was not a solution, because if Billy wasn't watched closely, in a flash he could be running out into the street after a ball, without any regard for traffic. When playing indoors with neighborhood children, Billy was bossy, continually grabbing their toys or refusing to share his own. Thus, his play dates had to be closely supervised by his parents to avoid their breaking down into a squabble. Due to these problems, Billy had few friends to play with. Instead, most of his leisure time was spent watching television or playing video games, activities that Marie and Stan were reluctant to encourage, but which they felt forced to accept since the 8-year-old could do little else without supervision.

Billy at School: A Teacher's Perspective

Around 5% of schoolchildren manifest ADHD (APA, 1994, 2000).

Billy's third-grade teacher, Mrs. Pease, found his behavior intolerably disruptive in school. She was also concerned that Billy's behavior problems were interfering with his ability to learn. He was a bright child, in her judgment, but due to his attention and behavior problems, he was failing to complete his lessons and hampering the other children's ability to attend to theirs.

A day at school in mid-April illustrated Billy's difficulties. Mrs. Pease had called the class to attention to begin an oral exercise: reciting a multiplication table on the blackboard. The first child had just begun her recitation when, suddenly, Billy exclaimed, "Look!" The class turned to see Billy running to the window.

"Look," he exclaimed again, "an airplane!"

A couple of children ran to the window with Billy to see the airplane, but Mrs. Pease called them back, and they returned to their seats. Billy, however, remained at the window, pointing at the sky. Mrs. Pease called him back, too.

"Billy, please return to your desk," Mrs. Pease said firmly. But Billy acted as though he didn't even hear her.

"Look, Mrs. Pease," he exclaimed, "the airplane is blowing smoke!" A couple of other children started from their desks.

"Billy," Mrs. Pease tried once more, "if you don't return to your desk this instant, I'm going to send you to Miss Warren's office." Billy, seemingly oblivious to her threats, remained at the window, staring excitedly up at the sky.

Mrs. Pease, her patience wearing thin, addressed Billy through gritted teeth. "Billy, come with me back to your seat!" she said. She took him by the hand and led him there. She also considered making good on her threat to send him to Miss Warren, the principal, but she glanced at the clock and realized Miss Warren would not be in her office now. Finding someone else to supervise Billy would probably be more disruptive than disciplining him within the class, so she settled for getting him back in his seat, then took her place once more in front of the class. By now she was almost 10 minutes into the lesson period and still had not finished a single multiplication table.

Mrs. Pease tried to resume the lesson. "Who can tell me 3 times 6?" she asked.

Fifteen children raised their hands, but before she could call on anyone, Billy blurted out the correct answer. "Thank you, Billy," she said, barely able to contain her exasperation, "but please raise your hand like the others."

Mrs. Pease tried again. "Who knows 3 times 7?" This time Billy raised his hand, but he still couldn't resist creating a disruption.

"I know, I know," Billy pleaded, jumping up and down in his seat with his hand raised high.

"That will do, Billy," Mrs. Pease admonished him. She deliberately called on another child. The child responded with the correct answer.

"*I knew that!*" Billy exclaimed.

"Billy," Mrs. Pease told him, "I don't want you to say one more word this class period."

Billy looked down at his desk sulkily, ignoring the rest of the lesson. He began to fiddle with a couple of rubber bands, trying to see how far they would stretch before they broke. He looped the rubber bands around his index fingers and pulled his hands farther and farther apart. This kept him quiet for a while; by this point, Mrs. Pease didn't care what he did, as long as he was quiet. She continued conducting the multiplication lesson while Billy stretched the rubber bands until finally they snapped, flying off and hitting two children, on each side of him. Billy let out a yelp of surprise, and the class turned to him.

"That's it, Billy," Mrs. Pease told him, "You're going to sit outside the classroom until the period is over."

"No!" Billy protested. "I'm not going. I didn't do anything!"

"You shot those rubber bands at Bonnie and Julian," Mrs. Pease said.

"But it was an accident."

"I don't care. Out you go!"

Billy stalked out of the classroom to sit on a chair in the hall. Before exiting, however, he turned to Mrs. Pease. "I'll sue you for this," he yelled, not really knowing what it meant.

Soon, the school bell rang, signaling the end of the period and the beginning of recess. Mrs. Pease was thankful to get some relief from the obligation of controlling Billy, but was frustrated that almost the entire math period had been wasted on his disruptions.

Out in the schoolyard, during recess, Billy's difficulties continued. As the children lined up for turns on the slide, Billy pushed to the head of the line, almost knocking one child off the ladder as he elbowed his way up. After going down the

The number of children diagnosed with ADHD more than doubled during the 1990s (Robison et al., 1999).

Symptoms of ADHD are typically most pronounced during the elementary school years. They become less conspicuous by late childhood and early adolescence (APA, 1994, 2000).

slide, Billy barged into a dodgeball game that some younger children were playing; he grabbed the ball away from one child and began dribbling it like a basketball, while the other child cried in frustration. The supervising teacher told Billy to give the ball back, but Billy kept dribbling, oblivious to her demands. Finally, she took the ball physically, and Billy wailed in protest.

"Hey, give that back!" he insisted.

"You took that ball from someone else," the teacher explained.

"But you took it from me. That's not fair!" Billy argued.

The teacher sent Billy to sit on a bench, where he remained sulking and feeling mistreated for the rest of the recess period.

This was an average day for Billy at school. On some of his better days, he was less physically disruptive, but he still had his problems, particularly in attending to and completing his schoolwork. In a typical case, Mrs. Pease would give the class an assignment to work on, such as completing a couple of pages of arithmetic problems. While most of the children worked without supervision until the assignment was completed, Billy was easily distracted. When he got to the end of the first page, he would lose his momentum and, rather than continuing, would begin fiddling with some object on his desk. Other times, if another child asked the teacher a question, Billy would stop his own work to investigate the situation, getting up to view the other child's work while failing to complete his own.

Finally, at a parent–teacher conference, Mrs. Pease told Billy's parents that she thought Billy's problems might be attributable to an "attention deficit disorder." Concerned about Billy's growing academic and social problems—not to mention feeling exhausted from continually having to remind, encourage, and threaten their son to get him to do the most elemental things—Marie and Stan decided to seek professional assistance. They arranged for a consultation at the Child Development Center.

Billy in Treatment: The Therapist in Action

After repeatedly observing a child's tornadoes of activity, inattention, and recklessness, teachers or parents often conclude that he or she suffers from *attention-deficit/hyperactivity disorder* (*ADHD*). However, 25 years of practice had taught Dr. Sharon Remoc, a child psychiatrist, that such a conclusion is often premature and inaccurate, leading to incorrect and even harmful interventions. Thus, when Billy's parents brought him to the Child Development Center, Dr. Remoc was careful to conduct lengthy interviews with the child, his parents, and his teacher; to arrange for him to be observed at home and at school by an intern; to set up a physical examination by a pediatrician to detect any medical conditions (for example, lead poisoning) that might be causing the child's symptoms; and to administer a battery of psychological tests. In addition to obtaining a description of Billy's current

> Only 33 to 50% of children who receive a diagnosis of ADHD from pediatricians actually undergo psychological or educational testing to support the diagnosis (Leutwyler, 1996).

problems and his history from his parents, Dr. Remoc had Billy's mother respond to questions from three different assessment instruments: the *Diagnostic Interview Schedule for Children (DISC)*, which contains questions pertaining to a wide range of childhood disorders represented in DSM-IV; the *Swanson, Nolan, and Pelham Checklist (SNAP-IV)*, which contains questions pertaining specifically to disruptive behavior problems; and the *Conners Parent Rating Scale*, which contains questions specifically for assessing ADHD. Similarly, Dr. Remoc sent the teacher's versions of the SNAP-IV and Conners scale to Mrs. Pease.

Billy's battery of tests included the Wechsler Intelligence Scale for Children (WISC) and the Wechsler Individual Achievement Tests (to provide scores in reading, mathematics, language, and written achievement). The results of these tests confirmed the impression already supplied by Billy's parents and Mrs. Pease: Billy's intelligence was above average, and his academic achievement was lower than his intelligence scores would predict. These findings established that Billy's academic problems were not due to intellectual limitations.

After completing this comprehensive assessment, Dr. Remoc was confident that Billy's difficulties met the criteria in DSM-IV for a diagnosis of *attention-deficit/hyperactivity disorder* (ADHD). He exhibited a majority of the symptoms listed both for *inattention* (for example, difficulty sustaining attention, failure to follow instructions, oblivious to verbal commands, easily distracted) and for *hyperactivity-impulsivity* (for example, difficulty remaining seated, excessive motor activity in inappropriate situations, difficulty waiting his turn). The symptoms were apparent before the age of 7, occurred both at home and school, and caused significant impairment in both the social and academic spheres.

Over the years, research has indicated that many children with ADHD respond well to either stimulant drugs or systematic behavioral treatment. Although some therapists prefer one of these approaches over the other, Dr. Remoc had come to believe that a combination of the interventions increases a child's chances of recovery. By helping the child to focus better and slow down, the medications may help him or her to profit from the procedures and rewards used in the behavioral program.

Stimulant drugs, which now include *methylphenidate* (Ritalin), *d-amphetamine* (Dexedrine), and *pemoline* (Cylert), were first used with ADHD children decades ago, when clinicians noted that the drugs seemed to have a "paradoxical" tranquilizing, quieting effect on these children. Subsequent research has shown that all children—both those with and those without ADHD—experience an increase in attentional capacity when taking stimulant drugs, resulting in behavior that is more focused and controlled. This may create the appearance of sedation, but the children are actually not sedated at all.

On the other hand, most forms of the medications must be taken every four hours, requiring the child to take at least one dose at school in order to maintain

> Children with low intelligence who are placed in an academic school setting that is beyond their intellectual development often show symptoms of inattention similar to those found in ADHD. Children of high intelligence placed in unstimulating academic settings may also display symptoms of inattention (APA, 1994, 2000).

> It has been estimated that as many as 10% of all American boys may take Ritalin or other stimulant medications for ADHD.

the benefits for the afternoon. If the parents want the benefits extended to the home environment, then additional doses have to be taken later in the day.

Unfortunately, none of the drugs are effective for all children, and only partially effective for others. And even when a drug is optimally effective, other areas of behavioral adjustment may still need to be addressed, because the ADHD child may have little practice in the more appropriate behaviors that he or she now is theoretically capable of producing. This is where behavioral programs may come into play.

In the ideal case, both parents and teachers are involved in implementing a behavior modification program, which is based on the ABC model of behavior. The *A* in the model denotes *antecedents,* the conditions that provide the occasion for a particular behavior; *B* denotes the *behavior* itself; and *C* denotes the *consequences* of the behavior. Thus, a given behavior is seen as prompted by certain antecedents, and maintained by its consequences. For example, Billy's sprint to the window was prompted by the antecedent condition of a boring classroom exercise and the appearance of an exciting stimulus (the airplane). It was maintained, according to the model, by the rewarding effect of viewing the airplane, which was much greater than the punishing effect of Mrs. Pease's warnings or even of being sent out of the room. In a behavior modification program, the usual strategy is to increase the rewards for engaging in *alternative behaviors* under the same antecedent conditions. Thus, if the reward for remaining seated can be made to exceed the reward for viewing the airplane, then, theoretically, the child will be more inclined to remain seated.

Learning alternative behaviors may involve more than just adjusting incentives or antecedents. Some skills may have to be taught directly. A child who has never practiced asking politely for a toy, as opposed to grabbing it, will need to learn this skill before he or she can respond to incentives to implement it. Direct behavioral skills training usually follows a standard sequence. First, the child receives an explanation of the skill; next, he observes a model demonstrating the skill; then, he practices performing the skill, first through role-playing in the training session and then through real-life behavioral practice. After the skill is learned, both parents and teachers can prompt the child to employ it in a given situation. For example, after the skill of *sharing* is well learned, the parent can prompt the child to "share" in a situation calling for cooperation with another child, and then praise the child appropriately for so doing. Theoretically, the more the skill is employed and reinforced in a variety of appropriate circumstances, the more the child will use the skill spontaneously, receiving naturalistic positive reinforcement from the environment in the form of friendly or gratified reactions from others.

Research suggests that a combination of drug therapy and behavioral therapy is often helpful to children with ADHD (Klassen et al., 1999).

Thus, Dr. Remoc outlined for Billy's parents four treatment components: (a) *stimulant medication,* (b) *parental training* in the use of behavioral modification principles, (c) *social skills training* for Billy, and (d) *token economy* in the school environment.

Dr. Remoc explained that stimulant medication was important for increasing Billy's attention and impulse control; this, in turn, would enhance his capacity to do what was expected of him, both in general and in response to the behavior modification plan. The parental training, she explained, would acquaint Marie and Stan with principles of behavior modification, allowing them to deal optimally with any remaining behavior problems, as well as with Billy's behavior during periods when he might not be taking medication (so-called drug holidays). Social skills training seemed necessary, Dr. Remoc said, in light of Billy's problems in getting along with other children and in cooperating at home. She explained that these skills often have to be learned directly, and do not result from medication alone. Finally, she explained that, since a large portion of Billy's difficulties occurred in the classroom, it would be helpful for both Billy and Mrs. Pease to have a behavioral program operating in that environment. Dr. Remoc spoke to Mrs. Pease about the matter, and the teacher was agreeable to instituting a program provided it wasn't too burdensome; but given Billy's problems up to now, Mrs. Pease said that almost anything seemed less burdensome than simply doing nothing.

Stimulant Medication   After ruling out any physical problems (e.g., motor tics) that might preclude the use of stimulant medication, Dr. Remoc discussed the basic rationale for use of the medication with Billy's parents. She explained that the medication had been used for years to treat children with symptoms of inattention, impulsivity, and overactivity. She also explained that, contrary to certain popular misconceptions, the medication is not a tranquilizer. On the contrary, the medication stimulates the central nervous system for 3 to 4 hours after it is ingested. This stimulant effect, she explained, seems to increase the capacity of children with ADHD to maintain their attention and to control their impulses. As a result, they are better equipped to meet the requirements of school, home, and social life.

Around 8.5 tons of Ritalin are produced each year, with 90% of it used in the United States (Leutwyler, 1996).

In addition, she informed Billy's parents that certain side effects can develop, including weight loss, slowed growth, dizziness, insomnia, and tics. Dr. Remoc noted, however, that these effects usually are not severe and often disappear after the body becomes accustomed to the drug or whenever a "drug holiday" is scheduled. The clinician noted that since most children with ADHD respond well to Ritalin without prohibitive side effects, she was inclined to try Ritalin first rather than other stimulant medications.

Dr. Remoc pointed out that the decision to take medication was not carved in stone. Indeed, the parents should consider the initial medication regimen as a trial period; if, during this time, they concluded that the medication was not worthwhile, then it should be discontinued. Either a different medication could be tried or they could rely on the behavioral methods alone.

Once Billy began taking the medication, it was apparent that his behavior improved substantially, although not totally. In class, for example, Billy still blurted out some answers and turned around to talk to his neighbors during silent reading period, but he did these things only about one fourth as often as before. Most noticeable from Mrs. Pease's standpoint, simply saying his name was often enough to get him to cease what he was doing.

Out in the schoolyard, Billy was now less inclined to barge into other children's games or push others aside. On the other hand, he still did not have a good social sense. Either he drifted off by himself or, if he did join a game, he failed to abide by the rules consistently, which ended up provoking arguments. For example, in joining a game of catch with four other children, Billy was inclined to hog the ball after he received it; he would then hold it and giggle in spite of the other children's yells that he was supposed to throw the ball to the next receiver.

At home, Billy seemed less driven physically. He sat at the dinner table for the entire meal, without constant requests to be excused and without getting up repeatedly to grab things or to play under the table. Also, his passion for jumping on the beds was gone, and he became more dependable in carrying out instructions. For example, if his parents sent him to wash up and sit at the table, they now could count on his following through 75% of the time (as opposed to 25%, as before). On the other hand, tendencies such as stubbornness and defiance remained a problem; it remained a struggle to get him to do chores, to get started on his homework, or to follow household rules in general. He continued to barge in on his mother when she was on the phone, shouting his insistent requests for snacks, toys, and videos.

Overall, however, the medication seemed to have many advantages.

Parental Training To gain some knowledge of behavioral management techniques, Billy's parents enrolled in a training group for parents of children with ADHD (at about the same time that Billy began medication). The group, led by a psychologist, Dr. James Grendon, was designed to educate parents about both ADHD and the principles of behavior modification for managing it. Group sessions were held three times a month, and once a month Dr. Grendon met alone with Billy's parents to discuss the child's individual situation.

At the very first group session, Billy's parents found comfort in learning that other parents' experiences closely paralleled their own. Pretty soon, all the parents were sharing their experiences, and found that they were dealing with very similar concerns. Many parents were able to see humor in some of the situations, and this helped to soften the impact of what they had all been going through.

> The use of Ritalin has increased as much as 300% since 1990 (Robison et al., 1999).

> Family conflict and negative parent–child interactions often characterize cases of ADHD. Such negative interactions frequently lessen markedly with successful treatment (APA, 2000).

It also helped Marie and Stan to know that some of their marital disputes were shared by the other parents. Like the others in the group, Billy's parents often argued over how to deal with their child. Although it didn't solve the problem, it helped them to know that even their arguments were "normal," given the circumstances.

In additional group sessions, Marie and Stan were progressively introduced to the ABC principles of behavior management. Among the points emphasized that they found helpful, was that parents can become unduly focused on discouraging problem behaviors through criticism or punishments; the punishments, in turn, are often ineffective and just fuel resentment. A different approach, Dr. Grendon explained, was to think in terms of the alternative behaviors (B) that parents would like their children to perform under the same circumstances (A), and to provide praise and rewards (C) accordingly.

Billy's parents explored this principle in greater detail in individual sessions with the group leader, as they felt it applied particularly to the way they were handling (or mishandling) many situations with their son. For example, a regular problem with Billy was that he interrupted his mother when she was on the phone. It had gotten so she practically had to lock herself in the bedroom in order to have a coherent conversation with a pediatrician, repairman, friend, relative, or anyone she needed to talk to. Often, even locking herself in was not enough to insure peace and quiet, as Billy might start pounding on the door in order to convey his demands, in spite of repeated scolding.

To address the problem, the psychologist asked Billy's parents to think specifically of what alternative actions they would like Billy to carry out under these conditions. At first, all Marie and Stan could think of was "not interrupt," but Dr. Grendon reminded them of the stipulation that they think of a tangible alternative behavior for Billy to carry out under the same circumstances. After some discussion, they came up with the idea of having Billy write down his requests whenever his mother was on the phone. They noted that their son loved to write notes, so this might be a tangible thing he could do to satisfy his demands temporarily, and allow him to resist interrupting. With further discussion, Billy's parents and the psychologist worked out the following procedure: Before Marie made a call or answered the phone, she would hand Billy a special message pad, reminding him to write down any questions or problems that he had while she was talking; Marie would then give prompt attention to Billy's messages as soon as she was off the phone; finally, if Billy succeeded in using the pad, instead of interrupting, for the majority of calls in a given week (his mother would keep a checklist to tabulate Billy's compliance), he would be given a special reward on the weekend (eating out at his favorite restaurant).

This was the first behavioral plan that Billy's parents put into effect, and after ironing out a few wrinkles, Billy was able to follow the procedure, even to the

> Children whose parents or other close relatives have had ADHD are more likely than others to develop the disorder (APA, 1994, 2000).

point of fetching the message pad himself whenever the phone rang. Eventually, he resisted interrupting almost entirely.

Other behavioral plans were then put into effect for other matters, such as household chores and homework completion. In both cases, Billy's parents found an effective formula by reversing antecedent conditions and behavioral consequences. For example, they saw to it that television viewing would always follow the completion of homework, rather than vice versa.

Social Skills Training Marie and Stan also enrolled their son in a class where he could learn skills for getting along better with other children. The class was in fact composed of other children receiving treatment at the center for ADHD.

During each class the focus was on learning one particular social skill, such as *sharing.* First, the group leader explained the concept of sharing, and then asked the children their own opinions of what it meant. Next, she demonstrated the implementation of the skill with several children in different, contrived, situations: sharing toys, sharing food, or sharing a seat. Then each child came up, one by one, and practiced sharing in each of these hypothetical circumstances. The group leader and the other children then gave the child corrective feedback on how well he or she had shared. Similar classes were devoted to other social skills, such as cooperating, speaking calmly, making polite requests, and following rules.

Billy's parents and Mrs. Pease received written guidelines for discussing the social skills training sessions at home and in school and for guiding Billy to use the skills in everyday situations. Many of the opportunities to prompt him arose at home in his interactions with his 5-year-old sister. With continued prompting, Billy started to share things with his sister spontaneously on many occasions, which increased the harmony in the household.

With these successes, and additional successes using the social skill of *cooperating,* Marie and Stan actually took the bold step of inviting one of Billy's schoolmates over to play. The last time a child had come over to play, it had been a disaster, as Billy had refused to relinquish any of his toys to his guest. Needless to say, no child was likely to return after such treatment. Although far from perfect, and in need of constant observation, the visit turned out to be reasonably pleasant.

> About half of children with ADHD who are referred for treatment also display oppositional defiant disorder or conduct disorder (APA, 2000).

Token Economy The token economy is an example of the ABC behavior modification system, but uses *tokens* to reinforce desired behavior rather than immediate, tangible rewards. The tokens are exchanged for an actual reward at a later time. Token reinforcement is particularly advantageous for ADHD children, who can get so wrapped up in the attractiveness of the actual reward that they find it difficult to remain mindful of the behaviors that the reward is designed to encourage.

For Billy, there were several behaviors that Mrs. Pease felt she would like to have some additional assistance in regulating, by means of some form of behavior modification. Accordingly, she and the therapist decided to focus on encouraging three specific school behaviors in Billy: raising his hand to answer questions (instead of blurting out answers), staying in line, and finishing in-class assignments. As token reinforcers, Mrs. Pease would use dinosaur stickers affixed to a piece of paper, with the number of stickers in each of three columns reflecting Billy's compliance with the three behavioral objectives. According to the plan (explained to Billy in a meeting with his parents and Mrs. Pease), Mrs. Pease would keep track of Billy's compliance separately for the morning period and the afternoon period, and award him one sticker if he achieved full compliance with a given behavioral objective in a given period. He would receive his morning stickers at lunchtime, and his afternoon stickers upon dismissal. The stickers could then be redeemed at home for special privileges (going out to eat, going out to a movie, an extra half hour of television or a video game, and others).

Billy liked the idea of getting stickers, and he agreed to the plan. On the first morning of the program, he received only one sticker: for finishing his assignment within the allotted time (he had blurted out a couple of answers and had wandered off from the line in going to art class). In the afternoon, however, he received two stickers: for staying in line and for finishing assignments. After a few more days on the program, Billy was averaging five stickers per day, a level that he was able to maintain, and which reflected a substantial improvement in all three areas.

Within 2 months of the combined treatment program, Billy had improved considerably. Increasingly he was conforming to classroom rules by staying in his seat, not talking, and finishing his assignments most of the time. When he deviated, he required only gentle reminders from Mrs. Pease in order to get back on track. Similarly, at home, he was less frenetic. He rarely jumped on the beds and remained seated at dinner most of the time; also, he could carry out instructions more dependably, and he usually accepted his household responsibilities without too much argument. In peer relations, Billy was still learning the culture of give and take, but with periodic guidance and further experience he was becoming increasingly effective. As a result, he was getting along well with his sister, and he now had a couple of friends who would come over regularly to play, and who invited him to their homes as well.

In DSM-II, ADHD was known officially as *hyperkinetic reaction of childhood,* and it was commonly referred to simply as *hyperactivity* or *hyperkinesis* (the latter term from the Greek for *over* and *motion*).

Unfortunately, after about 4 months of this improved functioning, Billy began to slip into some of his old patterns both at home and at school. His parents felt that the problems had to be addressed, as he seemed to be losing ground.

The recurrence of problems seemed to have coincided with the birth of his new baby brother. In a discussion with Dr. Remoc, Billy's parents wondered whether their total preoccupation with the birth of the baby, and their consequent inability to implement many features of the behavioral program (including not following through on redeeming Billy's dinosaur tokens), was responsible for the slippage in his progress. A renewed effort by the parents to apply the behavioral program, and an adjustment in the dosage of Billy's medication, helped the child to re-achieve his previous gains within a few weeks.

Epilogue

After 18 sessions of group parental training (over a 6-month period), 6 sessions of individual parent training, 6 sessions of social skills training for Billy, and 4 meetings at school with Billy's teacher, his ADHD symptoms stabilized at an improved level.

Billy himself reported that he was happier at school and enjoying the time at home with his family. He was still receiving medication and saw Dr. Remoc for regular checkups (every 4 months). Billy's parents planned to take him off medication in the summer (for a drug holiday) and felt confident of their ability to manage his behavior during that time with just the behavioral techniques. They were, in fact, a family again—sometimes concerned about things, and often harried—but, overall, enjoying their lives and activities together.

> In addition to being viewed negatively by peers and parents, children with ADHD often view themselves quite negatively as well (McCormick, 2000).

CASE 17

Conduct Disorder

Table 17-1

DSM-IV Checklist

Conduct Disorder

1. A repetitive and persistent pattern of behavior in which the basic rights of others or major age-appropriate societal norms or rules are violated, with at least three of the following present in the past twelve months (and at least one in the past six months):

   a. Frequent bullying or threatening of others.

   b. Frequent provoking of physical fights.

   c. Using dangerous weapons.

   d. Physical cruelty to people.

   e. Physical cruelty to animals.

   f. Stealing while confronting a victim.

   g. Forcing someone into sexual activity.

   h. Fire-setting.

   i. Deliberately destroying others' property.

   j. Breaking into a house, building, or car.

   k. Frequent manipulation of others.

   l. Stealing items of nontrivial value without confronting a victim.

   m. Frequent staying out beyond curfews, beginning before the age of 13.

   n. Running away from home overnight at least twice.

   o. Frequent truancy from school, beginning before the age of 13.

2. Significant impairment.

Based on APA, 1994, 2000.

Between 1 and 10% of children and adolescents display conduct disorder (APA, 2000).

Administrators at Billy Franklin's public school decided that the 17-year-old's presence there not only interfered with the education of other students but also posed a threat to their welfare. The officials feared that his increasingly destructive and harmful behavior might soon result in serious injury to one or many of Billy's classmates if immediate action were not taken. Billy's mother, Jennifer Franklin, who had raised her son without the help of his father, begged for one last chance, but a decision to expel the boy had been made. "Only property was damaged. No one was hurt," she pleaded, but she knew that her words were wasted on the school board. Billy had, after all, set the fire in the library, and although he had not intended to hurt anyone, he had certainly placed his classmates in danger. Granted, no one was hurt—this time. Next time, the outcome might be very different.

Although neighborhood parents had come to view Billy as an "uncaring, brutal, young devil," Jennifer could not let go of the image of her "little angel." At 8 years old, he had been everyone's sweetheart. "Mr. Manners"—as Billy's grandmother would refer to him—was always sure to say "please" and "thank you" and to give a hand to help his mother. His smile captured the hearts of everyone, and all of the neighborhood mothers were more than pleased when their children wanted to play with him.

Billy: The Seeds of a Problem

Early in his education, at parent-teacher conferences, Billy's teachers would do nothing but praise him, often suggesting that the classroom would run better if more children were like him. The teachers would go on about how sweet the young boy was, without addressing his inability to grasp many of the concepts that the other children were picking up with ease. When Billy was 9 years old, his 3rd-grade teacher, Mrs. O'Dwyer, spent the entire 45-minute conference with Jennifer fawning over the engaging child. The teacher failed to mention that he was barely passing mathematics.

During those early years, Billy was watched each day after school by his grandmother (who lived with them), and while his mother worked her evening job waiting tables at Jay's Diner. "Mr. Manners" and "Grammy" used to laugh for hours, while putting together puzzles, watching cartoons on TV, or doing other activities together. While all of his classmates loved him, it was Grammy whom Billy considered his "best friend." Most nights, both Billy and his grandmother were sound asleep by the time Jennifer returned from Jay's Diner.

It upset her greatly to come home and find the two of them sleeping. She knew that her aging mother did not have the mental ability to ensure that Billy was doing and understanding his schoolwork, but she had no choice. With Billy's father gone—he had disappeared when Billy was only 6 months old—she was forced to work two jobs, leaving much of the child care to her mentally declining mother.

During the weekends, Billy's mother made it a point to take him on trips. She felt that he needed a weekly break from their small house in southern New Jersey. For his 9th birthday, she took him to the Philadelphia Zoo, where he seemed to appreciate the polar bears most. He watched them with amazement for more than an hour, while other people came and went. One woman approached Jennifer and said, "Oh, you've got such a little angel there!" Billy's mother could not have agreed more.

> Conduct disorder has been linked to factors such as parental rejection or neglect, inconsistent and often harsh child-rearing practices, physical or sexual abuse, lack of supervision, early institutional living, frequent changes of caretakers, peer rejection, a delinquent peer group, and neighborhood exposure to violence (APA, 1994, 2000).

The first clear sign of trouble came toward the end of 3rd grade, when Billy was still 9 years old. Jennifer received a phone call at her day job in a grocery store. It was the vice principal informing her that Billy had been in a fight and was going to have to sit out recess for the rest of the week. Jennifer could not hide her disbelief and indignation. Why should Billy be punished if another child hit him? The vice principal informed her that Billy had thrown the first punch; the other child had apparently called him a "retard" when he had trouble reading a word in class, and Billy ran over and hit him.

As it turned out, this was not the only classmate to make fun of Billy's learning difficulties. Sally, once a friend, took to calling him "DoDo Brain." Other children, who once had enjoyed playing with him, offered similar names for him. Many of the children did this as a form of payback. It was becoming increasingly apparent to them that he was getting away with more than the rest of his classmates did, with his angelic smile. A teacher's favorite, Billy was becoming an outcast among his peers.

When the bus dropped him off at home in the afternoon each day, he would continue to display a glowing smile, knowing that just inside the door was Grammy, who loved him so much. He would not tell her of the names he was being called, nor that he was failing mathematics, writing, and reading. Although his grandmother had assured Jennifer that Billy was completing his homework each night, she would usually forget to enforce this house rule. Each day, within 20 minutes of his walking through the door, the two of them would be sitting in front of the television, engrossed and entertained.

One day, Billy's 4th-grade teacher, Teresa Goodwin, sent a letter home with Billy to alert his mother that he was failing several subjects. The letter indicated that he never did his homework and that there were increasing tensions between him and the rest of the class. The teacher requested that Jennifer come in to discuss a plan for helping Billy get back on track. Unfortunately, the letter never reached her. Billy gave it to his grandmother, who later threw it out in a state of confusion.

Thus, Billy's problems at school continued. His nickname officially became "Retardo," and he came to resent Ms. Goodwin, thinking that she could put a stop to his mistreatment if she really wanted to. Once, when she called on him for an answer, he called her a "bitch." Horrified, she revoked his recess for a week.

> By the age of 18, the average child in the United States has viewed 200,000 acts of violence on television (American Academy of Pediatrics, 1999).

Jennifer: A Mother Withdraws

At the end of that school year, Billy received three Fs on his final report card, and, according to the rules of the school district, he had to repeat the 4th grade. His mother sobbed, not only because of his school problems, but because she was accused by his teacher and school administrators of having little interest in helping her son to succeed.

Filled with guilt that she was failing her child, Jennifer grew anxious and depressed. She considered herself worthless, reasoning that if she had been a better spouse, Billy's father would never have left, and that the burden of raising him would not now lie solely with her. She knew that her mother was incapable of providing proper care for Billy, yet she needed to make money to support them all. Jennifer's depressive style increasingly affected her interactions with Billy. She grew withdrawn and filled with self-doubt, and she stopped taking him on trips or spending time with him on weekends. When Billy did "good" things, she would not acknowledge them with praise of any kind. When he misbehaved, she provided him with, at most, a muted reprimand.

At the same time, Grammy was growing more confused and disabled. She began to refer to Billy as Thomas, the name of her dead husband. Often she would wake in the middle of the night wondering where she was. Billy felt her slipping away. She no longer found the cartoons funny, and she often lost her temper. Her confusion and physical decline prevented the two of them from having meaningful interactions. That summer, she passed away, suffering a heart attack in her sleep. Billy, trying to wake her for breakfast, found her to be cold and stiff, and quickly realized that she was not waking up.

School began only a few weeks after the death of his grandmother. Repeating the 4th grade, Billy was now older than the other children in the class. He still had trouble with the academic material, however, and was quickly identified by his new classmates as the "weirdo." Now bigger than his classmates, he made it a regular habit to pick on the smaller children in class. He would tease them, call *them* names, and even hit them. In part, it was his way of retaliating, of expressing his anger, and of defending himself.

Jennifer quit her evening job at Jay's Diner. With only two people to support now, she was able to work at the grocery store during the day and be at home to make sure that Billy did his homework in the late afternoon. He greatly missed the fun that he used to have with his grandmother. Moreover, by the time he now finished his homework, there were no more cartoons to laugh at. All of this fueled a burning resentment of his mother.

Billy passed 4th grade that year, receiving four Cs and a B. But the year had taken a toll on his relationship with his mother. His anger, combined with his mother's hopelessness and despair, resulted in almost constant fighting between the two of them. In addition, the boy continued to have uncontrollable temper outbursts and to get into fights outside of the house.

Billy entered the 5th grade the next fall at the age of 12. His class was filled with all of the children whom he had teased and hit the previous year. They had stopped calling him "Weirdo" by now—perhaps they had learned their lesson—and, in fact, they paid him little attention at all. Now he would misbehave just to get noticed, throwing things in the middle of class, for example, or yelling out ob-

Individuals with conduct disorder have a heightened prevalence of learning disorders, communication disorders, attention-deficit/hyperactivity disorder, anxiety disorders, mood disorders, or substance-related disorders (APA, 1994, 2000).

scenities. Once he threw a dictionary at his teacher, hitting him in the stomach. Billy was punished, but at least he was noticed.

At home, too, his mother took to ignoring her son's disturbing behaviors. She would work on the bills, for example, even as Billy ran around in the background calling her names and breaking things. He was able to get a rise out of his mother only if he behaved outrageously enough. One night, for example, he pulled his mother's most expensive dress from her closet and tore it in half. In a moment of uncontrolled anger, she grabbed his arm, digging her nails deep into his skin, shook him, and slapped him twice across the face. They both cried themselves to sleep that night.

> **Boys with conduct disorder outnumber girls with the disorder (APA, 2000).**

Billy: A Disorder Blossoms

When Billy was 13, his 6th-grade class went on a field trip to New York City. The itinerary included a tour of the United Nations and a Broadway musical. Billy pleaded with his mother, begging her not to make him go. "The kids in my class are stupid! I don't want to go anywhere with those a...holes!" But she was not hearing any of it. Perhaps Billy would enjoy a big city like New York, she thought, or perhaps he could bond with some of his classmates. Anyway, she knew that she could not deal with him at home that day. Billy cried as she forced him onto the bus that morning. The other children saw him crying and teased him.

The school bus parked across from the United Nations building and the children got out. Everyone was assigned to "pick a buddy"—a simple task for most of the children, but no one wanted to be Billy's buddy. The teacher allowed a "four-way buddy system" so that "no one would be stuck alone with a buddy whom they did not like." Billy knew this referred to him. All of the children seemed to be watching him, expecting him to react. He didn't, however; he just kept his head down.

About 6 minutes into the tour, Mrs. Barnett, one of the teachers supervising the trip, noticed a buddy group with only three children. Billy was missing. A wave of panic spread among the teachers. An announcement was made over the building's loudspeakers, informing all tourists of the missing teen. Police searched the local neighborhood. Hours went by, but Billy was nowhere to be found. The children grew restless waiting on the bus all morning while the teachers were looking for Billy. Chants grew loud from the back of the bus: "Leave the retard here! Leave the retard here!" As time passed, the class's hopes of making the 2:00 p.m. Broadway musical on the other side of town were crushed.

> **Boys with conduct disorder frequently exhibit fighting, stealing, vandalism, and school discipline problems. Girls with this disorder are more likely to exhibit lying, truancy, running away, substance use, and prostitution (APA, 2000).**

At 3 o'clock, a policeman approached the teachers with a resistant Billy in hand. The officer had found the boy in a movie theater around the corner. He had been able to sneak into an R-rated film through a back entrance. He had also been spotted earlier in the day slashing the tires of parked cars. The teachers screamed at the troubled boy in front of the entire school bus. The children chanted, "Retard! A . . . hole! Retard! A . . . hole!" Rather than hushing the children, the teachers looked as though they wanted to join in the chant—and Billy knew this. Predictably, he was banned from future class trips.

Over time, the other mothers in the neighborhood stopped speaking to Jennifer. She stopped going to the neighborhood supermarket, where she was certain everyone was judging her, and shopped instead at stores a couple of towns away, where no one knew her or her son. She also quit her job at the local grocery store, and began working at a similar store farther away.

Billy recognized his mother's depression, but rather than feeling sympathy for her, he saw her as weak. He knew just what to do or say in order to make her cry. If he did not want to do his homework, for example, he might throw things at her and tell her that he hated her. She would burst into tears, and he would run out of the house. Often, he would go to a nearby lake. Sometimes he would cry, other times he would find rocks and throw them as hard as he could at ducks gathered by the lake. He knew he was hurting them, sometimes even killing them. But he didn't care. When he returned home at night, his mother might be asleep at the kitchen table, with an open liquor bottle sitting out.

Billy's downward slide continued in the 8th grade when, at age 15, he was permanently kicked off the school bus. One morning on the bus ride to school, a child had remarked under his breath that Billy "stunk like shit." In fact, Billy had been developing an odor. Without adult supervision, he would bathe about once a week. When Billy overheard this remark, he took out a textbook from his backpack and repeatedly banged the child over the head with it. The other children immediately got out of the way. It was not until the bus driver was able to pull the bus over, get to the back, and break things up that the child was rescued from the beating. The vice principal suspended Billy for 10 days, and ruled that it was now Jennifer's responsibility to transport her son to and from school. Billy spent most of his suspension hanging out by the lake near his house. He expressed delight with the vice principal's decision. As he saw it, he would not have to ride with those "punks" anymore.

Billy's mother was not as pleased. She would have to arrive at work late and leave early each day if she were to drive Billy to and from school. Her job was already in jeopardy. Customers had been complaining to the manager that she was losing her patience with them and acting rudely. In addition, her breath often smelled of alcohol. She decided that she could not drive Billy, and told him that he must walk the 2-mile distance each day. This, too, was fine with Billy. He did not want to spend any more time with his "weak" mother than he had to.

On his walks home, Billy would pass the township's high school, where a group of five or six students always hung out on the corner, laughing, talking loudly, frequently cursing, and smoking cigarettes. Their rebellious nature attracted Billy. The leader of this group, Ty, always wore the T-shirt of a band that Billy liked, Machine Pulse. On one of his walks home, Billy asked Ty whether he had bought the new

> Conduct disorder usually begins at between 7 and 15 years of age (APA, 2000).

album by Machine Pulse yet. Ty had not, but was very impressed that this kid from the middle school knew about the band. Instead of continuing on his journey home, Billy next went to a local record store. There he grabbed a copy of Machine Pulse's new album, put it discreetly in his jacket, and calmly walked out of the store.

The next day, Billy excitedly walked by Ty's group on his way home. He handed Ty a copy of the album and told him that it was a gift. "You're all right, kid." Ty's friends agreed, and handed Billy a cigarette. He put the cigarette in his mouth and lit it the way that he had seen people do in movies. After he coughed nonstop for a few minutes, Ty's girlfriend patted the smoking novice on the back, asking, "First cigarette?" He responded with a nod. With a smile, she said, "You're gonna be just fine."

By the time Billy entered high school, he and his mother were barely talking. She would have dinner ready for him in the refrigerator, and it was up to him to microwave it when he got home. It was not uncommon for him to hang out with Ty and Joe, another older boy, until late, and to return home after his mother was already asleep. Sometimes Ty and Joe would come home with him; and while Jennifer was asleep at the kitchen table, they would pour alcohol from her "secret" stash into their water bottles and refill her bottle with water. Although she would later notice that Billy had switched her alcohol with water, she never reprimanded him for it, or even addressed the matter. That would mean admitting that she kept a stash of alcohol. And so there was an unspoken understanding between the two of them.

Increasingly, Billy skipped classes each day to hang out with Ty and Joe. They would go to the mall for hours and visit the arcade. In the late afternoons, he might threaten smaller children, forcing them to give him the money in their pockets. Sometimes he would hit them anyway, just because he could. One day, he spotted a Walkman on the passenger seat of a parked car. He smashed the passenger window and took the Walkman. In the background, he heard Joe say, "What the f... is he thinking?" and Ty respond, "The kid's a f...ing moron."

That year, Billy skipped too many classes to pass any courses, and he had to repeat the 9th grade the following year. Almost 17, he was easily the oldest freshman in the high school. An entire foot taller than anyone else in his class, he was in remedial courses and still unable to understand the material. Privately, he too thought of himself as "Retardo."

When Billy did go to classes, he was a major disruption. He would throw things to the front of the classroom as the teacher was trying to teach. When the teacher turned to write on the chalkboard, Billy would shoot rubber bands at his classmates. The classroom had to be set up so that he was on one side and the rest of the students on the other. At lunchtime, he would sit alone.

One day, he handed in a test to his math teacher, Mrs. Cooper, without having answered any of the questions. Across the answer sheet he had written: "MRS.

Boys commit many more juvenile crimes than girls. More than half of the children or teenagers who are arrested each year are *recidivists*, meaning they have records of previous arrests. Arrests of teenagers for serious crimes have at least tripled since 1980 (U.S. Department of Justice, 1994).

COOPER F...S GOATS." The teacher sent him to the library to study math until she and the vice principal decided on his punishment. In the library, before shutting his eyes to rest, Billy opened his math textbook out of curiosity. As usual, the material made no sense. Impulsively, he took a lighter from his pocket and set the book on fire. He then left the book on the table and proceeded to go to the bathroom. By the time the fire alarm rang, the entire desk at which Billy had been sitting, and an adjacent wooden bookshelf, were in flames. The school was emptied while the sprinkler system put out the fire. By the time the fire department arrived, the fire was out. Within two weeks, the school board expelled Billy.

Billy in Treatment: Working on Several Fronts

In the wake of the fire incident, school officials asked Dr. James Constanti, a consulting child psychiatrist who specialized in disruptive disorders, to assess Billy and to design a treatment plan for him. Billy refused at first to meet with the "shrink," so Dr. Constanti began his work with the despondent Jennifer.

The meeting began with the psychiatrist administering a series of structured assessments, including the *Child Behavior Checklist* (*CBCL*) and the *Eyberg Child Behavior Inventory*. As Jennifer completed these inventories, it became clear to Dr. Constanti that Billy manifested a range of disruptive symptoms. Such symptoms are often referred to as "externalizing," because the individual is directing his or her inner problems outward at others—for example, by acting aggressively. Following the administration of these inventories, an unstructured clinical interview with Jennifer revealed further details of Billy's external symptoms.

The boy, who had defiantly remained in the waiting room with the receptionist, soon demanded to speak with the "shrink," as he feared that his mother's accounts of his behavior might be unfair and biased. After Jennifer had finished and returned to the waiting room, the troubled teenager was invited in to tell his story. Dr. Constanti's nonjudgmental style put Billy at ease. He was soon revealing behaviors that his mother did not know about, such as his efforts to hurt the ducks and various thefts.

By the end of the visit, with the school reports also in hand, Dr. Constanti arrived at a diagnosis of *conduct disorder*. Billy's persistent pattern of serious violations of rules, thievery, and aggression toward people and animals met the criteria of DSM-IV. Given that at least one of his symptoms had been present before the age of 10, the psychiatrist further categorized the conduct disorder as *"childhood-onset type."* Finally, based on the number of conduct problems displayed, along with their effects on others, Dr. Constanti determined that the conduct disorder was of *"moderate"* severity.

Jennifer almost begged Dr. Constanti to place her son on medication. However, the psychiatrist did not believe that this was an appropriate intervention at this

If no symptom of conduct disorder has appeared before 10 years of age, the disorder is characterized as *adolescent-onset type*. Individuals with this pattern are less likely to be aggressive and tend to have more normal peer relationships than those with the *childhood-onset type*. Those with the adolescent-onset type are more likely to improve.

A less severe pattern of defiant behavior by children and adolescents is *oppositional defiant disorder.* Here, the individuals repeatedly argue with adults, lose their temper, and feel great anger and resentment. They often ignore adult rules and requests, deliberately annoy others, and blame others for their mistakes and problems (APA, 1994, 2000). They do not, however, repeatedly violate the basic rights of others, as those with conduct disorder do.

stage. Drugs, he informed her, are rarely used as a first step in treating children with conduct problems such as Billy's. In fact, he explained, research has rarely found medications to be effective in cases of conduct disorder. If the disorder is further accompanied by depression, anxiety, or attention-deficit/hyperactivity disorder, medications may be helpful for those other problems. For example, an antidepressant such as Prozac may help alleviate an accompanying depression, or a stimulant such as Ritalin may help address accompanying attention-deficit problems. However, Dr. Constanti did not see any comorbid disorders at work in Billy's case.

Jennifer had seen an episode of a talk show in which "out-of-control" teens were sent to a "boot camp." She asked if such a camp might be an appropriate treatment for Billy. Again, Dr. Constanti informed her that such an intervention would probably not be appropriate in her son's case. The psychiatrist had concluded from his reading of the literature that punitive interventions such as boot camps or incarceration tended to be ineffective. In fact, bringing together individuals with conduct disorders in such settings may sometimes sabotage their progress.

Finally, Jennifer asked whether putting Billy into a weekly psychotherapy program would be appropriate. Once again, the psychiatrist informed her that psychotherapy alone tends to be ineffective in cases of conduct disorder. Treating Billy's conduct disorder was going to require a comprehensive, multilevel intervention program.

One thing that Dr. Constanti had noticed in meeting with Jennifer was her pattern of self-blame and self-criticism, feelings of hopelessness, inability to make decisions, and general lack of energy. The psychiatrist gently pointed out that not only were Billy's behavior patterns affecting her, but that her behavior patterns were affecting the boy. Dr. Constanti discussed his belief that Jennifer might, in fact, be suffering from clinical depression, and he suggested that she too might benefit from treatment, especially given the lack of social support in her life. Jennifer was very receptive to the psychiatrist's suggestions. She had always been so burdened by Billy's problem behaviors that she had not really thought about her own problem behaviors. Dr. Constanti pointed out that Billy's treatment program was going to require a clear head on her part, free of depressed or anxious feelings, or distorted thinking. He placed her on an antidepressant and referred her to a psychologist who specialized in cognitive therapy.

At the same time, Dr. Constanti organized a wide-ranging treatment program for Billy that took place at the family, school, and individual levels. In the *family* realm, Jennifer participated in a number of *psychoeducational* sessions designed to help her recognize that Billy's behaviors were not due to fixed, stable traits. Rather than thinking of his conduct problems as the result of a global disposition—that Billy was intrinsically bad—she learned that each behavior was the result of a situational antecedent. By repeatedly paying careful attention to the interactions between Billy and herself, she learned how to monitor the impact of antecedents and consequences, and she came to appreciate that she had in fact stopped responding to her son after years of witnessing his problem behaviors. Her withdrawal—including her lack of discipline in response to his undesirable behaviors—was crucial in shaping his behavior. In fact, it served to reinforce his inappropriate conduct.

The next step in the family realm was *parent management training,* in which Jennifer was taught how to modify, through consistent rewards and punishments, Billy's behavior at home. She learned how to offer positive reinforcements, such as attention and praise, consistently whenever Billy behaved positively, and to offer punishments, such as the revoking of privileges, whenever he exhibited negative behaviors. Overall, she learned the importance of a consistent, responsive home environment with a clear set of rules and consequences.

Finally, in the family realm, Dr. Constanti organized *interaction and communication training* for both Billy and his mother. After about a month of Jennifer's psychoeducational treatment, mother and son began weekly meetings with a family therapist and worked on their communications and interactions.

Dr. Constanti's treatment program also included interventions at *school.* It was apparent that the school had not met Billy's academic needs. Along with a conduct disorder, it was probable that he had a learning disorder. The psychiatrist arranged for a school psychologist to assess the teenager's specific learning disorder; subsequently, school officials agreed to provide the boy with several hours of individual, specialized tutoring each day. Simply placing Billy in the overcrowded remedial courses, as the school system had done previously, was surely not the answer.

In another aspect of the school intervention, Dr. Constanti met several times with Billy's teachers to consider in greater detail the teenager's misbehaviors in the classroom. Specifically, what were the antecedents and consequences of his misbehaviors there? As with Billy's mother, the teachers came to see what role their own withdrawals had been playing in his problem behaviors.

Finally, the treatment program included *individual* interventions. Dr. Constanti knew that changes to the family and academic environments alone are often sufficient in cases of conduct disorder in younger children, but that in adolescent cases the individual's autonomy and power needs typically must be addressed in treatment. The psychiatrist believed that Billy would benefit from an *impulse-control* and *problem-solving intervention.* Recognizing the teenager's appreciation of music, Dr. Constanti suggested that every two times Billy met with a communications and problem-solving counselor, his mother should buy him a CD of his choosing. Jennifer agreed, and Billy enthusiastically met with the counselor each week. In fact, he took a more and more active role in his therapy as the weeks went by. He developed a genuine rapport with his counselor and, within a few months, was tackling difficult social situations during the therapy discussions.

The most successful family interventions for cases of conduct disorder include such features as: (a) teaching parents more effective ways of dealing with their children, or (b) having parents and children meet together for behavior-oriented family therapy (Kazdin & Wassell, 1999).

Conduct disorders tend to become more resistant with age, so treatments for them are generally more effective when offered to children younger than 13 years of age (Burnette & Murray, 1996).

Epilogue

As is often the case with adolescents with conduct disorder, Billy did not make a complete recovery. There were some important improvements, however. The school, after consulting with Dr. Constanti, eventually accepted the boy back with the modified academic program. Working with a tutor who was sensitive to his learning disabilities, Billy passed the following marking period with 5 Cs—his best grades in years. In addition, his bullying behavior decreased dramatically. Eventually, he graduated from high school.

Other areas did not improve as much, however. Although Billy developed a clearer understanding of what was and what was not acceptable at home, his communications with his mother changed only modestly. He was, indeed, better behaved, but considerable tension remained between the two of them. Similarly, Billy continued to display a number of impulsive behaviors throughout his adult years.

Such progress hardly seemed miraculous to Jennifer, or fully satisfying to Billy. On the other hand, Dr. Constanti recognized that, as such cases go, Billy and his mother had in fact done fairly well. Jennifer now had a more normal home life, where she was able to experience some semblance of control and dignity. And Billy was able to obtain his high school diploma, which later opened the door to better job opportunities. Moreover, in the improved climate of his life, Billy developed several positive friendships, which were built on common interests and mutual respect rather than on dares and counterdares. His chances of winding up in prison or developing an antisocial personality disorder—common outcomes of conduct disorder—had been greatly reduced. It may have been too late to fully reverse Billy's early direction, but, at least, treatment had altered its course.

Although most cases of conduct disorder do improve over time, a substantial number of severe cases continue into adulthood, developing into antisocial personality disorder or other psychological problems (Myers et al., 1998).

You Decide: The Case of Julia, Age 17, Excessive Weight Loss

This case is presented in the voices of Julia and her roommate, Rebecca. Throughout the case, you are asked to consider a number of issues and to arrive at various decisions, including diagnostic and treatment decisions. Appendix A lists Julia's probable diagnosis, the DSM-IV criteria, clinical information, and possible treatment directions.

Julia: Measuring Up

I grew up in a northeastern suburban town, and I've lived in the same house for my entire life. My father is a lawyer, and my mother is the assistant principal at our town's high school. My sister, Holly, is 4 years younger than I am.

My parents have been married for almost 20 years. Aside from the usual sort of disagreements, they get along well. In fact, I would say that my entire family gets along well. We're not particularly touchy-feely: It's always a little awkward when we have to hug our grandparents on holidays, because we just never do that sort of thing at home. That's not to say that my parents are uninterested or don't care about us. Far from it; even though they both have busy work schedules, one of them would almost always make it to my track and cross-country meets and to Holly's soccer games. My mother, in particular, has always tried to keep on top of what's going on in our lives.

In high school, I took advanced-level classes and earned good grades. I also got along quite well with my teachers, and ended up graduating in the top 10% of my class. I know this made my mother really proud, especially since she works at the school. She would get worried that I might not be doing my best and "working to my full potential." All through high school, she tried to keep on top of my homework assignments and test schedules. She liked to look over my work before I turned it in, and would make sure that I left myself plenty of time to study for tests.

In addition to schoolwork, the track and cross-country teams were a big part of high school for me. I started running in junior high school because my parents wanted me to do something athletic and I was never coordinated enough to be good at sports like soccer. I was always a little bit chubby when I was a kid. I don't know if I was actually overweight, but everyone used to tease me about my baby fat. Running seemed like a good way to lose that extra weight. It was hard at first, but I gradually got better and by high school I was one of the best runners on the team. Schoolwork and running didn't leave me much time for anything else. I got along fine with the other kids at school, but I basically hung out with just a few close friends. When I was younger, I used to get teased for being a goody-two-shoes, but that had died down by high school. I can't remember anyone whom I ever had problems with.

I did go to the prom, but I didn't date very much in high school. My parents didn't like me hanging out with boys unless it was in a group. Besides, the guys I had crushes on were never the ones who asked me out. So any free time was

> Are the family dynamics and school pressures described by Julia particularly unusual? Under what circumstances might such family and school factors become problematic or set the stage for psychological problems?

mostly spent with my close girlfriends. We would go shopping or to the movies, and we frequently spent the night at each other's houses. It was annoying that although I never did anything wrong, I had the earliest curfew of my friends. Also, I was the only one whose parents would page me throughout the night just to check in. I don't ever remember lying to them about what I was doing or who I was with. Although I felt like they didn't trust me, I guess they were just worried and wanted to be sure that I was safe.

Julia: Coping With Stress

Now I am 17 years old and in the spring semester of my first year at college. I was awarded a scholar-athlete full scholarship at the state university. I'm not sure of the exact cause of my current problems, but I know a lot of it must have to do with college life. I have never before felt so much pressure. Because my scholarship depends both on my running and on my maintaining a 3.6 grade point average, I've been stressed out much of the time. Academic work was never a problem for me in the past, but there's just so much more expected of you in college.

It was pressure from my coach, my teammates, and myself that first led me to dieting. During the first semester, almost all my girlfriends in college experienced the "freshman 15" weight gain—it was a common joke among everyone when we were up late studying and someone ordered a pizza. For some of them it didn't really matter if they gained any weight, but for me it did. I was having trouble keeping up during cross-country practices. I even had to drop out of a couple of races because I felt so awful and out of shape. I couldn't catch my breath and I'd get terrible cramps. And my times for the races that I did finish were much worse than my high school times had been. I know that my coach was really disappointed in me. He called me aside about a month into the season. He wanted to know what I was eating, and he told me the weight I had gained was undoubtedly hurting my performance. He said that I should cut out snacks and sweets of any kind, and stick to things like salads to help me lose the extra pounds and get back into shape. He also recommended some additional workouts. I was all for a diet—I hated that my clothes were getting snug. In addition, I was feeling left out of the rest of the team. As a freshman, I didn't know any of the other runners, and I certainly wasn't proving myself worthy of being on the team. At that point, I was 5'6" and weighed 145 pounds. When I started college I had weighed 130 pounds.

Dieting was surprisingly easy. The dining hall food bordered on inedible anyway, so I didn't mind sticking to salads, cereal, or yogurt. Occasionally I'd allow myself pasta, but only without sauce. I completely eliminated dessert, except for fruit on occasion. If anyone commented on my small meals, I just told them that I was in training and gearing up for the big meets at the end of the season. I found ways to ignore the urge to snack between meals or late at night when I was studying. I'd go for a quick run, check e-mail, take a nap—whatever it took to distract myself.

Was the advice from Julia's coach out of line, or was it her overreaction to his suggestions that caused later problems?

Sometimes I'd drink water or Diet Coke, and if absolutely necessary I'd munch on a carrot.

Most eating disorders follow a period of intense dieting. Is dieting inevitably destructive? Are there safeguards that can be taken during dieting that can head off the development of an eating disorder?

Once I started dieting, the incentives to continue were everywhere. My race times improved, so my coach was pleased. I felt more a part of the team and less like an outsider. My clothes were no longer snug; and when they saw me at my meets my parents said I looked great. I even received an invitation to a party given by a fraternity that only invited the most attractive first-year women. After about a month, I was back to my normal weight of 130 pounds.

At first, my plan was to get back down to 130 pounds, but it happened so quickly that I didn't have time to figure out how to change my diet to include some of the things that I had been leaving out. Things were going so well that I figured it couldn't hurt to stick to the diet a little longer. I was on a roll. I remembered all the people whom I had seen on television who couldn't lose weight even after years of trying. I began to think of my frequent hunger pangs as badges of honor, symbols of my ability to control my bodily urges.

I set a new weight goal of 115 pounds. I figured if I hit the gym more often and skipped breakfast altogether, it wouldn't be hard to reach that weight in another month or so. Of course this made me even hungrier by lunchtime, but I didn't want to increase my lunch size. I found it easiest to pace myself with something like crackers. I would break them into several pieces and only allow myself to eat one piece every 15 minutes. The few times I did this in the dining hall with friends I got weird looks and comments. I finally started eating lunch alone in my room. I would simply say that I had some readings or a paper to finish before afternoon class. I also made excuses to skip dinner with people. I'd tell my friends that I was eating with my teammates, and tell my teammates that I was meeting my roommate. Then I'd go to a dining hall on the far side of campus that was usually empty, and eat by myself.

I remember worrying about how I would handle Thanksgiving. Holidays are a big deal in my family. We get together with my aunts and uncles and grandparents, and of course there is a huge meal. I couldn't bear the stress of being expected to eat such fattening foods. I felt sick just thinking about the stuffing, gravy, and pies for dessert. I told my mother that there was a team Thanksgiving dinner for those who lived too far away to go home. That much was true, but then I lied and told her that the coach thought it would be good for team morale if we all attended. I know it disappointed her, but I couldn't deal with trying to stick to my diet with my family all around me, nagging me to eat more.

Julia: Spiraling Downward

I couldn't believe it when the scale said I was down to 115 pounds. I still felt that I had excess weight to lose. Some of my friends were beginning to mention that I was actually looking too thin, as if that's possible. I wasn't sure what they meant—

I was still feeling chubby when they said I was too skinny. I didn't know who was right, but either way I didn't want people seeing my body. I began dressing in baggy clothes that would hide my physique. I thought of overweight people whom my friends and I had snickered about in the past. I couldn't bear the thought of anyone doing that to me. In addition, even though I was running my best times ever, I knew there was still room there for improvement.

Around this time, I started to get really stressed about my schoolwork. I had been managing to keep up throughout the semester, but your final grade basically comes down to the final exam. It was never like this in high school, when you could get an A just by turning in all your homework assignments. I felt unbearably tense leading up to exams. I kept replaying scenarios of opening the test booklet and not being able to answer a single question. I studied nonstop. I brought notes with me to the gym to read on the treadmill, and I wasn't sleeping more than an hour or two at night. Even though I was exhausted, I knew I had to keep studying. I found it really hard to be around other people. Listening to my friends talk about their exam schedules only made me more frantic. I had to get back to my own studying.

The cross-country season was over, so my workouts had become less intense. Instead of practicing with the team, we were expected to create our own work-out schedule. Constant studying left me little time for the amount of exercise I was used to. Yet I was afraid that cutting back on my workouts would cause me to gain weight. It seemed logical that if I couldn't keep up with my exercise, I should eat less in order to continue to lose weight. I carried several cans of Diet Coke with me to the library. Hourly trips to the lounge for coffee were the only study breaks I allowed myself. Aside from that, I might have a bran muffin or a few celery sticks, but that would be it for the day. Difficult though it was, this regimen worked out well for me. I did fine on my exams. This was what worked for me. At that point, I weighed 103 pounds.

After finals, I went home for winter break for about a month. It was strange to be back home with my parents after living on my own for the semester. I had established new routines for myself and I didn't like having to answer to anyone else about them. Right away, my mother started in; she thought I spent too much time at the gym every day and that I wasn't eating enough. When I told her that I was doing the same thing as everyone else on the team, she actually called my coach and told him that she was concerned about his training policies! More than once she commented that I looked too thin, like I was a walking skeleton. She tried to get me to go to a doctor, but I refused.

Dinner at home was the worst. My mother wasn't satisfied when I only wanted a salad—she'd insist that I have a "well-balanced meal" that included some protein and carbohydrates. We had so many arguments about what I would and wouldn't eat that I started avoiding dinnertime altogether. I'd say that I was going to eat at a friend's house or at the mall. When I was at home I felt like my mother was

---

Look back at Case 9, Bulimia Nervosa. How are Julia's symptoms similar to those of the individual in that case? How are her symptoms different?

Based on your reading of either DSM-IV or a textbook, what disorder might Julia be displaying? Which of her symptoms suggest this diagnosis?

Was there a better way for Julia's mother to intervene? Or would any intervention have brought similar results?

watching my every move. Although I was worried about the upcoming semester and indoor track season, I was actually looking forward to getting away from my parents. I just wanted to be left alone—to have some privacy and not be criticized for working out to keep in shape.

When I returned to school, I vowed that I would do a better job of keeping on top of my classes. I didn't want to let things pile up for finals again. With my practice and meet schedule, I realized that the only way to devote more time to my schoolwork would be to cut back on socializing with friends. In fact, I haven't seen much of my friends this semester. I don't go to meals at all anymore; I grab coffee or a soda and drink it on my way to class. I've stopped going out on the weekends as well. I barely even see my roommate. She's asleep when I get back late from studying at the library, and I usually get up before her to go for a morning run. Part of me misses hanging out with my friends, but they had started bugging me about not eating enough. I'd rather not see them than have to listen to that and defend myself.

All of which brings me to the present time. Even though I'm running great and I'm finally able to stick to a diet, everyone thinks I'm not taking good enough care of myself. I know that my mother has called my coach and my roommate. She must have called the dean of student life, because that's who got in touch with me and suggested that I go to the health center for an evaluation. I hate that she's going behind my back after I told her that everything was fine. I realize that I had a rough first semester, but everyone has trouble adjusting to college life. I'm doing my best to keep in control of my life, and I wish that I could be trusted to take care of myself.

Julia seems to be the only person who is unaware that she has lost too much weight and developed a destructive pattern of eating. Why is she so unable to look at herself accurately and objectively?

Rebecca: Losing a Roommate

When I first met Julia back in August, I thought we would get along great. She seemed a little shy but she'd be fun once you got to know her better. She was really cool when we were moving into our room. Even though she arrived first, she waited for me so that we could divide up furniture and closet space together. Early on, a bunch of us in the dorm started hanging out together, and Julia would join us for meals or parties on the weekends. She's pretty and lots of guys would hit on her, but she never seemed interested. The rest of us would sit around and gossip about guys we met and who liked whom, but Julia just listened.

From day one, Julia took her academics seriously. She was sort of an inspiration to the rest of us. Even though she was busy with practices and meets, she always had her readings done for class. But I know that Julia also worried constantly about her studies and her running. She'd talk about how frustrating it was to not be able to compete at track at the level she knew she was capable of. She would get really nervous before races. Sometimes she couldn't sleep, and I'd wake up in the middle of the night and see her pacing around the room. When she told me her coach suggested a new diet and training regimen, it sounded like a good idea.

I guess I first realized that something was wrong when she started acting a lot less sociable. She stopped going out with us on weekends, and we almost never saw her in the dining hall anymore. A couple of times I even caught her eating by herself in a dining hall on the other side of campus. She explained that she had a lot of work to do and found that she could get some of it done while eating, if she had meals alone. When I did see her eat, it was never anything besides vegetables. She'd take only a tiny portion and then she wouldn't even finish it. She didn't keep any food in the room except for cans of Diet Coke and a bag of baby carrots in the fridge. I also noticed that her clothes were starting to look baggy and hang off her. A couple of times I asked her if she was doing okay, but this only made her defensive. She claimed that she was running great, and since she didn't seem sick, I figured that I was overreacting.

I kept believing her until I returned from Thanksgiving. It was right before final exams, so everyone was pretty stressed out. Julia had been a hard worker before, but now she took things to new extremes. She dropped off the face of the earth. I almost never saw her, even though we shared a room. I'd get up around 8:00 or 9:00 in the morning, and she'd already be gone. When I went to bed around midnight, she still wasn't back. Her side of the room was immaculate: bed made, books and notepads stacked neatly on her desk. When I did bump into her, she looked awful. She was way too thin, with dark circles under her eyes. She seemed like she had wasted away; her skin and hair were dull and dry. I was pretty sure that something was wrong, but I told myself that it must just be the stress of the upcoming finals. I figured that if there were a problem, her parents would notice it and do something about it over winter break.

When we came back to campus in January, I was surprised to see that Julia looked even worse than during finals. When I asked her how her vacation was, she mumbled something about being sick of her mother and happy to be back at school. As the semester got under way, Julia further distanced herself from us. There were no more parties or hanging out at meals for her. She was acting the same way she had during finals, which made no sense because classes had barely gotten going. We were all worried, but none of us knew what to do. One time, Julia's mother called while she was out. As I was writing down the message, she asked me if I had noticed anything strange going on with Julia. I wasn't sure what to say. I felt guilty, like I was tattling on her, but I also realized that I was in over my head and that I needed to be honest.

I told her mother about Julia's odd eating habits, how she was exercising a lot and how she had gotten pretty antisocial. Her mother had spoken with their family doctor. Julia was extremely underweight, even though she still saw herself as chunky and was afraid of gaining weight. After I got off the phone with her

> Why was Rebecca inclined to overlook her initial suspicions about Julia's behaviors? Was there a better way for the roommate to intervene?

> How might high schools and universities better identify individuals with serious eating disorders? What procedures or mechanisms has your school put into operation?

mother, I looked in the back of Julia's closet. A few months ago I had asked to borrow a tampon. She opened a new box and gave me one. The same box was still there with only that one missing. For the first time, I realized how serious Julia's condition could be.

A few days later, Julia approached me. Apparently she had just met with one of the deans, who told her that she'd need to undergo an evaluation at the health center before she could continue practicing with the team. She asked me point-blank if I had been talking about her to anyone. I told her how her mother had asked me if I had noticed any changes in her over the past several months, and how I honestly told her yes. She stormed out of the room and I haven't seen her since. I know how important the team is to Julia, so I am assuming that she'll be going to the health center soon. I hope that they'll be able to convince her that she's taken things too far, and that they can help her to get better.

How might the treatment approaches used in Cases 3, 4, and 9 be applied to Julia? How should they be altered to fit Julia's problems and personality? Which aspects of these treatments would not be appropriate? Should additional interventions be applied?

CASE **19**

You Decide: The Case of Fred, Age 75, Memory Problems

This case is presented in the voices of Fred and his wife, Margaret. Throughout the case, you are asked to consider a number of issues and to arrive at various decisions, including diagnostic and treatment decisions. Appendix B lists Fred's probable diagnosis, the DSM-IV criteria, clinical information, and possible treatment directions.

Margaret: "My Husband's Brain Stopped Working Properly"

About 8 years ago, my life changed 100%. The reason? My husband's brain stopped working properly. We had been married 34 years and Fred was 67 years old. He had worked for the same construction company for 32 years, first as a laborer, then as a security supervisor and union leader. He was a big strong man, a good husband, and a good father to our son, Mark. Together, we had managed a good living—the original odd couple, our friends would call us—with him in construction and me an actress in television commercials. Life was good. And then his brain went downhill, taking Fred and me and Mark along with it.

The problem seemed small at first, hardly noticeable really. Sometimes, when telling me about his day at work, Fred would talk about the foreman, Jimmy, driving a "tractor" when he meant "bulldozer," or he'd say that he had made a "revision" instead of "decision." Little stuff, and he'd catch himself. I didn't think much of it at all, but it was odd. It doesn't sound like much, but it wasn't like him. I even thought, "Oh, well, the old boy's slipping," and I would laugh to myself. But when he forgot the anniversary of our first date, well . . . I knew something was wrong. I gave him all kinds of hell for that—accused him of having an affair, cried, and I let him have it. But I was also scared. I mean, maybe an anniversary like that doesn't mean much to other people, but for us—well, over the years, he'd taken me to Atlantic City for shows, to dinners in expensive restaurants. Once, after Mark was grown, he even got us a hotel room in the Catskills for a weekend. There was always some sort of surprise. So, 8 years ago, in anticipation of a special evening, I got all dressed up. When he got home from work that night and sat down on the sofa, I knew he'd forgotten; and when he saw the disappointment in my eyes, he realized the same thing pretty quickly. In fact, he was beside himself, and took me out to a very fancy Italian restaurant after I calmed down. But it was a bad sign. That year turned out to be a rough one.

It wasn't that he suddenly forgot everything, but it seemed like he was suddenly forgetting a bunch of things when he'd never been forgetting things before. I had always been the one with my head in the clouds, forgetting and losing things, not Fred. He'd be the one telling me, "Maggie, you've got to stay more on the ball. If you forget to pay the bills they're gonna shut off our electricity." Or he'd chew me out about forgetting to make a doctor's appointment for Mark. Of course, I'd joke, "Why don't we switch jobs and you'll see who's got it tougher," but he definitely had a sharper head, no denying that. Now, suddenly, he was losing his wallet

Forgetfulness is universal, and increases in forgetfulness are a normal part of aging. How might we distinguish normal forgetting or normal aging from the symptoms of a clinical disorder?

and we'd find it later in the study, where he'd sworn he hadn't been in days. Or he would leave half-drunk glasses of juice on the floor of the living room, and when I'd chide him about it he'd say, "Oh, I'm sorry," and change the subject. This was Mr. Neat Freak who, in past times, couldn't stand it if a dirty dish sat on the kitchen table more than a half hour after dinner.

He also had little accidents, spilling food on himself, or knocking over a pile of papers or the jar of pencils from the counter. Then he started asking me to drive him to work all the time. He said that he'd caught himself veering off the road a few times and had just barely avoided an accident. "It's all the stress," he'd tell me. "We've got a new contract coming up and I don't think it's gonna go our way. I've just got too much on my mind."

As the forgetfulness and unusual behavior mounted, it couldn't be ignored any more. Yet somehow I found a way to do just that. I wanted to believe him. Then, one day, he missed a meeting with an important contractor; just didn't show up. Instead, he went to his office like it was any other day. The company lost the contract and a lot of money, and it also was bad for their image. Actually, by that point in time, I wasn't all that surprised by his error. This strong and organized man, who had taken care of me for so many years, was by then becoming a different person, and I was becoming used to taking care of him. That's when I told him that he must see a doctor. And Fred did something I hadn't ever seen him do: He burst into tears.

Despite his emotional outpouring that evening, Fred managed to put off medical treatment for nearly a year. Eventually, however, the incidents caught up with him—for example, leaving his glasses in the mailbox or mowing only half the lawn—and he went for a neurological exam. A battery of tests revealed some cerebral damage, and the neurologist, Dr. Schoenfeld, broke the news to us that he was suffering from a form of progressive dementia. He explained to us that we would be facing a very difficult battle—that Fred would over the course of years become further incapacitated and less and less able to take care of himself. He also told us that very little could be done to stem the progress of Fred's condition. Fred was going to have to be very reliant on the support of his loved ones, particularly me, to see him through this.

Fred had already planned to retire, as his position in the company had been scaled down drastically after the contract debacle. The doctor's diagnosis simply made it official in our minds. Within 3 months, he was thrown a retirement party by his coworkers, many of whom he had mentored. By then he was having trouble remembering people's names, but that party meant a lot to him. He knew just how lucky he was to have so many caring friends and colleagues. He was still embarrassed about having lost that contract, but everybody tried their best to show him that they had nothing but gratitude for his years of service. He wasn't walking too well by then, either, so I helped him to a chair, where he sat for most of the party, sometimes crying quietly to himself—he no longer had full control of his

What might be the most difficult aspects of observing a spouse, parent, or other close relative gradually lose their memory or other cognitive faculties?

Dementia is an organic syndrome, marked by major problems in memory and at least one other cognitive function. Based on your reading of either the DSM-IV or a textbook, what form of dementia might Fred be displaying? Which of his symptoms suggest this diagnosis?

According to research, caring for a loved one with a severe form of dementia takes an average of 69 to 100 hours per week, leading to a range of psychological problems for caregivers. What kinds of problems would you expect caregivers to develop?

emotions. I think that was really his last great time, the last time he had a real special night out.

At the party, Fred gave a short talk to his coworkers, thanking them for the event. He had been worried about this speech beforehand. He feared attempting to reminisce or trying to be too specific, because he'd been having so much trouble remembering things, and he didn't want to read a speech off of a paper, so he preferred to kept it short. It broke my heart when I heard him say, "This is really a special night. I want to thank you all for this and for helping me out the way you've done the last few months. I'm not the kinda guy who talks a lot and makes big speeches to his friends. And that's what you are—my friends. That's why I've had a great time all these years. That's why I've loved my job, and going to work in the morning. We've had a lot of good times, and I'll miss you, my friends."

It was more than a retirement speech. It was a farewell speech, and it broke my heart. But, as painful as that was, the impromptu speech that he gave to me alone just 2 days later hurt even more. He was lucid that day. He was clear and organized and sharp as a tack, just like the old Fred. And he was hurting.

Fred: "Preparing for a Trip to Nowhere"

I'm mad, I'm frustrated, I'm everything in between. It's sure embarrassing, Maggie, it sure is. Can you imagine what it's like to have to think for 2 whole minutes before remembering our own grandchild's name? A child I held in my arms when he was born, and said, "This, this boy—Robert—is a perfect child." I watched him grow and played ball with him, and now I can see his face in front of me like he is in the room with me, but when I reach for his name, there's nothing there. Blank. How do I convince an 8-year-old child that his grandpa loves him and cares about him when I can't even be bothered to know his name?

I spend my whole life trying to be sharp, but I turn out a failure. I'm a 69-year-old man who needs a woman to take care of him like he's 90. What use am I? I provide for my family. I earn money. I do my job and help keep Wellstone Construction running. And now that's all gone. All gone. I can't do any of it. Lying in bed, sitting down all day. My wife and son, they provide for me. The company takes care of me. I'm a drain. No one will ever again think of trusting me with anything. Anything. "No, it would be too taxing for the poor guy." That's what they'll say. But they mean, "He'll just screw it up like he screws everything up."

Consider Case 4, Major Depressive Disorder: Did Fred show any symptoms of clinical depression as his disorder unfolded? Did Margaret? Would any of the treatment techniques described in Case 4 be helpful to either of them?

Right in the middle of the day, I all of a sudden don't know what time of day it is, or even what day it is. I don't even know what I had for breakfast this morning. If I want to go over there to pick up that book off that table, I have to ask you if you can help me walk. I can't walk without leaning on someone. Otherwise, I'll fall or have to stop and sit down.

Why should I even want to get up in the morning? Being up isn't all that different from being asleep, only a bit more confusing. Nothing in the world is more infuriating than knowing that you know the thing you can't remember. Knowing that you're not stupid, but that everything you once knew is being stripped away from you, little by little. God knows how long I'll even know who you are, Maggie. How long will it be before it's all just shapes and colors? How long before everyone else is making plans for me. Putting me in a home. Putting me out to pasture. Putting me to sleep. I feel like I'm preparing for a trip to nowhere.

I don't even know if I'll mind that so much. When I don't remember anything, it won't be so hard. Probably then I won't feel so stupid. I won't realize how much I am forgetting. That's what gets me—the forgetting. It gets me mad, but it gets me scared, too. I reach for a pen that I thought I was just writing with and I realize that it's not there. I look for it and then I realize that I'm not writing anything. Now I can't find the pen, and I don't even remember why I'm looking for it, and nothing makes any damned sense. It's like this dream that's real upsetting because I don't know what's going on but I know I should know. Oh, God!

When this all started, you know, I didn't believe it. A man can get used to a lot if he's trying to convince himself that nothing is wrong. Every time I'd forget something, or lose something, or drive off the road, it got to me for exactly 5 minutes. I'd be scared for 5 minutes and I'd admit to myself for 5 minutes that there was a serious problem here—that these things were happening more and more and that something was very wrong and that I should get this taken care of somehow. But after those 5 minutes, I would laugh it off and conclude that everything was fine—everyone forgets things, everyone loses concentration driving, everyone loses things—and I'd be fine. I'd come home, and I wouldn't think about it until the next thing happened. Then I'd be upset for another 5 minutes.

I want you to put me away, Maggie—you know what I mean—let me go, if I ever don't remember who you are. I don't want to forget my beautiful wife, and if I don't know who you are anymore, have them just inject me or give me whatever is necessary in order to get it over with. Don't worry about whether it's the right thing, because it is. I'm afraid that you won't do this, that you'll let me go on when I'm not myself anymore. I don't want you to have to see me and not know that I love you and need you with me. I don't want you to have to doubt my love for you because of this damned disease. Please, Maggie, don't let that happen. Please promise me.

Margaret: "A Long Goodbye"

I heard that speech from Fred several other times during the next 2 years. But then, he became less clear and less interested, and less able, and he stopped saying those things. The last 4 years really have been a long goodbye for us.

As the years have passed, Fred has been less and less able to do for himself. He has been increasingly unsteady on his feet. Furthermore, he lost control of his motor functions and is now unable to feed or clothe himself, or to use the

> If you were to lose your memory and cognitive faculties, bit by bit, how might that feel? What fears and worries might you experience?

> Why might Fred and Margaret have tried to overlook his symptoms, even as they were worsening?

> Unlike most of the other disorders in this casebook, Fred's problem was organic, progressive, and largely irreversible. What role might psychological treatments play in disorders of this kind?

bathroom on his own. At first, this was very upsetting to Fred; he was still aware enough to feel that his incapacitation made him ridiculous in some way, and he often lashed out at me in anger—even accusing me at times of trying to drug him so that he couldn't take care of himself. Later, he would tearfully apologize after these outbursts.

About 4 years ago, I bought him a walker to make it easier for him to get around. But about a year later, he fell while trying to walk across the hall to take a bath. He broke his hip and couldn't leave his bed for 4 months. More and more depressed, Fred began spending days staring at the wall or the bedsheets, refusing to talk even when I tried to speak to him. After his hip had healed, he still remained in bed, refusing to try to walk. He even began hearing voices and seeing people who weren't really in the room. Sometimes he would believe that long-gone relatives were in front of him and talking to him. Eventually, it seemed like it was just too taxing for him to try to distinguish the real from the imagined, and Fred began to treat everyone and everything around him with indifference or doubt. He treated real people who were talking to him as though they might be figments of his imagination, and he just turned away.

Our son, Mark, visited regularly, at least once every other weekend, from his New Hampshire home. Even seeing Fred this often, Mark was always surprised by the speed of his deterioration. After breaking his hip, Fred, who had always looked so forward to Mark's visits, often failed to get out of bed to greet our son, sometimes sleeping through the entire visit. Mark noticed that his father appeared to get less pleasure from the visits. He had prepared himself for the ravages of Fred's condition, but as his father deteriorated more and more, he, like I, became very shaken.

During one visit, Fred looked Mark in the eye, then turned to me and asked, "Who is this, Maggie? Who's he? Is that Jimmy? What's *he* doin' here?" Mark faced his father and said in a quiet voice, "Dad, it's me. Your son, Mark. And I love you." As he said this, however, Fred fell asleep, and Mark left the room dejected. Later, after Mark and I ate lunch, Fred awoke again, and called out. When Mark entered the room and stood over his father's bed, Fred touched his hand to Mark's face and after a minute said, quietly and hoarsely, "Son . . ." And they held hands without saying a word for an hour. I almost couldn't bear it.

Also, about 3 years ago, Fred started having violent nightmares, and he would sometimes wake me with his screaming. During and after some of the nightmares, he seemed a completely different person, with a crazed passion behind his frightened eyes. He was growing more and more convinced that I or others were plotting against him. During one of our visits to the neurologist, he complained, "She's stealing things from me. She steals my clothes so that when I can't find them she can make me feel foolish. I was eating a banana, and she wanted the banana. I put it down and turned my back for a minute, and that banana was gone. She's taking my food. This is all her fault. I know it is."

What role might psychotherapists play in helping close relatives cope with the deterioration of a loved one? What therapy approaches described throughout this casebook might be particularly helpful to such relatives?

People with a disorder such as Fred's often become angry, suspicious, and accusatory. What might be some of the reasons for such reactions and personality changes?

It's now been 8 years of taking care of him. At this point, I have to feed him and help him use the bathroom. I clean him, and I take him to the doctor. Thanks to his retirement package, we're okay financially. Still, we need to spend every penny we have on Fred's care. I can't work myself, since I have to be with him. The worst is when he looks at me and I know he doesn't know who I am, when he yells at me as if I'm an enemy and accuses me of stealing his things. At other times, however, he looks at me and his eyes say, "Thanks, Maggie," and I know he hasn't forgotten—even if he's remembering for only a moment.

Fred's decline seemed to reach a new level beginning around 6 months ago. Since then, he has been completely incontinent and barely able to speak. He has also been unable to leave our bedroom or the hallway of our house. He hasn't shown any recognition of Mark during his visits, and has barely even acknowledged me. About 3 weeks ago, he developed a cold that would not go away, and last week I had to take him to the hospital. He's still there, suffering from a respiratory infection and on a ventilator. He is in such a weakened condition that doctors are not sure that he will last the week.

I must admit that Mark and I each privately hope that the doctors' prognoses are accurate and Fred will die within the week. Neither of us has dared express this to the other, but we will both be relieved when Fred is gone—that is, the bedridden Fred whose spirit has already left us, who is a prisoner of his own body. When he is gone, he and we will finally be delivered from this long ordeal. And we will be able to remember our beloved Fred again as he once was—strong of mind and body.

After a long ordeal such as Fred's, it is common for close relatives to find themselves almost wishing for or looking forward to the person's death. What factors might explain such feelings and reactions?

**You Decide: The Case of Suzanne,
Age 21, Hair Pulling**

This case is presented in the voices of Suzanne and her mother, Sherry. Throughout the case, you will be asked to consider a number of issues and to arrive at various decisions, including diagnostic and treatment decisions. Appendix C lists Suzanne's probable diagnosis, the DSM-IV criteria, clinical information, and possible treatment directions.

Suzanne: A Sign of Things to Come

I don't know when I started doing it. I guess I've always hated school and I've always been really nervous about things. A lot of the time, even before college, I used to play with my hair a lot and pull on it, tighter and tighter the more nervous I became. But I didn't think there was anything unusual about it. You know, everyone has nervous habits that they turn to when they get all stressed out, right?

My parents were . . . let's say "difficult." They were always making me feel like I didn't do well enough. "Couldn't you have gotten an A? Couldn't you play basketball or soccer? Couldn't you have won the game? What could you have done to prepare for the test better? What can we learn from this? Why don't you have a boyfriend? Maybe if you dressed differently? You know, we just want you to be happy."

I guess this whole thing really started a long time ago. When I was in 7th grade, I used to pluck out my eyelashes. I don't know why I started: I just remember that it used to relax me when I was tense. I also got the idea in my head that my eyelashes and my eyes were really irritated. I thought that maybe I had some dirt caught in there, and it was stuck between my eyelashes. So I would loosen it and stop the irritation by pulling the eyelash out. I actually remember thinking that there were microscopic living bacteria—like I had seen in a science film—on the end of the eyelash, wiggling around under my skin, and the bad eyelashes needed to be pulled out. The little pain of pulling the lash out was something I actually looked forward to, like when you have a hanging fingernail that hurts and you need to pull it out: a second of pain and instant relief. Once I started noticing that I was doing it, I would be really nervous right before I would pull it, and I would think that maybe I shouldn't pull this one. Then, when I was pulling it out, I imagined I could feel the irritating inside part coming out. After it was over, I felt relieved, all the nervousness gone. I would look at the lash I had pulled, almost trying to see the little bacteria wiggling like a worm on a fishhook.

Soon, my eyelids were running out of hair, but no one seemed to notice, so I thought it wasn't a big deal. Maybe I wasn't really plucking them all out, I thought. Maybe I was just plucking out the bad ones, and the eyelashes now looked exactly the way they were supposed to. Maybe, I thought, I'm just sensitive to the way it looks because I keep thinking about it so much. Of course, I couldn't help but notice that I wasn't able to pluck any long eyelashes anymore, only little stubby ones. Also, my eyelids were hurting all the time.

> Many loving parents are described as being "overconcerned" about their children, or "overcontrolling" or "overinvolved." Where do such patterns of behavior come from? What can parents do to avoid crossing the line in their efforts to guide and protect their maturing children?

One night at dinner, my mom just turned to me after we'd been sitting together the whole dinner, and screamed out, "What the hell happened to your eyelashes? You look horrible!" Boy, that was so embarrassing. I wanted my parents to just go away. They wouldn't understand why I had to do it. I just wanted to crawl into a hole and die. I promised her that I would stop, but it was easier said than done. I'd catch—or should I say *Mom* would catch—myself doing it, reaching for the eyelashes even when there wasn't anything there. Eventually, my embarrassment became so great that it helped me to stop. Whenever I would reach for my eyelashes, I was able to catch myself before I touched them.

My lashes grew back, and the eyelids weren't as irritated all the time. After about 6 months, I didn't even have to think about it anymore. When I did think back on my behavior, I couldn't believe that I had plucked out every eyelash that I had. It didn't make sense anymore, and it seemed so unnatural. I was glad I had stopped, but I didn't want to think about it too much because I didn't want to consider the possibility that I wasn't "normal."

After my victory over eyelash plucking, I found myself trying to cope with school and other stresses in other ways. Throughout high school, I bit my nails and often stayed up all night worrying myself to the point of tears, walking around half asleep with a headache during the day from the exhaustion. During my junior and senior years, I was always concerned about whether I would get into a good college. Then, after I was accepted, there were all these preparations to make, while at the same time trying to finish my senior year in good standing. And then I had to get ready to move away from home. All the while, in the back of my mind, I was worried that there was something different about me from everyone else. I really didn't get along that well with most people; I just got too nervous around them, and relationships with boys never seemed to go anywhere.

Suzanne: Entering the Big Leagues

When I first got to college, I was really scared. I'd never been away from home for more than a couple of weeks, and never so far from my parents. Even though I couldn't wait to get away from them, I didn't know how I was going to get through life without them telling me how to do everything and how to get by in the real world. My next-door neighbor in the dorm, Jon, was a big help. He was from New York, so he was independent and sure of himself. He taught me how to take care of things like bills and money, how to get through classes and get food for myself. It was really a lot of fun; we made a little family out of our suite. Jon and I spent tons of time together and I was happy that I had wound up with him; it seemed like a stroke of luck.

Then one day he kissed me. Gosh, it seems so simple just to say it like that: *"He kissed me."* But that was how it happened. And I didn't think twice; I just kissed him back. Even though I had never really kissed a boy before. Not like that. We moved

Entering college is a major life stress that seems to trigger or exacerbate psychological difficulties for many persons. Why might this be such a difficult period in life?

on from there and had sex. I had always wondered what that would be like. How would it feel? But it felt wonderful—so right, so natural. I was so very happy with Jon, and I was feeling things that I had never felt for anyone.

One day, after we had been going together for about a month, Jon suddenly told me he thought we shouldn't be doing what we were doing anymore. He said it just like that, and just like that it was all over. He talked about expanding our horizons, exploring other relationships, and other such things. None of it made much sense or comforted me. I was totally devastated. And I was shocked by the suddenness with which the relationship ended. That alone would have been enough to crush me, but there was more. Jon wouldn't even talk to me or hang out with me anymore. It was a nightmare. At night I knew he was having girls come over and he was sleeping with them—each of them a reminder of how undesirable I was, of my failure at love, of my loss. I felt terrible about myself because Jon didn't love me like I loved him, and terrible because I had loved him in the first place. I was so depressed that I started failing two of my classes.

I think it was around this time, about midway through that first semester, that I first became aware that I was pulling my hair out. I say "first became aware," because I have no idea how long I'd actually been doing it. I just suddenly noticed, while in the middle of pulling my hair one time, that there were already a few strands of blond hair on the floor. This time it wasn't my eyelashes, but actual hair from the scalp on my head.

I realized immediately that the hair pulling was the same kind of thing that my eyelashes had been. I didn't feel so much the itchy, irritated feeling, but I would feel very uncomfortable. If I tried not to do it, I'd get really nervous and tense. I'd get this cramped, tight feeling in my stomach, and I'd worry that something bad was going to happen. By pulling out a hair, I would feel instant relief. When the hair came out, the knot in my stomach would pass and my heart would stop pumping so heavily. I could lean back in my chair or bed, and breathe much more easily. Unfortunately, this feeling of relief wouldn't last for long. In fact, as I said, the hair pulling would happen so often that I usually didn't know I was doing it—I would simply catch myself in the act.

Recalling the eyelash thing, I'd say to myself, "Remember, that was just a phase. You didn't have any trouble stopping," and I'd feel reassured. But of course I had had trouble stopping the eyelash plucking; it had just faded from my memory. As I paid more attention to my hair pulling, I observed that I tended to pull it from my right temple, on the side of my head, with my right hand. But I honestly couldn't be sure that that was the only hand I ever used.

A month or two after I first noticed what I was doing, I was in the shower and I felt a little patch of skin exposed around my favorite plucking spot. I think I was running the shampoo through my hair and I was rubbing it through my scalp. When I felt the patch where there was less hair, I panicked immediately. I could

Everyone has certain habits that they exhibit when they are under stress. Only occasionally do such habits blossom into a disorder such as Suzanne's. Are there ways of distinguishing innocent bad habits from signs of problems to come?

Based on your reading of either the DSM-IV or a textbook, what disorder might Suzanne be displaying? Which of her symptoms suggest this disorder?

feel my face turn bright red, and I think I was more embarrassed than anything else, even though I was alone. I thought, here I am doing this bizarre and perverse thing that no one else does, and now I must look like a freak. It occurred to me that everyone must know, and I just wanted to run and hide. In those first few moments of shock, I started breathing heavily, and I silently promised myself that I would never do this horrible thing again, that I was immature and stupid and disgusting, and I had to stop. When I rinsed out my hair I toweled it off. Then, terrified, I moved to the mirror to see just how bad I looked. Peeking from between squinted eyelids, I couldn't see a difference at first. Then I opened my eyes wide, and saw that there was definitely a hairless patch, although not as bad as it had felt to my fingers in the shower.

Good, I thought, with a feeling of relief. It seems silly in retrospect, but I remember thinking that if I just combed my hair over a certain way, everything would look fine. It relieved me enough that I went right back into this same routine again. Time and again, I'd catch myself plucking hair from the same spot. Eventually, I could no longer pretend to myself that I didn't have a noticeable bald patch. I invented newer, more elaborate hairstyles to cover it, while always thinking to myself, "Oh, I'm never going to do this again," or "I'm phasing it out." The truth was I hadn't slowed down a bit. It was probably becoming apparent to the people around me that there was something peculiar going on with my hair. But I kept on going, even checking to see if any hair was growing back.

When I went home for the winter break, I was terrified. I didn't want to risk my parents seeing this ugly bald spot on their "perfect" little daughter. For the entire month prior to winter break, I kept thinking, "Okay, stop pulling the hair. It needs to grow back." Then I'd think, when the urge had its grip on me, "Well, it's still 3 weeks away." And so I'd pull out the hair. And pull. And pull. And 3 weeks became 2, and 2 became 1, and the problem was as bad as ever when I had to fly home. I bit my nails the whole flight home, trying not to give in to the urge to pull my hair. I also didn't want to mess up the deceptive hairdo I had worked on so hard. Of course, there was Mom at the terminal waiting area, screaming, "Oh, my God! What did you do to your hair? You look terrible!" I told her to mind her own business and leave my hairdo alone. It was all I could do, however, to stop her from touching it.

I was only kidding myself that I could keep this a secret for 4 weeks. Within 1 week, Mom noticed the bald spot. In her typical way, she made me feel as if I had cut off an arm, and I turned bright red and cried. I didn't want to talk to her about it, both because she was horrible and because I didn't want to face it myself. So I left the room and said, "I won't talk about this now." But I knew that the damage had been done, and later I went down and told her that, as she could see, I had been pulling out my hair. I explained that I didn't know why, but I was going into therapy (to get her off my back) and I wanted to deal with it on my own. And

Suzanne's disorder is listed with impulse control problems in DSM-IV, as opposed to obsessive-compulsive disorders. Yet some clinicians believe that problems like hers are really a kind of compulsion. How are her symptoms similar to those displayed by the individual in Case 3, Obsessive-Compulsive Disorder? How are they different?

then I refused to discuss it further. I was surprised at how well I had handled my mother, but I knew that I had yet to handle my hair problem.

I went back to school, and I kept on doing it. My hair looked so bad I wasn't even trying to date. It wasn't until 2 more years passed that I decided to try therapy. I've been in counseling for 8 months now. I've come to appreciate that I have a lot of anxiety issues and problems with myself and my parents, and that's probably why I do this—at least in part. At the same time, my therapist has explained that many people have this disorder. I couldn't believe that at first. I really thought I was the only one.

I'm going to graduate this coming spring, and I'm doing very well at school and in basketball (Mom and Dad are SO happy!). I haven't pulled any hair out in, I think, close to 4 months, and I'm not feeling the urge much anymore, which is great. I feel better about the way I look. I've also started seeing a really nice guy named Mark. It's going great, although, after the disaster with Jon, I'm trying to take it slow. All in all, things are pretty good, but I do wonder whether I am prone to pulling my hair: Will I revert to this whenever I face a crisis? That worries me, and for now that's why I am continuing in therapy.

How might the treatment approaches used in Cases 3 and 4 be applied to Suzanne? Which aspects of these approaches would not be appropriate for her? Should additional interventions be applied?

A Mother's View: "You've Got to Stop This"

I think Suzanne was about 13 when I first noticed the problem with her eyelashes. We were sitting at the dinner table—this was about, oh, 8 years ago—and talking about her cheerleading practice. She was excited that she'd been picked to be the top of the pyramid. Tom and I were also happy about that. We'd been encouraging Suzie to try out for this cheerleading team because she had seemed unhappy. Sometimes she'd cry, and when we'd ask her what was wrong, she'd say, "I don't know," or "School is really hard." Tom and I talked about it and thought she might want to get involved in an extracurricular activity. We gently tried to get her to go out for a sport, like basketball, which she was so good at, but she insisted she didn't like playing sports. Finally, in desperation, I suggested that since she really liked gymnastics, she might want to try cheerleading. Suzie loved the idea. Apparently, she herself had thought about cheerleading, but she had been afraid to ask us if she could be a part of the team. She was concerned that we'd be disappointed; she thought we might look down on it, compared to basketball, soccer, or field hockey. Can you imagine that?

Anyway, the eyelashes... She was telling us about this pyramid thing at the table, and I wanted to give my little girl a big hug. When I leaned in, I thought something looked peculiar about her face. At first, it seemed like she looked really sad, and her eyes were bigger than usual. I hugged her, and told her that I was so proud of my little girl. Tom looked up from the paper and said he thought it was just great. Later, during dessert, when I was passing out the ice cream, I looked at her again. We were talking about her test the next day in social studies and how

Are the family, school, and social pressures described by Suzanne particularly unusual? Why might they have led to dysfunctioning in Suzanne's case, but not in the lives of other persons?

much studying she should do after dinner. At one point, she looked up, and that's when I noticed it.

"What happened to your eyelashes?!" I exclaimed, before I could stop myself. Suzie tried to turn her head away and look outside the room, in the opposite direction. She muttered, "I don't know." But I said, "Tom, look at this! She doesn't have any eyelashes."

He looked over, leaned in, and said, "You're right, Sherry. What's going on here, Suze?" Suzie took a deep breath and just said she sometimes plucked her eyelashes out. She didn't know why she did it. She said she just did—they itched her, maybe. I figured it was some sort of nervous habit, and I told her she had to stop. I told her it wasn't normal. She got upset, but finally promised she would try to stop doing it. I tried to give her some more incentive. "You're so beautiful," I told her, "but you look terrible without your eyelashes. You could look so much better. You've got to stop this, okay?"

For a while after that, I'd see her rubbing her eyelids where the lashes used to be. Tom and I tried to help out by stopping her whenever we saw her playing with her eyelids or eyelashes. After a while, and with some effort, it seemed to pay off. Her eyelashes eventually grew back, and she didn't seem to be plucking them anymore. We all forgot about it after a few years. I know I stopped thinking about it.

When she went off to college in Florida years later, the last thing on my mind was the way she had plucked out her eyelashes at the age of 13. Tom and I had been hoping she would go to a good school, with a strong girls' basketball team, but she didn't do very well on her SATs, and never did well enough in basketball to interest the scouts from the big schools. Anyway, the school she went to was fine, and we were proud that Suzie was going to college.

She never called us when she first went away. I guess it was the excitement of being somewhere new. Anyway, girls are like that at that age. When we would call her to see how she was doing in her classes, she never seemed to want to talk—she would talk very softly, say things were fine, and yes, she was making friends. She would then rush off the phone; once, I was sure that she was holding back tears.

When she came home for her first winter break, she had the most ridiculous hairdo I'd ever seen: a weird type of beehive combed over from the left. It was just horrible. I asked her why she did that to her hair, and she just said she liked it that way. After she'd been home a few days, she literally let her hair down, and when she tilted her head back once, right before she quickly brushed the hair back over, I saw it—her scalp! A horrifying, huge bald spot. I asked her what was wrong. "Are you sick?" But she just got really serious and said she didn't want to talk about it. Then she left the room.

Later, she admitted that she had started pulling her hair out. She said she didn't know why she did it, but she was going into therapy, for that and for a lot of other

On the surface, Suzanne and her mother had a close and loving relationship, but they also had some serious problems in their interactions. What were some of these problems, and how might they have contributed to Suzanne's disorder?

things. She explained that it was somehow connected to the eyelash thing from years ago, and I thought, "Of course, it all makes sense now." This is really strange, but she told me that it wasn't my problem, and I should just let her try to work on it herself.

After that, once she was back at school, whenever I would ask her on the phone how she was doing with the hair problem, she would mumble a short answer like "Fine." Sometimes she wouldn't come home at all on vacations. But I guess she's made things right and put it all behind her now. She was home just last month and she certainly seemed to have a full head of lovely blond hair. We had a great visit, and she's looking forward to graduating. And guess who's the starting guard on the girls' basketball team!

What defense mechanisms did Suzanne and her mother seem to use in order to cope with her eyelash problem and, later, her hair-pulling problem? How did such mechanisms help Suzanne? How did they hurt her?

Appendix A:
You Decide: The Case of Julia

The individual in *Case 18: The Case of Julia* would receive a diagnosis of *anorexia nervosa*.

DSM-IV	Checklist

Anorexia Nervosa

1. Refusal to maintain body weight above a minimally normal weight for age and height (that is, above 85% of proper weight).
2. Intense fear of gaining weight, even though underweight.
3. Disturbed body perception, undue influence of weight or shape on self-evaluation, or denial of the seriousness of the current low weight.
4. In postmenarcheal females, amenorrhea.

Based on APA (1994, 2000)

Clinical Information*

1. Typically, anorexia nervosa begins after a person who is slightly overweight or of normal weight has been on a diet.

2. People with anorexia nervosa typically also struggle with feelings of depression, anxiety, low self-esteem, and the need to be perfect. Some further experience sleep disturbances, obsessive-compulsive patterns, and substance abuse.

3. Although anorexia nervosa can occur at any age, the peak age of onset is between 14 and 18 years.

4. Prevalence: Around 0.5% of all females in Western countries develop anorexia nervosa in their lifetime. Approximately 90 to 95% of all cases occur among females.

5. Surveys suggest that more than 9% of female college athletes may suffer from an eating disorder, including around 20% of all college gymnasts.

6. The mothers of people with eating disorders are more likely to diet themselves and to be perfectionistic than mothers in other families.

Common Treatment Strategies*

1. First step: Increase calorie intake and quickly restore the individual's weight, using a strategy such as supportive nursing care.

2. Second step: Deal with underlying psychological problems by offering a mixture of psychoeducation and psychotherapy (individual, group, and family). Cognitive-behavioral approaches, which seek to change the client's misconceptions and attitudes about eating and weight, are particularly common.

3. Aftermath: About 83% of people who receive successful treatment for anorexia nervosa continue to show full or partial improvements years later. However, some of them relapse along the way, many continue to worry about their weight and appearance, and half continue to experience some emotional or family problems. Teenagers seem to have a better recovery rate than older persons, and females have a better recovery rate than males.

* **Sources:** Andersen (1995); APA (1994, 2000); Bastiani et al. (1995, 1996); Fichter & Pirke (1995); Halmi (1995); Herzog et al. (1999); Johnson et al. (1995); Lehoux et al. (2000); Pike & Rodin (1991); Pyle (1999); Strober et al. (1997); Treasure et al. (1995); Wiederman & Pryor (2000); Wright (2000).

Appendix B:
You Decide: The Case of Fred

The individual in *Case 19: The Case of Fred* would receive a diagnosis of *dementia of the Alzheimer's type.*

DSM-IV **Checklist**

Dementia of the Alzheimer's Type

1. The development of multiple cognitive deficits manifested by both memory impairment and at least one of the following cognitive disturbances:

   a. Aphasia.

   b. Apraxia.

   c. Agnosia.

   d. Disturbance in executive functioning (that is, planning, organization, sequencing, abstracting).

2. Significant impairment in social or occupational functioning, along with significant decline from a previous level of functioning.

3. Gradual onset and continuing cognitive decline.

4. Deficits are not due to other central nervous system conditions, systemic conditions, or substance-induced conditions.

5. Disturbance is not better accounted for by another mental disorder.

Based on APA (1994, 2000)

Clinical Information*

1. Alzheimer's disease is the most common form of dementia, accounting for at least half of all cases.

2. The disease sometimes appears in middle age, but most often occurs after the age of 65, particularly among people in their late 70s and early 80s.

3. After its onset, the disease progresses gradually, ranging in duration from 2 to as many as 20 years.

4. Sufferers may at first deny that they have a problem, but they may soon become anxious or depressed; many also become agitated.

5. Around 3% of the world's adult population suffer from some form of dementia, including more than 25% of all people over the age of 85.

6. Structural changes in the brains of people with Alzheimer's disease include an excessive number of *neurofibrillary tangles* (twisted protein fibers found within the cells of the hippocampus and certain other brain areas) and of *senile plaques* (deposits of a small molecule known as the *beta-amyloid protein* that form between cells in the hippocampus, cerebral cortex, and certain other brain regions).

7. The disease often has a genetic basis.

8. Victims of the disorder usually remain in fairly good health until the later stages of the disease. With less activity, however, they may become prone to illnesses such as pneumonia, which can result in death. Alzheimer's disease leads to 23,000 deaths each year in the United States.

Common Treatments*

1. No single approach or set of approaches is highly effective in all cases of Alzheimer's disease.

2. Certain drugs, such as *tacrine* (Cognex) and *donepezil* (Aricept), bring modest improvements in short-term memory, reasoning ability, language use, and coping ability for some patients. Such drugs prevent the breakdown of *acetylcholine* in the brain, a neurotransmitter essential to memory.

3. Behavioral interventions may help change everyday patient behaviors that are stressful for the family, such as wandering at night or urinary incontinence.

4. The needs of the caregivers must also be met by approaches such as psychoeducation, psychotherapy, support groups, and regular time-outs.

5. Alzheimer's disease *day-care facilities* (providing outpatient treatment programs and activities during the day) are becoming common. In addition, many *assisted-living* facilities are being built—apartments which provide supervision and are tailored to the needs and limitations of people with the disease.

---

* **Sources:** Alzheimer's Association (1997); APA (1994, 2000); Clyburn et al. (2000); Cowley, 2000; Fisher & Carstensen (1990); Kalb (2000); Krall et al. (1999); Lorenzo & Yankner (1996); Muir (1997); NCHS (1999); Pinkston & Linsk (1984); Selkoe (1992, 1996, 1998, 1999, 2000); St. George-Hyslop (2000); Zal (1999).

Appendix C:
You Decide: The Case of Suzanne

The individual in *Case 20: The Case of Suzanne* would receive a diagnosis of *trichotillomania.*

DSM-IV **Checklist**

Trichotillomania

1. Recurrent pulling out of one's hair resulting in noticeable hair loss.
2. An increasing sense of tension immediately before pulling out the hair or when attempting to resist the behavior.
3. Pleasure, gratification, or relief when pulling out the hair.
4. Disturbance is not better accounted for by another mental disorder and is not due to a general medical condition.
5. Significant distress or impairment.

Based on APA (1994, 2000)

Clinical Information*

1. Trichotillomania is listed as one of the *impulse-control disorders* in DSM-IV, a group of disorders marked by a failure to resist an impulse, drive, or temptation to perform harmful acts.
2. Some clinicians believe that the disorder is actually a form of *obsessive-compulsive disorder,* because the hair-pulling, like the compulsions found in obsessive-compulsive disorder, is compulsive in nature, feels involuntary to sufferers, and is recognized as senseless by sufferers.
3. Contrasts between trichotillomania and the compulsions of obsessive-compulsive disorder: Compulsions are most often performed in response to obsessions, performed in a rigid or even ritualistic way, aimed at preventing

some dreaded event, done with full awareness by the sufferer, and span beyond a single behavior.

4. Research on trichotillomania and its treatments is very limited.

5. The disorder often first appears during early adolescence.

6. The disorder may last only weeks or months, or may be chronic (years or even decades).

7. Prevalence: About 0.6% of college students exhibit the disorder. Females seem to heavily outnumber males.

8. In children, self-limited periods of hair-pulling are a common, temporary habit. In addition, as many as 10 to 15% of college students pull hair regularly, without meeting the clinical criteria of trichotillomania.

9. Most sufferers of trichotillomania also exhibit another psychological disorder, either concurrently or at another point in their lives, particularly a mood disorder or an anxiety disorder. Only 15% exhibit obsessive-compulsive disorder.

Common Treatments*

1. Self-help groups.

2. Certain antidepressant medications, such as *clomipramine* (Anafranil).

3. Cognitive-behavioral therapy, featuring:

   a. Self-monitoring of hair pulling behaviors.

   b. Exposure to situations that trigger hair-pulling.

   c. Performance of alternative or competing behavior during exposure, until the urge to pull hair passes.

   d. Identification and alteration of beliefs about the appearance of one's hair that may be contributing to the behavior.

4. Psychotherapy for any feelings of depression that may accompany trichotillomania.

5. Relapse-prevention strategies.

* **Sources:** APA (1994, 2000); Azrin et al. (1980); Christenson et al. (1991); Christenson et al. (1991); Friman et al. (1984); Rothbaum et al. (1993); Stanley et al. (1994); Stein et al. (1999); Swedo et al. (1989).

References

AA World Services. (1998, 2000).
Personal communication. Statistics branch. New York.

Ackerman, M. D., & Carey, M. P. (1995).
Psychology's role in the assessment of erectile dysfunction: Historical precedents, current knowledge, and methods. *J. Consult. Clin. Psychol., 63*(6), 862–876.

Adler, J. (1998, May 4).
Take a pill and call me tonight. *Newsweek,* p. 48.

Allan, C., Smith, I., & Mellin, M. (2000).
Detoxification from alcohol: A comparison of home detoxification and hospital-based day patient care. *Alcohol Alcohol., 35*(1), 66–69.

Alzheimer's Association. (1997, February 17).
Survey: Stress on Alzheimer's care givers. Cited in *USA Today,* p. 1D.

American Academy of Pediatrics. (1999).
Media alert: AAP addresses Colorado shooting.

Andersen, A. E. (1995).
Sequencing treatment decisions: Cooperation or conflict between therapist and patient. In G. Szmukler, C. Dare, & J. Treasure (Eds.), *Handbook of eating disorders: Theory, treatment, and research.* Chichester, England: Wiley.

Angst, J. (1995).
The epidemiology of depressive disorders. *Eur. Neuropsychopharmacol.,* Suppl., pp. 95–98.

Angst, J. (1999).
Major depression in 1998: Are we providing optimal therapy? *J. Clin. Psychiatry, 60*(Suppl. 6), 5–9.

APA (American Psychological Association) (1994).
Diagnostic and statistical manual of mental disorders (4th ed.). Washington, DC: Author.

APA (American Psychological Association) (1996).
Interim report of the working group on investigation of memories of childhood abuse. In K. Pezdek & W. P. Banks (Eds.), *The recovered memory/false memory debate.* San Diego: Academic Press.

APA (American Psychological Association) (2000).
DSM-IV text revision. Washington, DC: Author.

Ash, R. (1999).
Fantastic book of 1001 facts. New York: DK Publishing.

Atlas, J. A. (1995).
Association between history of abuse and borderline personality disorder for hospitalized adolescent girls. *Psychol. Rep., 77,* 1346.

Awad, A. G., & Voruganti, L. N. (1999).
Quality of life and new antipsychotics in schizophrenia: Are patients better off? *Int. J. Soc. Psychiatry, 45*(4), 268–275.

Azrin, N. H., Nunn, R. G., & Frantz, S. E. (1980).
Treatment of hairpulling: A comparative study of habit reversal and negative practice training. *J. Behav. Ther. Exp. Psychiat., 11,* 13–20.

Baldessarini, R. J., Tondo, L., & Hennen, J. (1999).
Effects of lithium treatment and its discontinuation on suicidal behavior in bipolar manic-depressive disorders. *J. Clin. Psychiatry, 60*(Suppl. 2), 77–84.

Barak, Y., Kimhi, R., & Weizman, R. (2000).
Is selectivity for serotonin uptake associated with a reduced emergence of manic episodes in depressed patients? *Inter. Clin. Psychopharmacology, 15*(1), 53–56.

Bastiani, A. M., Altemus, M., Pigott, T. A, Rubenstein, C., et al. (1996).
Comparison of obsessions and compulsions in patients with anorexia nervosa and obsessive-compulsive disorder. *Biol. Psychiat., 39,* 966–969.

Bastiani, A. M., Rao, R., Weltzin, T., & Kaye, W. H. (1995).
Perfectionism in anorexia nervosa. *Inter. J. Eat. Disorders, 17*(2), 147–152.

Bates, G. W., Thompson, J. C., & Flanagan, C. (1999).
The effectiveness of individual versus group induction of depressed mood. *J. Psychol., 133*(3), 245–252.

Baucom, D. H., Shoham, V., Mueser, K. T., Diauto, A. D., & Stickle, T. R. (1998).
Empirically supported couple and family interventions for marital distress and adult mental health problems. *J. Consult. Clin. Psychol., 66*(1), 53–88.

Berrettini, W. H. (2000).
Susceptibility loci for bipolar disorder: Overlap with inherited vulnerability to schizophrenia. *Biol. Psychiatry, 47*(3), 245–251.

Bowden, C. L. (1995).
Treatment of bipolar disorder. In A. F. Schatzberg & C. B. Nemeroff (Eds.), *Textbook of psychopharmacology* (pp. 603–614). Washington, DC: American Psychiatric Press.

Burnette, E., & Murray, B. (1996).
Conduct disorders need early treatment. *APA Monitor, 27*(10), 40.

Burney, J., & Irwin, H. J. (2000).
Shame and guilt in women with eating-disorder symptomatology. *J. Clin. Psychol., 56*(1), 51–61.

Bushman, B. J., Baumeister, R. F., & Stack, A. D. (1999).
Catharsis, aggression, and persuasive influence: Self-fulfilling or self-defeating prophecies? *J. Pers. Soc. Psychol., 76*(3) 367–376.

Button, E. (1993).
Eating disorders: Personal construct therapy and change. Chichester, England: Wiley.

Cahill, S. P., Carrigan, M. H., & Frueh, B. C. (1999).
Does EMDR work? and if so, why? A critical review of controlled outcome and dismantling research. *J. Anx. Dis., 13*(1–2), 5–33.

Cameron, P. M., Leszcz, M., Bebchuk, W., Swinson, R. P., Antony, M. M., Azim, H. F., Doidge, N., Korenblum, M. S., Nigam, T., Perry, J. C., & Seeman, M. V. (1999).
The practice and roles of the psychotherapies: A discussion paper. *Cana. J. Psychiatry, 44*(Suppl. 1), 18S-31S.

Canty, G. F. (1996).
Therapists at work. *The Institute Notebook, 5*(2), 1,4.

Canty, G. F. (1996).
A heart to heart on depression. *The Institute Notebook, 5*(3), 1,4.

Chan, S., MacKenzie, A., Ng, D. T., & Leung, J. K. (2000).
An evaluation of the implementation of case management in the community psychiatric nursing service. *J. Adv. Nurs., 31*(1), 144–156.

Christenson, G. A., Mackenzie, T. B., & Mitchell, J. E. (1991).
Characteristics of 60 adult chronic hair pullers. *Am. J. Psychiatry, 148,* 365–370.

Christenson, G. A., Pyle, R. L., & Mitchell, J. E. (1991).
Estimated lifetime prevalence of trichotillomania in college students. *J. Clin. Psychiatry, 52,* 415–417.

Clark, D. M., & Wells, A. (1997).
Cognitive therapy for anxiety disorders. In L. J. Dickstein, M.B. Riba, & J. M. Oldham (Eds.), *Review of psychiatry* (Vol. 16). Washington, DC: American Psychiatric Press.

Clarke, J., Stein, M. D., Sobota, M., Marisi, M., & Hanna, L. (1999).
Victims as victimizers: Physical aggression by persons with a history of childhood abuse. *Arch. Intern. Med., 159*(16), 1920–1924.

Cloninger, C. R., Bohman, M., & Sigvardsson, S. (1981).
Inheritance of alcohol abuse. Cross fostering analysis of adopted men. *Arch. of Gen. Psychiatry, 30,* 861–868.

Clyburn, L. D., Stones, M. J., Hadjistavropoulos, T., & Tuokko, H. (2000)
Predicting caregiver burden and depression in Alzheimers disease. *J. Ger. B Psychol. Sci. Soc. Sci., 55*(1), S2–13.

Cole, D. A., & Turner, J. E., Jr. (1993).
Models of cognitive mediation and moderation in child depression. *J. Abnorm. Psychol., 102*(2), 271–281.

Compas, B. E., Haaga, D.A.F., Keefe, F. J., Leitenberg, H., & Williams, D. A. (1998).
Sampling of empirically supported psychological treatments from health psychology: Smoking, chronic pain, cancer, and bulimia nervosa. *J. Consult Clin. Psychol., 66*(1), 89–112.

Courchesne, R., & Courchesne, E. (1997).
From impasse to insight in autism research: From behavioral symptoms to biological explanations. *Dev. Psychopathol.,* special issue.

Cowley, G. (2000).
Alzheimer's: Unlocking the mystery. *Newsweek,* pp. 46–51.

Craddock, N., & Jones, I. (1999).
Genetics of bipolar disorder. *J. Med. Genet., 36*(8), 585–594.

Craske, M. G., & Barlow, D. H. (1993).
Panic disorder and agoraphobia. In D. H. Barlow (Ed.). *Clinical handbook of psychological disorders* (2nd ed., pp. 1–47). New York: Guilford Press.

Davis, L. L., Ryan, W., Adinoff, B., & Petty, F. (2000).
Comprehensive review of the psychiatric uses of valproate. *J. Clin. Psychopharmacol., 20*(Suppl. 1), 1S-17S.

Davis, T., Gunderson, J. G., & Myers, M. (1999).

Borderline personality disorder. In D.G. Jacobs (Ed.), *The Harvard Medical School guide to suicide assessment and intervention.* San Francisco: Jossey-Bass.

Dawson, G., & Castelloe, P. (1992).

Autism. In C. E. Walker (Ed.), *Clinical psychology: Historical and research foundations.* New York: Plenum Press.

DeRubeis, R. J., Tang, T. Z., Gelfand, L. A., & Feeley, M. (2000).

Recent findings concerning the processes and outcomes of cognitive therapy for depression. In S. L. Johnson, A. M. Hayes, et al. (Eds.), *Stress, coping, and depression.* Mahwah, NJ: Erlbaum.

DeSilva, P. (1995).

Cognitive-behavioural models of eating disorders. In G. Szmukler, C. Dare, & J. Treasure (Eds.), *Handbook of eating disorders: Theory, treatment and research.* Chichester, England: Wiley.

Eigan, L. (1991, February).

Alcohol practices, policies, and potentials of American colleges and universities. An OSAP White Paper. Rockville, MD: Office for Substance Abuse Prevention.

Ekman, P., O'Sullivan, M., & Frank, M. G. (1999).

A few can catch a liar. *Psychol. Sci., 10*(3), 263–266.

Everson, S. A., Goldberg, D. E., Kaplan, G. A., Cohen, R. D., et al. (1996).

Hopelessness and risk of mortality and incidence of myocardial infarction and cancer. *Psychosom. Med., 58,* 113–121.

Express Scripts, Inc. (1999, June 29).

1998 Express Scripts Trend Report. St. Louis, MO: Author.

Fairburn, C. G., Cooper, Z., & Cooper, P. J. (1986).

The clinical features and maintenance of bulimia nervosa. In K. D. Brownell & J. P. Foreyt (Eds.), *Handbook of eating disorders* (pp. 389–404). New York: Basic Books.

Fairburn, C. G., Jones, R., Peveler, R. C., Hope, R. A., & O'Connor, M. (1993).

Psychotherapy and bulimia nervosa: Longer-term effects of interpersonal psychotherapy behavior therapy, and cognitive behavior therapy. *Arch. Gen. Psychiat., 50,* 419–428.

Fairburn, C. G., Marcus, M. D., & Wilson, G. T. (1993).

Cognitive-behavioral therapy for binge eating and bulimia nervosa: A Comprehensive Manual. In C. G. Fairburn & G. T. Wilson (Eds.), *Binge eating: Nature, assessments, and treatment* (pp. 361–404). New York: Guilford Press.

Fairburn, C. G., Peveler, R. C., Jones, R., Hope, R. A., & Doll, H. A. (1993).
Predictors of 12-month outcome in bulimia nervosa and the influence of attitudes to shape and weight. *J. Consult.Clin. Psychol., 61,* 696–698.

Falloon, I.R.H., & Liberman, R. P. (1983).
Behavioral family interventions in the management of chronic schizophrenia. In W. McFarlane (Ed.), *Family therapy of schizophrenia* (pp. 325–380). New York: Guilford Press.

Fava, M., Rankin, M. A., Wright, E. C., Alpert, J. E., Nierenberg, A. A., Pava, J., & Rosenbaum, J. F. (2000).
Anxiety disorders in major depression. *Compr. Psychiatry, 41*(2), 97–102.

Feldman, H. A., Goldstein, I., Hatzichristou, D. G., Krane, R. J., & McKinlay, J. B. (1994).
Impotence and its medical and psychosocial correlates: Results of the Massachusetts Male Aging Study. *J. Urol., 151,* 54–61.

Fichter, N. M., & Pirke, K. M. (1995).
Starvation models and eating disorders. In G. Szmukler, C. Dare, & J. Treasure (Eds.), *Handbook of eating disorders: Theory, treatment, and research.* Chichester, England: Wiley.

Fisher, J. E., & Carstensen, L. L. (1990).
Behavior management of the dementias. *Clin. Psychol. Rev., 10,* 611–629.

Foa, E. B., & Kozak, M. J. (1995).
Field trial: Obsessive-compulsive disorder. *Am. J. Psychiatry, 152*(1), 90–96.

Foreyt, J. P., Poston, W.S.C., & Goodrick, G. K. (1996).
Future directions in obesity and eating disorders. *Addict. Behav., 21*(6), 767–778.

Frank, E., Grochocinski, V. J., Spanier, C. A., Buysse, D. J., Cherry, C. R., Houck, P. R., Stapf, D. M., & Kupfer, D. J. (2000).
Interpersonal psychotherapy and antidepressant medication: Evaluation of a sequential treatment strategy in women with recurrent major depression. *J. Clin. Psychiatry, 61*(1), 51–57.

Friedman, M. (1984).
Alteration of type A behavior and reduction in cardiac recurrences in postmyocardial infarction patients. *Am. Heart J., 108,* 237–248.

Friedman, M., & Rosenman, R. (1974).
Type A behavior and your heart. New York: Knopf.

Friedman, M. J. (1999)

Pharmacotherapy for post-traumatic stress disorder. In M.J. Horowitz et al., *Essential papers on post-traumatic stress disorder. Essential papers in psychoanalysis.* New York: New York University Press.

Friman, P. C., Finney, J. W., & Christophersen, E. R. (1984).

Behavioral treatment of trichotillomania: An evaluative review. *Behav. Ther., 15,* 249–265.

Fulwiler, C., & Pope, H. G., Jr. (1987).

Depression in personality disorder. In O. G. Cameron (Ed.), *Presentations of depression: Depressive symptoms in medical and other psychiatric disorders.* New York: Wiley.

Garner, D. M., Garfinkel, P. E., & O'Shaughnessy, M. (1985).

The validity of the distinction between bulimia with and without anorexia nervosa. *Am. J. Psychiatry, 142,* 581–587.

Garssen, B., & Goodkin, K. (1999).

On the role of immunological factors as mediators between psychosocial factors and cancer progression. *Psychiatry Res., 85*(1), 51–61.

George, E. L., Friedman, J. C., & Miklowitz, D. J. (2000).

Integrated family and individual therapy for bipolar disorder. In S. L. Johnson, A. M. Hayes, et al. (Eds.), *Stress, coping, and depression.* Mahwah, NJ: Erlbaum.

Goetzel, R. Z., Anderson, D. R., Whitmer, R. W., Ozminkowski, R. J., Dunn, R. L., & Wasserman, J. (1998).

The relationship between modifiable health risks and health care expenditures. An analysis of the multi-employer HERO health risk and cost database. The Health Enhancement Research Organization (HERO) Research Committee. *J. Occup. Environ. Med., 40*(10), 843–854.

Gorfinkle, K., & Redd, W. H. (1993).

Behavioral control of anxiety, distress, and learned aversions in pediatric oncology. In J. C. Holland & W. Breitbart (Eds.), *Psychiatric aspects of symptom management in cancer patients* (pp. 129–146). Washington, DC: American Psychiatric Press.

Gottesman, I. I. (1991).

Schizophrenia genesis. New York: Freeman.

Grant, B. F., & Dawson, D. A. (1997).

Age at onset of alcohol use and its association with DSM-IV alcohol abuse and dependence: Results from the National Longitudinal Alcohol Epidemiologic Survey. *J. Subst. Abuse, 9,* 103–110.

Grilo, C. M., Becker, D. F., Fehon, D. C., Walker, M. L., et al. (1996).
Gender differences in personality disorders in psychiatrically hospitalized adolescents. *Am. J. Psychiatry, 153*(8), 1089–1091.

Halmi , K. A. (1995).
Current concepts and definitions. In G. Szmukler, C. Dare, & J. Treasure (Eds.), *Handbook of eating disorders: Theory, treatment, and research.* Chichester, England: Wiley.

Hardy, J. D., & Smith, T. W. (1988).
Cynical hostility and vulnerability to disease: Social support, life stress, and physiological response to conflict. *Health Psychol., 7,* 447–459.

Harrington, R. C., Fudge, H., Rutter, M. L., Bredenkamp, D., Groothues, C., & Pridham, J. (1993).
Child and adult depression: A test of continuities with data from a family study. *Br. J. Psychiatry, 162,* 627–633.

Hermann, C., Kim, M., & Blanchard, E. B. (1995).
Behavioral and prophylactic pharmacological intervention studies of pediatric migraine: An exploratory meta-analysis. *Pain, 60*(3), 239–255.

Herzog, D. B., Dorer, D. J., Keel, P. K., Selwin, S. E., Ekeblad, E. R., Flores, A. T., Greenwood, D. N., Burwell, R. A., & Keller, M. B. (1999).
Recovery and relapse in anorexia and bulimia nervosa: A 7.5-year follow-up study. *J. Amer. Acad. Child Adol. Psychiatry, 38*(7), 829–837.

Hill, H. E., Kornetsky, C. H., Flanary, H. G., & Wikler, A. (1952).
Effects of anxiety and morphine on discrimination of intensities of painful stimuli. *J. Clin. Invest., 31,* 473–480.

Hill, H. E., Kornetsky, C. H., Flanary, H. G., & Wikler, A. (1952).
Studies of anxiety associated with anticipation of pain. *Arch. Neurol. Psychiatry, 67,* 612–619.

Hirschfeld, R. M. (1999).
Efficacy of SSRIs and newer antidepressants in severe depression: Comparison with TCAs. *J. Clin. Psychiat., 60*(5), 326–335.

Hunicutt, C. P., & Newman, I. A. (1993).
Adolescent dieting practices and nutrition knowledge. Health values. *J. Health Behav., Edu. Promotion, 17*(4), 35–40.

Inskip, H. M., Harris, E. C., & Barraclough, B. (1998).
Lifetime risk of suicide for affective disorder, alcoholism and schizophrenia. *Brit. J. Psychiat., 172,* 35–37.

James, W. M. (1890).
Principles of psychology (Vol. 1). New York: Holt, Rinehart & Winston.

Jay, S. M. (1988).
Invasive medical procedures. In D. K. Routh (Ed.), Handbook of pediatric psychology (pp. 401–426). New York: Guilford Press.

Johnson, W. G., Schlundt, D. G., Barclay, D. R., Carr-Nangle, R. E., et al. (1995).
A naturalistic functional analysis of binge eating. Special series: Body dissatisfaction, binge eating, and dieting as interlocking issues in eating disorders research. Behav. Ther. 26(1), 101–118.

Johnston, L. D., O'Malley, P. M., & Bachman, J. G. (1993).
National survey results on drug use from the Monitoring the Future Study, 1975–1992.

Johnston, L. D., O'Malley, P. M., & Bachman, J. G. (1999).
Cited in press release. Drug trends in 1999 among American teens are mixed. Ann Arbor: University of Michigan News and Information Services.

Kalb, C. (2000, January 31)
Coping with the darkness: Revolutionary new approaches in providing care for helping people with Alzheimer's stay active and feel productive. Newsweek, pp. 52–54.

Kanner, B. (1995).
Are you normal?: Do you behave like everyone else? New York: St. Martin's Press.

Kanner, B. (1998, February).
Are you normal? Turning the other cheek. Am. Demographics.

Kanner, L. (1943).
Autistic disturbances of affective contact. Nerv. Child. 2, 217.

Kaplan, H. S. (1987).
The illustrated manual of sex therapy (2nd ed.). New York: Brunner/Mazel.

Kate, N. T. (1998, April).
Two careers, one marriage. Am. Demographics.

Katon, W. J., & Walker, E. A. (1998).
Medically unexplained symptoms in primary care. J. Clin. Psychiatry, 59 (Suppl. 20), 15–21.

Kazdin, A. E., & Wassell, G. (1999).
Barriers to treatment participation and therapeutic change among children referred for conduct disorder. J. Clin. Child Psychol., 28(2), 160–172.

Keel, P. K., & Mitchell, J. E. (1997).

Outcome in bulimia nervosa. *Am. J. Psychiatry, 154,* 313–321.

Kessler, R. C., & Zhao, S. (1999).

The prevalence of mental illness. In A.V. Horwitz & T. L. Scheid (Eds.), *A handbook for the study of mental health: Social contexts, theories, and systems.* Cambridge, England: Cambridge University Press.

Kessler, R. C., McGonagle, K. A., Zhao, S., Nelson, C. B., Hughes, M., Eshleman, S., Wittchen, H. U., & Kendler, K. S. (1994).

Lifetime and 12-month prevalence of DSM-III-R psychiatric disorders among persons aged 15–54 in the United States: Results from the National Comorbidity Survey. *Arch. Gen. Psychiatry, 51*(1), 8–19.

Kiecolt-Glaser, J. K., Glaser, R., Gravenstein, S., Malarkey, W. B., & Sheridan, J. (1996).

Chronic stress alters the immune response to influenza virus vaccine in older adults. *Proc. Natl. Acad. Sci. U.S.A., 93,* 3043–3047.

Kiecolt-Glaser, J. K., Page, G. G., Marucha, P. T., MacCallum, R. C., & Glaser, R. (1998).

Psychological influences on surgical recovery. Perspectives from psychoneuroimmunology. *Am. Psychologist, 53*(11), 1209–1218.

Kirn, W. (1997, August 18).

The ties that bind. *Time,* pp. 48–50.

Klassen, A., Miller, A., Raina, P., Lee, S. K., & Olsen, L. (1999).

Attention-deficit hyperactivity disorder in children and youth: A quantitative systematic review of the efficacy of different management strategies. *Can. J. Psychiatry, 44*(10), 1007–1016.

Kocsis, J. H., Friedman, R. A., Markowitz, J. C., Miller, N., Gniwesch, L., & Bram, J. (1995).

Stability of remission during tricyclic antidepressant continuation therapy for dysthymia. *Psychopharmacol. Bull., 31*(2), 213–216.

Krall, W. J., Sramek, J. J., & Cutler, N. R. (1999).

Cholinesterase inhibitors: A therapeutic strategy for Alzheimer's disease. *Ann. Pharmacother., 33*(4), 441–450.

Laumann, E. O., Paik, A., & Rosen, R. C. (1999).

Sexual dysfunction in the United States: Prevalence and predictors. *JAMA, 281*(6), 537–544.

Lecrubier, Y., Bakker, A., Dunbar, G., and the collaborative paroxetine panic study investigators. (1997).
A comparison of paroxetine, clomipramine, and placebo in the treatment of panic disorder. *Acta Psychiatr. Scandin., 95,* 145–152.

Lehoux, P. M, Steiger, H., & Jabalpurlawa, S. (2000).
State/trait distinctions in bulimic syndromes. *Inter. J. Eat. Disorders, 27*(1), 36–42.

Leutwyler, K. (1996).
Paying attention: The controversy over ADHD and the drug Ritalin is obscuring a real look at the disorder and its underpinnings. *Sci. Am., 272*(2), 12–13.

Liberman, R. P., Kopelowicz, A., & Young, A. S. (1994).
Biobehavioral treatment and rehabilitation of schizophrenia. *Behav. Ther., 25,* 89–107.

Lieberman, J. A. (1998).
Maximizing Clozapine therapy: Managing side effects. *J. Clin. Psychiatry, 59*(Suppl. 3), 38–43.

Linehan, M. M. (1993).
Cognitive-behavioral treatment of borderline personality disorder. New York: Guilford Press.

Linehan, M. M. (1993).
Skills training manual for treating borderline personality disorder. New York: Guilford Press.

Linehan, M. M., Armstrong, H. E., Suarez, A., Allmon, D., & Heard, H. L. (1991).
Cogntive-behavioral treatment of chronically parasuicidal borderline patients. *Arch. Gen. Psychiatry, 48,* 1060–1064.

Linehan, M. M., Heard, H. L., & Armstrong, H. E. (1993).
Naturalistic follow-up of a behavioral treatment for chronically parasuicidal borderline patients. *Arch. Gen. Psychiatry, 50,* 971–974.

Lloyd, G. G., & Lishman, W. A. (1975).
Effect of depression on the speed of recall of pleasant and unpleasant experiences. *Psychol. Med., 5,* 173–180.

LoPiccolo, J. (1991).
Post-modern sex therapy for erectile failure. In R. C. Rosen & S. R. Leiblum (Eds.), *Erectile failure: Diagnosis and treatment.* New York: Guilford Press.

Lorenzo, A., & Yankner, B. A. (1996).
Amyloid fibril toxicity in Alzheimer's disease and diabetes. In R. J. Wurtman, S. Corkin, J. H. Growdon, & R. M. Nitsch (Eds.), *The neurobiology of Alzheimer's disease.* New York: New York Academy of Sciences.

Manne, S. L., Redd, W. H., Jacobsen, P. B., et al. (1990).
Behavioral intervention to reduce child and parent distress during venipuncture. *J. Consult. Clin. Psychol., 58,* 565–572.

Mariani, M. A., & Barkley, R. A. (1997).
Neuropsychological and academic functioning in preschool boys with attention-deficit/hyperactivity disorder. *Dev. Neuropsychol., 13*(1), 111–129.

Masters, W. H., & Johnson, V. E. (1970).
Human sexual inadequacy. Boston: Little, Brown.

McCormick, L. H. (2000).
Improving social adjustment in children with attention-deficit/hyperactivity disorder. *Arch. Fam. Med., 9*(2), 191–194.

McCrady, B. S. (1990).
The marital relationship and alcoholism treatment. In R. L. Collins, K. E. Leonard, B. A. Miller, & J. S. Searles (Eds.), *Alcohol and the family: Research and clinical perspectives* (pp. 338–355). New York: Guilford Press.

McGuire, P. A. (2000, February).
New hope for people with schizophrenia. *Monitor on Psychology, 31*(2), 24–28.

McKenzie, S. J., Williamson, D. A., & Cubic, B. A. (1993).
Stable and reactive body image disturbances in bulimia nervosa. *Behav. Ther., 24,* 195–207.

Meichenbaum, D. (1977).
Cognitive-behavior modification: An integrative approach. New York: Plenum Press.

Melzack, R., Weisz, A. Z., & Sprague, L. T. (1963).
Strategems for controlling pain: Contributions of auditory stimulation and suggestion. *Exp. Neurol., 8,* 239–247.

Miklowitz, D. J., Goldstein, M. J., & Nuechterlein, K. H. (1995).
Verbal interactions in the families of schizophrenic and bipolar affective patients. *J. Abnorm. Psychol., 104*(2), 268–276.

Miller, K. J., Gleaves, D. H., Hirsch, T. G., Green, B. A., Snow, A. C., & Corbett, C. C. (2000).
Comparisons of body image dimensions by race-ethnicity and gender in a university population. *Int. J. Eat. Disord., 27*(3), 310–316.

Miller, I. W., Norman, W. H., & Keitner, G. I. (1999).
Combined treatment for patients with double depression. *Psychother. Psychosom., 68*(4), 180–185.

Miller, L. S., Wasserman, G. A., Neugebauer, R., Gorman-Smith, D., & Kamboukos, D. (1999).
Witnessed community violence and antisocial behavior in high-risk, urban boys. *J. Clin. Child Psychol., 28*(1), 2–11.

Montgomery, S. A., Bebbington, P., Cowen, P., Deakin, W., et al. (1993).
Guidelines for treating depressive illness with antidepressants. *J. Psychopharmacol., 7*(1), 19–23.

Moos, R. H., & Cronkite, R. C. (1999).
Symptom-based predictors of a 10-year chronic course of treated depression. *J. Nerv. Ment. Dis., 187*(6), 360–368.

Muir, J. L. (1997).
Acetylcholine, aging, and Alzheimer's disease. *Pharmacol. Biochem. Behav., 56*(4), 687–696.

Myers, M. G., Stewart, D. G., & Brown, S. A. (1998).
Progression from conduct disorder to antisocial personality disorder following treatment for adolescent substance abuse. *Am. J. Psychiatry, 155*(4), 479–485.

Narrow, W. E., Regier, D. A., Rae, D. S., Manderscheid, R. W., & Locke, B. Z. (1993).
Use of services by persons with mental and addictive disorders: Findings from the National Institute of Mental Health Epidemiologic Catchment Area Program. *Arch. Gen. Psychiat., 50*, 95–107.

NCHS (National Center for Health Statistics). (1999).
Fastats A to Z. Chronic liver disease/cirrhosis. Washington, DC: Centers for Disease Control and Prevention.

NCHS (National Center for Health Statistics). (2000).
Births, marriages, divorces, and deaths: Provisional data for January 1999, National Vital Statistics Reports, Vol. 48, No. 1. Washington, DC: Centers for Disease Control and Prevention.

NHSDA (National Household Survey on Drug Abuse). (1998).
1998 national estimates of rates of use and other measures related to drugs, alcohol, cigarettes, and other forms of tobacco. Washington, DC: U.S. Department of Health and Human Services.

Nolen-Hoeksema, S. (1995).
Gender differences in coping with depression across the lifespan. *Depression, 3*, 81–90.

Nolen-Hoeksema, S. (1998).
The other end of the continuum: The costs of rumination. *Psychol. Inquiry, 93*, 216–219.

North, C. S., Nixon, S. J., Shariat, S., Mallonee, S., McMillen, J. C., Spitznagel, E. L., & Smith, E. M. (1999).
Psychiatric disorders among survivors of the Oklahoma City bombing. *JAMA 282*(8), 755–762.

Novaco, R. W. (1975).
Anger control. Lexington, MA: Lexington.

PORT (Patient Outcomes Research Team). (1998).
Cited in S. Barlas, Patient outcome research team study on schizophrenia offers grim indictment. *Psychiatr. Times, XV*(6).

Patrick, C. J., Cuthbert, B. N., & Lang, P. J. (1990).
Emotion in the criminal psychopath: Fear imagery. *Psychophysiology, 27*(Suppl.), 55.

Patrick, C. J., Bradley, M. M., & Lang, P. J. (1993).
Emotion in the criminal psychopath: Startle reflex modulation. *J. Abnorm. Psychol., 102*(1), 82–92.

Paxton, S. J., & Diggens, J. (1997).
Avoidance coping, binge eating, and depression: An examination of the escape theory of binge eating. *Int. J. Eat. Disord., 22,* 83–87.

Penn, D. L., & Mueser, K. T. (1996).
Research update on the psychosocial treatment of schizophrenia. *Am. J. Psychiatry, 153,* 607–617.

Pickens, R., & Fletcher, B. (1991).
Overview of treatment issues. In R. Pickens, C. Leukefeld, & C. Schuster (Eds.), *Improving drug abuse treatment.* Rockville, MD: National Institute on Drug Abuse.

Pickett, S. A., Cook, J. A., & Razzano, L. (1999).
Psychiatric rehabilitation services and outcomes: An overview. In A. V. Horwitz & T. L. Scheid (Eds.), *A handbook for the study of mental health: Social contexts, theories, and systems.* Cambridge, England: Cambridge University Press.

Pike, K. M., & Rodin, J. (1991).
Mothers, daughters and disordered eating. *J. Abnorm. Psychol., 100*(2), 198–204.

Pinkston, E. M., & Linsk, N. L. (1984).
Behavioral family intervention with the impaired elderly. *Gerontologist, 24,* 576–583.

Psychiatric Rehabilitation Consultants. (1991).
Modules for training and independent living skills for persons with serious mental disorders. Available from Dissemination Coordinator, Camarillo-UCLA Research Center, Box 6022, Camarillo, CA 93011–6022.

Pyle, R. L. (1999).
Dynamic psychotherapy. In M. Hersen & A. S. Bellack (Eds)., *Handbook of comparative interventions for adult disorders* (2nd ed.). New York: Wiley.

Rachman, S. (1993).
Obsessions, responsibility and guilt. *Behav. Res. Ther., 31* (2), 149–154.

Redd, W. H., Jacobsen, P. B., Die-Trill, M., et al. (1987).
Cognitive/attentional distraction in the control of conditioned nausea in pediatric cancer patients receiving chemotherapy. *J. Consult. Clin. Psychol., 55,* 391–395.

Regehr, C., Cadell, S., & Jansen, K. (1999).
Perceptions of control and long-term recovery from rape. *Amer. J. Orthopsychiat., 173*(supp.34), 24–28.

Regier, D. A., Narrow, W. E., Rae, D. S., Manderscheid, R. W., Locke, B. Z., & Goodwin, F. K. (1993).
The de facto US Mental and Addictive Disorders Service System: Epidemiologic Catchment Area prospective 1-year prevalence rates of disorders in services. *Arch. Gen. Psychiatry, 50,* 85–94.

Regier, D. A., Rae, D. S., Narrow, W. E., Kaelber, C. T., & Schatzberg, A. F. (1998).
Prevalence of anxiety disorders and their comorbidity with mood and addictive disorders. *Br. J. Psychiatry, 173*(Suppl. 34), 24–28.

Riggs, D. S., & Foa, E. B. (1993).
Obsessive-compulsive disorder. In D. H. Barlow (Ed.), *Clinical handbook of psychological disorders: A step-by-step treatment manual* (2nd ed.). New York: Guilford.

Roazen, P. (1992).
The rise and fall of Bruno Bettelheim. *Psychohist. Rev., 20*(3), 221–250.

Robison, L. M., Sclar, D. A., Skaer, T. L., & Galin, R. S. (1999).
National trends in the prevalence of attention-deficit/hyperactivity disorder and the prescribing of methylphenidate among school children: 1990–1995. *Clin. Pediatr., 38*(4), 209–217.

Rosen J. C., & Leitenberg, H. (1982).
Bulimia nervosa: Treatment with exposure and response prevention. *Behav. Ther., 13*(1), 117–124.

Rosen, J. C., & Leitenberg, H. (1985).
Exposure plus response prevention treatment of bulimia. In D. M. Garner & P. E. Garfinkel (Eds.), *Handbook of psychotherapy for anorexia nervosa and bulimia.* New York: Guilford Press.

Rossow, I., & Amundsen, A. (1995).
Alcohol abuse and suicide: A 40-year prospective study of Norwegian conscripts. *Addiction, 90*(5), 685–691.

Rothbaum, B. O., Shaw, L., Morris, R., & Ninan, P. T. (1993).
Prevalence of trichotillomania in a college freshman population. *Journal of Clinical Psychiatry, 54,* 72.

Sacks, O. (2000, May).
An anthropologist on Mars: Some personal perspectives on autism. Keynote address. Eden Institute Foundation's Sixth Annual Princeton Lecture Series on Autism.

Selkoe, D. J. (1991).
Amyloid protein and Alzheimer's disease. *Scientif. Amer., 265,* 68–78.

Selkoe, D. J. (1992).
Alzheimer's disease: New insights into an emerging epidemic. *J. Geriat. Psychiat., 25*(2), 211–227.

Selkoe, D. J. (1998).
The cell biology of beta-amyloid precursor protein and presenilin in Alzheimer's disease. *Trends Cell Biol., 8*(11), 447–453.

Selkoe, D. J. (1999).
Translating cell biology into therapeutic advances in Alzheimer's disease. *Nature, 399*(Suppl. 6738), A23–31.

Selkoe, D. J. (2000).
The origins of Alzheimer's disease: A is for amyloid. *JAMA, 283*(12), 1615–1617.

Selkoe, D. J., Yamazaki, T., Citron, M., Podlisny, M. B., Koo, E. H., Teplow, D. B., & Haass, C. (1996).
The role of APP processing and trafficking pathways in the formation of amyloid B-protein. In R. J. Wurtman, S. Corkin, J. H. Growdon, & R. M. Nitsch (Eds.), *The neurobiology of Alzheimer's disease.* New York: New York Academy of Sciences.

Shea, T., Elkin, I., Imber, S., Sotsky, S., Watkins, J., Colins, J., et al. (1992).
Course of depressive symptoms over follow-up: Findings from the National Institute of Mental Health treatment of depression collaborative research program. *Arch. Gen. Psychiatry, 49,* 782–787.

Shisslak, C. M., Crago, M., McKnight, K. M., Estes, L. S., Gray, G., & Parnaby, O. G. (1998).
Potential risk factors associated with weight control behaviors in elementary and middle school girls. *J. Psychosom. Res., 44*(3/4), 301–313.

Smith, T. W. (1992).

Hostility and health: Current status of a psychosomatic hypothesis. *Health Psychol., 11,* 139–150.

Spanier, C. A., Frank, E., McEachran, A. B., Grochocinski, V. J., & Kuprer, D. J. (1999).

Maintenance interpersonal psychotherapy for recurrent depression: Biological and clinical correlates and future directions. In D. S. Janowsky et al. (Eds.), *Psychotherapy indications and outcomes.* Washington, DC: American Psychiatric Press.

Spector, I. P., & Carey, M. P. (1990).

Incidence and prevalence of sexual dysfunctions: A critical review of the empirical literature. *Arch. Sex. Behav., 19*(4), 389–408.

Spiegel, D., & Classen, C. (2000).

Group therapy for cancer patients: A research-based handbook of psychosocial care. New York: Basic Books.

Spoont, M. R. (1996).

Emotional instability. In C. G. Costello (Ed.), *Personality characteristics of the personality disordered.* New York: Wiley.

Stallard, P., Velleman, R., & Baldwin, S. (1998).

Prospective study of post-traumatic stress disorder in children involved in road traffic accidents. *Br. Med. J., 317*(7173), 1619–1623.

Stanley, M. A., Borden, J. W., Bell, G. E., & Wagner, A. L. (1994).

Nonclinical hair pulling: Phenomenology and related psychopathology. *J. Anx. Dis., 8,* 119–130.

Stein, D. J., Christenson, G. A., & Hollander, E. (Eds.). (1999).

Trichotillomania. Washington, DC: American Psychiatric Press, Inc.

St. George-Hyslop, P. H. (2000).

Molecular genetics of Alzheimer's disease. *Biol. Psychiatry, 47*(3), 183–199.

Striegel-Moore, R. H., Silberstein, L. R., & Rodin, J. (1993).

The social self in bulimia nervosa: Public self-consciousness, social anxiety, and perceived fraudulence. *J. Abnorm. Psychol., 102*(2), 297–303.

Strober, M., Freeman, R., & Morrell, W. (1997).

The long-term course of severe anorexia nervosa in adolescents: Survival analysis of recovery, relapse, and outcome predictors over 10–15 years in a prospective study. *Int. J. Eat. Disord., 22*(4), 339–360.

Swedo, S. E., Leonard, H. L., Rapoport, J. L., Lenane, M. C., Goldberger, E. L., & Cheslow, C. L. (1989).
A double-blind comparison of clomipramine and desipramine in the treatment of trichotillomania (hair pulling). *N. Eng. J. Med., 321,* 497–501.

Taylor, S. (1995).
Anxiety sensitivity: Theoretical perspectives and recent findings. *Behav. Res. Ther., 33*(3), 243–258.

Taylor, S. E., Kemeny, M. E., Reed, G. M., Bower, J. E., & Gruenewald, T. L. (2000).
Psychological resources, positive illusions, and health. *Am. Psychol., 55*(1), 99–109.

Teichman, Y., Bar-El, Z., Shor, H., Sirota, P., et al. (1995).
A comparison of two modalities of cognitive therapy (individual and marital) in treating depression. *Psychiat. Interpers. Biol. Process., 58*(2), 136–148.

Telch, C. F., & Agras, W. S. (1993).
The effects of a very low calorie diet on binge eating. *Behav. Ther., 24,* 177–193.

Tkachuk, G. A., & Martin, G. L. (1999).
Exercise therapy for patients with psychiatric disorders: Research and clinical implications. *Profess. Psychol.: Res. Pract., 30*(3), 275–282.

Treasure, J., & Szmukler, G. I. (1995).
Medical complications of chronic anorexia nervosa. In G. I. Szmukler, C. Dare, & J. Treasure (Eds.), *Handbook on eating disorders: Theory, treatment and research.* Chichester, England: Wiley.

Treasure, J., Todd, G., & Szmukler, G. (1995).
The inpatient treatment of anorexia nervosa. In G. Szmukler, C. Dare, & J. Treasure (Eds.), *Handbook of eating disorders: Theory, treatment, and research.* Chichester, England: Wiley.

U.S. Department of Justice/Bureau of Justice Statistics. (1994).
Violence between inmates: Domestic violence. Annapolis Junction, MD: Bureau of Justice Statistics Clearinghouse.

Van Bourgondien, M. E., & Schopler, E. (1990).
Critical issues in the residential care of people with autism. *J. Autism Dev. Disord., 20*(3), 391–399.

Walsh, B. T., Wilson, G. R., Loeb, K. L., Devlin, M. J., et al. (1997).
Medication and psychotherapy in the treatment of bulimia nervosa. *Am. J. Psychiatry, 154,* 523–531.

Weissman, M. M., & Olfson, M. (1995).

Depression in women: Implications for health care research. *Science, 269*(5225), 799–801.

Wiederman, M. W., & Pryor, T. (1996).

Substance use and impulsive behaviors among adolescents with eating disorders. *Addic. Behav., 21*(2), 269–272.

Wilsnack, R. W., Vogeltanz, N. D., Wilsnack, S. C. & Harris, T. R. (2000).

Gender differences in alcohol consumption and adverse drinking consequences: Cross-cultural patterns. *Addiction, 95*(2), 251–265.

Wilson, K. A., & Chambless, D. L. (1999).

Inflated perceptions of responsibility and obsessive-compulsive symptoms. *Behav. Res. Ther., 37*(4), 325–335.

Wooley, S. C., & Wooley, O. W. (1985).

Intensive outpatient and residential treatment for bulimia. In D.M. Garner & P. E. Garfinkel (Eds.), *Handbook of psychotherapy for anorexia nervosa and bulimia.* New York: Guilford Press.

Wright, I. C., Rabe, H. S., Woodruff, P. W. R., David, A. S., Murray, R. M., & Bullmore, E. T. (2000).

Meta-analysis of regional brain volumes in schizophrenia. *Am. J. Psychiatry, 157*(1), 16–25.

Wright, S. (2000).

Group work. In B. Lask, R. Bryant-Waugh et al. (Eds.), *Anorexia nervosa and related eating disorders in childhood and adolescence* (2nd ed). Hove, England: Psychology Press/Taylor & Francis.

Zal, H. M. (1999).

Agitation in the elderly. *Psychiat. Times, XVI*(1).

Zisook, S., Zisook, S., Goff, A., Sledge, P., Shuchter, S. R. (1994).

Reported suicidal behavior and current suicidal ideation in a psychiatric outpatient clinic. *Ann. Clin. Psychiatry, 6,* 27–31.

Name Index

Subject Index